A

COMMON-SCHOOL GRAMMAR

OF THE

ENGLISH LANGUAGE.

BY

SIMON KERL, A. M.,

AUTHOR OF "COMPREHENSIVE GRAMMAR," "FIRST LESSONS IN GRAMMAR," ETC.

Sacred Interpreter of human thought,
How few respect or use thee as they ought!"

COWPER, on *Language.*

NEW YORK:
IVISON, PHINNEY, BLAKEMAN, & CO.
CHICAGO: S. C. GRIGGS & CO.
1868.

KERL'S SERIES OF GRAMMARS.

Kerl's First Lessons in English Grammar. — Designed as an introduction to the Common-School Grammar. The plan, definitions, observations, and exercises, are in the simplest style, and suited to the capacity of children.

Kerl's Common-School Grammar. — A simple, thorough, and practical grammar of the English language. Great care has been taken to make it, if possible, the best treatise of its kind now before the public. The parts relating to Idioms, Analysis, and False Syntax, will be found particularly valuable.

Kerl's Comprehensive Grammar. — An original work, that breaks up the old stereotyped method of English grammars, and re-arranges matter more nearly in accordance with the genius of the language. The articles on Versification, Punctuation, and Capital Letters, throw new light on these subjects; and in False Syntax, and the Analysis of Sentences, the exercises are fresh, pithy, and exhaustive. The work is especially useful to every speaker, writer, or teacher, as a book of reference.

PREFACE.

"LANGUAGE," said Sheridan, "is the great instrument by which all the faculties of the mind are brought forward, moulded, and polished." He who travels over our extensive country can easily observe that wherever the people have a limited and obscure knowledge of language, there all the other elements of civilization and refinement are in a correspondingly undeveloped state; but that wherever a home is surrounded by the beauties of nature and art, there is also generally heard such language as reveals the presence of literature and the cultivation of thought and sensibility.

Language is at once the most useful, powerful, delicate, and durable instrument wielded by man. It materializes thought, so as to make it tangible, permanent, and transmissible; and it thus carries civilization into every nook and corner of the world. It receives the intellect, heart, and achievements of every generation; and bears forward the responsible burden to be judged by every future generation. While the marble crumbles, and the canvas fades, an embodiment of great thoughts in glorious language lives through all time; renewing its youth, like the phœnix, with every edition from the printing-press, and, like the sun, spreading its light and beneficence round the whole globe.

But how many literary productions are more or less disfigured with inaccuracies of grammar; and what an injurious influence is often exerted on the language of the people, by the hasty and crude literature of the daily press! How often do men express their thoughts, even on important occasions, inaccurately, obscurely, ambiguously, or ridiculously; and what a multitude of bickerings, lawsuits, and contentions arise from language misapplied or misunderstood! It was the opinion of a late Attorney-General of the United States, that the people of this country pay at least twenty millions of dollars a year for the abuse of the English language in matters of contract and legislation alone.

Till the excellent treatise of Murray made its appearance, the study of English grammar had hardly become a branch of common-school education; but since that time the importance of the science has been so far established in the convictions of the public, that grammar is now everywhere one of the leading studies in common schools. Corresponding text-books have constantly increased, until we have a superabundance; yet there is doubtless always room for an improved system in every science.

Most readers prefer to ascertain the plan and contents of a book by simply turning over its leaves; but the following features of this treatise are some of those which the author has endeavored to make worthy of special notice: —

1. The simple and scientific nature of the general plan, and the methodical arrangement of matter throughout the book.

2. The clearness, brevity, and uniformity of the definitions.

3. The abundance and appropriateness of the illustrations and exercises.

4. The careful development of every part in proportion to its importance; so that the book is unusually symmetrical and comprehensive.

5. The introduction of the historical element of our language; and the careful regard for those laws which underlie the fabric of language, and make it what it is.

6. The treatment of infinitives and participles.

7. The Rules of Syntax, in regard to both meaning and brevity.

8. The collection of idioms and other difficult constructions.

9. The system of Analysis, and the progressive development of sentences according to its principles.

10. The classification of False Syntax; and the lessening of so great a number of little rules, which are seldom learned and always soon forgotten.

11. The critical remarks on syntax, punctuation, and capital letters.

12. The superior mechanical execution of the work.

The relative importance of the matter has been carefully distinguished by different sizes of type; and what is designed only for reading or reference, has been placed at the end of each Part, or so distinguished from the portions to be committed to memory as not to embarrass the learner or distract his attention. The pages to be studied make thus but a comparatively small book. Yet for those pupils who may need a smaller or an introductory treatise, a book called "First Lessons in English Grammar," and made on the same plan as this work, has been expressly prepared.

If any teacher wishes his pupils to "analyze and parse" as soon as possible, he can require them to commit the Rules of Syntax to memory, and he can then drill them, as they advance from the commencement of the book, on the sentences which begin page 241.

Brevity has been constantly studied; and great care has been taken to make this grammar as simple, progressive, and interesting as such a book can be made without injuring its scientific value.

In closing this Preface, the author desires to express his grateful acknowledgment for valuable suggestions received from the Masters of the Boston Public Schools; of whom he would especially mention Daniel C. Brown, Joshua Bates, and James A. Page, as the gentlemen to whom he is mostly indebted.

INDEX.

For nice points, see Observations, pp. 58, 209, 311, 346.

SYNOPSIS.

Part I.—An Outline for Beginners.

THIS Part shows the connection between thought and language, and how the latter is developed from a few great or fundamental ideas. It contains a familiar explanation of the chief ideas in grammar, which is followed by a series of exercises that show the general construction of sentences.

For a mode of using these exercises, the teacher may consult Kerl's "First Lessons."

Part II.—Words Uncombined.

This Part begins with a presentation of the subject and its divisions; it then treats of letters, elementary sounds, accent, pronunciation, syllables, spelling, and derivation, or it teaches what can be learned about words before they are combined in sentences.

Part III.—Words Grammatically Combined.

This Part shows what we must learn about words in order to know how they should be put together to make sentences. It treats of the parts of speech and their properties, the rules of syntax, and parsing; or it shows into what classes we must divide words, and what jointings we must make, or by what ideas we must be governed, in order to put words rightly together in sentences.

Part IV.—Words Logically Combined.

This Part supposes that the jointings and small combinations of words are already made; and that we are now ready to put the larger parts together so as to get sentences for all kinds of thoughts. It therefore treats of phrases and clauses, as well as of words; of subjects, predicates, modifiers, connectives, simple sentences, complex sentences, and compound sentences.

Part V.—Words Improperly Combined.

This Part treats of the errors which can arise under both the preceding Parts. It implies that there may be some excess, deficiency, wrong choosing, or improper arrangement, in regard to the words which are to show precisely what we mean.

Part VI.—Ornament and Finish.

This Part supposes that we have already learned to express thoughts intelligibly and correctly, but that we now seek to express them in the most interesting and impressive manner; or it shows by what means thoughts are imparted to the best advantage. Hence it treats of figures, versification, utterance, and punctuation.

Remarks.— | denotes separation. = is placed between equivalent expressions.

A number placed over a word shows which Rule of Syntax should be applied to it.

W means *wrong:* sentences beginning with this letter are to be corrected.

What is to be committed to memory by the pupil, is printed in large type, or is distinguished by being numbered with heavy black figures.

The few technical or difficult words which we have been obliged to use, the teacher should explain; or he should give out a number of them to the pupils from time to time, and require them to learn the meanings in some large dictionary.

English Grammar.

PART I.

AN OUTLINE FOR BEGINNERS.

"I am convinced that the method of teaching which approaches most nearly to the method of investigation, is incomparably the best; since, not content with serving up a few barren and lifeless truths, it leads to the stalk on which they grow."

BURKE.

THOUGHT AND ITS EXPRESSION.

1. We *think*, or have *thoughts*.

2. We express our thoughts by means of *words*.

3. Words are either spoken or written.

4. The expressing of our thoughts by means of words, is called *language*, or *speech*.

5. Language is made to suit the world, and consists of many thousands of words; but, like trees or persons, they can all be divided into a small number of classes.

6. To express our thoughts, we use nine classes of words, which are therefore called the *Parts of Speech*.

7. The PARTS OF SPEECH are *Nouns*, *Pronouns*, *Articles*, *Ad'jectives*, *Verbs*, *Adverbs*, *Prĕpositions*, *Conjunctions*, and *Interjections*.

8. To these nine classes of words belong eight chief

properties; *Gender*, *Person*, *Number*, *Case*, *Voice*, *Mood*, *Tense*, and *Comparison*.

9. These classes of words, and their properties, are based mainly on the following ten things or ideas: *Objects*, *Actions*, *Qualities*, *Sex*, *Number*, *Relation*,* *Manner*, *Time*, *Place*, and *Degree*.

Let us now see by what natural process we shall get thoughts, and then words to express them.

Parts of Speech.

NOUNS.

When we look around us, we naturally first notice objects. The words *John*, *Mary*, *tree*, *house*, *street*, *man*, *horse*, *apple*, *flower*, *rose*, *chair*, *desk*, *book*, *paper*, *pencil*, are, all of them, words that denote objects, and such words are called *nouns*.

10. A **Noun** is a name.

Tell what trees grow in the woods. What flowers grow in gardens? What animals are on farms? What things can boys eat? What things do children play with? What objects did you see this morning, on your way to school? Who are your classmates? What would you call the words you have mentioned?

You can generally tell whether a word is a noun or not, by considering whether it denotes something that you can see, hear, taste, smell, or feel, or think of as being a person or thing.

PRONOUNS.

When objects are near to us, or already known by having been mentioned, we do not always use their names, but cer-

* Considered here chiefly as applied to Case and Person.

tain little words in stead of the names. If I say, "William promised Mary that William would lend Mary William's grammar, that Mary might study the grammar," you can easily see that the sentence is clumsy and disagreeable, because I have repeated the words *William*, *Mary*, and *grammar*. But if I say, "William promised Mary that *he* would lend *her his* grammar, that *she* might study *it*," you notice that the sentence is much more simple and agreeable, because I have used the little words *he*, *she*, and *it*, for the nouns *William*, *Mary*, and *grammar*, in stead of repeating these nouns. *Pronoun* means *for a noun;* and pronouns are so called because they are used *for nouns*, or *in stead of nouns*.

11. A **Pronoun** is a word used in stead of a noun.

The most common pronouns are *I*, *my*, *myself*, *mine*, *me*, *we*, *our*, *ourselves*, *ours*, *us*, *you*, *your*, *yourself*, *yours*, *ye*, *thou*, *thy*, *thyself*, *thine*, *thee*, *he*, *his*, *him*, *himself*, *she*, *her*, *herself*, *hers*, *it*, *itself*, *its*, *they*, *theirs*, *them*, *themselves*, *who*, *whose*, *whom*, *which*, and *that*. The easiest way in which you can generally distinguish a pronoun from a noun, is to consider whether the word denotes an object, without being itself the name of the object. "*I* saw *you*." Here *I* denotes me, without being my name; and *you* denotes the person spoken to, without being his name.

Put suitable pronouns for the words in Italic letters:—

John has learned *John's* lesson. Mary has torn *Mary's* book. The apple lay under the *apple's* tree. The apples lay under the *apples'* tree. Thomas has come home, and *Thomas* is well. Lucy is pretty, and *Lucy* knows it. The gun was brought, but the *gun* was out of order. Laura was disobedient, and therefore *Laura's* teacher punished *Laura*. Julia will buy you a basket, if *Julia* can buy the *basket* cheap. Joseph and Mary went to meet *Joseph and Mary's* father, but *Joseph and Mary's father* came another way.

ARTICLES.

Most objects exist in classes; and when we use merely the ordinary name of something, we generally mean the class or object at large or indefinitely; as, *tree, apples, water.* To show that we mean only one object of a kind, and no particular one, or that we mean some particular object or objects, we generally place the word *a* or *an,* or *the,* before the name; as, *a* tree, *the* tree, *the* trees. If I say, "Give me *a* book, *an* apple," you understand that any book or apple will answer my purpose; but if I say, "Give me *the* book, *the* books," you understand that I want some particular book or books. These words, *a* or *an* and *the,* which are very often used before nouns, and which generally show how we select the objects of which we are speaking, are called *articles.*

12. An **Article** is the word *the, a,* or *an,* placed before a noun to limit its meaning.

Place A *before each of the following nouns; then* THE:—

Man, book, pen, boy, parrot, pink, school-house, newspaper.

Place AN *before each of the following nouns; then* THE:—

Ax, eagle, Indian, ox, owl, arbor, undertaker.

VERBS.

We can not think of an object, without thinking something of it. Therefore every thought or saying implies at least two things; something of which we think or speak, and something that we think or say of it: the former is called the *subject,* and the latter the *prĕd'icate.* "Rivers flow"; here *rivers* is the subject, and *flow* is the *predicate.* "Deep rivers flow smoothly"; here *deep rivers* is the subject, and *flow smoothly* is the predicate.

13. A **Subject** is a word or phrase denoting that of which something is said.

14. A **Predicate** is a word or phrase denoting what is said of the subject.

15. A **Proposition** is a subject combined with its predicate.

When we speak of any object, we generally tell either what it *is*, what it *does*, or what *is done* to it.

1. Flowers *are beautiful.* The ant *is an insect.*
2. Birds *sing.* Boys *play.* Carpenters *build houses.*
3. Fields *are ploughed.* The corn *was ground.*

The words *are*, *is*, *sing*, *play*, *build*, etc., by means of which we say things of the subjects, are called *verbs.*

16. A **Verb** is a word used to express the act or state of a subject.

"The river washes away the soil"; here *washes* is a verb, because it tells what the river does. "The river *is* deep"; here *is* is a verb, because it tells something of the river, or helps to show in what state it is. Sometimes we say that the verb *affirms* or *predicates* something of its subject. This is nearly the same as to tell you that it says something of that about which we are talking. We are sometimes obliged to use hard words in books, for the sake of greater accuracy or exactness. By dressing soldiers in a different style from that in which citizens are dressed, we can easily distinguish them from citizens. So every science has generally, in its words, a dress of its own.

Mention the subjects, the predicates, the verbs of the predicates, and why: —

Frogs leap. Fishes swim. The wind whistles. The thunder rolls. The lightning flashed. Clouds were moving. He recited his lesson. The door creaked. The snake crept into the grass. Out flew the partridges. Lilies and roses were blooming together.

Put a suitable subject to each of the following predicates: —

Is happy; knows nothing; am sick; art released; grew

rapidly; was neglected; were neglected; went away; spoke sensibly; replied; stepped forth; retreated; should obey their parents; was a great man.

Say something of each of the following objects, by telling what they are: —

Street, grass, hay, ice, stars, mountains, room, table.

Say something of each of the following objects, by telling what they do: —

Horse, farmers, trees, servant, hogs, tailor, teacher, scholar.

Say something of each of the following objects, by telling what is done to them: —

Lesson, bonnet, bridge, yard, window, John, newspaper.

ADJECTIVES.

We notice every day that objects are not all alike, even when of the same general kind. Some roses, for instance, are *red;* some are *white;* and some are *yellow.* An apple may be *large* or *small; red, green,* or *yellow; hard* or *mellow; mealy* or *juicy.* Sometimes we notice several things of interest in the same object. A river, for instance, may be *deep, broad, clear,* and *swift.* The value of objects, or the regard we have for them, depends not a little on their qualities; and hence it is necessary for us to have words that will show the qualities of objects, or describe the objects. These words are called *adjectives.* Sometimes we use words that do not express the qualities of objects, but that still serve to show what objects are meant. Such words are *this, that, each, every, either, first, second, one, two, three,* etc. These words are also called *adjectives.* The word *adjective* means *throwing* or *joining to;* an adjective generally modifies the idea of an object, by joining to it that of some quality.

17. An **Adjective** is a word used to qualify or limit the meaning of a noun or pronoun.

"A *good* pupil will be *industrious.*" *Good* and *industrious* are adjectives, because they describe the pupil; that is, they describe the object *meant* by the word *pupil.* "*This* tree bore *five* bushels of apples." *This* is an adjective, because it makes the indefinite word *tree* mean a particular one; and *five* is an adjective, because it makes the indefinite word *bushels* mean a particular number.

Tell which are the adjectives, and why: —

Warm weather; dark clouds; shady lawns; tall trees; a white cloud; yonder house; a hollow tree; a steep bluff.

Put suitable adjectives to each of the following nouns; and then tell what each of the objects is, by using the same adjective: —

Man, boy, workman, star, rose, river, book, day, crow, swan, pink, winter, snow, wood, stones, lead.

ADVERBS.

Not only are objects different, but their actions are also different, even when of the same general kind. People do not all walk alike, nor talk alike, nor write alike. Hence we often use such words as *well, badly, fast, slowly, gracefully, awkwardly, sweetly, harshly, hastily,* etc., to describe the actions of persons, or to distinguish their actions from one another. These words are called *adverbs,* because they are generally *added* to *verbs.* Sometimes we distinguish actions by telling simply where or when they are done; as, "It rained *everywhere*"; "It rained *seldom.*"

We not only use words to describe objects and their actions, but we often use words to show in what degrees objects or actions have their qualities; as, *very* good; *tolerably* fast; *more* rapidly; *most* rapidly. And these words, which express degree, and are joined to adjectives and adverbs, are also called *adverbs.*

18. An **Adverb** is a word used to modify the meaning of a verb, an adjective, or another adverb.

"John studies *diligently"; here diligently* is an adverb, because it shows the manner of studying, or it shows the *mode* of doing that act which is *meant* by the word *studies*. "The apple is *very* good"; here *very* is an adverb, because it shows in what degree the apple is good. "The cars ran *uncommonly* fast"; here *uncommonly* is an adverb, because it shows in what degree the cars ran fast.

PREPOSITIONS.

By looking around us, we can easily see that the great mass of objects composing this world, is held together in a thousand different ways. "Houses are *on* the ground; cellars are *under* houses; and trees grow *around* houses." "Boats run *up* and *down* rivers, and rivers flow *between* hills." "The morning star rises *before* the sun, and night comes *after* sunset."

To describe objects and all their actions and states, we have not a sufficient number of words made especially for this purpose, or we should have to use these words disagreeably often. Hence we often describe objects, actions, or their qualities, by showing simply how they are related to other objects; or we make our thoughts pictures of parts of the world, by showing in these pictures how the corresponding things are linked together. Such linking words, that express relation, are the words *on, under, around, up, down, before,* and *after,* used above; and such words are called *prepositions,* because they are generally placed before the nouns and pronouns with which they make descriptive phrases. *Preposition* comes from *pre,* before, and *positio,* placing; the word therefore means *placing before.*

19. A **Preposition** is a word used to show the relation between a following noun or pronoun and some other word.

"The roses *by* my window are *in* full bloom." *By* is a preposition, because it shows the relation between *roses* and *window*, or the phrase *by my window* shows what roses are meant;

and *in* is a preposition, because it shows the relation between *are* and *bloom*, or the phrase *in bloom* shows in what condition the roses are or exist.

CONJUNCTIONS.

We frequently use certain words simply to connect words, phrases, clauses, or sentences, and to show the dependence of the parts thus connected. When you hear such words as *and*, *but*, *because*, you at once know that something more is to come, and that it bears a certain relation to what has been said. If I say, "John writes *and* ciphers"; "John spilt his ink on the desk *and* on the floor"; "John writes every day, *and* I generally look at his writing"; you see that the word *and* adds something more to what has been said, or joins two words, two phrases, or two propositions together; and since *conjunction* means *joining together*, this word, and others like it, have been called *conjunctions*.

20. A **Conjunction** is a word used to connect words, phrases, or propositions.

"He rides, *if* he is sick." "He rides, *though* he is sick." "He rides, *because* he is sick." Here *if*, *though*, and *because* are conjunctions, because each connects two propositions.

INTERJECTIONS.

When we see, hear, or in any other way notice things, our feelings are often suddenly excited, and we utter, almost unconsciously, certain little words that show these emotions. Words of this kind are such as *O*, *oh*, *ah*, *pish*, *tut*, *aha*, *whew*, etc., which you have doubtless often heard. They generally express surprise, wonder, joy, grief, anger, or contempt. *Interjection* means *throwing between*; and since these words are loosely thrown between other words in speaking, they have been called *interjections*.

21. An **Interjection** is a word that expresses an emotion, and is not connected in construction with any other word.

"Day broke; but then, oh! what a spectacle was that battle-field!" *Oh* is an interjection, because it expresses the sudden emotion of the speaker, and is not related to any of the other words of the sentence.

SUGGESTION TO THE TEACHER. — Take a walk with your class during some leisure interval, and teach them the parts of speech from the surrounding scenery.

Properties of the Parts of Speech.

GENDER.

When I say *John*, I mean a male; when I say *Mary*, I mean a female; when I say *child*, I can mean either a male or a female; and when I say *knife*, I mean neither a male nor a female. Hence some nouns are the names of males; some are the names of females; some are the names of either males or females; and some are the names of neither males nor females. From this distinction in the use of words, we get that property of nouns and pronouns which is called *gender*.

22. **Gender** is that property of nouns and pronouns which distinguishes objects in regard to sex.

23. There are four genders; the *masculine*, the *feminine*, the *common*, and the *neuter*.

24. A noun or pronoun is of the *masculine gender*, when it denotes a male. *Man.*

25. A noun or pronoun is of the *feminine gender*, when it denotes a female. *Woman.*

26. A noun or pronoun is of the *common gender*, when it denotes either a male or a female. *Person.*

27. A noun or pronoun is of the *neuter gender*, when it denotes neither a male nor a female. *House.*

The nouns *man*, *boy*, and *king* are of the masculine gender, because they denote males; the nouns *woman*, *girl*, and *queen* are of the feminine gender, because they denote females; the nouns *parent*, *cousin*, and *neighbor* are of the common gender, because they can be applied to either males or females; and the nouns *house*, *tree*, and *chair* are of the neuter gender, because they are the names of neither males nor females.

PERSON.

In speaking, we can refer either to ourselves, to the person spoken to, or to the person or thing spoken of; and there are no other ways of speaking. From this distinction in the use of words, we get that property of nouns, pronouns, and verbs, which is called *person*.

28. Person is that property of words which shows whether the speaker is meant, the person spoken to, or the person or thing spoken of.

29. There are three persons; the *first*, the *second*, and the *third*.

30. A noun or pronoun is of the *first person*, when it denotes the speaker. *I* saw you.

31. A noun or pronoun is of the *second person*, when it denotes the person spoken to. *You* saw me.

32. A noun or pronoun is of the *third person*, when it denotes the person or thing spoken of. *He* saw *it*.

"*I Paul* have written it"; here *I* and *Paul* are of the first person, because they denote the person speaking. In the sentence, "*Thomas*, *your* | *horse* has run away," *Thomas* and *your* are of the second person, because they denote the person spoken to; while the word *horse* is of the third person, because it denotes the object spoken of.

NUMBER.

There are not only many kinds of objects in the world, but generally many objects of each kind. In speaking, we often wish to show that we mean one object of a kind, or more than one; and we use words accordingly. From this distinction in the use of words, we get that property of words which is called *number*.

33. Number is that property of words which shows whether one object is meant, or more than one.

34. There are two numbers; the *singular* and the *plural*.

35. A noun or pronoun is of the *singular number*, when it denotes but one object. *Book*.

36. A noun or pronoun is of the *plural number*, when it denotes more objects than one. *Books*.

The nouns *Albert*, *tree*, and *girl* are of the singular number, because each denotes but one object; the nouns *boys*, *trees*, and *girls* are of the plural number, because each denotes more objects than one.

CASE.

When we speak of an object, we either say that it *is* something, that it *does* something, or that something *is done* to it; as, "The dove *is white*"; "The dove *coos*"; "The dove *was caught*." This relation of an object to what is said of it, is called *case*. When something is done, the act often affects some object; as, "The dove eats *corn*." This relation of the act to what is acted upon, is also called *case*. Almost every object in the world belongs to some other object, or is a part of some other; as, "*Mary's* dove"; "The *dove's* feathers."

All these relations of objects produce, in the expression of our thoughts, those relations between words which are called *cases*.

37. Case is that property of nouns and pronouns which shows how they are used in the construction of sentences.

38. There are three cases; the *nom'inative*, the *possessive*, and the *objective*.

39. A noun or pronoun is in the *nominative case*, when it is the subject of a predicate-verb. *I* run.

40. A noun or pronoun is in the *possessive case*, when it denotes possession. *My* hat.

41. A noun or pronoun is in the *objective case*, when it is the object of a transitive verb or a preposition. He sent *me* to *him*.

"*John* shot some *squirrels* in my *father's* | *field*." Here the word *John* is said to be in the nominative case, because it denotes the doer of something, or the person of whom something is said; the words *squirrels* and *field* are said to be in the objective case, because *squirrels* shows what he shot, and *field* shows in what; and the word *father's* is in the possessive case, because it denotes the owner of something.

The teacher should explain the subject of *Case* more fully.

VOICE.

When an act is done by one person or thing to another, we can state the fact in two ways, — either by telling what the doer does, or by telling what is done to the person or thing acted upon; as, "Brutus *killed* Cæsar"; "Cæsar *was killed* by Brutus." From this distinction in the use of words, we get that property of verbs which is called *voice*.

42. Voice is that property of verbs which shows whether the subject does, or receives, the act.

43. There are two voices; the *active* and the *passive*.

44. A verb is in the *active voice*, when it represents its subject as acting. I *struck*.

45. A verb is in the *passive voice*, when it represents its subject as acted upon. I *was struck*.

If I say, "The servant *scoured* the floor," *scoured* is said to be in the active voice, because it represents the subject, servant, as acting upon the floor; but if I say, "The floor *was scoured* by the servant," *was scoured* is said to be in the passive voice, because it represents the subject, floor, as acted upon.

MOOD.

Many actions really take place; but many actions are only in the mind, or people are in certain relations to them. If I say, "I *write*," I express something as a matter of fact; "I *may* or *can write*," I express not what is matter of fact, yet may become such, or I simply declare my relation to the act; "If I *were writing*," I express a mere supposition; "*Write*," I request it to be done; "*To write*," "*Writing*," I simply speak of the act. These different modes of expressing the verb, grammarians call moods; or, from this distinction in the use of verbs, we get that property of verbs which is called *mood*.

46. **Mood** is that property of verbs which shows how the act or state is referred to its subject.

47. There are four moods; the *indicative*, the *subjunctive*, the *potential*, and the *imperative*.

48. A verb in the *indicative mood* expresses an actual occurrence or fact. I *go*.

49. A verb in the *subjunctive mood* expresses a future contingency, or a mere wish, supposition, or conclusion. If I *go*. If I *were*.

50. A verb in the *potential mood* expresses power, possibility, liberty, inclination, duty, or necessity. I *may*, *can*, or *must go*.

51. A verb in the *imperative mood* expresses command, entreaty, exhortation, or permission. *Go* (thou).

52. There are two other forms of the verb, the *infinitive* and the *participle;* but it is hardly necessary to call them *moods.* See pp. 131, 217.

"I *study*"; here *study* is in the indicative mood, because it expresses something as really taking place. "If I *study*," "If I *were studying*"; here *study* and *were studying* are in the subjunctive mood, because the former expresses only what may take place hereafter, and the latter a mere supposition. "I *can study*"; here *can study* is in the potential mood, because it expresses only my ability in regard to studying. "*Study*"; here *study* is in the imperative mood, because it is given as a command to the person spoken to. "*To study*," "*Studying*"; here the actions are spoken of abstractly, that is, without referring them to any particular person or thing.

TENSE.

We can not separate our actions from time. Besides, the time of an act, or whether the act is completed or not, is often a matter of great importance to us. Time may naturally be divided into three great divisions, — *present, past,* and *future;* and in each of these periods we may speak of an act as simply taking place, or as completed. Thus: "I *write*," "I *have written*"; "I *wrote*," "I *had written*"; "I *shall write*," "I *shall have written*." These different ways of using verbs to distinguish time, are called *tenses.*

53. **Tense** is that property of verbs which shows the distinctions of time.

54. There are six tenses: the *present,* the *present-perfect;* the *past,* the *past-perfect;* the *future,* and the *future-perfect.*

55. A verb in the *present tense* expresses a present act or state. I *see.*

56. A verb in the *present-perfect tense* represents

something as completed in present time; or as past, but connected with present time. I *have seen.*

57. A verb in the *past tense* expresses simply a past act or state. I *saw.*

58. A verb in the *past-perfect tense* represents something as completed in past time. I *had seen.*

59. A verb in the *future tense* expresses simply a future act or state. I *shall see.*

60. A verb in the *future-perfect tense* represents something as completed in future time. I *shall have seen.*

The following sentences illustrate the six tenses: "The tree *blossoms*," "The tree *has blossomed*"; "The tree *blossomed*," "The tree *had blossomed*"; "The tree *will blossom*," "The tree *will have blossomed*."

COMPARISON.

Objects not only have qualities, but they often differ in their qualities, especially in degree; and not a little of our regard for objects depends on whether they have more or less of the qualities which we like or dislike. I may prefer, for instance, one apple to another because it is *larger* or *better* than the other. Actions also differ, and not unfrequently in degree. "John may study *diligently*, but Mary may study *more diligently*."

When we thus compare qualities, actions, and their circumstances, we usually make but three chief distinctions. We may speak of the quality itself, of a higher or a lower degree of it, or of the highest or the lowest degree; as, *wise, wiser, wisest; wise, less wise, least wise.* From these distinctions in the use of qualifying words, we get that property of adjectives and adverbs which is called *comparison.*

61. Comparison is that property of adjectives and adverbs which expresses quality in different degrees.

62. There are three degrees of comparison; the *positive*, the *comparative*, and the *superlative.*

63. An adjective or an adverb is in the *positive degree*, when it expresses simply the quality. *Wise.*

64. An adjective or an adverb is in the *comparative degree*, when it expresses the quality in a higher or a lower degree. *Wiser*, *less wise.*

65. An adjective or an adverb is in the *superlative degree*, when it expresses the quality in the highest or the lowest degree. *Wisest*, *least wise.*

"Jane is *tall*"; "Alice is *taller*"; "Louisa is the *tallest.*" "Jane writes *carefully*"; "Alice writes *less carefully*"; "Louisa writes *least carefully.*"

Fundamental Ideas, and Grammatical Development of Sentences.

OBJECTS.

1. Horse, dog, man, boys, lady, monkey, parasol.

The *horse* runs. The *dog* barks. The *man* works. *Boys* study and play. The *lady* lost *her* | *parasol.* The *monkey* had taken the *lady's* | *parasol.* I bought a *barrel* of *flour.* *Life* has *its* | *pleasures* and *its* | *troubles.*

2. For me to go. To die for one's country.

For me to go is impossible. (What is impossible?) He wishes *to sell the farm.* It is glorious *to die for one's country.*

3. That he will ever return. That you are not very attentive.

That he will ever return, is doubtful. (What is doubtful?) He says *that you are not very attentive to your business.* Is it not a pity, *that she knows so little?*

From the examples under this head, we can infer that a fundamental idea may show itself in a *word*, a *phrase*, or a *clause.* And from some of the examples under the following heads, it will be evident that it sometimes shows itself in the *changes* which it causes in the *forms of words.*

66. A **Phrase** is two or more words rightly put together, without making a proposition.

67. A **Clause** is a proposition that makes but a part of a sentence.

68. A **Sentence** is a thought expressed by a proposition, or a union of propositions, followed by a full pause.

ACTIONS.

Roll, read, climb, fly, swim, dance, sing.

The ball *rolls.* The boy *reads.* Squirrels *climb* trees. Pigeons *fly* rapidly. Ducks *swim.* The girls *sing* and *dance.* The girls *sing*, *walk*, and *dance.* The lightnings *dart* from cloud to cloud. The dew *bends* and *refreshes* the flowers.

Changes in Form. — The bell *tolls.* The bell *is tolling.* The bell *has tolled.* The bell *tolled.* The bell *had tolled.* The bell *will toll.* The bell *will have tolled.* The bell *may toll.* The bell *may have tolled.* The bell *should have tolled.* *Toll*, sweet bell!

I *strike.* I *am striking.* I *am struck.* I *was struck.* I *was striking.* I *struck.* I *have been striking.* I *have been struck.* I *shall strike.* I *shall be struck.* I *shall have been striking.* I *could strike.* I *could have been struck.* See Manner and Time, pp. 23 – 25.

QUALITIES, OR ATTRIBUTES.

1. **Words.** — A *green* meadow. The meadow is *green.* A *fragrant* pink. The pink is *fragrant.* *Warm* weather. The weather is *warm.* *Blue* hills. The hills are *blue.* *Long* lessons. The lessons were *long.* An *idle* boy. The boy is *idle.* A *bleak* and *frosty* morning. The morning is *bleak* and *frosty.*

She has *black* eyes, *rosy* cheeks, and *pearly* teeth. The *windy* summit, *wild* and *high*, rises against the *distant* sky. *Rosy* child, with forehead *fair*, *coral* lip, and *shining* hair.

Changes in Form. — A *cold* day; a *colder* day; the *coldest* day. The day was *cold.* The day was *colder.* The day was the *coldest.* *Large* fish live in *deep* water. *Larger* fish live in *deeper* water. The *largest* fish live in the *deepest* water. This tree has *many* apples. That tree has *more* apples. Yonder tree has *most* apples. See Degree, p. 26.

2. **Phrases.** — The flowers *of spring* and the stars *of heaven.* (What flowers?) Beauty is *like the flowers of spring,* but virtue is *like the stars of heaven.* The song *of the robin* was clear and tender. A bough *with red berries* floated on the water. The time *of danger* is the time *for courage.* It is the knell *of the departed year.* She has a bouquet *of rare and beautiful flowers.* The shady lawn *between the house and the river* is the most delightful part *of the farm.*

3. **Clauses.** — The lady *who sings so well,* is now in the house. (What lady?) He *who is fond of solitude,* is generally fond of studying. Those people *who flatter you,* are not your friends. The rain *which we have had this week,* has been very refreshing. We gathered every year large quantities of nuts, *which grew in great abundance in the forest | that surrounded our little farm.*

SEX.

He is a *boy.* *She* is a *girl.* *It* is a *tree.* I met *him.* You met *her.* We met *them.* *He* is my *father.* *She* is my *mother.* My *uncle* came on *his* pony. My *aunt* came in *her* carriage. His *brother* is a *duke.* His *sister* is a *duchess.* *He* married a *Jewess.* *She* married a *Jew.* *He* was *administrator.* *She* was *administratrix.* *He* is an *actor.* *She* is an *actress.* If *Joseph* was a *hero,* *Josephine* was a *heroine.* *Beaus* wait upon *belles.* The *prince* and the *princess* are now *king* and *queen.* Miss

Julia Brooks is the niece, not the nephew, of Mr. Julius Brooks. *Ganders* are white, and *geese* are gray. Ganders and geese are often called geese; drakes and ducks, ducks; horses and mares, horses; and heirs and heiresses, heirs. Two *sons* were all the *male descendants*, and three *daughters* all the *female descendants*, of the family. The *landlady* was very polite to the *gentlemen* and the *ladies;* but I assure you the *landlord* made them all pay for their titles the next morning.

NUMBER.

One *is.* Two or more *are.* One was. Two or more were. One has been. Two or more have been. One reads. Two or more read. The man works. The men work. My tooth is sound. My teeth are sound. That goose is wild. Those geese are wild. The boy has lost his knife. The boys have lost their knives. The girl has recited her lesson. The girls have recited their lessons. Only one half was accepted, though both halves were offered. The fox is a cunning animal. Foxes are cunning animals. The lady is modest. Ladies are modest. My foot is sore. My feet are sore. Our feet are sore. The mouse ran into its hole. The mice ran into their holes. The child sleeps. The children sleep. He bought an ox. They bought a yoke of oxen. I am busy. We are busy. Thou art. Ye are. I know myself. We know ourselves. He knows himself. They know themselves. He, she, or it, is good. They are good. The deer is a pretty creature. Deer are pretty creatures. The sheep is timid. Sheep are timid. The swine is greedy. Swine are greedy. I bought one dozen. He bought five dozen. This species of flowers is beautiful. These species of flowers are beautiful. The committee was large. The committee were not unanimous. The whole flock of partridges was caught. A multitude of people were assembled. The news is good. By this means he lost all. By these means he lost all. His lungs were diseased. Riches are seldom well spent. The embers were hot. The dregs were at the bottom. The tongs have been more useful than the snuffers. An *ash* is a tree; but *ashes* are the remains of burned wood or coal. *Geniuses* are men of genius, but *genii* are spirits. *Dice* are used for gaming, and *dies* are used for stamping. A *memorandum* denotes one thing, but *memorandă* denote more. A *rádius* is a single line, but *radĭī* are more. *Silk* is a kind of stuff, but *silks* are different kinds of silk. *Tea* is a kind of drink, but *teas* are different kinds of tea. By *spices* we usually mean different kinds of *spice*. The Misses Bates are sisters to Dr. Bates; and the Messrs. Barnes are brothers to Miss Barnes. Ten spoonfuls made a cupful; and twenty cupfuls made two pitchers nearly full. My brothers-in-law live at my father-in-law's residence. The court-martial appealed to all the preceding courts-martial's decisions.

Every boy has brought his books. All the boys have brought their books. All sugar is sweet. All ripe oranges are yellow. Either place is suitable. Both places are suitable. Neither place is suitable. Some children are industrious. Most children are lazy. Some one is talking. Some others are shutting their desks. Many were invited, but only a few came. Two make a pair; twelve make a dozen; and twenty make a score. Five pair were sold for fifty cents. Man's years are three score and ten.

PERSON.

This subject belongs more properly to the next head, Relation; but it is probably best to consider it in connection with Number.

I am. Thou art. He is. We are. You are. They are. I was. Thou wast. He was. We were. You were. They were. I have been. You have been. He has been. They have been. I write. He writes. *I* know *my* lessons. *He* knows *his* lesson. *You* know *your* lesson. *We* know *our* lessons. *They* know *their* lessons. *I* take care of *myself.* *You* take care of *yourself.* *We* take care of *ourselves.* *You* take care of *yourselves.* *He* takes care of *himself.* *They* take care of *themselves.* This is *mine;* that is *yours;* and the other is *his* or *hers.* The responsibility must fall upon *him,* upon *you,* or upon *me.* *We* have deceived *ourselves;* *you* have deceived *yourselves;* and *they* have deceived *themselves.*

RELATION.

Things have many relations to one another, and there are as many corresponding relations in the use of words; but we shall here notice only the chief of those relations which afford us the cases of nouns and pronouns.

Nominative Case. — The *tree* fell. (What fell?) The *flower* is unfolding. The *partridges* flew away. The *ship* moves. The *bell* rings. The *storm* roars. *She* laughed. (Who laughed?) *He* is reading. *I* shall return soon. The *boys* skate. The *trees* wave. The *fire* crackles and flames.

The *ocean* is blue. (What is blue?) This *map* is beautiful. The *well* was deep. Her *dress* was white and neat. The *lark* is a singing-bird. A *thief* is also a liar. Our *corn* is gathered. The *bread* is baked. *Brass* is made of zinc and copper.

Objective Case. — The fisherman catches *fish.* (Catches what?) The boy broke the *looking-glass.* My mother spins *flax.* The carpenter mended the *door.* The caterpillars devoured the *buds.* The weaver weaves *yarn* into cloth. The barber shaved *me.* I invited *him.* They hid *themselves.* The sun is warming the *garden.* Snow has covered the *hills.* She sang us a *song.*

I was going down the *street.* (Down what?) The Mississippi river rises in *Minnesota.* The book lay on the *table.* The child fell into the *well.* The bridge extends over the *river.* There is a plank-road from the *church* to the *college.* Several railroads run through *Pennsylvania.* The garden lies behind the *house.* The swallows flutter about the *eaves.*

Possessive Case. — Here is the *boy's* book. Here are the *boys'* books. This is the *man's* hat. These are the *men's* hats. I have cleaned *my* desk. We have cleaned *our* desks. You have broken *your* slate. He has bruised *his* thumb. She has torn *her* book. They had lost *their* way. This is *mine;* that is *yours;* and the other is *hers*. *Yours* are better than *ours*. My *brother's* estate belongs to one person only. My *brothers'* estate belongs to two or more persons. My *friend's* request comes from one person only. My *friends'* request comes from two or more persons. It is *our* duty, not *theirs*, to supply the *people's* wants. For *goodness'* sake, help me out of my troubles. He resides near *St. James's* Place.

MOOD OR MANNER.

We shall notice manner here, only so far as it relates to the different modes of expressing the verb in regard to its subject.

Indicative Mood. — John is at home. The glass was broken. The servant has made a fire. I had bought a farm. You shall see him to-morrow. The miller will have ground the corn before we return.

Subjunctive Mood. — If John were at home. If the glass be broken, you may throw it away. If the servant had made a fire, we should have been comfortable. If I bought the farm, I should have to sell it again. If you see him to-morrow, tell him to visit me. Had the miller ground the corn, we should have returned sooner.

Potential Mood. — John may be at home. The glass may have been broken. The servant could have made a fire. I would buy the farm, if he would sell it. You must see him to-morrow. The miller should have ground the corn.

Imperative Mood. — John, be at home. Peter, make a fire. Miller, grind the corn. Buy the farm. See him to-morrow, if you can. Behave yourself well. Be always kind and obliging. Do not grieve over unavoidable calamities.

INFINITIVES AND PARTICIPLES. — A servant came *to make* a fire. I ought *to have bought* the farm. It seems *to have rained* last night. Two hundred cannons, *flashing* and *thundering* continually, seemed *to shake* the very earth to its centre. The glass *having been broken*, we threw it away.

Akin to the forms of the verb known as MOODS, *are the forms of the verb called* VOICES.

John hit James. James was hit by John. He told the story. The story was told by him. The puppy tore the book. The book was torn by the puppy. The water turns the wheel. The wheel is turned by the water. The winds fan the flowers and ruffle the waters. The flowers are fanned and the waters are ruffled by the winds.

Akin to the MOODS *are also the* INTERROGATIVE *and the* NEGATIVE FORM *of the verb.*

He has read the book. He has not read the book. Has he read the book? Has he not read the book? You have been at home. You have not been at home. Have you been at home? Have you not been at home? Life is a burden. Life is not a burden. Is life a burden? Is not life a burden?

Akin to the MOODS *are also the* FORMS *of the tenses.*

He teaches. He teacheth. He is teaching. He does teach. He doth teach. You know him. Thou knowest him. You are a sinful people. Ye are a sinful people. I write. I am writing. I do write. I wrote. I was writing. I did write. Visit me. Do visit me. Are you the traitor? Art thou the traitor?

TIME.

A chief idea sometimes displays itself in the changes which it causes in a certain class of words. When this occurs, the idea becomes a grammatical property. Hence *time* affords us the *tenses*.

Changes in Form. — PRESENT TENSE. — The rose blooms. The boy studies. The work is done. The leaves are falling. The cars do not move. The journey is expensive.

PRESENT-PERFECT TENSE. — The rose has bloomed. The boy has studied. The work has been done. The leaves have been falling. The journey has been expensive.

PAST TENSE. — The rose bloomed. The boy studied. The work was done. The leaves were falling. The cars did not move. The journey was expensive.

PAST-PERFECT TENSE. — The rose had bloomed. The boy had studied. The work had been done. The leaves had been falling. The journey had been expensive.

FUTURE TENSE. — The rose will bloom. The boy will study. The work will be done. The leaves will be falling. The journey will be expensive.

FUTURE-PERFECT TENSE. — The rose will have bloomed. The boy will have studied. The work will have been done. The train will have left. The journey will have been expensive.

Time may show itself more definitely in *words phrases*, or *clauses*, that are used to express it.

Words. — The paper comes *weekly*. Go *instantly*. It rains *daily*. Your class is *now* reciting. He will return *late*. I shall see you *to-morrow*. He was here *yesterday*. Jonquils bloom *early*. The oak lives *long*. We shall *soon* reach the shore. He visits us *frequently*. She is *always* cheerful.

Phrases. — He remained *till morning*. A great storm arose *after sunset*. They were treated well *that night*, and *the next day* they departed. *At the break of day*, our horses were saddled. He rode a hundred miles *in twenty-five hours*. *For many a returning autumn*, this Indian visited the graves of his fathers. *Within twenty years from the foundation of this village*, deer had become scarce.

Clauses. — He knocked at the door, *before any one was awake*. We shall have peace, *after we have subdued the enemy*. Great

2

was the alarm in the colony, *while these children were lost.* We traveled through dim paths, *until the day drew to its close.* She smiled *when I told her how I had fallen into the water.*

Frequently, the changed form, the word, the phrase, and the clause, are all found in the same sentence; as, "He *came* | *early* | *in the morning,* | *while we were at breakfast.*"

PLACE.

Words. — The man is *here.* My horse stands *yonder.* I went *home.* I have seen him *somewhere.* I shall go *abroad.* The wall fell *inwards.* The birds flew *away.* The dog came *up.* Beautiful mansions gleamed *far* and *near.*

Phrases. — Melons grow *on vines.* Tea is brought *from China.* The child slept *in its mother's lap.* I was *at the same school.* You reside *in a pleasant part of the city.* Let us take a ramble *in the woods.* The cascade tumbled *from the rocks.* The army marched *round the hill.* We went *through swamps, thickets, and endless mud.* The Indians bore them *far beyond the limits of the settlement.* She sat *below us,* | *at the same table.*

Clauses. — We caught the minnows *where the water ripples over the rocks.* He remains *wherever he finds good company.* Thou hearest the sound of the wind; but thou canst not tell *whence it cometh*, and *whither it goeth.*

Frequently, two or more chief ideas are combined in the same sentence. A recent French novel begins thus: "*In the gloomy month of November,* | *when the English drown and hang themselves*, a disconsolate lover walked *forth* | *into the fields*, and seated himself *under a juniper-tree.*" (Time and place.)

DEGREE.

The river is *deep.* The lake is *deeper.* The ocean is the *deepest* body of water in the world. This one is *good;* that one is *better;* but the other is the *best.* Want is *bad;* but debt may be *worse*. A *good* name is *better* than riches. The *worst* gambler won the money. Who has *more* enemies and *fewer* friends, *more* trouble and *less* pleasure, than the miser? The pink is *more beautiful* than the marigold, and one of the *most fragrant* of flowers. He sat *next* to me, though I was *nearer* to the speaker. I said an *elder* soldier, not a *braver*. The *upper* room is already occupied. The *hindmost* man was left in the *utmost* distress. Most men judge others *more severely* than themselves. The weather is somewhat colder. The weather is so cold that I need my overcoat. There was so much noise that we could hear but very little of what was said.

Logical Development of Sentences.

Persons are often perplexed in determining how they shall arrange the words by means of which they express their thoughts. We generally express our thoughts as we naturally think them. That of which we think or speak, is naturally first thought of; and therefore it is generally first put down. To this we add, either before or after, all the descriptive words, phrases, and clauses, that belong to it; as, "The boy," "The little boy," "The little boy from the country," "The little boy from the country, who was here yesterday." Having thus got the subject, we next put down, in like manner, what is said of it; as, "wept," "wept bitterly," "wept bitterly for a long time," "wept bitterly for a long time because he could not find his father." "The little boy from the country, who was here yesterday, wept bitterly for a long time because he could not find his father." From this sentence it is obvious that we naturally first put down the subject, then the predicate, adding to each, or rather, including with each, the various qualities or secondary ideas which enter into the thought. We do not, however, always arrange our words in this way; but we sometimes put down first that which is first or most thought of, or makes the greatest impression upon us, even if it is not the object itself of which we are speaking. "The whole shelf of china fell down with such clattering and breaking as startled us all." In an occurrence of this kind, the fall is naturally the most striking part; and therefore we would probably say, "Down fell the whole shelf of china, with such clattering and breaking as startled us all."

We have many different thoughts. Our thoughts are made thus different because they are made up of many different ideas. Hence we get many different sentences; but nearly all of these sentences come more or less within the following description, or their parts answer to some of the following questions: —

Which one? How many? Of what kind?	**Subject.** Who? What?	Is what? Does what? Has what done to it?	When? Where? How? Why? As to what?

Let us now develop sentences accordingly.

SUBJECT.

Simplest Form. Who? What?

Columbus discovered America. *Galile'o* invented the telescope. *Capt. John Smith* colonized Virginia. *The Romans* destroyed Jerusalem. *Washington* is called the father of our country. *The Mayor* did not sign the bill.

Iron is the most useful metal. *Wealth* is not the greatest blessing. *A pen* may be more dangerous than a sword. *Poplars* grow rapidly. *Beauty* is a perishing flower.

Which one?

This TREE is an oak. *That* TREE is an elm. *Yonder* FARM belongs to me. *The first* MAN was shot. *The last* SQUADRON had arrived. *The youngest* CHILD is a daughter. *The eldest* SON is in the army. *Albert's* BOOKS are new. *My neighbor's* HORSES ran away. *Your* CAP fits me. *The* RIVER *Hudson* is in New York. *The* POET *Cowper* lived at Olney, in England. *The* STEAMSHIP *Arctic* was wrecked at sea. DAVID, *the son of Jesse,* became king of Israel. *The* TREE *dead at the top* was first cut down. *The* APPLE *highest on the tree* is not always the best. *The* ELM *before the house* must be a thousand years old. *The* PALING *around the garden* cost a hundred dollars. *The* FIELD *below the hill* is sometimes overflowed. *The* HILLS *beyond the river* are blue and beautiful. *The* HOUSE *erected by the church* is a parsonage. *The* TREES *planted along the river* grow rapidly. *The* LINES *written by Coleridge* are the most beautiful in the collection. *The* MAN *who sits next to the speaker,* is the president. *The* SUM *which was collected last Sunday,* has already been expended. *The* EVIL *about which you have said so much,* I have myself noticed.

How many?

Seven MEN were wounded. *A thousand* SOLDIERS make a regiment. *Twenty-five* CARRIAGES followed the hearse. *Only one* PERSON was seen in the canoe.

Of what kind?

A terrible THUNDER-STORM passed over the city. *A beautiful* LAKE lay in front of the house. *Silvery* CLOUDS fringed the horizon. *Iron* RAILING is very durable. *Small and beautiful* FLOWERS hung from the rocks. *A Colt's* REVOLVER was in his belt. *A hunter's* RIFLE was the only gun we had. ISABELLA, *a pious and noble queen,* assisted Columbus. COLLINS, *a poet of the most delicate sensibilities,* died in the prime of life. *A* SHIP *of the largest size* was sunk by this rifled cannon. *A* MAN *of good habits* generally enjoys good health. *The* FEATHERS *of ducks and geese* are used for beds. *A* PERSON *governed by his inclinations only,* is apt to be fickle. *A* LADY *admired and praised for her beauty,* is apt to become vain. PLANTS *reared in cellars* are seldom strong. LAWS *to prevent such outrages* should be enacted. *A* DINNER *to suit the occasion* was prepared. *The* MAN *who does not keep his word,* should not be trusted. *The* TREES *which are of the smallest size,* generally grow on high places. There arose, about this time, from the lower ranks of the people, *a* MAN *named Cromwell, of incredible depth of understanding, strict integrity, and unwavering resolution,* | *who with one hand held successfully the reins of civil authority, and with the other hurled victoriously the thunderbolts of war.*

PREDICATE.

Is what?

Life *is short.* Time *is precious.* War *is ruinous.* Cotton *is dear.* Farmers *are generally industrious.* Tomatoes *are wholesome.* Tomatoes *are red or yellow.* The pine-apple *is sweet and juicy.* The cat *is a useful animal.* John *is an idle boy.* The turkey *is a native of America.* The eagle *is a bird of great power.* The home of the brave *is the home of the free.* Gratitude *is the memory of the heart.* Hope *is the blossom of happiness.*

Does what?

Lambs *play.* Eagles *soar.* Cars *run.* Bears *growl* and *bite.* My head *aches.* James IS GATHERING *hazel-nuts.* Mary IS PARING *apples.* These islands PRODUCE *spices.* Cæsar FOUGHT *many battles.* You HAVE MADE *an enemy* of *him.* George GAVE *me a piece of his apple.* He TOLD *the story to his brother,* and *then* they both LAUGHED.

Has what done to it?

The door *was shut.* The stranger WAS BITTEN *by the dog.* The book WAS SENT *by mail.* The field *had been reaped.* The meat WILL BE COOKED *in a few hours.* The treasures of the pirates WERE BURIED *on an island.* The cargo *was landed.* The bells *were rung.* The old house WAS TORN *down by the workmen.* Our apples MUST BE GATHERED *next week.* The book IS *well* PRINTED *and* BOUND. Most people ARE *easily* DECEIVED *by fair appearances.*

When?

Words. — Come *soon.* I called *afterwards.* I have *never* seen him. He has *always* been in debt. Let us start *early.*

Phrases. — He visits us *every day.* I go to school *in the morning.* The robber was hanged *before noon,* | *about ten o'clock.*

Clauses. — Remain *till I return.* We often deceive ourselves, *while we try to deceive others. When wolf eats wolf,* there is nothing else in the woods to eat. We used to go to bed at nine o'clock, *when we lived in the country.* My heart dilated with honest pride, *as I recalled to mind the stern yet amiable characters of our Revolutionary fathers.*

Where?

Words. — Stop *here.* I called *there. Yonder* comes your father. I found no amusement *anywhere.* He lives *above.*

Phrases. — He visited us *at home.* We went *into the country.* There is a railroad *across the Isthmus of Darien.* Have you made a fire *in my room? On the banks of the Ganges* we can see the ebony in bloom.

Clauses. — The enemy put their cannons *where no enemy could approach them. Where honesty takes root,* the blessing of God makes it a tree. Wherever there is honey, *there you will also find bees. As far as we went,* there was nothing but desolation.

How?

Words. — Move *briskly.* I knocked *gently.* The boatmen sang *merrily.* Did your goods sell *well?* The procession moved *slowly* and *solemnly.*

Phrases. — It rained *in torrents.* She dresses *after the Spanish fashion.* We keep *without remorse* that which we acquire *without crime.* Half the people in the world live *at the expense of the other half.* Here comes the body of Cæsar, *mourned by Mark Antony.* The Assyrian came down *like the wolf on the fold.*

Clauses. — She behaved *as every modest young lady should behave.* The honest man speaks *as he thinks;* the flatterer, *as others like to hear. As you work,* so shall you thrive. The storm howled and tore *as if it would uproot the forest altogether.*

Why?

Words. — *Therefore* go. *Why* did you knock? *Wherefore* did you not write? *Hence* we parted.

Phrases. — She died *of grief.* The soldiers perished *from hunger and thirst.* The accident happened *through carelessness.* He went *for pleasure.* I want money *to buy books.* He called *to see you.*

Clauses. — He feels very much dejected, *for he cannot find employment.* I sent for the doctor, *because the child was very sick. Since you will have it so,* I will go with you. Live virtuously, *that you may be happy.*

As to what?

Phrases. — She is ashamed *to dance.* She has not the courage *to speak to him.* He is poor *in money,* but rich *in knowledge.* I am fond *of strawberries and raspberries.* I paid the bookseller *for the books.* He is indolent *about every thing.* I am able *to pay him.*

Clauses. — I consent *that you go and see him.* I feared *lest I should lose it.* I am glad *that we have peace again.*

Propositions, or Simple Sentences, combined.

Our thoughts consist of propositions, either single or combined. Propositions are combined in many different senses. The following are the principal modes of combining them.

Addition.

The coffee was good, *and* the rolls were excellent. I was alone, *and* the night was dark and stormy. That boy is very studious, *and* he is loved by all his classmates. The rivulet rested clear as crystal in the rocky urn, *and* large blue violets hung over the surrounding moss.

Contrariety.

He is a small man, *but* he is very strong. We started early, *but* we came an hour too late. He is stout and healthy in appearance, *yet* he has always been sickly. We lost the battle, *notwithstanding* we did our utmost to win it. *Although* he is accused, *yet* he is innocent.

Alternation, or Choice.

I will *either* send you my horse, *or* you may hire one at my expense. *Neither* spend your money before you have it, *nor* buy what you do not need. *Either* he will hate the one, and love the other; *or* else he will hold to the one, and despise the other.

Cause.

This field will produce well, *because* the soil is fertile. I refused his present, *for* I knew he offered it from selfish motives. He is angry; *therefore* let him alone. *As* it is impossible to go, let us remain contentedly at home. *Since* we cannot enjoy this world long, is it not strange that most people are so very avaricious?

Sometimes a sentence will consist of a combination of differently connected propositions; as, "Great men undertake great things, *because* they are themselves great; *but* fools undertake them, *because* they think them easy." (Cause and contrariety.)

Condition.

If I were in your place, I would join the army. Would you go, *if* you should be invited? *If* there were no evil listeners, there would be no evil talkers. *So* it answers the purpose, it will matter little how indifferent it is.

No Connective expressed.

When no connective is expressed, the connecting sense generally is that of *and*, *for*, *but*, *if*, or *that is*.

The woods are hushed, the waters rest. Every age has its pleasures; every situation has its charms. It is not too late: it is only nine o'clock. He who renders a service, should forget it; he who receives it, should remember it. That concerns you, does it not? Would you thrive? rise at five. (If you would thrive, etc.) Had he done his duty, he would not now be in disgrace.

PART II.

WORDS UNCOMBINED.

GRAMMAR AND ITS DIVISIONS.

69. Grammar is the science which teaches how to speak and write correctly.

70. English Grammar is the science which teaches how to speak and write the English language correctly.

Every language can be investigated according to the following particulars: —

1. The sounds of its words.
2. The forms of its words.
3. The classification of its words, according to their meanings and variations.
4. The combination of its words, in the construction of sentences.
5. The finish and ornament of sentences. Hence, —

71. ENGLISH GRAMMAR is divided into five parts; *Pronunciation*, *Orthog'raphy*, *Etymol'ogy*, *Syntax*, and *Pros'ody*.

72. Pronunciation treats of the sounds of letters, and of the sounds and stress of syllables in uttering separate words.

73. Orthography treats of the forms of letters, and teaches how to spell words correctly.

74. Etymology treats of the derivation, classes, and properties of words.

75. Syntax treats of the relations and arrangement of words in sentences.

76. Prosody treats of figures, versification, utterance, and punctuation.

77. The basis of grammar, or the test of correctness in the use of language, is the usage of the best writers and speakers.

PRONUNCIATION.

LETTERS AND SOUNDS.

78. LANGUAGE consists of a great variety of sounds, which are used as the signs of ideas, and are called words.

79. These sounds can all be reduced to a small number of simple sounds, which are represented to the *eye* by means of *letters*.

80. A **Letter** is a character that denotes one or more of the elementary sounds of language, or it is the least, distinct part of a written word.

EXAMPLES. — A, b, c; *age*, *at*, *art*; *bubble*; *cent*, *cart*.

81. The English language contains about forty elementary sounds, which are represented by twenty-six letters, called the *alphabet*.

The Phoneticians make *forty-three* elementary sounds.
LONG VOWELS *: *eel*, *ale*, *arm*, *all*, *ope*, *food*.
SHORT VOWELS: *ell*, *an*, *odd*, *up*, *foot*.
SHADE VOWELS: *earth*, *air*, *ask*.

* That the pupil may not confound the letters with their powers, let him substitute "VOCALS" for "VOWELS," "DIPHTHONG VOCALS" for "DIPHTHONGS," and "LIQUID SOUNDS" for "LIQUIDS."

DIPHTHONGS: *i*sle, *oi*l, *ow*l, m*u*le.

COALESCENTS: *y*ea, *w*ay.

ASPIRATE: *h*ay.

EXPLODENTS: ro*p*e, ro*b*e, fa*t*e, fa*d*e, et*ch*, ed*g*e, lo*ck*, lo*g*.

CONTINUANTS: sa*f*e, sa*v*e, wrea*th*, wrea*th*e, bu*ss*, bu*zz*, vi*ci*ous, vi*si*on.

LIQUIDS: fa*ll*, fa*r*.

NASAL LIQUIDS: see*m*, see*n*, si*ng*.

If we consider the foregoing "diphthongs" composite, equivalent to *ä-ĭ*, *ŏ-ĭ*, *ä-oo*, and *ĭ-oo*, our language will have but *thirty-nine* simple sounds. If we regard *c* as a more slender sibilant than *s;* and if *o*, as heard in *form*, is broader or more orotund than *a*, as heard in *fall*, then we shall have *forty-one* simple sounds in all. — See p. 61.

82. Some letters represent several sounds each; as *a* in *ăt*, *ärt*, *all*, etc.

83. Sometimes different letters represent the same sound; as *c* and *s* in "sin*c*e" and "sen*s*e."

84. Sometimes two or more letters represent but one sound; as *ph* = *f*, in *ph*leme; *eau* = *o*, in *beau;* *ch*, in *church.*

85. Hence our alphabet is both *defective* and *redundant;* for a perfect alphabet should have one letter, and but one, for every simple sound.

86. The *name* of a letter is what it is called in the alphabet.

87. The *power* of a letter is the sound, or oral element, which it represents. Some letters have several powers each.

The name of a letter is generally one of its powers, or a syllable that shows the power; but the name and the power should not be confounded. Thus, *a* represents the sounds of *ā*, *ă*, *ä*, *a*. *Kay* shows the power, or oral element, represented by *k*.

CLASSIFICATION OF LETTERS.

88. The **Letters** are divided into *vowels* and *consonants;* the consonants are divided into *mutes* and *semivowels*, and some of the semivowels are called *liquids*.

Vowels.

89. A **Vowel** is a letter that denotes pure tone.

The vowel sounds are formed by keeping the organs of speech more or less apart or open, or by letting the voice flow out freely. The organs of speech are the *lips*, the *teeth*, the *tongue*, the *palate*, and the *glottis*.

90. The vowels are *a*, *e*, *i*, *o*, and *u*. Also *w* and *y* are vowels, when equivalent to the vowels *u* and *i;* as in *now* and *tyrant*.

91. A **Diphthong** is the union of two vowels to denote one sound.

Ex. — PROPER: o*i*l, fr*au*d, gr*ou*nd. IMPROPER: *ē*ar, p*ō*ur, yo*ū*r, dec*ē*it, sl*ē*ight.

92. A diphthong is *proper*, if the two vowels are heard, or denote a sound different from that of either; *improper*, if only one vowel is heard.

93. A **Triphthong** is the union of three vowels to denote one sound.

Ex. — B*eau*ty, bur*eau*, v*iew*, l*ieu*, bu*oy*.

94. Triphthongs are also divided, like diphthongs, into *proper* and *improper*.

Consonants.

95. A **Consonant** is a letter that can be fully uttered only with the aid of a vowel sound. It denotes a contact of some of the organs of speech, called an *articulation*.

Some of the consonant sounds we modify by emitting breath; as in the sounding of *th* or *f*. *H* denotes only an emission of breath.

Some of the consonant sounds we modify by using the head as a sort of drum; as in the sounding of *m* or *l*.

96. The consonants are all the letters except the vowels.

97. *W* or *y* is a consonant, when a vowel sound follows it in the same syllable; as in *water*, *I'-o-wa*, *year*, *Bun-yan*.

98. *U* and *i* are consonants, when equivalent to the consonants *w* and *y*; as in *per-suade*, *pon-iard*, u-*nit* (consonant and vowel).

X is equivalent to *ks*, *gz*, or *z*; as in *tax*, ex-*act*, X*erxes*.

99. A **Mute** is a consonant that has no sound whatever without the aid of a vowel, and at the end of a word stops the voice entirely.

100. The mutes are *b*, *p*, *d*, *t*, *k*, *q*u (=*k*w); also *c* and *g* hard, as in *lac* and *gig*.

101. A **Semivowel** is a consonant that has some sound of its own, being in its nature between a vowel and a mute.

102. The semivowels are all the consonants except the mutes.

103. The **Liquids** are *l*, *m*, *n*, *r*; and perhaps *s* and *z*, which are sometimes called sibilants.

The liquids are so called from their soft sound, which easily flows into and unites with that of other letters.

Ex. — String, brilliance. "Lull with Amelia's liquid name the Nine." — *Pope*.

---

104. A letter is said to be *silent*, when it is suppressed in pronunciation.

Ex. — Wa*l*k, kil*n*, ni*gh*t, vict*u*als, *h*our, *ph*t*h*isic.

105. In singing, vowel sounds are made most prominent; and clear and distinct utterance is attained chiefly by pronouncing the consonants with exactness.

ACCENT.

106. Accent is a stress of voice on a certain syllable of a word that has two or more syllables.

Ex.—*Bak′*-er, a-*muse′*; an *en′*-trance, to en-*trance′*. "An *Au-gust′* procession in the month of *Au′*-gust."

Accent sometimes serves to distinguish words that are spelled alike, or to show the chief part of the word.

107. Words of three or more syllables generally have a chief accent, called the *primary accent;* and one or more inferior accents, called the *secondary accent* or *accents.*

Ex.—Lu′-mi-na′-ry, an′-te-ce′-dent, in-com′-pre-hen′-si-bil′-i-ty.

108. Some words, mostly compounds, have two accents of nearly equal stress.

Ex.—A′-men′, fare′-well′ (interjection), knit′-ting-nee′-dle.

109. The *penult* syllable of a word is the second syllable from the end; and the *antepenult* is the third syllable from the end.

110. Most words used in our language have the chief accent either on the penult or else on the antepenult.

PENULT: Con′-quest, at-tor′-ney, dis-a-gree′-ment, Jer-e-mi′-ah.

ANTEPENULT: Tem′-per-ate, con-tin′-u-al, mu-ta-bil′-i-ty, Je-ru′-sa-lem.

111. RULES FOR PRONUNCIATION.

1. Give to every syllable its proper sound.

Do not say *ben* for *been*, *wāre* for *wĕre*, *blāte* for *blēat*, *dreen* for *drain*, *keow* for *cow*, *toon* for *tūne*, *săssy* for *saucy*, *rench* for *rinse*, *hŭf* for *hoof*, *pīnt* for *point*, *larn* for *learn*, *ŏnly* for *ōnly*, *guīne* for *going*, *atter* for *after*, *winder* for *window*, *meader* for *meadow*, *hostīle* for *hostĭle*, *genuīne* for *genuĭne*, *Americā* for *Americă*, *Canader* for *Canadă*.

2. Be careful not to omit any letter or letters of a syllable, nor any syllable or syllables of a word, that are not silent.

Do not say *kep* for *kept*, *ness* for *nests*, *lenth* for *length*, *strenth* for *strength*, *srub* for *shrub*, *sriek* for *shriek*, *mornin* for *morning*, *shinin* for *shining*, *chile* for *child*, *wuss* for *worse*, *goverment* for *government*, *hickry* for *hickory*, *particler* for *particular*, *spose* for *suppose*.

3. Place the accent on the proper syllable.

Do not say *fan'-atic* for *fanat'-ic*, *interest'-ing* for *in'-teresting*, *i'-dea* for *ide'-ä*, *mu'-seum* for *muse'-um*, *indus'-try* for *in'-dustry*, *in'-quiry* for *inqui'-ry*, *hospit'-al* for *hos'-pital*.

4. Bear in mind that derivative words are not always accented or pronounced like their primitives.

Pyr'-amid, *pyram'-idal*, not *pyr'-amidal; converse'*, *con'-versant*, not *convers'-ant; lament'*, *lam'-entable*, not *lament'-able; prē-serve'*, *prĕs-ervation*, not *prē-servation; a-pos'-trophe*, *ăp-os-troph'-ic*, not *a-pos'-trophic*.

5. Remember that a change in the part of speech sometimes requires a change in the accent.

To absent', to be ab'-sent; to escort', an es'-cort; to perfume', a per'-fume.

But sometimes we suppose such words differ in pronunciation, when they really do not. To *ally'*, an *ally'*, not *al'-ly;* to *consent'*, my *consent'*, not *con'-sent*.

6. In doubtful cases, pronounce words according to their spelling or according to analogy.

Lieutenant is better pronounced *loo-ten'-ant* than *lev-ten'-ant*.

ORTHOGRAPHY.

FORMS OF THE LETTERS.

112. The letters are used in different styles; as, Roman, *Italic*, *Script*, and **Old English**.

113. The letters are printed in types of various sizes:

Great Primer, English, Pica, Small Pica, Long Primer, Bourgeois, Brevier, Minion, Nonpareil, Agate, Pearl, Diamond.

114. The letters are used either as capital letters or as lower-case or small letters.

CAPITAL LETTERS.

115. Small letters are preferred in all ordinary writing, except where capital letters are needed for distinction.

116. Words that begin with capital letters, may be divided into two classes; *First Words*, and *Words that are themselves Words of Distinction.*

First Words.

117. The first word of every sentence or its equivalent, or the first word after a full pause, should begin with a capital letter.

For examples, see any page of this book.

118. Within a sentence, the first word of any important beginning may commence with a capital letter.

Ex. — "*Resolved*, That our senators be requested," etc.

"One truth is clear: Whatever is, is right." — *Pope.*

W. *Be it enacted by the Legislature of New York*, that a tax, etc.

1. Any part of a sentence, especially in enumeration, that is broken off to begin a new line for the purpose of making it more conspicuous, should begin with a capital letter.

Ex. — "Our citizens have contributed —
"To the support and improvement of schools, . $12,275;
"To the building and repairing of bridges, . . . 5,130."
"I am, Sir, with sincere esteem,
"Your faithful servant,
"ROBERT PEEL."

W. The work is admirably adapted to the use of schools, —
by thorough and varied exercises;
by frequent and complete reviews;
by simplicity of terms and arrangement.

2. The first word of a direct quotation, an example, or other saying, so introduced as to imply a transition from one speaker to another, should begin with a capital letter.

Ex. — Solomon says; "Pride goeth before destruction." Remember this ancient maxim: "Know thyself." She called out, "Why did you go?" He answered, No. *Stare* is often used in a bad sense; as, "The impudent fellow *stared* at me."

W. They shouted, "victory." Every tongue shall exclaim with heartfelt joy, welcome! welcome! La Fayette.

But indirect quotations or questions, resumed or partial quotations, and words quoted merely as language, should not begin with capitals.

Ex. — Solomon says, that pride goes before destruction. She asked me why I went. This is indeed, as Chatham says, "a perilous and tremendous moment."

With Mr. Headley, an event always "transpires." — *Poe.*

3. The first word of every line of poetry should begin with a capital letter.

Ex. — "But now the smiles are thicker,
Wonder what they mean;
Faith, he 's got the Knicker-
Bocker Magazine!" — *Saxe.*

W. Now bright the sunbeam on St. Lawrence smiles,
her million lilies, and her thousand isles.

Words of Distinction.

119. The words *I* and *O* should always be capitals.

Ex.—"For *I* will not forsake thee, *O* friend of my youth."

W. He knew i was there. Such, o music! is thy heavenly power.

120. Every word denoting the Deity should begin with a capital letter.

Ex.—The Most High; the Supreme; the Infinite One; to God and his angels; Divine Providence; our Lord Jesus Christ; the Father, the Son, and the Holy Ghost.

"The hope of my spirit turns trembling to *Thee*."—*Moore*.

W. The holy spirit; the eternal; the omnipotent; our saviour; to him who is the friend of the widow and the orphan.

1. A common word that merely relates to God, must sometimes begin with a capital letter, to show its reference to the Deity.

Ex.—"The *Hand* that made us is divine."—*Addison*. "He who is the *Mind* of the universe, overlooks no small things."—*John Wilson*.

2. A pronoun used in connection with a name that is the chief word denoting the Deity, usually requires no capital.

Ex.—"God provides for all *his* creatures."—*Blair*. "O *thou* merciful God!"—*Book of Common Prayer*.

W. O Lord, Thou Who art merciful and omnipotent, save us.

3. An ordinary adjunct used as a part of a name that denotes the Deity, or a word that describes rather than denotes the Deity, usually requires no capital.

Ex.—The *all-seeing* Searcher *of our hearts*; *great* Parent *of good*; to Him who is the *friend* of the widow and the orphan.

W. The King of Kings, and lord of lords; the judge of the world. They were made by the Wisdom and Goodness of thy Hand.

121. Every proper name, or each chief word of a proper name, should begin with a capital letter.

Ex. — Thomas, Susan, Sunday, Monday, May, Alabama; George Washington; Amelia B. Welby; the Duke of Wellington; Charles the First. When a word implying distinction or honor is constantly used with a proper name, it becomes a part of the name itself. (The teacher should explain to the pupil what a proper noun is.)

W. mary, george, march, saturday, kentucky, henry l. gaylor.

122. Every title, whether used alone or in connection with a proper noun, should begin with a capital letter.

Ex. — *Mr.* Brown; *Mrs.* Elizabeth B. Browning; *Dr.* Vaughan; *Maj.* Holt; *Gen.* Washington; *Sir* Isaac Newton; James M. Marlow, *Esq.*; Alexander the *Great;* a letter from the *Hon.* Robert Wells. "The petty governor of Shiraz has the title of 'Flower of Courtesy,' 'Nutmeg of Consolation,' and 'Rose of Delight.'" — *Gazetteer.* "'You are old, *Father* William,' the young man replied." — *Southey.* "So *Master* Dick went off on his travels." — *O. W. Holmes.* "The *Doctor* now heard the approach of clattering hoofs." — *Id.*

W. From capt. Jones; lord Byron; Joseph Allen, esq.; a speech from gov. Andrew. John bull can tell brother Jonathan what are the consequences of being too fond of glory.

Proper names consist chiefly of the names of persons, places, and time. They are therefore very numerous, amounting to millions. And since it is not always easy to make a new and acceptable proper name, a common word or phrase of the language, whose meaning is supposed to suit, is often taken and made a sort of proper name.

1. When a new proper name is made from an old one, by the addition of some common word, the common word generally begins with a capital.

Ex. — Orleans, *New Orleans;* Cambridge, *East Cambridge;* Boston, *South Boston, Boston Neck;* Scott, *Gen. Scott;* Jefferson, *Jefferson City;* Madison, *Madison Square;* Astor, *Astor House;* Vernon, *Mount Vernon;* Pike, *Pike's Peak;* Mexico, *the Gulf of Mexico;* Britain, *the British Channel.*

W. Rhode island; Miller's landing; lower California; Japan sea; Harper's ferry; Lafayette place; Hudson's bay; the bay of Honduras; lake Erie; cape Ann; mount Auburn; Cook's inlet; Behring's strait; the strait of Magellan; Queen Charlotte's sound; Faneuil hall; William and Mary's college.

2. When a common word or phrase of the language is raised to the dignity of a proper name for a particular object, the word or chief words should begin with capitals.

Ex. — The Park; Salt River; Great Bear Lake; Lake Superior; the Black Sea; Big Sandy; Land's End; the Cape of Good Hope; the United States; the Western States; the Mountains of the Moon; the Old South Church; the City Hall; a book called — The Temple of Truth.

To this head may be referred the titles of books and topics.

W. The laurel hills; the dead sea; white river; sandy hook; a hill called cedar crest; the lake of the woods; point lookout; the five points; pea ridge; the white sulphur springs; the rocky mountains; union square; central park; on fifth avenue, near spruce street; from the common, to the dry dock.

---

123. An ordinary noun applied to a personified object, often becomes a proper noun in sense, and should then begin with a capital letter.

Ex. — "The *Wind* and the *Sun* loved the *Rose*,
But the *Rose* loved but one;
For who recks the *wind* where it blows,
Or loves not the *sun*." — *Bulwer*.

W. Pride, poverty, and fashion, once undertook to keep house together.

124. Every word derived from a proper name should begin with a capital letter.

Ex. — Columbia, American, Roman, Jesuit, Christian, Scotchman. "He is the *Cicero* of his age." "A *Southern* man is from the South."

W. These spaniards joined the italian army.

125. But when such a word has lost its reference to

the proper name, and has become a common word of the language, it should not begin with a capital.

Ex.—A guinea, sandwiches, damask, daguerrotype, galvanize, china-ware.

126. A word of special importance or emphasis, or a word so peculiarly or technically applied as not to be sufficiently definite if written otherwise, should begin with a capital letter.

Ex.—The General Assembly; the excellence of our Constitution; the War Department; William Penn with several Friends; the American Revolution. "The Reform Bill." — *London Times.* "Education is the great business of the Institute." — *Holmes.* "The other member of the Committee was the Rev. Mr. Butters, who was to make the prayers before the Exercises of the Exhibition." — *Id.*

W. Put this motto upon the banner: "The union, the constitution, and the enforcement of the laws."

Frequently, in accordance with the foregoing rule, the subject of discourse is commenced with a capital letter; as, "The disasters which this little band of Puritans encountered." — *Everett.*

127. In capitalizing phrases or sentences, whether used as titles or as headings, distinguish the nouns by capitals; also important adjectives, participles, or other words; but always write the mere particles in small letters.

Ex.—*Episcopal Innovation; or, the Test of Modern Orthodoxy, in Eighty-seven Questions, imposed as Articles of Faith, upon Candidates for Licenses and Holy Orders, in the Diocese of Peterborough; with a Distinct Answer to each Question, and General Reflections relative to their Illegal Structure and Pernicious Tendency.* — SIDNEY SMITH.

128. Names, titles, or mottoes, when very emphatic, or when designed to catch the eye from a distance, are frequently printed or painted wholly in capitals. And in Advertisements or Notices, the liberty of capitalizing is carried to a great and almost indefinite extent.

Examples to be Corrected.

Formula. — Incorrect: the word ——, beginning with a small —, should begin with a capital —; because ——. (Give the precept violated, as presented on some preceding page; and vary the Formula when a variation is needed.)

1. These Birds go South in Winter, but return in Spring or Summer. — *Audubon.*

2. for Rent or Sale. balance, $ 9.25.

3. When Laud was arraigned, "can any one believe me a traitor?" exclaimed the astonished prelate. — *Bancroft.*

4. The question is, which of them can best pay the penalty?

5. The answer may be, yes or no.

6. The bible says, children, obey your parents.

7. The blood of those who have Fallen at concord, lexington, and Bunker hill, cries aloud, "it is time to part."

8. Lindley murray teaches, "when a quotation is brought in obliquely after a comma, a Capital is unnecessary; as, solomon observes, That the child is spoiled by sparing the rod." — *octavo grammar*, P. 284.

9. Washington city, the Capital of the united states, is in the district of Columbia.

10. This chief had the sounding appellation of white thunder.

11. In ancient days there dwelt a sage called discipline.

12. There lay madam partlet, basking in the sun, breast-high in sand.

13. Falsehood sheltered herself among the passions.

14. This County was settled by welsh emigrants, who were zealous christians, and entered heartily into our revolutionary struggle.

15. New year's day and the fourth of July are holidays.

16. Cowper, the Author of the Task, was a good Poet.

17. The secretary of state visited fortress Monroe.

18. The president lives in the white house.

19. He was President of the Massachusetts historical society, and the Editor of the Boston daily advertiser.

20. The Missouri compromise was discussed in the senate.

21. A presbyterian minister preached every sunday at west Brookfield.

22. She is gone to him who comforteth as a father comforteth.

23. The Guests were entertained by mayor Rice, at his residence, no. 34, union park.

24. Believe not each aspersing tongue,
as most weak people do;
but still conclude that story wrong
which ought not to be true.

SYLLABLES.

129. A **Syllable** is a letter, or a union of letters, pronounced as one unbroken sound.

Ex. — A, on, no, stretched, barb'dst, a-e-ri-al, pro-fu-sion.

130. Every syllable must consist of one or more vowels, or of one or more vowels enclosed on one or both sides by one or more consonants.

Ex. — O, i-dle, au-tumn, bro-ker, an, ants, dot, breast.

SYLLABICATION.

131. **Syllabication** is the division of words into syllables.

132. Words are divided into syllables, to show their pronunciation or derivation.

Ex. — De-pose, dep-o-si-tion, re-in-force-ment, lov-er, rain-bow.

Syllabication thus enables us, in writing, to divide words properly at the ends of lines.

133. In dividing words into their syllables, we should give to every syllable precisely those letters which the correct pronunciation of the word gives to it.

Ex. — Su-prem-a-cy, pro-cras-ti-nate, pref-ace, oth-er, ma-ter-nal, as-tron-o-my, twin-kle, tic-kle, Rob-ert, E-liz-a-beth.

W. Plan-ting, un-loa-ding, ma-keth, or-ga-ni-zing, e-squire, go-vern, cons-ti-tu-tion, va-le-tu-din-a-ri-an, mark-et.

134. Words should generally be divided according to their prefixes, suffixes, or grammatical endings, if they have any; and compound words should be divided into their simple ones.

Ex. — Re-new, ring-let, great-er, wis-est, ful-ly, boat-swain.

W. Dril-ling, wea-ver, a-noth-er, wi-ser, ren-ted.

135. When derivation and pronunciation conflict, the division must be made according to the *pronunciation.*

Ex. — Ap-a-thy, not a-path-y; rec-ol-lec-tion (remembrance), ap-os-tol-ic-al, ther-mom-e-ter, pred-i-cate, prop-o-si-tion.

W. A-scribe, or-tho-graph-y, pre-fer-ence, de-po-si-tion, par-ti-ci-pi-al.

136. A word that has more syllables than one, may be divided at the end of a line, but only at the close of a syllable.

The part in either line should consist of at least more letters than one, and be of such a nature that it is not likely to be misconceived at the first impression. Such words as *a-long*, *a-gain*, *o-lio*, *craft-y*, *read-y*, *curv-ed*, should rather stand wholly in one line; and such words as *accompli-ces*, *advanta-ges*, should rather be divided *accom-plices*, *advan-tages*.

Divide into syllables: —

Artery, sorcery, luscious, varnish, blanket, pickle, musket, extraordinary, possession, decision, nevertheless, western, monkey, paternal, unserviceable, reformation, recreate, reëlect, grafter, rafter, charter, chanter, waiter, traitor, felony, felonious, active, picture, pitcher, lounger, noisy, knitting, shilling, willing, azure, national, siren, soldier, associate, pronunciation, Boston, Diana.

RULES FOR SPELLING.

137. Spelling is the art of expressing words by their right letters, properly arranged. This art must be learned chiefly from spelling-books, dictionaries, and observation in reading.

Rule I.—Doubling.

Words of one syllable, ending in a single consonant preceded by a single vowel; and words of more syllables, ending in the same way, with the accent fixed on the last syllable,—double the consonant before a vowel in the derivative word.

Ex.—Sad, *sadder, saddest;* rebel′, *rebelled, rebellion;* rob, *robber;* win, *winning;* fop, *foppish;* drum, *drummer;* up, *upper;* admit, *admittance;* quiz, *quizzed.*

In other cases, no doubling takes place.

Ex.—Seal, *sealed;* gild, *gilded;* hard, *harder;* infer′, (*infer′red,*) *in′fer ence;* bigot, *bigoted;* tax, *taxed.* *X* final = two consonants, *ks* or *gz;* therefore never doubled.

There is a difference between *robed* and *robbed*, *planing* and *planning*, *hater* and *halter*.

Good writers sometimes double *l*, contrary to the Rule above.

Ex.—"Traveller"—*Prescott, Bryant;* "carolled"—*Irving.*

Rule II.—Final Y.

Final **Y**, preceded by a consonant and followed by any letter except *i*, is changed into *i* in the derivative word.

Ex.—Fly, *flies;* glory, *glories, glorify, glorified, glorifying, glorifi-*

cation; try, *trial;* pretty, *prettier, prettiest;* merry, *merrily, merriment;* pity, *pitiable;* ivy, *ivied.*

Exceptions: Most of the derivatives of *sly, dry,* and *shy* usually retain *y;* as, *dryly, slyness.*

Final **Y**, preceded by a vowel, or followed by *i*, remains unchanged in the derivative word.

Ex. — Chimney, *chimneys;* gay, *gayer, gayest, gayety;* cry, *crying,* crier; buoy, *buoyant;* destroy, *destroyer;* annoy, *annoyance;* joy, *joyful.*

Exceptions: Pay, *paid; said, laid, daily; staid* (remained), *stayed* (checked).

Rule III. — Final E.

Final **E**, when silent, is *rejected* before a *vowel* in the derivative word. But it is *retained* when needed to keep *c* or *g* soft, or to preserve the identity of the word.

Ex. — Bite, *biting;* force, *forcible;* sale, *salable;* rogue, *roguish.* Agree, *agreeable;* peace, *peaceable;* singe, *singeing;* glue, *gluey.*

There is a difference between *dying* and *dyeing, singing* and *singeing.*

Words ending with *ie* change *i* into *y*, before *i*, to prevent the doubling of *i;* as, Die, *dying;* vie *vying;* tie, *tying;* lie, *lying.*

Final **E** is *retained* before a *consonant* in the derivative word. Sometimes it is *rejected* when not needed.

Ex. — Base, *baseless;* rue, *rueful;* definite, *definitely;* eye, *eyelet;* whole, *wholesome,* but *wholly.* Due, *duly;* true, *truly;* awe, *awful;* judge, *judgment.* (*D* softens the *g*, and renders the *e* unnecessary.)

Monosyllables that end with *f, l,* or *s*, preceded by a single vowel, generally have this consonant double, as *cliff, mill, pass;* words that end with any other consonant in the same way, generally have it single, as *man, cat, map.* The final consonant of a primitive word generally remains double, but should not be trebled, in the derivative word, as in *blissful, skillful, fully.*

One *l* is often dropped from *ll*, especially when the accent is on some other syllable; as in *shalt*, *always*, *welcome*, *fulfill'*, *use'ful*. Derived verbs generally prefer the ending *ize* to *ise*, as *legal*, *legalize*. *Ei* after *c*, as in *ceiling*, *deceive;* generally *ie* after any other letter, as in *siege*, *lien*, *sieve*. *Specie*, *seize*, *inveigle*, and a few other words, are exceptions.

Compound words generally retain the spelling of the words from which they are formed; as, *housewife*, *juryman*, *illness*, *wherein*. Where, *wherever;* whose, *whosever;* sheep, *shepherd;* feet, *fetlock;* pass, *pastime;* well, *welfare;* holy, *holiday*, — are some of the exceptions.

138. Generally speaking, spelling and pronunciation are the better, the better they agree, and serve to distinguish words that differ in meaning.

Ex. — *Gray* is preferable to *grey;* *haul*, to *hale;* and *show*, to *shew*.

139. **Contraction**, in spelling, is the omission of some letter or letters from a word. An apostrophe (') is generally put in the place of what is omitted.

Ex. — *E'er*, ever; *o'er*, over; *'gainst*, against; *o'clock*, of the clock. Sometimes two or more words are contracted into one, and the parts combined are occasionally changed in spelling. *'Tis* or *it's* is used for *it is;* *won't*, for *will not;* *I'd*, for *I would* or *I had*.

Exercises in Spelling.

Rule I.	Rule II.	Rule III.	Miscellaneous.
Swimming,	Witticism,	Pining,	Scarred,
steaming,	laziness,	pinning,	scared,
thinned,	gayety,	valuable,	solely,
learned,	wearisome,	chargeable,	wholly,
airy,	moneyed,	striving,	till,
starry,	allies,	fusible,	until,

druggist,	alleys,	sedgy,	truly,
acquittal,	reliable,	smoky,	singeing,
benefited,	relying,	stylish,	gluing,
dreaded,	thriftily,	paroled,	hoeing,
referred,	gayly,	patrolled,	recall,
reference,	daily,	vying,	willful,
regretted,	likelihood,	advertisement,	countryman,
propeller,	holiday,	traceable,	receipt,
shopping,	spied,	servilely,	siege,
galloping.	spy-glass.	acknowledgment.	colonize.

140. The most ludicrous blunders in spelling are usually made by the misapplication of those words which agree in pronunciation, but differ in spelling and meaning.

Correct the errors: He was *bread* for the church. Hawks *pray* on other birds. The judge immediately *baled* the prisoner. The benches were all in *tears*, one above another. All those barrels for *sail*, at ten o'clock.

ETYMOLOGY.

WORDS.

141. Letters make syllables, syllables make words, words make sentences, and sentences express thoughts.

142. A **Word** is a syllable, or a union of syllables, used as the sign of some idea.

Ex. — Man, horse, pink, green, strikes, down, because.

143. WORDS are divided, according to their number of syllables, into *monosyllables*, *dissyllables*, *trisyllables*, and *polysyllables*.

A monosyllable is a word of one syllable. *Act.*

A dissyllable is a word of two syllables. *Active.*

A trisyllable is a word of three syllables. *Actively.*

A polysyllable is a word of four or more syllables. *Activity.*

144. WORDS are divided, according to their formation, into *primitive*, *derivative*, and *compound.*

A primitive word is not formed from another word. *Breeze.*

A derivative word is formed from another word. *Breezy.*

A compound word is composed of two or more words. *Sea-breeze, never*the*less.*

145. WORDS are divided, according to their use, into nine classes, called *parts of speech.* — See p. 70.

DERIVATION OF WORDS.

146. The elements of words, in derivation, are *roots*, *prefixes*, and *suffixes.*

147. A **Root** is the chief part of a word, or that part which receives the prefix or the suffix.

148. A **Pre′fix** is a letter or letters joined to the beginning of a word, to modify its meaning.

149. A **Suf′fix** is a letter or letters joined to the end of a word, to modify its meaning.

PREFIXES.	ROOTS.
De, down.	*De* - press; to press down.
Re, again.	*Re* - build; to build again.
Ex, out.	*Ex* - pel (drive); to drive out.
Con, together.	*Con* - nect (join); to join together.
Un, not.	*Un* - sound; not sound.

SUFFIXES.	ROOTS.
Able, can be.	Read-*able*; can be read.
Er, person or thing.	Read-*er*; one who reads, a reading-book.
En, to make.	Black-*en*; to make black.
Ness, state or quality.	Happi-*ness*; the state of being happy.
Y, having, resembling.	Ston-*y*; having stones, hard as stone.

Sometimes a word has two or more prefixes or suffixes; as, *re-pro*-duct-*ive-ness*.

150. Roots are either native or foreign, and sometimes much disguised.

Ex.—*Bakery* is derived from *bake*. *Attract'* is derived from the Latin *ad*, to, and *traho*, I draw. *Ide'a*, from the Greek *eïdo*, I see, denotes something "in the mind's eye."

151. Derivative words are formed from primitives, by means of prefixes or suffixes; and compound words are formed by uniting primitives or derivatives.

Ex.—Plant, *re*-plant, *trans*-plant, *im*-plant. Act, act-*or*, act-*ive*, act-*ivity*; great, great-*est*. *Blacksmith*, *spelling-book*.

152. There are different prefixes capable of expressing the same sense, and there are also different suffixes capable of expressing the same sense. The choice of prefixes or suffixes is therefore determined not merely by their meaning, but also by euphony, analogy, and the character of the root.

Ex.—Generous, *un*-generous; accurate, *in*-accurate; throne, *de*-throne, *un*-throne; confess, confess-*ion*; acknowledge, acknowledg-*ment*.

153. Frequently, in making derivative or compound words, some of the parts must be altered for the sake of euphony or analogy. Hence there occurs sometimes a *change*, an *omission*, or an *insertion* of some letter or letters. The last letter of the prefix must often be the same as the first letter of the root.

Ex. — Con-lect, *col-lect;* dis-fer, *dif-fer;* in-moderate, *im-moderate;* con-operate, *co-operate;* dis-vulge, *di-vulge;* a-archy, *an-archy;* mucilage-ous, *mucilag-inous.*

Compound Words.

154. Two or more words, expressing but one conception, or habitually used together as the term for one object or idea, should be compounded.

Ex. — Horseman, gooseberry, rainbow, to-morrow, four-footed. "A five-cent savings-bank;" "blue-eyed, golden-haired Mary."

A crow is a *black bird*, but not a *blackbird*. A *glass house* is made of glass; but a *glass-house* is a house in which glass is manufactured. A *live oak* is simply a living oak; but a *live-oak* is a species of evergreen oak. A *dancing master* is a master that dances; but a *dancing-master* teaches dancing. A *white washed* house may not be a *white-washed* house. *Many-colored* birds have many colors each; *many colored* birds are numerous, though they may all be of one color. A *dog's-ear* is the corner of a leaf turned over; but a *dog's ear* is the ear of a dog. A *lady's slipper* is a shoe; but *lady's-slipper* is a plant.

155. When a compound word is first formed or but little used, a hyphen is generally placed between its parts.

Ex. — Night-robber, rosy-fingered; the tree-and-cloud-shadowed river.

156. By long and general use, most compound words lose the hyphen, provided the parts coalesce like the syllables of one word and under one chief accent.

Ex. — Statesman, steamboat, railroad, inkstand, no′bleman, book′-seller, home′sickness, notwithstand′ing.

For more, in regard to compound words see pp. 260 and 345.

[A sufficient knowledge of prefixes, suffixes, and roots is so generally obtained from spelling-books and other sources, that we have followed the advice of many eminent teachers, and omitted the rest of this subject.]

QUESTIONS FOR REVIEW.

1. What is Grammar? . . . ¶ 69
2. What is English Grammar? . 70
3. Into what parts is it divided? . 71
4. Of what does Pronunciation treat? 72
5. Of what does Orthography treat? 73
6. Of what does Etymology treat? . 74
7. Of what does Syntax treat? . 75
8. Of what does Prosody treat? . 76
9. What is the basis of grammar? 77
10. Of what does language consist? . 78
11. To what can these sounds be reduced? 79
12. What is a letter? 80
13. How many elementary sounds has the English language? and how many letters to represent them? 81
14. What is the name of a letter? . 86
15. What is the power of a letter? . 87
16. Our alphabet is both defective and redundant: explain how it is so. 82-5
17. How are the letters classified? . 88
18. What is a vowel? 89
19. Which letters are vowels? . 90
20. What is a diphthong? . . . 91
21. A proper diphthong? An improper? 92
22. What is a triphthong? . . . 93
23. What is a consonant? . . 95
24. Which letters are consonants? . 96
25. When are *w* and *y* vowels? and when consonants? . . . 90, 97
26. What is a mute? 99
27. Which letters are mutes? . . 100
28. What is a semivowel? . . . 101
29. Which are the semivowels? . 102
30. Which letters are called liquids? and why? 103
31. When is a letter silent? . . 104
32. What is accent? . . . 106
33. What is said of primary accent and of secondary accent? . . 107
34. What is said of two equal accents on the same word? . . . 108
35. Which syllable of a word is the penult? which is the antepenult? 109
36. Give the first rule for pronunciation; — the second; — the third; — the fourth; — the fifth; — the sixth. 111
37. In what styles are the letters used? 112
38. In what sizes of type? . . . 113
39. How are they distinguished in form? 114
40. How are small letters used? and for what are capitals used? . 115
41. How may words beginning with capital letters be classified? . 116
42. What is said of the first word of every sentence? . . . 117
43. When are capital letters used within sentences? 118
44. What is said of parts of a sentence that begin anew?
45. Of direct quotations?
46. Of indirect quotations?
47. Of lines of poetry?
48. Of *I* and *O*? 119
49. Of words denoting the Deity? . 120
50. When does a pronoun, denoting the Deity, not require a capital?
51. What is said of proper names? . 121
52. Of titles? 122
53. Of new proper names made from old ones?
54. Of common phrases made proper names?
    Of titles of books?
55. Of the names of personified objects? 123
56. Of words derived from proper names? 124
57. When should such a word not begin with a capital? 125
58. What is said of words that are particularly important or emphatic, or that are used in a technical sense? 126
59. How are phrases or sentences capitalized? 127
60. What is a syllable? . . . 129
61. Every syllable must have, at least, what kind of letter? . . . 130
62. What is syllabication? . . 131
63. Why are words divided into syllables? 132
64. How are words divided into syllables? 133-5
65. What is said of dividing words at the ends of lines? 133
66. What is spelling? 137
67. From what must this art be learned? 137
68. What is the first Rule?
69. What is the second Rule?
70. What is the third Rule?
71. What is said of contraction, in spelling? 139
72. What is a word? 142
73. How are words classified according to their syllables? . . . 143
74. What is a monosyllable?
75. What is a dissyllable?
76. What is a trisyllable?
77. What is a polysyllable?
78. How are words classified according to their formation? . . . 144
79. What is a primitive word?
80. What is a derivative word?
81. What is a compound word?
82. How are words classified according to their use? 145
83. What are the elements of words, in derivation? 146
84. What is a root? 147
85. What is a prefix? 148
86. What is a suffix? . . . 149
87. What is said of roots? . . . 150
88. From what are derivative and compound words formed? . . 151
89. What variations do the elements of words sometimes undergo, in derivation? 153
90. When are words compounded? . 154
91. When is the hyphen used? . . 155
92. When is the hyphen omitted? . 156

OBSERVATIONS.

Grammar. — Since the different nations of the earth speak different languages, — as, English, French, German, Italian, Spanish, etc., — every language has many peculiarities of its own; and these peculiarities, which generally make the burden of its grammar, are sometimes called the *particular grammar* of the language to which they belong. But since people and the world are everywhere much alike, and since people therefore think everywhere nearly in the same way, it follows that all languages have much in which they agree, and this is sometimes called *universal grammar.*

We have said that the basis of grammar is the usage of the best writers and speakers. This usage is merely a convenient test for determining what is proper or improper; for the real basis of grammar must be sought in the laws of mind and in the requirements of thought, or it is the philosophy of thought and language applied to the requirements of human knowledge in all its extent and variety.

As to the two kinds of language, spoken and written, spoken language has the advantage in the power of enforcing its meaning by means of voice, emphasis, and gestures; but written language, in modern times, by the help of the press and other facilities, has greatly the advantage in durability and the almost unlimited powers of circulation.

Pronunciation. — Among the educated, the pronunciation of the English language is everywhere nearly the same; but, among the uneducated, there is considerable diversity. In the United States, however, there is less deviation from the literary standard than in Great Britain.

The modern pronunciation of the English language differs also very much from that which prevailed about five hundred years ago, or in the time of Chaucer. This is evident from the old spelling, and from the requirements of the rhyme and metre in old verse.

"The soun of briddès for to hear,
That on the bushes singen clear." — *Chaucer.*
"And she was clepèd Madam Eglantine;
Full well she sangè the servíce divine." — *Id.*
"He stodè the bright moonè to beholde,
And alle his sorrowe to the moone he tolde." — *Id.*
"Me thinketh it accordant to reasón,
To tellen you allè the conditión." — *Id.*
"And whanne this alchymister saw his timè,
Ris'th up, Sir Priest, quod he, and stondeth by me." — *Id.*

Here final *e's*, and other endings not now in use, are made syllables. *Reason* and *condition* are pronounced with the accent on the last syllable, somewhat as in French. *Time* is pronounced *ti-mè;* for it was made to rhyme with *by me.*

From the foregoing and other examples we may infer three things:—

1. Pronunciation formerly had more syllables than it now has. Most of these extra syllables consisted of faint or draggling syllables at the ends of words. In some German dialects the people have even at the present day the habit of annexing obscure *ă* to most of their words, (somewhat as bad readers annex *ers*,) by which they apparently make their speech more rhythmical. *Query:* Was the English language ever pronounced as these German dialects?

2. Accent was formerly more Continental, or French, than it now is; that is, it has since glided more from syllables near the end to syllables near the beginning: it has also become more permanent. In Chaucer we have *virtúe* and *vírtue*, *natúre* and *náture*, *langáge* and *lángage*.

3. The sounds of certain words are now different from what they were, and the vowel sounds have generally run into greater variety. *An* was sounded *ain; heart, hert; gōld, goold*; *greăt, grēat*, etc. ("None but an Irishman would say *greăt*." — *Chesterfield*.) Even within our recollection, the broad sound of *gräss, hälf*, and *läst*, has passed into *gràss, hàlf*, and *làst*.

English pronunciation has a hasty air, tends to brevity, slides its accents toward the left, and gradually improves in melody, or musical variety. An *omnibus* has become a mere *'bus; Brougham* is pronounced *Broom; Worcester, Woos-ter;* and *Michilimackinac* loses its serpentine length in *Mack'-e-naw*. A *balco'-ny* has become a *bal'-cony; con'-template* is now more common than *contem'-plate; o-be-je-ent* has yielded to the more euphonious *o-be-di-ent;* and *pro-nun-ci-a-tion* is becoming more common than *pro-nun-she-a-tion*.

Poetry sometimes adopts antiquated modes of expression because they tend to give it an elegant quaintness. But poetry, written long ago, must sometimes be pronounced, for the sake of the rhyme, as the language was pronounced when the verse was written.

> "Lo! the poor Indian, whose untutored mind
> Sees God in clouds or hears him in the wind." — *Pope*.

> "Tell me, where is fancy bred, —
> In the heart, or in the head?
> How begot, how nourishèd?" — *Shakespeare*.

Here *wĭnd* must be pronounced *wīnd*, to rhyme with *mīnd;* and *ed* must be sounded, so as to rhyme with *head*.

The verbal ending *ed* is yet heard in the speech of some very old people; but, unless the word is used adjectively, as in the phrase *a learnèd man*, this ending is now generally blended with the preceding syllable when it will coalesce with it in sound.

Accent. — 1. Words ending with the sound of *shun*, *zhun*, or *chun*, or with any kindred sound, have the chief accent on the *penult;* as, *contempla'-tion, decis'-ion, conven'-tion, artifi'-cial, coura'-geous, insuffi'-cient.*

2. Words ending with *cive, sive, ic, ics,* or with *tive* preceded by a consonant, have the chief accent on the *penult;* as, *deci'-sive, hero'-ic, sulphu'-ric, calisthen'-ics, collec'-tive.*

Exceptions: Arith'-metic, ar'-senic (noun), ad'-jective, bish'-opric, cath'-olic, chol'-eric, ephem'-eric, her'-etic, lu'-natic, pol'-itic, pol'-itics, rhet'-oric, sub'-stantive, tur'-meric, and perhaps pleth'-oric and splen'-etic.

3. Words that have the following endings, have the chief accent on the *antepenult:* —

Acal, acy, athy. Heli'-acal, theoc'-racy, sym'-pathy.
E-al, e-an, e-ous. Or'-deal, Hercu'-lean, sponta'-neous.
Efy, ety, erous. Stu'-pefy, sati'-ety, aurif'-erous.
Fluent, fluous. Circum'-fluent, super'-fluous.
Gonal, graphy. Diag'-onal, orthog'-raphy.
I-a, i-ac, i-al. Rega'-lia, demo'-niac, armo'-rial.
I-an, ical, i-ous. Colle'-gian, astronom'-ical, contume'-lious.
Inous, ify, ity. Om'-inous, person'-ify, solid'-ity.
Logy, loquy, lysis. Anal'-ogy, col'-loquy, paral'-ysis.
Meter, metry. Barom'-eter, trigonom'-etry.
Orous, ulous. O'-dorous, sed'-ulous.
Phony, tomy, thropy. Eu'-phony, anat'-omy, misan'-thropy.

Exceptions: Adamante'-an, antipode'-an, colosse'-an, cano'-rous, empyre'-an, hymene'-al, hymene'-an, pygme'-an.

4. Words of three or more syllables, ending with *ative,* have the accent on the *antepenult,* or on the preceding syllable; as, *demon'-strative, op'-erative, nom'-inative, pal'-liative, spec'-ulative.*

Exceptions: Crea'-tive, colla'-tive, dila'-tive.

Letters. — There is not, perhaps, any other language in the world that has experienced so many revolutions as the English; but, like the political institutions of the people by whom it is spoken, it seems to have gained strength and excellence by every change.

About a thousand years ago, our ancestors used what is called the Anglo-Saxon Alphabet. This alphabet is as follows: —

A a, B b, C c, D ꝺ, E e, F ꝼ, G ᵹ, H h, I i, L l, M m, N n, O o, P p, R ꞃ, S ꞅ, T ꞇ, U u, W ƿ, X x, Y ẏ. Þ þ (*th* aspirate), Ð ð (*th* vocal).

Then followed the Old English, or Black Letter.

A a, B b, C c, D d, E e, F f, G g, H h, I i, J j, K k, L l, M m, N n, O o, P p, Q q, R r, S s, T t, U u, V v, W w, X x, Y y, Z z.

These were superseded by the much more beautiful Roman Alphabet, which is the alphabet now generally used.

Powers of the Letters. — In considering the alphabet, we should notice, and keep distinct, two things: —

1. The *written elements* of language, which are *letters*.
2. The *oral elements* of language, which consist of *tone, articulation,* and *breath.*

Hence the oral elements have been sometimes classified into *vocals, subvocals,* and *aspirates.* But this classification does not present the truth beyond the vocals; for nearly all the elements denoted by consonants are composite. The following is probably as minute an analysis of the oral elements as the pupil can understand: —

Pure tone.

Ex. — *A*le, *a*t, *a*rt, *a*ll, m*e*, m*e*t, p*i*ne, p*i*n, *o*ld, *o*dd, m*o*ve, *u*se, *u*s, th*ou*, *oi*l.

Pure breath.

Ex. — *H*at.

Toned articulation.

Ex. — *B*i*b*, *d*i*d*, *g*i*g*, *j*u*dg*e, *l*o*ll*, *m*u*m*, *n*u*n*, ri*ng*, *r*oa*r*, *th*us, *v*an, *w*e, *y*et, *z*one, a*z*ure.

Aspirated articulation.

Ex. — *F*i*f*e, *k*i*ck*, *p*o*p*, *s*in*c*e, *t*i*t*, *th*eme, *sh*eep, *ch*eap, *wh*ip.

The powers of the consonants are most readily obtained by simply omitting the vowel sounds with which they are uttered. The element denoted by *s* consists of a whistling sound made purely of breath. Admit tone, and you have *z*. The sounds denoted by the consonants *w* and *y* are very nearly vowel sounds. The same is true of *h*; or, denoting mere breath, *h* leaves the vowel after it nearly bare.

Capital Letters. — Formerly, every noun was commenced with a capital letter; and other important words of the sentence were sometimes commenced in the same way. The following is a specimen of the usage in fashion a hundred years ago: —

"A Deadly Feud had long ſubſiſted between the Houſes of Malcolm and Douglas; but it happened that the Heir of Malcolm ſaved the Heir of Douglas in Battle, and this Act produced an Inviolable Friendſhip between them." — *London Chronicle.*

Beginnings. — Persons of not much skill in composition frequently find a difficulty in determining when they have a sentence, or in deciding how to divide their thoughts into sentences. This difficulty must be overcome mainly by skill in grammar and composition. A proposition (see p. 5) can not be partly in one sentence and partly in another; and modifying words or phrases should remain with the parts which they modify. Propositions closely bound together in sense, should make but one sentence; but propositions loosely connected may often be either gathered into one sentence or divided into two or more sentences.

Examples. — When an example consists of a proposition, or of something used in the sense of a proposition, it should begin with a capital letter. But when words or phrases, used for illustration, occur in the body of a sentence, they need not begin with capitals if the meaning is sufficiently obvious without them; though usage is divided in regard to such expressions, and capitals sometimes distinguish the parts better than small letters.

Verse. — When verse is written in the form of prose, it should generally have only the capitals which are suitable to prose.

Words of Distinction. — The Indian always says, "Great Spirit," or uses both words to denote God; but when Pope wrote, "Thou great First Cause," he used *great* in its ordinary descriptive sense. The *King of kings* shows pre-eminently God's relation to worldly kings; but the *Angel of Death* does not show the relation of any angel to death. The *Devil* denotes *Satan*; but a *devil* may be simply a bad person or spirit. When the words *god, goddess, deity, divinity*, etc., are applied to the heathen deities, they do not begin with capitals. When *Muses, Graces, Naiads*, etc., are regarded in the splendor of ancient imagination, they are generally favored with capitals; but our own *fairies, sylphs, ghosts, hobgoblins*, etc., are rather too puny and undignified in idea to be thus distinguished.

The names of important individual objects, as *spring, summer, autumn, winter, time, eternity, space, seasons, morning, evening, day, night, earth, heaven, hell, sun, moon, world, universe, nature, equator, zodiac, north, east*, etc., when used in their most ordinary sense, or when their ordinary meaning predominates, do not usually begin with capitals; but when they are used in a specific or personified sense, they should begin with capitals. When *Heaven* denotes God, it should always begin with a capital letter; and when it denotes the abode of the blessed, it is also frequently written with a capital.

Lord's Day is equivalent to *Sunday*. *New Year's Day*, the *Fourth of July*, *Good Friday*, or any other holiday, is as much a particular day as *Sunday*, or any other day of the week. The phrases *Elegy in a Country Churchyard, Battle of Hohenlinden, The Task*, are as much the names of particular poems as *John, James*, and *Henry*, are the names of particular boys. "Gray took hardly more pains with his Elegy," not *elegy*. The *gospel* denotes the Christian doctrines; but the *Gospels* and the *Revelation* denote parts of the New Testament. A *Methodist*, a *Republican*, a *Mussulman*, or a *Roarer*, belongs to some religious, political, or social sect or party. "The President sent the document to Congress; and the Senate returned it to the General Assembly, or Legislature, of New York."

Hence, the names of holidays, the names of the days of the week or months of the year, the chief words in the titles of books, the names of sects, parties, associations, or public bodies, should begin with capital letters.

Should the word *park* be constantly applied to a particular place in stead of a proper name, then the place should be called the *Park*, not the *park*. If I should use the phrase *Old Dominion* for the proper name *Virginia*, I would begin each word of the phrase with a capital letter; but if I should call Goldsmith's *Deserted Village* Goldsmith's *great poem*, I would not begin the latter words with capitals. We must often judge whether the specific or titular sense, or else the ordinary meaning of the words, is uppermost in the speaker's mind, and use capitals or small letters accordingly. *Webster's Speeches* refers to a book, or to their title; while *Webster's speeches* refers simply to the speeches as such. "I went with him to visit the Lakes;" *i. e.*, a celebrated group of lakes. We can see *white mountains* in almost any mountainous country; but the *White Mountains* are in New Hampshire. A Cambridge Professor speaks of his *Essay*, in referring to a book called *Cambridge Essays;* and, having introduced *Captain Marryatt*, he afterwards speaks of him as the *Captain*, not as the *captain*. When I speak of the *principal* of a school, I refer to his duties; but when I speak of the *Principal* of a school, I refer to his title. A chapter in your *history* refers to your life; but a chapter in your *History* refers to a book so named. "Part 1, Remark, Observations, Rules for Spelling," refer to certain divisions or headings of a book. Our *Club*, *President*, *Treasurer*, and *Secretary*, are such in title as well as in fact. The *London Times* says, "Her Majesty, the Prince Consort, the Bride, the Prince of Wales, and the other members of the Royal Family, were present." Common folks would not have been thus honored with capitals. An astronomer writes, "The Sun is the centre of the System;" because these capitalized words denote subjects of which he treats.

When I speak of the *Company* or the *Convention*, I mean to guard you against thinking of the wrong one, or to make you think of a particular one. Missouri is a part of the *South*, though it lies *west*. If the *North*, *East*, *South*, and *West*, make the United States, then any one of these *states* is a *State*, being derived from a proper noun. We may speak, however, in general terms, of the *states*, *kingdoms*, and *empires* of the earth. The *Insurrection* was printed with a capital letter only while the excitement lasted; but the *Reformation* and the *Revolution* are still matters of interest, and retain their capitals.

Hence, the names of great events, of important places, or of persons in high official positions, even when they consist of common words of the language, should generally begin with capitals.

When a term consists of two or more words, and especially if they are linked together in the sense of apposition, it is sometimes difficult to determine how many capitals should be used. In such cases we should carefully consider how much makes the name, or whether the parts are separately significant. The *Ohio river* is as well denoted by the *Ohio*, which is a sufficient name to call it by, and which implies the word *river;* but the *Red River* is not usually called the *Red*, nor is the *Blue Ridge* ever called the *Blue*, for it takes both words to make the name. The *city of New York*, or *New York city*, is generally called *New York;* but *Jersey City* needs both words to make the name. The *Erie Canal* is wholly a name; but the *Erie and Ohio canal* is understood as being simply the canal between Lake Erie and the Ohio river. In the phrase, "the *prophet Jonah*," the words are separately significant, or but temporarily united; but in the terms *Lake Erie, Mount Vernon, Cape Hatteras, Penobscot Bay, Queen Elizabeth, Loch Gyle, Ben Lomond*, both words are so commonly used as the name, that each begins with a capital letter. "Victoria, the *queen* of Great Britain;" "Mary, *Queen* of Scots:" the former phrase is explanatory, but the latter is also titular. In this country, *Esq.* is always used as a title, and therefore it properly begins with a capital letter; but, in England, *esq.* is often used merely as a term of rank, and therefore in English journals we often find it beginning with a small *e*. *Harper's ferry* was once a *ferry* belonging to a man named *Harper;* but now *Harper's Ferry* is a town.

When objects are very common and comparatively insignificant, we often find that only the specific words, and not the general words,—especially when the latter are plural,—begin with capital letters; as, "in Cass and Butler *counties*." The words *county, township, hill, creek, river*, when used in connection with specific words, are not generally commenced with capital letters. *Street* we find written—Fifth *Street*, Fifth and Madison *Streets;* Fifth-*street*, Walnut-*street*, Fifth and Walnut *streets* (the hyphen being omitted from the plural phrase, to show the common reference of *streets* to the two words before it); and, lastly, Fifth *street*. The first two modes are best authorized. The same remark applies occasionally to the words *place, square, house, church*, etc. But, in all cases in which the specific word is also a common word of the language, the tendency is, to begin the general word with a capital letter too; as, "Black *Sea*," "Long *Island*," "White *River*." The English, in many cases, compound some kinds of the foregoing terms; as, "*Spring-gardens, Leceister-place, Hampden-street, Arklow-house.*" Only the first part of a compound word is usually commenced with a capital letter, as in the foregoing terms; but when the term has a titular sense, each part is more generally commenced with a capital, as "*Attorney-General.*"

Personification. — A word denoting a personified object is commenced with a capital, only when it has strictly the sense of a proper noun that is applied to a person; as, "And *Hope* enchanting smiled, and waved her golden hair." But, "The *ship* lost her cargo." "'Will you walk into my parlor?' said the Spider to the Fly," represents the spider and the fly as if they were Mr. A and Mr. B.

Derivatives. — The word *Christian*, though it has become a common word of the language, begins with a capital on account of its highly honorable derivation. The word *Italic*, applied to letters, is often commenced with a small *i*; but the analogy of the word *Roman* rather tends to sustain the capital *I*.

After all, in regard to capital letters, something must be left to taste, or to the nice intuitive perceptions of the writer.

Syllables. — Formerly, words were divided into syllables according to their derivation and vowels; as, *or-tho-gra-phy, ha-bit:* but now the highest rule is, to divide them as they are pronounced; as, *or-thog-ra-phy, hab-it.* In dividing words into syllables, we should endeavor, first, to show the exact pronunciation; secondly, to make neat syllables; and, thirdly, to show the derivation of the words. Quite a number of words are still variously and sometimes inconsistently divided in our best dictionaries. The following additional rules may be useful to the learner.

Vowels. — *Diphthongs* and *triphthongs*, not severed; as, *loy-al, buoy-ant: vowels making different syllables,* separated; as, *a-e-ri-al, co-op-e-rate: vowels changed to consonants,* to their own syllables; as, *un-ion, liq-uid, brill-iant.*

Consonants. — *Single consonant between two vowels, and not shortening the former nor sounded with it,* to the latter syllable; as, *re-bel', ha-zy, ea-sy: shortening the former vowel or joined to it,* to the former syllable; as, *reb'-el, heav-y, fraud-u-lent: mute and liquid, not shortening the syllable preceding,* joined to the latter; as, *pa-trol: shortening it,* separated; as, *cit-ron: liquid and mute, blending with former vowel,* joined to it; as, *post-age:* not both blending with former vowel, separated; as, *dan-ger, pas-tor: two consonants, in other cases,* generally separated; as, *sup-per, mem-ber, mos-sy, col-lec-tive, pic-ture, pic-kle,* etc. *Ch, sh, th, gh, ph, wh,* and *tch,* are regarded as single letters; and *tion, sion, cious, tient,* etc., as single syllables.

Spelling. — The spelling of the English language, several hundred years ago, was much more clumsy and variable than it now is. *It* was spelled *it, itt, yt, ytt, hit, hitt, hyt,* or *hytt; when, whanne* or *whan; company, compagnie; truly, treulyche; earth, eorthe; hands, hondes; unkind, unkuynde; should, scholden; which, quhiche* and *whiche; since, syghthen; gathered, y-gadered.* In the course of time there was introduced a Rule to double the consonant, whenever the vowel before it was short; and to leave it single, when the vowel was long. Accordingly, we find *hadde, thanne, starre*, etc., for *had, than, star*. The effect of this rule can still be seen in such words as *mill, less, cliff;* and our existing rule for doubling the final consonant in certain cases, is probably an offshoot from the same rule.

Formerly, *parlor, labor, vapor*, etc., were spelled *parlour, labour, vapour;* but the superfluous *u* is now rejected. Formerly, *public, music, arithmetic*, etc., were spelled *publick, musick, arithmetick;* but the superfluous *k* is now omitted from nearly all such words except monosyllables. A few verbs of two or more syllables retain or assume the *k* for the sake of the pronunciation; as, *traffic, mimic, mimicked, mimicking*, not *mimicing*.

Some words can be spelled in two or more different ways, with good authority for each; as, *keg* and *cag; plough* and *plow; inquire* and *enquire; traveler* and *traveller; hominy, homony*, and *hommony*. But this diversity is now confined to a comparatively small number of words; and the better forms of these words will probably soon exterminate the other forms. Generally speaking, the spelling of the English language is so irregular that it is safer and better to learn the words themselves than to depend upon rules.

Derivation. — The English language is a composite, derived from a number of other languages. Hence it is full of conflicting analogies. The chief languages from which it has been formed, are, in the order of time, about as follows: —

Celtic, Saxon, Danish, French, Latin, and **Greek.**

Its groundwork, its syntax and idiomatic pith, are essentially Saxon. Nearly all the most common words, as *earth, heaven, water, fire, wind, wood, grass, man, boy, ox, cow, sheep, hen, goose, house, mouse, rat, hand, heart, soul, love, hate, grief, sorrow, eye, ear, hair, arm, fist, finger, breast, foot, day, night, morning, evening, month, year, summer, winter, word, way, speak, say, whisper, smile, laugh, weep, walk, wash, watch, lie, stand, run, dance, creep, fly, come, go, have, hold, good, bad, long, short, near, far, deep, wide, old, young, thin, thick, sour, bitter, sweet, I, my, you, he, she, it, who, which, that, this, so, as, thus, here, there, where, ever, never, in, on, under, up, to, from, with, by, and, both, for, if, since, then, than, or, but*, etc., are Saxon. The other languages which have contributed most words, are the French and the Latin. The French has furnished most of the words pertaining to refinement and fashion. The Latin and the Greek have furnished most of the terms required in the great circle of sciences and arts. From the Latin *duco, ductum*, to lead; *capio, captum*, to take; *fero, latum*, to carry; *mitto, missum*, to send; *tendo, tensum*, to stretch; *teneo, tentum*, to hold; *plico, plicatum*, to fold; *pono, positum*, to place; *specio, spectum*, to look; and from the Greek *logos*, discourse; and *graphè*, writing, — are derived about 2,000 English words.

It is said that the English language has about 100,000 words, and that about 13,000 of these are derived from 154 Latin and Greek primitives.

That spirited, that glorious little poem, Campbell's *Hohenlinden*, contains 198 words. Of these, 170 are Saxon; 19, French; and 9, Latin; making about 86 per cent of Saxon words. Probably no other specimen of English literature shows so well the simplicity and force of the Saxon element, and what preference should be given to Saxon words in our daily use of language.

A word can sometimes be traced through a number of languages. The Greek *aner*, the Latin *vir*, the German *Herr*, the French *sieur*, and the English *sir*, are all of them essentially the same word.

Words, like people, exist in families and kindreds. *Act, actor, action, active, activity, actuate, actual, actually*, etc., are a family; and *hide, hat, hood, hut*, and *house*, are all akin. So are *bind, band*, and *bond; rest* and *roost; scale, shell*, and *skull;* and *draw, drag, draggle, drawl, dray, dredge, drudge, drain, train*, and *draft*.

Words have been called *fossil poetry;* and it is sometimes very interesting to trace them to their originals and kindreds. An *acorn* is an *oak-corn;* a *berry* is what a bush *bears;* a *daisy* is a *day's-eye; clover* is something that has *cloven* leaves; a *field* is a place where the trees are *felled;* a *yard* is a piece of ground that *girds* a house; what is *wild*, is self-*willed*, or follows its own *will;* a *landscape* is a *land-shape; fodder* is *food* for *feeding* cattle; an *ore* is taken from the *earth*; *heaven* is what is *heaved* (heav-en, giv-en) or arched over; a *hamlet* is a dear little *home*, and a *satchel* is a small *sack;* a *neighbor* is one who lives *nigh;* what I *ought* to do, is *owed* by me as a duty; a *nostril* is a *nose-drill*, or nose-hole; a *husband* is the *house-band*, or support; a man's *wife* once was the *weaver* of his household; a *month* is measured by the *moon;* he who is *tantalized* is treated or mocked like *Tantalus;* a *meandering* river is as crooked as the *Meander*, a river of Phrygia; *umbra* is the Latin word for shade, and an *umbrella* is therefore a little shade; a *parasol* — from the Greek *para*, against, and the Latin *sol*, sun* — is something held against the sun; a *mansion* — from the Latin *maneo, mansum*, to remain — is a place to remain in; the first *clock* seemed to *cluck*, like a hen; and a *flea* is probably so called from the rapidity with which he *flees*, or tries to escape.

Ill is contracted from *evil*, and *ail* is akin to it; *dawn*, from *day-en* (*day-ing*), making day; *deed*, from *do-ed*, done, what is done; *first*, from *fore-est, for'st; last*, from *latest; lass*, from *laddess; alone*, from *all one; only*, from *one-like; flood*, from *flowed; fulsome*, from *foul-some; parboil*, from *part-boil; Naples* from *nea polis*, new city; *offal* is what falls off, or is cast away; and what I *doff*, I *do off*.

King Henry the Eighth, of England, became "the chiefe authour" of

* Perhaps rather from the Italian *parare*, to ward off, and *sole*, sun.

an English grammar, for "the childrene of his lovynge subjects," which he compelled the people to use; and thus originated the common phrase, *the King's English.* The Irishman may claim that his nickname has descended from "the senators of Rome, in Rome's best day." Thus, *pater, patres, patricians, Patricius, Patrick, Paddy, Pat.*

Many words, applied first to material things, have been extended to things intellectual or abstract. "The *spirit* in its literal import is *breath* or *wind, rectitude* is *straightness, error* is a *wandering, transgression* is a *going-over, education* is a *drawing-out,* a *language* is a *tongue;*" and we speak of "*bright* hopes, *unshaken* confidence, and *corroding* cares."

The two principles which guide us most in the use and formation of words, are *resemblance* and *relation.* The *leaf* of a book resembles the *leaf* of a plant; and the *key* to an arithmetic serves to *unlock* its mysteries. *Buzz, hiss, hum, roll, roar, rattle, clatter, click, clang, thin, burly,* are all imitative. Some letter combinations are eminently suggestive of the meaning. There is something decidedly nasal in the *sn* that begins *sneeze, sneer, snout, snore, snort, snuff, snuffle,* and *snicker. Spr* or *sp* implies expansion or unfolding; as in *spread, sprawl, sprinkle, sprout,* and *spring. St* implies firmness; as in *stout, stand, stool, stump, stay, stiff, strut, strong,* and *stack.* A *sceptre* indicates royalty; a *sword,* a soldier, or war; a *sail,* a ship; and a *head,* the ox that wears it.

There are many beautiful analogies in derivation, of which the following are specimens: —

Crack, *crackle;* crumb, *crumble;* curd, *curdle;* fond, *fondle;* game, *gamble;* grim or grum, *grumble;* nest, *nestle;* rank, *rankle;* roam, *ramble;* rough, *ruffle;* set, *settle;* shove, *shovel, shuffle;* spark, *sparkle;* stray, *straggle;* stride, *straddle;* throat, *throttle;* wade, *waddle;* wink, *twinkle;* writhe, *wriggle.*

Bind, *bundle;* gird, *girdle;* hand, *handle;* lade, *ladle;* seat, *saddle;* shoot, *shuttle;* spin, *spindle;* steep, *steeple;* thumb, *thimble.*

Beat, *batter;* spit, *sputter, spatter;* pest, *pester;* blow, *bluster;* climb, *clamber;* gleam, *glimmer;* shine, *shimmer;* gloss, *glisten;* wend, *wander;* long, *linger;* hang, *hanker;* whine, *whimper.*

(The foregoing examples show that a derivative word is sometimes a *diminutive,* a *frequentative,* or an *augmentative* of its primitive; that is, it may imply a lessening, a frequency, or an increase, in regard to the meaning of the primitive. And then, generally speaking, the stronger the sound, the stronger the meaning.)

Joined, *joint;* feigned, *feint;* waned, *want;* weighed, *weight;* cleaved, *cleft;* thieved, *theft;* drived, *drift;* gived, *gift;* waved, *waft;* deserved, *desert;* haved, *haft;* held, *hilt;* skim, *scum;* deem, *doom.*

Healeth, *health;* stealeth, *stealth;* groweth, *growth;* breweth, *broth;* gird-eth, *girth;* smiteth, *smith.* ("The *smith* that *smiteth* at the fire." — *Verstegan.*)

Deep, *depth;* long, *length;* strong, *strength;* young, *youth;* merry, *mirth;* wide, *width;* slow, *sloth.*

Bake, *batch;* wake, *watch;* make, *match;* break, *breach;* speak, *speech;* seek, *beseech;* stick, *stitch;* nick, *niche, notch;* drink, *drench;* crook, *crouch;* stark, *starch.*

There is often a shortening in spelling or pronunciation: —

Grāin, *grănary;* cāve, *căvity;* main*tain*, main*tenance*, please, *plĕasant;* zēal, *zĕalous;* shēep, *shĕpherd;* fēet, *fĕtlock;* hīnd, *hĭnder;* splēen, *splĕnetic;* prīme, *prĭmer;* crīme, *crĭminal;* goose, *gŏsling;* sour, *sŭrly;* bōor, *bŭrly;* south, *sŏuthern.*

The changes which words undergo, are such as tend to produce greater musical variety. There is ever a tendency, too, in derivation, to hold to some fundamental parts or analogies. Hence the Saxon prefix *ge* has in some of our words run into *a*, as in *arise* and *awake;* and the Saxon *lif-lâdu*, life-leading, has become *livelihood.* People are thus sometimes misled. *Aspáragus* is often improperly called *sparrow-grass;* and we often hear the improper forms *preventative, maintainance, proposial*, and *mountain'eous*, for the words *preventive, maintenance, proposal*, and *moun'tainous.*

Language not only exists, but lives, grows, and decays. It is not a dead mechanism, but a living organism. Words, and modes of expression, are constantly coming into use; others, passing out of use; and others, assuming new burdens of meaning, and probably losing the old. An old writer speaks of a "*polite* surface" (*polished* surface), and of "*resenting* a favor" (*re-feeling* it, or reflecting upon it with gratitude). Our expressive words *bulk, dose, opiate, ponderous, caress, thrill, grisly, tissue*, and *plumage*, were all denounced, at different times, either as being newfangled or as being obsolete.

Words become respectable or otherwise, according to the use made of them; but it is remarkable that they nearly always pass from good meanings to bad ones, and very seldom the other way. The word *knave* once denoted simply a lad; but as lads frequently became pages, attendants, or servants to persons of consequence, the word was gradually applied to attendants or servants; and as these were sometimes dishonest or not deemed respectable, the word gradually acquired its present meaning. The good, substantial *gentlewomen* of the olden times have been superseded by those who are all flattered, by the *gentlemen*, into *ladies* (wives or daughters of *lords*); and yet even this word will soon cease to be respectable if it should be frequently applied as in the following instance: "Stolen by a lady, from a little girl, a cashmere shawl," etc., etc. — *Newspaper Advertisement.*

PART III.

WORDS GRAMMATICALLY COMBINED.

PARTS OF SPEECH.

ETYMOLOGY AND SYNTAX.

157. A **Part of Speech** is a class of words, made according to their use and meaning in sentences.

By synecdoche, the term *part of speech* is often applied to a single word.

158. The English language has nine PARTS OF SPEECH; *Nouns*, *Pronouns*, *Articles*, *Adjectives*, *Verbs*, *Adverbs*, *Prepositions*, *Conjunctions*, and *Interjections*.

The *nouns*, *pronouns*, and *verbs*, are the chief classes; and next to them rank the *adjectives* and the *adverbs*. These five classes have, to some extent, what are called *inflections*; that is, they are sometimes changed in form to express a modification in the idea.

NOUNS AND PRONOUNS.*

Classification.

<table>
<tr><td rowspan="2">Nouns.</td><td rowspan="2">Proper.
Common;
including
Collective,
Abstract,
Verbal.</td><td rowspan="4">Properties.</td><td>GENDER.</td><td>Masculine,
Feminine,
Common,
Neuter.</td></tr>
<tr><td>PERSON.</td><td>First,
Second,
Third.</td></tr>
<tr><td rowspan="2">Pronouns.</td><td rowspan="2">Personal,
Relative,
Interrogative,
Adjective.</td><td>NUMBER.</td><td>Singular,
Plural.</td></tr>
<tr><td>CASE.</td><td>Nominative,
Possessive,
Objective.</td></tr>
</table>

* Nouns and Pronouns are sometimes called *Sub'stantives*.

NOUNS.

159. A **Noun** is a name.

Ex.—Martha, Columbus, river, wind, farm, farmer.

160. Sometimes a phrase is used as a noun.

Ex.—New York; Sir Walter Scott; Henry the Eighth; Duke of Marlborough. "*Toward the earth's centre* is down."

161. Sometimes a clause is used as a noun.

Ex.—"*That the war must soon end*, is plain." (What is plain?) "I will see *whether the fire is burning*." (See what?) "It is certain *that he will go*." (What is certain?)

162. Sometimes a word from another part of speech, or a mere sign, is used as a noun.

Ex.—"The proudest *she* in Christendom."—*Shakespeare*. "The *why* is plain as way to parish church."—*Id.* "The signs +, —, ×, and ÷."—*Robinson*.

CLASSES OF NOUNS.

163. Nouns are divided into two classes,—*proper* and *common;* and the common nouns include, as a part of their number, *collective* nouns, *abstract* nouns, and *verbal* nouns.

164. A **Proper Noun** is a name that distinguishes a particular one from the rest of a class.

Ex.—Mary, Henry, Boston, Connecticut; the *Iliad*.

Mary is a proper noun, because it is a name that distinguishes a particular girl or woman from others.

165. When a proper noun assumes meaning, or implies other objects that have the same name, it becomes a common noun.

Ex.—"Bolivar was the *Washington* of South America." (Great general and patriot.) "Some mute, inglorious *Milton* here may rest." (Great poet.) "I saw the *Russians*, and also a *Turk* and several *Persians*, at the Astor House."

Plural nouns that begin with capital letters, and distinguish groups as singular proper nouns distinguish individuals, should be considered proper nouns. Hence "the *Azores*," "the *Cherokees*," "the *Messrs. Harris*," denoting each the whole of a group, are proper nouns.

166. A **Common Noun** is a name common to all of the same kind or class.

Ex. — Girl, boy, city, river, mountain, man, horse.

Girl is a common noun, because it is a name that is common, or can be applied, to any one of a certain class of females.

167. When a common noun denotes an object in the sense of a proper noun, it becomes a proper noun.

Ex. — The Common; Niagara Falls. "Come, gentle *Spring*."

Sometimes there is no class, or but one object to be denoted by a proper noun or a common noun. When this is the case, the proper noun simply denotes the object; as, *God:* while the common noun denotes the object, and also shows what it is; as, *earth*, *sky*, *truth*.

168. A **Collective Noun** is a name that denotes, in the singular form, more than one object of the same kind.

Ex. — Family, army, swarm, class, congregation.

169. An **Abstract Noun** is the name of a quality, an action, or some other attribute.

Abstract means *drawn from*. The words *goodness*, *virtue*, *hope*, *wisdom*, *motion*, *rest*, *peace*, and *industry*, are *abstract* nouns; because they are not the names of objects that exist by themselves, but the names of qualities, actions, or states, belonging to objects, or of notions that we form in regard to them.

170. A **Verbal Noun** is a participle or an infinitive used as a noun. Verbal nouns belong to abstract nouns.

Ex. — "*To climb* is generally difficult." "The boy hurt himself by *climbing* a tree." (The teacher should give the pupil some idea of what a participle or an infinitive is.)

A participle, used as a noun, is sometimes called a *participial noun*.

A noun, and why; whether proper, common, or collective, and why: —

Boy, George, day, Saturday, month, September, flock, tribe, holiday, Christmas, island, Cuba, nations, city, Boston, people, multitude, river, Hudson, party, Azores, ashes.

PRONOUNS.

171. A **Pronoun** is a word used in stead of a noun.

Ex. — "The father and *his* son cultivated the farm *which* | *they* had purchased"; *i. e.*, The father and the *father's son* cultivated the farm *which farm* | *the father and the father's son* had purchased.

172. Pronouns enable us to avoid clumsy expressions, and especially the disagreeable repetition of nouns.

173. The word, phrase, or clause, which a pronoun represents, is called its *antece'dent.*

Ex. — "*James* saw his mistake." *James* is the antecedent of *his.* "*He* who is well, undervalues health." *He* is the antecedent of *who.* "I wished *to call him back;* but *it* was impossible." "*He sold his farm;* and now he regrets *it.*" Sometimes the antecedent *follows* the pronoun; as, "And there *her* brood the *partridge* led." — *Bryant.*

174. When a pronoun has a modified antecedent, it represents it with all its modifications.

Ex. — "The largest tree of the grove spread its shade over us." Here *its* represents not *tree* merely, but *the largest tree of the grove.*

175. The antecedent of a pronoun is sometimes omitted.

Ex. — "There are, who, deaf to mad Ambition's call,
Would shrink to hear the obstreperous trump of fame." — [*Beattie.*

Supply *those*, or *those persons*, after *are.*

176. The pronoun is sometimes omitted.

Ex. — "The lamb thy riot dooms to bleed to-day,
Had he thy reason, would he skip and play?" — *Pope.*

Supply *which* after *lamb.*

CLASSES OF PRONOUNS.

177. Pronouns may be divided into four classes; *personal*, *relative*, *interrogative*, and *adjective.*

Personal Pronouns.

178. A **Personal Pronoun** is one of those pronouns which distinguish the grammatical persons.

Ex. — "*I* saw *you* and *him*." *I* means the speaker; *you*, the person spoken to; and *him*, the person spoken of.

179. The chief personal pronouns are *I*, *thou* or *you*, *he*, *she*, and *it*.

For their declined forms and their compounds, see p. 103.

180. **You**, *your*, *yours*, and *yourself*, are now preferred in common usage to *thou*, *thy*, *thine*, *thee*, etc.

181. **Thou**, *thy*, *thine*, *thee*, *thyself*, and *ye*, are ancient and solemn forms. Hence they are still used, —

1. In the Bible.

Ex. — "*Thou* shalt not bear false witness against *thy* neighbor."

2. In prayers or other addresses to the Deity.

Ex. — "*Thou* Almighty Ruler, hallowed be *thy* name!" — *Prayer.*

3. Frequently, in poetry.

Ex. — "*Thou* art not false, but *thou* art fickle." — *Byron.*

182. **Ours**, *yours*, *hers*, *theirs*, and generally *mine* and *thine*, are respectively equivalent to *our*, *your*, *her*, etc., and the name of the object possessed. These two words should be parsed in stead of the other word.

Ex. — "He ate his apple, you ate *yours* [*your apple*], and I ate *mine*" [*my apple*]. *Yours* is not governed by a noun understood, for the noun could not be put after it; but it is equivalent to *your* and a noun. — See p. 103.

183. Before vowel sounds or the letter *h*, *mine* and *thine* are sometimes preferred, in the solemn or poetic style, to *my* and *thy*.

Ex. — "All *mine* iniquities." — *Bible.* "*Thine* altar." — *Whittier.*
"Time writes no wrinkles on *thine* azure brow." — *Byron.*

So, formerly, *none* to *no*. "Thou shalt have *none* other gods before me." — *Bible.*

184. **It** sometimes denotes merely the state or condition of things, or a point of time.

Ex. — *It* rains. *It* thunders. *It* is 12 o'clock.
"'*T* was moonlight on the Persian Sea." — *Moore.*

185. **It** sometimes introduces a sentence, and is explained by a following word, phrase, or clause.

Ex. — *It* is *he*. *It* is *she*. *It* was *they*. *It* is mean *to take advanage of another's distress*. *It* is perfectly plain *that a straight line must be the shortest distance between two points.*

It, in all the foregoing examples, has no antecedent.

186. A **Compound Personal Pronoun** is a word consisting, in the singular number, of *my*, *thy*, *your*, *him*, *her*, or *it*, compounded with *self;* in the plural, of *our*, *your*, or *them*, compounded with *selves*.

Ex. — Myself, yourself, himself; ourselves, yourselves, themselves.

187. These pronouns are used in two senses: —

1. For emphatic distinction.

Ex. — "He *himself* said so"; *i. e.*, no other person said so.

2. In a reflexive sense.

Ex. — "He hurt *himself*." "Said I to *myself*, I am *myself* again." That is, the act or state of the person terminates upon himself.

Relative Pronouns.

188. A **Relative Pronoun** is a pronoun that generally stands in close relation to an antecedent, and joins to it a descriptive clause.

Ex. — "The fur *which* warms the monarch, warmed a bear."
"Too low they build, *who* build beneath the stars." — *Young.*
"Spirit *that* breathest through my lattice." — *Bryant.*

Which means the fur; and *which warms the monarch* tells what fur.
Who relates to *they;* and its clause describes the persons meant by *they*.

189. The relative pronouns are *who*, *which*, *what*, *that*, and *as*, with their declined forms and their compounds.

190. Who is applied to persons, and to other objects when regarded as persons.

Ex. — "The *man who* feels truly noble, will become so." — *Chapin.* "Now a faint tick was heard below, from the *Pendulum*, *who* thus spoke." — *Jane Taylor.*

W. "The son of Esrom, which was the son of Seth." — *Bible.*

191. Which is applied to things, and to all animals inferior to man.

Ex. — The *rose which;* the *horse which;* the *army which.*

W. The lion who had killed the man, was shot the next day.

A group of persons regarded as one whole, and denoted by a collective noun, becomes a thing, and *who* should not be applied to it; as, "He instructed and fed the *crowds which* [not *who*] surrounded him."

192. What is used in place of *thing which* or *things which*, and it has therefore no antecedent.

Ex. — "I will take *what* [*the things which*] you send."

193. That is preferred to *who* and *which* in the following instances: —

1. When the antecedent denotes both persons and other objects.

Ex. — The ship and passengers *that* were lost at sea.

W. Was it the wind, or you, who shut the door?

2. Generally when a more specific or restrictive relative than *who* or *which* is needed.

Ex. — "In thoughts *that* breathe, and words *that* burn." — *Gray.* "Riches *that* are ill got, are seldom enjoyed." — *Johnson.* That is, not all riches, but only those which are ill got.

W. Adjectives which express number are called numerals.

3. After the superlative degree, when the sense is restrictive.

Ex. — This is the hardest lesson *that* we have yet had.

W. I was the first one who came to school this morning.

4. After *who*, used as an antecedent.

Ex. — Who *that* respects himself, would tell a lie?

5. After *same*.

Ex. — It is the same star *that* we saw last night.
W. These are the same sums which we had yesterday.

6. Generally, after *no*, *all*, *any*, *each*, *every*, *some*, or *very*.

Ex. — "And all *that* beauty, all *that* wealth, e'er gave." — *Gray*.
W. No man who knows him, would trust him.

7. Frequently, after personal pronouns, or after predicate-nominatives referring to *it*.

Ex. — "Fall he *that* must." — *Pope*. But, "*His* praise is lost *who* waits till all commend." — *Id*. "It is not grief *that* bids me moan."

8. Generally, where *who* or *which* would seem less proper.

Ex. — "A little child *that* lightly draws its breath." — *Wordsworth*. "A woman *who* had a daughter *that* was very beautiful." "A woman *that* had a daughter *who* was very beautiful."

194. The relative *that* does not allow a preposition to stand immediately before it; and hence *whom* or *which* must be used after a preposition, or the arrangement of the words must be varied.

Ex. — "He is the same man *with whom* I came"; or, "He is the same man *that* I came *with*."

195. *Which* and *that* have no possessive form of their own; and hence they sometimes borrow *whose*, the possessive of *who*.

Ex. — "The undiscovered *country*, from *whose* bourn [from the boundary *of which*] no traveler returns." — *Shakespeare*.

196. As is a relative pronoun when it follows *such*, *many*, or *same*, and relates to the objects thus specified.

Ex. —He has such friends *as* every one should wish to have.
As is also generally a relative pronoun after *as much*.

197. A **Compound Relative Pronoun** is *who*, *which*, or *what*, with *ever* or *soever* annexed to it.

Ex. — I will take *whatever* you send.

A compound relative pronoun is generally a little more emphatic or comprehensive than the simple one; and it dispenses with the antecedent when this is indefinite.

The indefinite *ever* or *soever* partly represents the antecedent, by being a sort of substitute for the indefinite adjective before it; and hence, when the antecedent is expressed or supplied, the *ever* or *soever* must generally be omitted.

Ex. — "*Whoever* [*he who*] cares not for others, should not expect their favors." — "The Gaul offered his own head to *whoever* [*any person who*] would bring him that of Nero." — *Gibbon.*

Interrogative Pronouns.

198. An **Interrogative Pronoun** is a pronoun used to ask a question.

Ex. — *Who* came with you? *Which* is he?

Interrogative pronouns have no antecedents; but the noun or pronoun which is given in answer to the interrogative pronoun, is sometimes called the *subsequent;* as, "Who came with you? — *John.*"

"An interrogative pronoun is a relative in search of an antecedent." — *Phil. Museum.*

199. The interrogative pronouns are *who*, *which*, and *what*, with their declined forms.

All these pronouns can be applied to either persons or things, except *who,* which is applicable to persons only.

200. **Who** inquires for the name of a person; but, when the name is given, for some description.

Ex. — "*Who* is he?" — *Wirt.* "*Who* was Blennerhasset?" — *Id.*

201. **Which** generally supposes the name known; and it is applied to persons or things, in asking for a particular one of two or more.

Ex. — "*Which* is Shylock?" — *Shakespeare.* "*Which* is yours?"
In this sense, *whether* was formerly used in asking for one of two; as, "*Whether* of the twain?" — *Spenser.* "*Whether* is greater, the gold or the temple?" — *Bible.*

202. **What** asks for the kind of thing; and hence, sometimes, for the character or occupation.

Ex. — "*What* can ennoble sots, or slaves, or cowards?
Alas! not all the blood of all the Howards." — *Pope.*
"*What* art thou?" — *Milton.* "*What* is he?"

203. An interrogative pronoun is sometimes used in a responsive sense; and it may then be called a *responsive pronoun*, or an *indirect interrogative pronoun.*

"Who is he? — I know not *who* he is."
"Which is it? — I can not tell *which* it is."
"What is truth?" "Tell me *what* truth is." — See p. 222.

Observe the difference: "*Who went?*" (*What person.*) Interrogative pronoun. "I do not know *who* went." (*What person.*) Responsive pronoun. "I do not know the person *who* went." Relative pronoun.

Adjective Pronouns.

204. An **Adjective Pronoun** is a common specifying adjective used as a pronoun.

Common specifying adjectives are such as *this*, *that*, *each*, *any*, *some*, *such*, *all*, etc.

Ex. — "The new *ones* [*edifices*] are larger." — *Addison.*
"Such men as *one* [*a person*] sometimes meets with." — *Taylor.*
"By *others'* faults, wise men correct their own." — *Proverb.*
"Where *either's* fall determines both their fates." — *Goldsmith.*
"It was the *latter*, not the *former*, that was in danger." — *Benton.*
"The age of chivalry is gone; *that* [*the age*] of," etc. — *Burke.*
"Virtue and vice are before you; *this* leads to misery, *that* to peace."
'*Some* put the bliss in action, *some* in ease:
Those call it pleasure; and contentment, *these.*" — *Pope.*
"They deemed *each other* oracles of law." — *Pope.*
"Husbands and wives are continually complaining of *each other.*" — [*Johnson.*
"Bear ye *one another's* burdens." — *Bible.*

Adjective pronouns frequently have no antecedents.

205. ADJECTIVE PRONOUNS may be divided into four classes; *distrib'utive, demon'strative, indefinite*, and *reciprocal.*

206. The *distributive pronouns* are *each, either*, and *neither.* They relate to objects taken singly.

Every, used as a pronoun, is nearly obsolete.

207. The *demonstrative pronouns* are *this, these, that, those, same, former*, and *latter.* They point out objects definitely.

208. The *indefinite pronouns* are *one, ones, other, others, any, some, such, all, both*, and *none.* They relate to objects indefinitely.

A few other adjectives may occasionally be called indefinite pronouns.

209. The *reciprocal pronouns* are *each other* and *one another.* They imply a reciprocal action or relation.

Each other and *one another* can generally be parsed in a different way. — See p. 100.

210. *Either, neither*, and *each other*, should be used in speaking of two only; *one another*, in speaking of more.

For correct examples, see the preceding page.

W. Either of the eight Professors. (Any one.)
The two Smiths are not related to one another.
Pupils should be polite to each other. — *N. Webster.*

211. When *this* and *that* are used in speaking of two, *that* should be applied to the more distant, the first-mentioned, or the absent; *this*, to the nearer, the last-mentioned, or the present.

The pronouns, and why; personal, relative, interrogative, or adjective, and why:—

I will go with you and him to see them.
It was the owner himself who killed the dog which bit us.
Who knows who he is? Some are lazy, and others stupid.

"Why is my sleep disquieted?
Who is he that calls the dead?" — *Byron.*

That is a relative pronoun when *who, whom*, or *which* can be put in its place, without destroying the sense.

PROPERTIES OF NOUNS AND PRONOUNS.

212. Nouns and Pronouns have *gender*, *person*, *number*, and *case*.

213. A pronoun must agree with its antecedent, in gender, person, and number.

Ex. — "John met *his* mother." *His* is of the same gender, person, and number as *John*.

W. Every one should attend to their own business.

GENDER.

214. **Gender** is that property of nouns ana pronouns which distinguishes objects in regard to sex.

215. There are four genders; the *masculine*, the *feminine*, the *common*, and the *neuter*.

216. A noun or pronoun is of the *masculine gender*, when it denotes a male. *Boy*.

217. A noun or pronoun is of the *feminine gender*, when it denotes a female. *Girl*.

218. A noun or pronoun is of the *common gender*, when it denotes either a male or a female. *Child*.

219. A noun or pronoun is of the *neuter gender*, when it denotes neither a male nor a female. *Book*.

The sex of an object denoted by a word of the common gender sometimes becomes more definitely known from some other word, and the words should then be parsed accordingly; as, "The *child* and *his* mother were in good health." Here *child* is masculine, as shown by *his*.

220. For the sake of brevity, nouns that are strictly masculine or feminine only, are sometimes applied to both sexes. The masculine term is generally preferred.

Ex. — "*Horses* are fond of green pastures"; *i. e.*, *horses*, and *mares* too. "The *Jews* are scattered over the whole world."
"We saw *geese* and *ducks*." "The *poets* of England."

But in connection with a proper noun, only the appropriate term will harmonize in sense; as, "The poet Homer." "The poetess Sappho."

221. On the same principle, the masculine pronoun is sometimes preferred to the feminine, or used for both.

Ex.—Every *person* should try to improve *his* mind.

W. "Almost everybody has their faults."—*Chapin.*

222. Sometimes animals are regarded as male or female, not from their sex, but from their general character.

Ex.—"The *lion* meets *his* foe boldly."—*Addison.*
"Every *ant* minds *her* own business."—*Id.*

On the same principle, sex is sometimes disregarded when the creature is small, unimportant, or imperfectly known; as, "The *child* has scorched *its* frock." "The *mouse* ran back when *it* saw me." In such cases it would probably be best to parse both the noun and the pronoun as being of the common gender.

223. Things without life are sometimes regarded as persons, and have then a suitable sex ascribed to them. Nouns thus used are said to be masculine or feminine by *personification.*

224. The masculine gender is preferred, if the object is noted for size, power, or domineering qualities.

Ex.—"Lo, steel-clad *War his* gorgeous standard rears!"—*Rogers.*
"The *sun* seemed shorn of *his* beams."—*Milton.*

225. The feminine gender is preferred, if the object is noted for beauty, amiability, productiveness, or submissive qualities.

Ex.—"Soon *Peace* shall come with all *her* smiling train."
"Earth, with *her* thousand voices, praises God."
"The *ship*, with *her* snowy sails and flaunting banner."

226. When a collective noun is used in the plural number, or when it denotes the whole collection as one thing, it is of the neuter gender; when it is used otherwise, its gender corresponds with the sex of the individuals composing the collection.

Ex.—"Six *families* settled on this river." "Every *generation* has *its* peculiarities." "The *congregation* will please to retain *their* seats."

Personal pronouns of the first or the second person are of the common gender, unless the sex becomes more definitely known from some other word.

How Gender is Expressed.

227. There are three methods of distinguishing the two sexes.

1. By different words.

Masculine.	*Feminine.*	*Masculine.*	*Feminine.*
Bachelor,	maid.	Man,	woman.
Beau,	belle.	Master,	mistress.
Boy,	girl.	Master,	miss.
Bridegroom,	bride.	Mr.,	Mrs.
Brother,	sister.	Monk, friar,	nun.
Buck,	doe.	Monsieur,	madame.
Bull,	cow.	Monsieur,	mademoiselle.
Bullock,	heifer.	Nephew,	niece.
Colt,	filly.	Papa,	mamma.
Drake,	duck.	Ram, buck,	ewe.
Earl,	countess.	Rooster,	hen.
Father,	mother.	Sir,	madam.
Gander,	goose.	Sire (horse),	dam.
Gentleman,	lady.	Sloven,	slattern.
Hart,	roe.	Son,	daughter.
He,	she.	Stag,	hind.
Horse,	mare.	Steer,	heifer.
Husband,	wife.	Swain,	nymph.
King,	queen.	Uncle,	aunt.
Lad,	lass.	Wizard,	witch.
Lord,	lady.	Youth,	maiden, damsel.
Male,	female.	Charles,	Caroline.

2. By different endings.

Most nouns of this class denote rank or occupation; and the feminine generally ends with *ess* or *trix*.

Ex. — Abbot, *abbess*; governor, *governess*.

Add ESS: Baron, count, viscount, dauphin, deacon, diviner, giant, god (see p. 50), heir, hermit, host, Jew, lion, mayor, patron, peer, poet, priest, prince (see p. 51), prior, prophet, shepherd, tailor, author.

Change RER *into* RESS: Adulterer, adventurer, caterer, murderer, sorcerer.

Change TER *or* TOR *into* TRESS, *and* DER *into* DRESS: Actor, arbiter, benefactor, chanter, enchanter, conductor, embassador, elector, founder, huckster, hunter, idolater, inventor, instructor, Mister, painter, porter, protector, proprietor, teamster, songster, traitor, victor, waiter, auditor, editor, orator.

Change TOR *into* TRIX: Administrator, exec′utor, testator.

Change TOR *into* TRESS *or* TRIX: Director, mediator, spectator.

Words not so Regular.

Masculine.	*Feminine.*	*Masculine.*	*Feminine.*
Emperor,	empress,	Margrave,	margravine.
Tiger,	tigress.	Joseph,	Josephine.
Negro,	negress.	Paul,	Pauline.
Votary,	votaress.	Goodman,	goody.
Duke,	duchess.	Widower,	widow.
Marquis,	marchioness.	Don,	donna.
Anchoret, Anchorite,	anchoress.	Infant,	infanta.
		Signor,	signora.
Doctor,	doctoress, doctress.	Sultan,	sultana, sultaness.
Tutor,	tutoress, tutress.	Tzar,	tzarī′na.
		Augustus,	Augusta.
Hero,	hĕr′oīne.	Cornelius,	Cornelia.
Landgrave,	landgravine.	Louis,	Louī′sa, -īse′.

John,	Joanna.	Jesse,	Jessie.
Henry,	Henrietta.	Frank, }	Frances.
Julius,	Julia, Juliet.	Francis, }	

Words derived or compounded from others, usually express gender in the same way.

Arch*duke*,	arch*duchess*.	Grand*father*,	grand*mother*.
Land*lord*,	land*lady*.	Step*son*,	step*daughter*.
School*master*,	school*mistress*.	Pea*cock*,	pea*hen*.

3. By using a distinguishing word.

Bear,	*he*-bear,	*she*-bear.	*Cock*-sparrow,	*hen*-sparrow.
Goat,	*he*-goat,	*she*-goat.	*Male* descendants,	*female* descendants.
Servant,	*man*-servant,	*maid*-servant.	*Mr.* Reynolds,	{ *Mrs.* Reynolds,
Rabbit,	*buck*-rabbit,	*doe*-rabbit.		{ *Miss* Reynolds.

Some masculine terms have rarely or never corresponding feminines, as *baker*, *brewer*, *lawyer*; and some feminine terms have rarely or never corresponding masculines, as *laundress*, *coquet*, *hag*.

The gender, and why: —

Person, corpse, corps, spirit, angel, they, I, hers, game, clergy, party, nations. *John* is a noun, and *she* is a pronoun.

PERSON.

228. Person is that property of words which shows whether the speaker is meant, the person spoken to, or the person or thing spoken of.

229. There are three persons; the *first*, the *second*, and the *third*.

230. A noun or pronoun is of the *first person*, when it denotes the speaker. "*I Paul* have written it."

231. A noun or pronoun is of the *second person*, when it denotes the person spoken to. "*Paul*, *thou* hast written it."

232. A noun or pronoun is of the *third person*, when

it denotes the person or thing spoken of. "*Paul* has written *it*."

233. The third person is sometimes elegantly used for the first or second.

Ex. — "The *king* is always willing to listen to the just complaints of *his* subjects"; for, "*I* am always willing," etc. "Surely, my mother does not mean to marry me to such an old miser"; for, "Surely, *mother*, *you* do not," etc.

When inanimate objects are addressed, they are of course personified, or regarded as persons; as, "O *Liberty!* what crimes are committed in thy name!" — *Madame Roland.*

When a noun comes after a verb and explains the nominative, it is of the third person, though the nominative may be of the first or second person; as, "I am the *sheriff*." (I am *he*.) "You are *heroes*."

The nouns and pronouns, and why; of what person, and why: —

You will find that many evils beset us mortals.

I said to him, Well, my little friend, how fare the school-boys?

Change into the other persons: —

John writes. The girls study. Henry, you may play.

Shall Hannibal compare himself with this half-year captain?

NUMBER.

234. Number is that property of words which shows whether one object is meant, or more than one.

235. There are two numbers; the *singular* and the *plural*.

236. A noun or pronoun is of the *singular number*, when it denotes but one object. *Tree*, *she*.

237. A noun or pronoun is of the *plural number*, when it denotes more objects than one. *Trees*, *they*.

238. A proper noun is made plural, when it is needed to denote a family, race, or group, or two or more individuals of the same name or character.

Ex. — The Dixons; the Cherokees; the Azores; the twelve Cæsars.

239. The names of qualities, states, actions, substances, arts, sciences, and diseases, when the reference is to the kind of thing, are generally used in the singular number only.

Ex. — Pride, peace, business, gold, grammar, painting, fever.

240. But such words may become plural, —

1. When different kinds are meant.

Ex. — Teas, fevers. "The *nationalities* and *religions* of the world." — *Chapin.*

2. When things are meant that have the property or substance, or consist of parts.

Ex. — Curiosities, marbles, paintings, proceedings. "The *heights* around the city." — *Gen. Scott.* "I had only a few *coppers* left." — *Franklin.* "I heard the *waters* roar down the cataract." — *Addison.*

241. Some nouns are always plural, especially the names of things consisting of two or many parts.

Aborig'inēs	Eaves	Măt'ins	Stairs
Annals	Embers	Nuptials	Statist'ics
Antip'odēs	Entrails	Nippers	Stilts
Ar'chīves	Goggles	Oats	Suds
Ashes	Hatches	Paraphernal'ia	Thanks
As'sets	Head'-quarters	Pinchers	Teens
Belles-let'tres	Hose	Ple'iads	Tongs
Billiards	Hyster'ics	Rega'lia	Tidings
Bitters	Ides	Riches	Trousers
Breeches	Lees	Remains	Tweezers
Cattle	Litera'ti	Scissors	Victuals
Clothes	Lungs	Shears	Vitals
Dregs	Mamma'lia	Snuffers	Withers.

To the foregoing list belong a few more words less common; also most of the scientific family names of animals and plants.

Some nouns, that have the singular, have acquired a plural that differs from it in meaning. Plurals of this kind also belong to the list above.

Ex. — *Arms*, weapons; *colors*, banner; *compasses*, dividers; *dividers*, an instrument; *drawers*, an article of clothing; *goods*, merchandise; *greens*, young leaves for cooking; *grounds*, dregs; *letters*, literature; *manners*, behavior; *morals*, morality; *shambles*, meat-market; *spectacles*, glasses; *stays*, a corset; *vespers*, evening hymn.

242. Sometimes such a word may be used in the singular number, to denote a part or an individual.

Ex. — "The left *lung* was diseased." — *Dr. Rush.* "A *mammal.*" — *Goldsmith.* "A valuable *statistic.*" — *Census.*

243. Some nouns have the same form for either number.

Deer	Series	News	Mathematics
Sheep	Species	Alms	Politics
Swine	Corps	Odds	Physics
Vermin	Appara'tus	Amends	Metaphysics
Grouse	Bellows	Wages	Mechanics
Head (cattle)	Gallows	Pains (care)	Glanders
Sail (ships)	Means	Ethics	Measles, etc.

It seems to us that *all* names of a plural form that denote sciences or diseases, should be classed under this head.

News, though analogous to *goods* and *odds*, seems to be now used in the singular number only. *Wages* and *pains* are generally plural.

Corps is pronounced *kōre* in the singular number, and *kōres* in the plural.

A word of the foregoing class, especially if applied to a science or a disease, often denotes what is singular in its essence but plural in its manifestations; and whether the word should be considered singular or plural, will therefore depend on our conception of the thing.

244. Some nouns of number, preceded by a numeral, and some nouns denoting small animals or other objects regarded as to their nature or in mass, are also often used in the singular form to express either number.

Ex. — "Twenty *pair* of eyes." — *Shakespeare.* "Three *score* and ten." — *Bible.* So, *brace*, *dozen*, *yoke.* "This creek abounds in *trout* and *perch.*" — *Exploring Expedition.* "The *foe!* they come; they come." — *Byron.* *Foot* and *horse*, meaning troops, are thus often used in a plural sense; and sometimes *cannon* and *shot* are thus used.

But the plural forms of most such nouns are also used, especially when the word implies number or individuals rather than kind or quantity.

Ex. — "*Trouts* and *salmons* swim against the stream." — *Bacon.* "As *pilchards* are to *herrings.*" — *Shakespeare.* "By *scores* and *dozens.*" — *Id.*

It seems, indeed, that some nouns, such as *fish* and *fowl*, have *two plurals*; a regular one, denoting individuals or kinds, and a collective one, denoting the kind of thing, in which the word remains unchanged as in the case of collective nouns.

245. A collective noun is *singular*, when the entire collection is regarded as one thing.

Ex. — The *army* was large.

246. A collective noun is *plural*, when it refers to the individuals composing the collection.

Ex. — Most *people* are too solicitous about the future.

247. A collective noun is *plural*, when it has the plural form.

Ex. — The *armies* were large.

How the Plural Number is Expressed.

248. Most nouns are made plural, by adding *s* to the singular.

Ex. — Book, *books;* chimney, *chimneys;* nation, *nations.*

249. Nouns that end with *s*, *x*, *z*, *sh*, or soft *ch*; and nouns that end with *i*, *o*, *u*, or *y*, preceded each by a consonant, — are made plural by adding *es* to the singular.

Ex. — Glass, *glasses;* fox, *foxes;* topaz, *topazes;* bush, *bushes;* church, *churches;* alkali, *alkalies;* negro, *negroes;* gnu, *gnues;* story, *stories.* (*Y* is changed to *i.* See p. 50.)

250. When a vowel precedes final *o* or *y*, *s* only is annexed; as, folio, *folios;* monkey, *monkeys.*

251. Proper nouns, foreign nouns, and unusual nouns, to prevent the liability of mistaking them, are varied as little as possible; and hence they merely assume *s*, or *es* when *s* will not coalesce in sound.

Ex. — Denny, the *Dennys;* Dennie, the *Dennies;* Peri, *Peris;* canto, *cantos;* "several *tos*" [or *to's*]; the two *Miss Foots.* But, Jones, the *Joneses;* Fox, the *Foxes.*

When words of these classes are so familiarly known as to be easily recognized in almost any form, they are often made plural like ordinary nouns; as, Henry, *Henries;* Nero, *Neroes;* no, *noes.*

Owing to their foreign tinge, we still find in good use *cantos*, *duodecimos*, *fandangos*, *frescos*, *grottos*, *halos*, *hidalgos*, *juntos*, *lassos*, *mementos*, *octavos*, *pianos*, *porticos*, *quartos*, *salvos*, *solos*, *tyros*, *zeros*, in stead of *cantoes*, *grottoes*, etc., which are also coming into use.

252. The following nouns change the ending into *ves*: —

Beef,	beeves.	Life,	lives.	Wife,	wives.
Calf,	calves.	Loaf,	loaves.	Wolf,	wolves.
Elf,	elves.	Self,	selves.	Wharf,	{ wharfs, wharves.
Half	halves.	Sheaf,	sheaves.		
Knife,	knives.	Shelf,	shelves.	Staff,	{ staves (sticks), staffs (officers).
Leaf,	leaves.	Thief,	thieves.		

Staff always makes *staffs* in compounds; as, flagstaff, *flagstaffs.*

253. For forming the plural of some words, no general rule can be given; and they are therefore said to be *irregular*.

Man,	men.	Goose,	geese.	I,	we.
Woman,	women.	Tooth,	teeth.	Thou,	ye.
Child,	children.	Mouse,	mice.	He, she, *or* it,	they.
Ox,	oxen.	Louse,	lice.	This,	these.
Foot,	feet.	Cow,	cows, kine.	That,	those.

The words ending with *man*, that are not compounds of *man*, are regular, or take *s;* as, German, *Germans;* talisman, *talismans;* Mussulman, *Mussulmans.*

254. Some nouns have both a regular and an irregular plural, but with a difference in meaning.

Brother,	*brothers* (of the same family),	*brethren* (of the same society).
Die,	*dies* (stamps for coining),	*dice* (small cubes for gaming).
Fish,	*fishes* (individuals),	*fish* (quantity, or the species).
Genius,	*geniuses* (men of genius),	*ge'nii* (spirits).
Index,	*in'dexes* (tables of contents),	*in'dicēs* (algebraic signs).
Penny,	*pennies* (pieces of money),	*pence* (how much in value).

Brothers is sometimes used in the sense of *brethren*, probably as a more affectionate term.

255. Most compound words are expressed in the plural number, by making plural only that part of the word which is described by the rest.

Mouse-trap,	mouse-trap**s**.	Brother-in-law,	brother**s**-in-law.
Cupful,	cupful**s**.	Sister-in-law,	sister**s**-in-law.
Spoonful,	spoonful**s**.	Billet-doux.	billet**s**-doux.
Wagon-load,	wagon-load**s**.	Court-martial,	court**s**-martial.
Ox-cart,	ox-cart**s**.	Aid-de-camp,	aid**s**-de-camp.

256. The pluralized part of a compound word is made plural in the same way as if it stood alone.

Ex. — Horse*man*, horse*men;* dor*mouse*, dor*mice;* *hanger*-on, *hangers*-on.

257. When a compound word is a foreign term or other phrase, of which the descriptive part is not very obvious, the whole term generally takes the regular plural ending.

Piano-forte,	piano-forte**s**.	Tête-a-tête,	tête-a-tête**s**.
Camera-obscura,	camera-obscura**s**.	Ipse-dixit,	ipse-dixit**s**.
Port-monnāie,	port-monnāie**s**.	Jack-a-lantern,	Jack-a-lantern**s**.

258. A few terms have both parts made plural.

Man-servant,	men-servants.	Ignis-fatuus,	ignēs-fatuī.
Woman-servant,	women-servants.	Knight Templar,	Knights Templars.

259. When the title *Mr.*, *Miss*, or *Dr.*, is used with a name, the whole term is made plural by making plural the title only.

Ex. — Mr. Harper, *Messrs. Harper;* Miss Brown, the *Misses Brown;* Dr. Lee, *Drs. Lee; Messrs.* John and James Morton; *Misses* Julia and Alice Clark.

260. When the title is *Mrs.*, or when the word *two*, *three*, etc., stands before the title, the latter noun is made plural.

Ex. — "The Mrs. Barlows." — *Irving.* "The two Miss Scotts had been gathering flowers." — *Id.*

Other terms, consisting of names and titles, follow sometimes one analogy, and sometimes the other. "From Dutchesses and *Lady Maries.*" — *Pope.* "I went to the *Ladies Butler.*" — *Swift.* "May there be *Sir Isaac Newtons* in every science." — *Watts.*

261. Words adopted from other languages usually retain their foreign plurals in our language. Some, however, take the English plural only; some, the foreign; and some, either.

No certain rule can be given for forming such plurals, but the following rules may be of some assistance: —

1. The ending *a* is changed to *æ* or *ata.*
2. The ending *us* is changed to *i.*
3. The ending *um* or *on* is changed to *a.*
4. The ending *is* is changed to *es* or *ides.*
5. The ending *x* or *ex* is changed to *ces* or *ices.*

R means that the word before it nas also the regular English plural.

Change final

A to **ae**: —	Fib′ula	Minu′tia	**A** to **ata**: —
Alum′na	Form′ula, R.	Nĕb′ula	Dogma, R.
(*alumnæ*)	Lam′ina	Sco′ria	(*dogmas, dogmata*)
Are′na, R.	Lar′va	Sĭm′ia	Stigma, R.
Cica′da, R.	Mac′ula	Ver′tebra	Mias′ma

Us to **i**:—

Alum′nus
(*alumnī*)
Cal′culus
Echi′nus
Focus, R.
Fungus, R.
Hippopot′amus, R.
Ma′gus
Nau′tilus, R.
Nu′cleus, R.
Pol′ypus, R.
Ra′dius, R.
Sarcoph′agus
Stim′ulus
Ter′minus
Tu′mulus

Um or **on** to **a**:

Animal′culum
(*animalculă*)
Aphe′lion,
Aqua′rium, R.
Arca′num
Autom′aton, R.
Corrigen′dum
Crite′rion, R.
Datum
Desidera′tum
Efflu′vium
Ephem′eron
Enco′mium, R.
Erra′tum
Fulcrum, R.
Gymna′sium, R.
Herba′rium, R.
Me′dium, R.
Memoran′dum, R.
Men′struum, R.
Momen′tum, R.
Parhe′lion
Perihe′lion
Phenom′enon
Rostrum, R.
Scho′lium, R.
Spectrum, R.
Spec′ulum, R.
Strătum, R.
Trape′zium, R.
Vin′culum, R.

Is to **es**:—

Amanuen′sis
(*amanuensēs*)
Anal′ysis
Antith′esis
Axis
Basis
Crisis
Diær′esis
Di′esis
Ellip′sis
Em′phasis
Hypoth′esis
Metamor′phosis
O′asis
Paren′thesis
Phasis
Praxis
Synop′sis
Syn′thesis
Thesis

Is to **ides**:—

Aphis
(*aph′idēs*)
Apsis
Can′tharis
Chrys′alis
Ephem′eris
Epider′mis
Iris, R.
Probos′cis

X to **ces**:—

Appendix, R.
(*appen′dixes*,
appendicēs)
Calx, R.
Ca′lyx, R.
Cica′trix, R.
He′lix, R.
Ma′trix, R.
Ra′dix, R.

Ex to **ices**:—

Apex, R.
(*a′pexes*, *ap′icēs*)
Vertex, R.
Vortex, R.

Less Regular.

Beau, R.,
beaux.
Bandit, R.,
banditti.
Cher′ub, R.,
cher′ubim.
Ge′nus,
gen′era.
Hia′tus, R.,
hiatus.
Lar′ynx, R.,
laryn′gēs.
Madame,
Mesdames.
Monsieur,
Messieurs.
Mr.,
Messrs.
Pha′lanx, R.,
phalan′ges.
Ser′aph, R.,
ser′aphim.
Sta′men, R.,
stam′ina.
Ver′tigo,
vertig′inēs.
Virtuo′so,
virtuosos,
virtuosī.

The English plurals of the foregoing words are generally preferred in familiar language; and the foreign, in scientific.

262. Letters, figures, and other characters, are made plural by annexing *'s*.

Ex.—"The *a's* and *n's* in the first line." "By 5's and 7's." "What mean those ʒ's and ϑ's?" The apostrophe is used to prevent ambiguity; thus, "Cross your *t's* and dot your *i's*," is not the same as "Cross your *ts* and dot your *is*." 5s might mean 5 shillings or five times *s*.

Numbers of Pronouns.

263. In editorials, speeches, and proclamations, *we*, *our*, *us*, etc., are frequently used to denote apparently but one.

Ex.—"*We* believe that the war can not last much longer."
London Times.

This manner of speaking gives generally an air of modesty or authority to the assertion; the speaker seeming to deliver his own sentiments as if they were also entertained or could be enforced by others as well as by himself.

To the foregoing manner of speaking, *ourself* is peculiarly adapted, and it is sometimes used accordingly. "What then remains? *Ourself*."—Pope's *Goddess of Dullness.*

264. *You*, *your*, and *yours*, are now singular as well as plural; but *yourself* is strictly singular.

265. *What*, in close connection with a plural, is sometimes used in the plural number.

Ex.—"We were now at the mercy of *what* are called guerillas."

266. *None* (*no-one*) is used in either the singular or the plural number.

Ex.—"*None* is good save One."—*Bible.* "*None* are completely happy."—*Blair.*

267. Relative, interrogative, and some adjective pronouns, have the same form for both numbers; and most other pronouns are irregular.

For the analogies which most pronouns follow, see paragraphs 243 and 253.

The number, and why:—

Rose, roses, molasses, ashes, family, families, I, we, him, them, two, a two, a pair, two pair, memoranda, miasma, cherubim, optics, commanders-in-chief, orang-outangs.

Spell the plural of the following words: —

Sofa, larva, house, mouse, feather-bed, booth, tooth, ox, box, root, foot, turf, wolf, genus, genius, isthmus, trio, cargo, valley, Tully, alley, ally, trellis, ellipsis, Mr. Jones, Mrs. Jones.

CASE.

268. Case is that property of nouns and pronouns which shows how they are used in the construction of sentences.

269. There are three cases; the *nominative*, the *possessive*, and the *objective*.

Nominative Case.

270. A noun or pronoun is in the *nominative case*, when it is the subject of a predicate-verb.

That is, when an act or state is predicated of it. — See page 5.

Ex. — "*John* struck James." (*Who* struck James?) "The *rose* is beautiful." (*What* is beautiful?) "*He* came after *I* left."

W. Him and me went to school together. — See p. 103.

271. A noun or pronoun is also in the *nominative case*, when it is used independently or absolutely.

272. A noun or pronoun is used *independently*, —

1. By direct address. "*John*, your father is here."
2. By exclamation. "Alas, poor *Yorick!*"
3. By pleonasm or specification. "*He* that hath ears, let him hear." "Worcester's *Dictionary*, Unabridged."

To this last head belong inscriptions, and generally those nouns which are used merely to name objects. — See p. 100.

273. A noun or pronoun is used *absolutely*, when, by some abridgment, it is set free, or *absolved*, from its nominative relation to a finite verb, but still remains with the participle or the infinitive.

"The *house* being sold, we removed." (When the *house* was sold, etc.)
"The vanity of being a *belle*." ("That she was a *belle*.")
"To become a *scholar*, requires exertion." ("He has become a *scholar*.")

W. Me being sick, the business was neglected. — See p. 103.

Possessive Case.

274. A noun or pronoun is in the *possessive case*, when it denotes possession.

Ex. — *John's* horse. (Whose horse?) *My* slate.

Possession may be past, or future and intended, as well as present and actual; as, "*Webster's* Dictionary"; "*Men's* boots for sale here." The former example implies *origin;* the latter, *fitness.*

275. The possessive case of nouns is formed by annexing to the name of the owner an apostrophe ('), and then the letter *s*.

Ex. — *Mary's* slate. *Burns's* poems. *Men's* affairs.

W. Henrys books. Brooks' translation. Childrens' playthings.

276. The apostrophe only is annexed to plural nouns that end with *s*.

Ex. — The *soldiers'* camp.

277. The possessive *s* is sometimes omitted from singular nouns that end with the sound of *s*, when so many hissing sounds would come together as to produce unusual harshness.

Ex. — "The defeat of *Xerxes'* army was the downfall of Persia."
Rollin.

A singular noun that ends with an *s*-sound, should generally have the apostrophe and *s;* as, "*Dennis's* Works." — *Pope.* "*Louis's* reign." — *Macaulay.* "*Charles's* affairs." — *Prescott.* "For *conscience'* sake," "For *goodness'* sake," are rather idiomatic exceptions to the rule, than fair illustrations of a general principle.

Possession may also be expressed by *of*, and sometimes by an adjective, or a noun made an adjective; hence, —

278. The meaning of the possessive case is sometimes more elegantly expressed by using *of*, or by making the possessive word an adjective.

"The death of Socrates" is a better expression than "Socrates's death"; and "Lucas Place" is quite as intelligible as Lucas's Place."

W. Essex's death. Demosthenes's orations.

279. The two possessive forms of such words as *deer* and *sheep* are distinguished by placing the apostrophe before the *s* in the singular number, and after it in the plural; as, *deer's*, *deers'*. This is a questionable rule.

280. A compound or complex term takes the possessive sign but once; generally at the end, or next to the name of what is owned.

Ex.—The *court-martial's* decisions; the *courts-martial's* decisions.

"The *Bishop of Landaff's* residence." "*Edward Everett's* oration." "At *Hall's, the baker.*" "At *Hall the baker's.*" Supply *residence* or *store*.

W. At Smith's, the bookseller's.

281. A pair or series of nouns, implying common possession, take the possessive sign at the end, and but once.

Ex.—"*Oakley* and *Mason's* store"; *i. e.*, the store of Oakley and Mason.

282. A pair or series of nouns, not implying common possession, or emphatically distinguished, take each the possessive sign.

Ex.—"*Webster's* and *Worcester's* Dictionary"; *i. e.*, Webster's Dictionary and Worcester's Dictionary. "By his *mother's* as well as his *father's* advice."

W. John and Mary's books.

In such expressions as all the foregoing, *of* is sometimes preferable.

Idiomatic Expressions. — "A discovery of Sir Isaac *Newton's*" is equivalent to "A discovery of Sir Isaac *Newton's discoveries.*" "That head of *yours,*" however, is not equivalent to "That head of *your heads*"; but the expression can be parsed by considering it equivalent to "That head of *your possession.*" — See p. 103.

Objective Case.

283. A noun or pronoun is in the *objective case,* when it is the object of a transitive verb or a preposition.

Transitive means *passing over.* A transitive verb generally denotes an act that passes over from one person or thing to another; as, *strike.* The object of a transitive verb or a preposition is the noun or pronoun which completes its relation.

Ex. — "The soldiers carried their bleeding *companion* to the *river.*" (Carried *whom?* to *what?*) "*Whom* did you send to *me?*"

W. Who do you want? Who did you send for? See p. 103.

284. A noun or pronoun is also in the objective case, when it is used in the sense of an adjunct.

An *adjunct* is a preposition with the noun or pronoun required after it to complete the sense; as, "*on the floor.*"

Ex. — "I do not care a *straw.*" Care not how much? "The street is a *mile* long, and sixty *feet* wide." Long and wide to what extent? "He went *home.*" Went to what place?

The objectives under the latter head are simply phrases from which the preposition has been dropped; as, "He remained *five days*" = He remained *during five days.* In many cases the preposition can be supplied: but when such an abridged mode of expression has struck root in a language, there springs up at once an *idiom;* and since the relation of the object to the other word is simply the known relation between the things, cases may occur in which no suitable preposition can be found, for that relation may never have been expressed by any preposition in the language.

285. There are expressions, however, obviously elliptical.

Ex. — "Dr. Rush, No. 340, Chestnut Street, Philadelphia, Penn."

To Dr. Rush, *at* No. 340, *on* Chestnut Street, *in* Philadelphia, *in* Pennsylvania.

Same Case.

286. A noun or pronoun is generally in the *same case* as another, when it denotes the same person or thing.

Ex. — "Cortez, the *conqueror* of Mexico, was a brave *man*."

Cortez may be called the leading or principal term; and the other, the subordinate or explanatory term.

287. The subordinate term may be, —

1. An emphatic word. "Brown *himself* went."
2. An explanatory word. "Brown the *merchant*."
3. A repeated word, repeated for emphasis or explanation. "I, *I*, am the man." "Company, villainous *company*, has been the ruin of me."

288. Under SAME CASE, two kinds of construction may be noticed; *predication* and *apposition*.

289. When an intransitive or passive verb joins the two terms, the latter is said to be *predicated* of the other, and may be called a *predicate nominative* or *substantive.*

Ex. — "He is *Governor*." "He was elected *Governor*." "The world is but a *stage*, and all the men and women [are] merely *players*." — *Shakespeare*.

"Tom struts a *soldier*." — *Pope*. "She walks a *queen*." — *Id*.

W. It was me. Is it him? I knew it was her. — See p. 103.

290. The verb declares the identity between the two terms, or shows how that identity is acquired or made known.

When an infinitive or a participle joins the explanatory term to an objective term, the relation is still predication rather than apposition; but the explanatory term should then be called simply a *predicate-substantive*, for it is not a nominative; as, "I know *it* to be *him*." After a participle, the explanatory term is generally a predicate-*nominative*; as, "He, being the *brother*, interceded."

291. When no verb joins the terms, the latter term is said to be in *apposition* with the other, and is called an *appos'itive.*

Ex. — "Webster, the *orator* and *statesman*, was not related to Webster the *lexicographer*." "At Smith's, the *bookseller*." "A firth, or *frith*." "As a *statesman*, HE had great ability." "IT is useless *to resist*." "IT is plain *that he must fail*." The terms in apposition sometimes differ in form, as *Smith's* and *bookseller* above. — See p. 211.

292. Two words are also in apposition, when both are objects of a verb that produces the identity.

Ex. — "They named *her Mary*." (*She* was named *Mary*.)
"They elected *him Mayor*." (*He* was elected *Mayor*.)

293. Two or more explanatory nouns are also in apposition, when used together to denote the same person; though they may not be explanatory of each other.

Ex. — Yonder lives a great *scholar* and *statesman*.

294. The explanatory term sometimes precedes the other, or the verb.

Ex. — "A *man* he was to all the country dear." — *Goldsmith.*
"*Who* is he?" He is *who?* (*Who* asks for explanation.)

295. It is not always necessary that the explanatory term should agree with the other in any thing else than case.

Ex. — "Our *liberties*, our greatest *blessing*, we shall not give up so easily." "*I* was *eyes* to the blind, and *feet* was *I* to the lame."

296. The whole is sometimes again mentioned by a distributive word, or by words denoting the parts; and sometimes the separate persons or things are summed up in one emphatic word denoting the whole.

Ex. — "THEY bore *each* a banner." "The two love *each* [loves the] other." (See p. 80.) "Time, labor, money, *all* were lost."

"But those that sleep, and think not of their sins,
Pinch THEM,—*arms*, *legs*, *backs*, *shoulders*, *sides*, and *shins*."—*Shak.*

297. The explanatory term is sometimes cut off from the other by a governing word, and may then be different in case.

Ex.—Yonder is the city of *St. Louis*.

Cases of Pronouns.

298. The compound personal pronouns, and some other pronouns, are used only in the nominative and the objective case; and for both they have the same form.

See the declension of pronouns, p. 103.

299. To express emphatic distinction in the possessive case, we use the word *own* in stead of *self* or *selves*.

Ex.—Every man should attend to *his own* business.

300. *Who* is declined, *what* is not declined, and *which* and *that* borrow *whose;* but all the relative pronouns have the same form for both numbers.

301. *What*, used as a common relative pronoun, and sometimes other expressions of the same kind, may supply two cases.

Ex.—"Take *what* suits you." Here *what* is the object of *take* and also the subject of *suits*.

302. When the form of the relative prevents it from furnishing two cases, it must take the form required for its own clause, and a suitable antecedent must be supplied for the other clause.

Ex.—"Give it to *whoever* needs it." *Whoever* can not be both objective and nominative; therefore its nominative form is preferred so as to suit the verb *needs*, and an antecedent is supplied for *to*.

"Give it to *any person who* [*that*] needs it." The *ever* or *soever* must generally be omitted when the antecedent is supplied. — See p. 78.

303. When *what* is interrogative or responsive, it has but one case, and that depends on some word in its own clause.

Ex. — "*What* is it? — I do not know *what* it is." *What* is in the nominative case agreeing with *it*. *Know* governs not *what*, but the entire clause beginning with *what*.

304. *One*, *other*, and *another*, are declined like nouns.

DECLENSION OF NOUNS AND PRONOUNS.

Having shown you what properties nouns and pronouns have, we shall next show you, briefly and regularly, how the different nouns and pronouns are written to express these properties. This process is called *declension*.

305. To **Decline** a noun or pronoun is to show, in some regular way, what forms it has to express its grammatical properties.

Observe that nouns sometimes remain unchanged, and that pronouns are sometimes wholly changed, to express their properties.

NOUNS.

Singular.			Plural.		
Nominative.	*Possessive.*	*Objective.*	*Nominative.*	*Possessive.*	*Objective.*
Boy,	boy's,	boy;	boys,	boys',	boys.
Man,	man's,	man;	men,	men's,	men.
Lady,	lady's,	lady;	ladies,	ladies',	ladies.
Fox,	fox's,	fox;	foxes,	foxes',	foxes.
Smith,	Smith's,	Smith;	Smiths,	Smiths',	Smiths.
John,	John's,	John.			

Decline *Mary*, *woman*, *duchess*, *state*, *farmer*, *Benjamin*, *city*.

PRONOUNS.

	SINGULAR.			PLURAL.		
	Nom.	*Poss.*	*Obj.*	*Nom.*	*Poss.*	*Obj.*
1st Pers.	I,	my, mine,	me;	we,	our, ours,	us.
2d Pers.	Thou,	thy, thine,	thee;	ye,	your, yours,	you.
	You,	your, yours,	you;	you,		
3d Pers.	*Mas.* He,	his,	him;	they,	their, theirs,	them.
	Fem. She,	her, hers,	her;			
	Neut. It,	its,	it;			

	Nom. or *Obj.*	*Nom.* or *Obj.*
1st Pers.	Myself (*or* ourself);	ourselves.
2d Pers.	Thyself *or* yourself;	yourselves.
3d Pers.	Himself, herself, itself;	themselves.

Nom.	*Poss.*	*Obj.*	*Nom.*	*Poss.*	*Obj.*
One,	one's,	one;	ones,	ones',	ones.
Other,	other's,	other;	others,	others',	others.

SINGULAR or PLURAL.	Who,	whose,	whom.	(-ever *or* -soever.)
	Which,	(whose,)	which.	"
	What,	———	what.	"
	That,	(whose,)	that.	
	As,	———	as.	
	None,	———	none.	

Decline *I, thou, you, he, she, it, myself, thyself, yourself, himself, herself, itself, one, other, who, whoever, whosoever, which, whichever, what, that, as, none.*

Exercises.

Tell which words are nouns, and why; which words are pronouns, and why:—
Tell what kind of noun, and why; what kind of pronoun, and why:—
Mention the gender, and why:—
Mention the person, and why:—

Mention the number, and why: —

Mention the case, and why; or show on what word it depends: —

It will probably be best to interrogate the pupil on but one thing at a time, through all the following sentences.

Jesus wept. Farmers plough. Iron rusts. Jerusalem was destroyed. He works. She studies. I thank you. John found Mary's book. Lucy's lamb nips the grass. Our friends are kind. Albert wrote his name in his book. Love and kindness go together. Colonel Thomas H. Benton died in the year 1858. Hannibal defeated the Romans. Hatred produces strife. Vain people love flattery. Must I leave thee, Paradise? Captain Cook sailed round the world. We went to Boston. Boston is the capital of Massachusetts. Youth, the morning of life, is often misspent. She seemed a creature fresh from the hands of God. A herd of buffaloes crossed the prairie. A flock of blackbirds is on the tree. The groves were God's first temples. There are lions and ostriches in Africa. She deceived herself. The lady who had been sick, received the peaches which were ripe. This is the same marble that you gave me, and it is the best one that I have. Is this apple yours, or mine? We bought only such mules as we needed. Who is perfect? Whom did you see? What you thoroughly understand, you can easily describe. Whatsoever comes from the heart, goes to the heart. Ferdinand and Isabella, the king and queen of Spain, enabled Columbus, a Genoese, to discover America. Liberty has God on her side. Bad boys spoil good ones. I am the captain, sir. There has been much severe fighting in crushing this rebellion. I like apples. I like to skate. Learn the *how* and the *why*. Why he went, is obvious. (What is obvious?) I know that you can learn. (I know what?) It is probable that he will be elected. (What is probable?) The storm having ceased, we renewed our journey.

"On that day of desolation, lady, I was captive made;
Bleeding for my Christian nation, by the walls of high Belgrade."

What is the objective corresponding to —

I? — thou? — we? — ye? — you? — he? — she? — it? — they? — who?

What is the nominative corresponding to —

Me? — us? — thee? — him? — whom? — her? — hers? — them? — themselves? — herself? — it? — which?

Form the compound pronoun: —

My, our, thy, your, him, her, it, them, who, which, what.

Of what gender, person, number, and case is each of the following pronouns?

Him, his, its, he, them, it, I, you, thy, their, she, thou, me, your, us, they, my, mine, thine, yours, hers, others, theirs, we, thee, our, ours, ye, myself, themselves, ourselves, thyself, yourselves, yourself, himself, itself, herself, one, none, one's, ones', other, others', who, what, which, whatever.

ARTICLES.

306. An **Article** is the word *the*, *a*, or *an*, placed before a noun to limit its meaning.

Ex. — Horses; *a* horse, *the* horse, *the* horses; *the* others.

Sometimes an article, as in the last example, is placed before a pronoun.

Classification. { *Definite*, **The.** / *Indefinite*, **A** or **An.** }

307. **The** is used to point out a particular object or class, or something as being a particular one, part, or group.

"*The* sun"; *i. e.*, not a particular sun, but a particular object that is called *sun*.

"Honor *the* soldier"; "Here lived *the* Cherokees." A particular class of persons.

"*The* first man"; "*the* lungs"; "*the* first men." One, part, group.

Sometimes *the* may point out either a particular one or part of a class, or else the entire class as distinguished from other kinds of objects; as, "*The bee* stung him"; "*The bee* is a pattern of industry."

W. Wisest and best men sometimes commit errors.
Sometimes one article is improperly used for another.

308. *The* sometimes precedes a proper noun, to render it sufficiently definite; or it points out an object as already known, or as pre-eminently distinguished.

Ex. — *Ohio* means a State; but *the Ohio*, a river.

" *The Fulton* went up the river this morning."

"*Fulton* went up the river this morning," may relate to a man.

" *The* generous *Lafayette* and *the* noble *Washington*."

" These are the sacred feelings of thy heart, O Lyttleton, *the friend*."

W. Connecticut is a beautiful river.

309. *The* may relate to a singular or a plural word.

Ex. — *The* river, *the* rivers; *the* fourth *man*, *the* four *men*.

310. A or **An** is used to show that no particular one of a class is meant.

A man, *an* insect; *a* small picture. " He was *a* merchant."

W. The interest is the fourth part of the debt.

311. *A* or *an* can be used to point out one only, or one aggregate. Sometimes more are spoken of, but they are still considered one by one.

Ex. — "*A pen*"; not, *a pens*. An eye; a large tree; a dozen apples; a wealthy people; a few dimes. " We paid for the mules *a* hundred dollars *a* head."

W. A winding stairs led us to the observatory. (A flight of, etc.)

When a noun is limited by other words, the indefinite article does not relate merely to the noun, but to the noun with its limitations. " A young man," " A man of fine sense," do not mean no particular *man*, but no particular *young man*, no particular *man of fine sense*.

312. *A* and *an* are both called the *indefinite article;* because they are but a later and an earlier form of the same word, have the same meaning, and differ in use only.

313. A should be used whenever the next word begins with a consonant sound.

U long, *eu*, *w*, *o* in *one*, and *y* articulated with a vowel after it, have each a consonant sound.

Ex. — *A* brother, *a* cup, *a* union, *a* eulogy; such *a* one.

W. An useful exercise. An hundred men. Such an one.

314. An should be used whenever the next word begins with a vowel sound.

That is, *an* should be used before *a*, *e*, *i*, *o*, *u* not equivalent to *yu*, *y* equivalent to *i*, silent *h*, and *h* faintly sounded when the next syllable has the chief accent.

Ex. — *An* arm, *an* ear, *an* inch, *an* oar, *an* hour; *an* hero'ic deed.

W. A interest. A adjective. A officer. A honor. A historian.

315. No Article is used when we refer chiefly to the nature of the object, to the class generally, or to only a part indefinitely; also when the substantive is sufficiently definite itself, or is rendered so by other words.

Ex. — *Meat* is dearer than *bread*. *Gold* is heavier than *silver*. *Peaches* are better than *apples*. *Virtue* and *vice* are *opposites*. *Working* is better than *starving*. He honors the name of *gentleman*. *Man* is endowed with *reason*. There are *fishes* that have *wings*. George; Post-Office; that tree; some tree; *words* that breathe. "*They* were the means by *which*"; not, *the which*.

W. A cypress is a curious species of a tree.
The highest officer of a State is styled a Governor.
Reason was given to a man to control his passions.

The article, and why; whether definite or indefinite, and why; and to what word it relates: —

The roses in the garden. (*The* what?) The rose is a beautiful flower. A fish from the river. A daughter of a duke. The daughter of the duke. A daughter of the duke. An eagle's nest.

Place the proper indefinite article before each of the following words or phrases: —

Razor, house, knife, humming-bird, chicken, ounce, insult, aunt, ox, ball, hundred, African, hexameter; interesting story; honest man; humble cottage.

ADJECTIVES.

316. An **Adjective** is a word used to qualify or limit the meaning of a noun or pronoun.

Ex. — A *mellow* apple; a *beautiful* woman; a *brilliant* star; *five* carriages; *yonder* mountains; *brass* buttons; *hoary-headed* men.

He is *brave* and *prudent.* To slight the poor is *mean.*

317. Words from other parts of speech are frequently used as adjectives.

Ex. — A *gold* ring; a *mahogany* table; *California* gold; *she* politicians; a *would-be* scholar; *parsing* exercises; the *far-off* future; the *above* remarks; a *farewell* address.

"The lightnings flashed *vermilion.*" — *Dante.* (Were *red.*)

CLASSES OF ADJECTIVES.

318. Adjectives are divided into two chief classes; *descriptive* and *definitive.*

319. A **Descriptive Adjective** describes or qualifies.

Ex. — White, good. "The *green* forest glowed in *golden* light."

320. A **Definitive Adjective** merely specifies or limits.

Ex. — There are *many* wealthy farmers in *this* country.

321. Adjectives may be divided into several smaller classes; namely, *common*, *proper*, *particip'ial*, *compound*, *numeral*, and *pronom'inal.*

This classification is not strictly logical, but it is convenient and instructive.

322. A **common adjective** is any ordinary adjective that expresses quality or circumstance; as, *good*, *upper*, *daily.*

323. A **proper adjective** is an adjective derived from a proper noun; as, *American*, *English*, *Newtonian.*

324. A **participial adjective** is a participle used as a descriptive adjective. "*Twinkling* stars." — See p. 221.

325. A **compound adjective** is a compound word used as an adjective. "*Thick-warbled* songs."

326. A **numeral adjective** is a definitive adjective that expresses number.

327. NUMERAL ADJECTIVES are divided into four classes; *cardinal*, *ordinal*, *multiplicative*, and *indefinite*.

1. A *cardinal numeral* tells how many; as, *one*, *two*.
2. An *ordinal numeral* tells which one; as, *first*, *second*.
3. A *multiplicative numeral* tells how many fold; as, *single*, *double*.
4. An *indefinite numeral* expresses number indefinitely; as, *few*, *many*.

328. **Pronominal adjectives** are definitive adjectives that are sometimes used as pronouns.

Not all the words usually called pronominal adjectives, can be used as pronouns.

329. PRONOMINAL ADJECTIVES are divided into three classes; *distrib'utive*, *demon'strative*, and *indef'inite*.

1. The *distributive* relate to objects taken *separately*.

Ex. — Each, every, either, neither, many a. — See p. 80.

2. The *demonstrative* point out objects *definitely*.

Ex. — This, these, that, those, yon, yonder, same, former, latter.

3. The *indefinite* relate to objects *indefinitely*.

Ex. — Any, other, another, one, both, all, some, such, several.

DEGREES OF COMPARISON.

330. **Comparison** is that property of adjectives and adverbs which expresses quality in different degrees.

Ex. — Lime is *white*; milk is *whiter*; snow is the *whitest*.
"Mules are *more hardy* and *less expensive* than horses."

331. There are three degrees of comparison; the *positive*, the *comparative*, and the *superlative*.

332. **Positive.** An adjective is in the *positive degree*, when it expresses simply the quality; as, *hard*, *good*.

333. **Comparative.** An adjective is in the *comparative degree*, when it expresses the quality in a higher or a lower degree; as, *harder*, *less hard*.

334. Superlative. An adjective is in the *superlative degree*, when it expresses the quality in the highest or the lowest degree; as, *hardest*, *least hard*.

The positive degree sometimes implies comparison from its syntax, but without referring to a higher or a lower degree of the same quality; as, "She is as *good* as he, and as *modest* as she is beautiful."

335. The **Comparative Degree** may imply, —

1. Two different objects with the same quality.

Ex. — Honey is *sweeter* than molasses.

W. This is the best of any other.
The youngest of the two sons is yet going to school.

2. Two different conditions of the same object.

Ex. — A nation is *happier* in peace than in war.

3. Two different qualities in the same object.

Ex. — A nation may be *more prosperous* than *virtuous*.

Sometimes, though seldom with elegance, different qualities of different objects can be compared; as, "My *horse* is *whiter* than *yours* is *black*."

336. The **Superlative Degree** usually implies three or more objects or conditions; and it may refer simply to the rest considered, or to all others.

Ex. — "The *least* of three evils."
"The *best* peaches are already taken from the tree."
"The *loveliest* flowers were there." — *Carlyle*.
"I am *happiest* at home." "The river is *highest* in June."

The degree of comparison is sometimes estimated from so low a positive that it falls even below a full positive; as, "Your claim is *better* than his, though neither is *good*"; "Your *largest* horse is not *large*." And comparatives and superlatives are sometimes estimated from other comparatives or superlatives; as, "My kite rose *higher*, and *higher*, and *higher*, until it was *highest*, and far *higher* than the *highest* of all the other kites."

"And in the *lowest* depth a *lower* deep,
Still threatening to devour me, opens wide." — *Milton*.

337. An adjective can not be compared with propriety, when it denotes a quality or property that can not exist in different degrees.

Ex. — Equal, level, perpendicular, square, naked, round, straight, one, two, second, deaf, dead, full, empty, perfect, right, honest, sincere, hollow, four-footed.

338. Good writers sometimes compare such adjectives when they do not take them in their full sense.

Ex. — "Our sight is the *most perfect* of our senses." — *Addison.* This means that it approaches nearer, than the rest, to perfection. "And love is still an *emptier* name." — *Goldsmith.* Most qualifying adjectives can be thus used either in a relative or in an absolute sense.

339. The positive is sometimes diminished by annexing *ish*, or by using such words as *rather*, *somewhat*, *slightly*, etc.

Ex. — Black, *blackish; somewhat* disagreeable; *rather* young.

340. A high degree of the quality, without implying direct comparison, is expressed by *very*, *exceedingly*, *almost*, etc.

Ex. — *Very* respectfully; *a most valiant* soldier.

How Adjectives are Compared.

341. To express degrees below the positive, we use *less* and *least*.

Positive, *good;* comparative, *less good;* superlative, *least good.*
Important, *less important, least important.*

342. To express degrees above the positive, we annex to it *er* and *est*, or place before it *more* and *most*.

Ex. — Positive, *rich;* comparative, *richer;* superlative, *richest.*
Deep, *deeper, deepest;* cheerful, *more cheerful, most cheerful.*

Which of these methods should be used, depends chiefly on the sound of the word, or on the number of its syllables.

343. Adjectives of one syllable are compared by annexing *er* for the comparative, and *est* for the superlative.

Large, larg*er*, larg*est;* sad, sad*der*, sad*dest;* dry, dri*er*, dri*est.*

While studying this section, the pupil should review the Rules for Spelling, pp. 50, 51.

344. Adjectives of two syllables, ending with *le* or *y*, or accented on the second syllable, are also compared by annexing *er* and *est.*

Able, *abler*, *ablest;* lovely, *lovelier*, *loveliest;* polite, *politer*, *politest.*

A few other adjectives of two syllables, especially those which end in a vowel or a liquid sound, are sometimes compared by *er* and *est;* as, narrow, *narrower*, *narrowest;* handsome, *handsomer*, *handsomest.* "The metaphor is the *commonest* figure." — *Blair.* "Philosophers are but a *soberer* sort of madmen." — *Irving.*

345. Other adjectives of two syllables, and all adjectives of more than two syllables, are compared by placing *more* and *most* before the positive.

Loyal, *more loyal*, *most loyal;* evident, *more evident*, *most evident.*

W. It was the beautifullest and curiousest thing I ever saw.

346. Some words are expressed in the superlative degree by *annexing* MOST to them.

Ex. — Fore*most*, ut*most* (*out*most), in*most*, inner*most*, hind*most.*

347. *More* and *most* can sometimes be used in comparing any word that admits of comparison.

Ex. — "A foot *more light*, a step *more true*,
Ne'er from the heath-flower dashed the dew." — *Scott.*

When several adjectives come together, of which some are properly compared by *er* and *est*, and others by *more* and *most*, the smaller are generally placed first, and all are compared as one, by *more* and *most;* as, "The *more nice* and *elegant* parts." — *Johnson.* "Homer's imagination was by far the *most rich* and *copious.*" — *Pope.*

348. *More, most, less*, and *least*, when used to compare other words, are usually parsed separately, and as adverbs.

It does not, however, seem to us improper, to parse the whole phrase as one word.

349. Those adjectives which can not be compared by means of a general rule, are said to be *irregular.*

Positive.	*Comparative.*	*Superlative.*
Good,	better,	best.
Bad, Ill, Evil,	worse,	worst
Much, Many,	more,	most.
Little,	less,	least.
Fore,	former,	foremost, first.
Hind,	hinder,	hindmost.
Far,	farther,	farthest.
(Forth,)	further,	furthest.

Positive.	*Comparative.*	*Superlative.*
(Up,)	upper,	uppermost.
(In,)	inner,	inmost, innermost.
(Out,)	outer, (utter,)	outmost, utmost, uttermost.
Near,	nearer,	nearest, next.
Late	later, latter,	latest, last.
Old,	older, elder,	oldest, eldest.

Elder and *eldest* are applied to persons only; *older* and *oldest*, to persons or things. *Later* and *latest* refer to time; *latter* and *last*, generally to order in place.

Lesser is sometimes used for *less*; as, "Lesser Asia"; better, "Asia Minor."

350. Some irregular adjectives have no positive.

Ex. — Nether. nethermost; under, undermost; hither, hithermost.

351. Some irregular adjectives have no comparative.

Top, topmost; head, headmost; southern, southernmost.

352. Some irregular adjectives have neither positive nor superlative.

Ex. — Minor, major, junior, senior, interior, exterior, anterior, posterior, superior, inferior, prior, ulterior. — See p. 214.

353. Most compound adjectives are compared by varying only the descriptive word, and in the usual way.

Ex. — Long-headed, *longer*-headed, *longest*-headed.
Good-natured, *better*-natured, *best*-natured.

Adjectives that have Number.

354. Some adjectives have number.

Ex. — This, these; that, those; few; many.

355. *One*, *each*, *every*, *either*, *neither*, *many a*, *this*, *that*, *another*, *much*, *all* (the whole), and *whole* (all the), are *singular*.

Ex. — "*Every creature* loves *its* like."

"*Neither combatant* recovered from *his* wounds."

"*Every four years* make an Olympiad." — *Lempriere.*

Sometimes, as in this last example, the adjective relates to an aggregate of objects.

356. The numerals above *one*, and the words *these*, *those*, *all* (number), *few*, *several*, *many*, *divers*, and *sundry*, are *plural*.

357. Adjectives that imply number, must agree in this respect with the substantives to which they belong.

Ex. — *Four feet;* not, *four foot.* "*That kind* of trees"; or, "Trees of *that kind*"; not, "*Those kind* of trees."

W. I never liked those sort of bonnets. Three cord of wood.

---

358. The substantive to which the adjective belongs, is sometimes understood.

Ex. — "She is using the *new book* in stead of the *old*" [*book*].

359. An adjective sometimes becomes a noun, —

1. To denote the quality abstractly.

Ex. — "Burke wrote on the *beautiful*."

2. To denote some object distinguished by the quality.

Ex. — "A home on the rolling *deep*."

3. To denote a class of persons distinguished by the quality.

Ex. — "Providence rewards the *good*, and punishes the *bad*."

360. Sometimes it is necessary to supply a noun.

Ex. — "The truly good" [*persons*]. The adverb *truly* can modify *good* as an adjective, but not as a noun. "Nearly all [*the soldiers*] were captured." "The tender and helpless" [*children*].

Pronominal and other Definitive Adjectives.

All; number or quantity. "*All* men." "*All* the land." [salt?"
Any; indefinite, opposed to *none*. "*Any* one may go." "Have you *any*
Both; *the two*. "*Both horses* are lame."
Divers; *several* or *many* and *different*. "*Divers philosophers* think so."
Each; two or more considered separately. "*Each* glove." "*Each* pupil."
Either; one or the other of two. "Take *either* road."
Else; *besides*. "Any one *else*." "Who *else*?"
Every; all of many considered separately. "*Every hour* of the day."
Few; a comparatively small number. "*Few* shall part where many meet."
Former; preceding in place or time. "The *former rule*." "A *former*
Latter; following in place or time. "The *latter position*." [*notice*."
Little; not *much*. "*Little* money." (*Little*, meaning small, is a descriptive
Many; a comparatively large number. — See *Few*. [adjective.)
Many a; many considered separately; to *many* as *every* to *all*. "*Many a*
Much; a comparatively large quantity. "*Much* money." [flower."
Neither; *not the one nor the other*. "*Neither* of my gloves."
No; *not any, not a*. "*No* ice." "He is *no friend* of mine."
None; *no one, no ones*. "*None* is needed." "*None* are needed."
One; a person or thing indefinitely considered, opposed to *other*. "*One* man or another."
Other, another; something different or distinct. "Some *other* person."
Own; possession with emphasis or distinction. "My *own* book."
Same; identity, similarity. "The *same* boat." "Built of the *same* stones."
Several; more than *two* and fewer than *many*. "*Several* boys."
Some; indefinite, and opposed to *all* or a *particular one*. "*Some* of the robbers." "*Some* one said so."
Such; the same as something else mentioned or described. "*Such a man* is he." "*Such writers* as Swift." This adjective is descriptive as well as definitive; and it is often a sort of *pro-adjective*.
Sundry; emphatically more than one or two. "*Sundry* foes assailed me."
That, those; distant or absent in time or place, the more remote of two, the first-mentioned, something indefinitely selected but definitely described.
This, these; near or present in time or place, the nearer of two, the last-mentioned. — See p. 80.

"*That affair* about which we talked yesterday." "*This affair* about which you are now talking." "*This chair* is better than *that*." "*Those pupils* who were absent, will please to give their names."

Very; equivalent to a compound personal pronoun. "Our *very* existence."
What, which; interrogative or responsive "*What* man." "*Which* man."
Yon or **yonder** points out something in sight. "*Yonder* hill."

Exercises.

The adjective, and why; whether descriptive or definitive, and why; and to what it belongs:—

The blue sky. The sky is blue. An aspiring man. The American flag. The star-powdered galaxy. A modest and beautiful woman, with eyes bright, blue, and affectionate. This is a broad, deep, clear, and winding river. The night grew darker and darker. The apples boiled soft. He is asleep. That field has been in cultivation four years. The first car is not full, having but one man in it.

Compare, of the following adjectives, those which can be compared:—

Wise, studious, near, good, evil, melodious, high, tuneful, saucy, eloquent, expressive, lovely, nimble, late, many, much, few, little, old, glowing, accomplished, expert, half-finished, full, counterfeit, graceful, worthless, bottomless, fundamental, ornamental, vernal, green, sluggish, sunburnt, free, first.

Mention and spell the three degrees of comparison:—

Strong, weak, light, gay, rough, nice, coarse, fierce, white, ripe, thin, slim, dim, fit, hot, fat, glad, big, droll, dry, sprightly, manly, gentle, noble, idle, discreet, remote, sublime, profound.

Compare by using LESS *and* LEAST*:—*

Broad, convenient, confident, oily, troublesome, thick, joyful, sorrowful, exorbitant, exact, indulgent, handsome.

Join suitable adjectives to each of the following nouns:—

Moon, field, fountain, trees, garden, horse, willow, man, woman, pen, ink, day, wood, boys, thoughts, feelings, conduct.

QUESTIONS FOR REVIEW.

1. What is a **Part of Speech**? . ¶ 157
2. How many and what are the parts of speech? 158
3. What is a **Noun**? Give examples. 159
4. Into what classes are nouns divided? 163
5. What is a *proper noun*? . . . 164
6. When does a proper noun become a common noun? . . . 165
7. What is a *common noun*? . . 166
8. When does a common noun become a proper noun? . . . 167
9. What smaller classes do the common nouns include?
10. What is a *collective noun*? . . 168
11. What is an *abstract noun*? . 169
12. What is a *verbal* or *participial noun*? 170
13. What is a **Pronoun**? . . 171
14. What is the *antecedent* of a pronoun? 173
15. Into what classes are pronouns divided? 177
16. What is a *personal pronoun*? . 178

17. Mention the chief personal pronouns? 179
18. What is said of *you*, *yours*, etc.? 180
19. What is said of *thou*, *thy*, *thine*, etc.? 181
20. Of *ours*, *yours*, etc.? 182
21. Of *it*? 184, 185
22. What is a *compound personal pronoun*? 186
23. How are these pronouns used? 187
24. What is a *relative pronoun*? 188
25. Mention the relative pronouns? 189
26. To what is the relative *who* applied? 190
27. To what is the relative *which* applied? 191
28. How is the relative *what* used? 192
29. When is the relative *that* preferred to *who* or *which*? 193
30. When is *as* a relative pronoun? 196
31. What is a *compound relative pronoun*? 197
32. What is an *interrogative pronoun*? 198
33. Mention the interrogative pronouns. 199
34. What is said of the interrogative *who*? 200
35. What is said of the interrogative *which*? 201
36. What is said of the interrogative *what*? 202
37. What is a *responsive* or an *indirect interrogative pronoun*? 203
38. What is an *adjective pronoun*? 204
39. Into what classes are the adjective pronouns divided? 205
40. What is said of the *distributive pronouns*? 206
41. Of the *demonstrative pronouns*? 207
42. Of the *indefinite pronouns*? 208
43. Of the *reciprocal pronouns*? 209
44. How should *either*, *neither*, *each other*, and *one another* be used? 210
45. How should *this* and *that* be used? 211
46. What properties have nouns and pronouns? 212

47. What is **Gender**? 214
48. How many genders are there, and what are they called? 215
49. When is a noun or pronoun of the *masculine gender*? 216
50. Of the *feminine gender*? 217
51. Of the *common gender*? 218
52. Of the *neuter gender*? 219
53. What is said of personified objects? 223
54. When is the masculine gender preferred? 224
55. When is the feminine gender preferred? 225
56. What is said of the gender of collective nouns? 226
57. How many methods are there of distinguishing the two sexes? 227
58. What is the first method? Give examples.
59. What is the second method? Give examples.
60. What is the third method? Give examples.

61. What is **Person**? 228
62. How many persons in grammar, and what are they called? 229
63. When is a noun or pronoun of the *first person*? 230
64. Of the *second person*? 231
65. Of the *third person*? 232

66. What is **Number**? 234
67. How many numbers in grammar, and what are they called? 235
68. When is a noun or pronoun of the *singular number*? 236
69. When is a noun or pronoun of the *plural number*? 237
70. When is a proper noun made plural? 238
71. What nouns are generally used in the singular number only? 239
72. What exception is mentioned? 240
73. Mention some nouns that are generally used only in the plural number. 241
74. Mention some nouns that have the same form for either number. 243
75. What is said, in regard to number, of *pair*, *dozen*, *fish*, *fowl*, *trout*, *salmon*, and similar words? 244, etc.
76. When is a collective noun singular? 245
77. When is a collective noun plural? 246, '7
78. How are most nouns made plural? 248
79. To what nouns is *es* added? 249
80. How are proper nouns made plural? Give examples. 251
81. What is the plural of *foot*, a part of the body; and of *Foot*, a man's name?
82. Give the plural of *beef*, *half*, *loaf*, *wife*, and *wolf*; and tell us what is said of such words. 252
83. Give the plural of *man*, *tooth*, and *mouse*; and tell us what is said of such words 253
84. Give the plurals of *brother*, *die*, *genius*, and *penny*; and tell us what is said of such words 254
85. How are most compound words made plural? 255
86. What exceptions? 257, 258
87. How is a name that begins with the title *Mr.*, *Miss*, or *Dr.* made plural? 259
88. What is said of the title *Mrs.*? 260
89. What is said of the plural of foreign words? 261
90. What is said of the ending *a*? Give examples.
91. Of the ending *us*? Give examples.
92. Of the ending *um* or *on*? Examples.
93. Of the ending *is*? Examples.
94. Of the ending *x* or *ex*? Examples.
95. How are letters and figures made plural? 262
96. What is said of the editorial *we*? 263
97. What is said of *you*, *your*, etc., in regard to number? 264
98. What is said of relative and other pronouns, in regard to number? 267

99. What is Case?
100. How many cases are there, and what are they called? . . . 269
101. When is a noun or pronoun in the nominative case? . . 270. 271
102. In what different ways is a noun or pronoun used independently? 272
103. When is a noun or pronoun used absolutely? 273

104. When is a noun or pronoun in the *possessive case?* . . . 274
105. How is the possessive case regularly formed? 275
106. When is the apostrophe only added, or when is the possessive *s* omitted? 276, 277
107. In what other ways can possession be expressed? 278
108. How is a compound or complex term expressed in the possessive case? 280
109. What is said of a pair or series of terms implying common possession? 281
110. What is said of a pair or series of terms not implying common possession? 282

111. When is a noun or pronoun in the *objective case?* . . . 283

112. When is a noun or pronoun in the *same case* as another? . . 286
113. What may the subordinate term be? 287
114. What two kinds of construction under same case? . . . 288
115. When is the explanatory term *predicated* of the other? 289
116. What is said of the connecting verb? 290
117. When are the two terms in *apposition?* 291
118. Must the terms agree in anything else than case? . . . 295
119. In what different ways are words in apposition sometimes applied to the same objects? . . 296

120. In what two cases are compound personal pronouns used? . . 298
121. What is said of *who*, *what*, *which*, and *that*, in regard to case and declension? 300
122. When may *what* have two cases? . 301
123. When does *what* have but one case? 303
124. How are *one*, *other*, and *another* declined? 304
125. What is it, to *decline* a noun or pronoun? 305
126. Decline *merchant*, *child*, *I*, *thou*, *you*, *he*, *she*, *one*, *it*, *who*, and *himself*.

127. What is an Article? . . 306
128. How are the articles classified?
129. How is *the* used? . . . 307
130. How is *a* or *an* used? . . . 310
131. Does *a* or *an* mean one, or more than one? 311
132. Why are *a* and *an* both considered the same word? 312
133. When should *a* be used? . . 313
134. When should *an* be used? . . 314
135. When should no article be used? . 315

136. What is an Adjective? . . 316
137. Into what two chief classes are adjectives divided? . . . 318
138. What is a *descriptive adjective?* . 319
139. What is a *definitive adjective?* 320
140. Into what smaller classes are adjectives divided? 321
141. What is a *common adjective?* . 322
142. What is a *proper adjective?* . . 323
143. What is a *participial adjective?* 324
144. What is a *compound adjective?* . 325
145. What is a *numeral adjective?* . 326
146. Into what classes are numerals divided? 327
147. What are *pronominal adjectives?* 328
148. Into what classes are they divided? 329
149. What is *comparison* in grammar? 330
150. How many degrees of comparison, and what are they called? . 331
151. When is an adjective in the *positive degree?* 332
152. When, in the comparative degree? 333
153. When, in the superlative degree? 334
154. What is said of the comparative degree? 335
155. Of the superlative degree? . . 336
156. When can an adjective not be compared? What exception? 337, 338
157. To express degrees below the positive, how are adjectives compared? 341
158. To express degrees above the positive, how are adjectives compared? 342
159. When are the endings *er* and *est* preferred? 343, 344
160. When are *more* and *most* preferred? 345
161. Compare *good*, *bad*, *much*, *many*, *little*, *kind*, *far*, *in*, *near*, *late*, *old;* and tell us what is said of such words. . . . 346, 349
162. Do adjectives have number? . . 354
163. Mention some adjectives that are singular, and some that are plural? 355, 356
164. What is said of adjectives in regard to their agreement with substantives in number? . . . 357
165. Is the substantive to which the adjective relates, always expressed? 358
166. When does an adjective become a noun? 359
167. Define *each*, *every*, *either*, *neither*, *this*, and *that*.

VERBS.

361. A **Verb** is a word used to express the act or state of a subject.

Ex. — The horse *ran*. The rose *blooms*. He *was elected*.

362. Frequently, a verb consists of two or more words.

Ex. — They *might have been captured*. He *was sent for*.

363. Sometimes words from other parts of speech are made verbs.

Ex. — "We have tried *to better* our condition." — *Shakespeare*. "This *out-Herods* Herod!" — *Id.* "I'll *fortune-tell* you!" — *Id.*

For exercises, see Part I.; p. 22, for instance.

Classification.

Verbs.

- IN FORM.
  - Regular,
  - Irregular.
- IN SYNTAX.
  - As related to Subjects.
    - Finite or Predicate Verbs.
    - *Not Finite.* Participles, Infinitives.
  - As related to Objects.
    - Transitive,
    - Intransitive.
  - As related to one another.
    - Principal,
    - Auxiliary.
- **Properties.**
  - VOICE. Active, Passive.
  - MOOD. Indicative, Subjunctive, Potential, Imperative.
  - TENSE. Present, Present-perfect; Past, Past-perfect; Future, Future-perfect.
  - PERSON. First, Second, Third.
  - NUMBER. Singular, Plural.

CLASSES OF VERBS.

Regular and Irregular.

364. VERBS are divided, according to their form, into *regular* and *irregular*.

365. A **Regular Verb** is a verb that takes the ending *ed*, to form its past tense and its perfect participle.

Ex. — Present, *plant;* past, *planted;* perfect participle, *planted.*
Carry, carri *ed*, carri *ed;* rebel′, rebel *led*, rebel *led.*

While studying this section, review the Rules for Spelling, pp. 50 and 51.

366. An **Irregular Verb** is a verb that does not take the ending *ed*, to form its past tense and its perfect participle.

Ex. — Sweep, *swept*, *swept;* cling, *clung*, *clung;* cut, *cut*, *cut.*

367. The **Principal Parts** of a verb are the *present tense*, the *past tense*, the *present participle*, and the *perfect participle.*

These are called the PRINCIPAL PARTS, because by means of them and the auxiliary verbs all the other parts of the verb can be formed.

368. The **Present Tense** is the simplest form of the verb; as, *go.*

369. The **Past Tense** is the simplest form that expresses a past fact; as, *went.*

370. The **Present Participle** is that form which ends always with *ing;* as, *go-ing.* It is therefore so well known that it hardly needs mentioning.

371. The **Perfect Participle** is that form which makes sense with the word *having* before it; as, *gone*, (having *gone*).

In general, only the simple participles are used in compound forms. — See p. 158.

The present tense and the past tense which we have just mentioned, are the present indicative or infinitive and the past indicative. For the sake of brevity, they are generally called simply the *present* and the *past;* and the *past* is sometimes called the *prĕt'erit.*

LIST OF IRREGULAR VERBS.

The following are the irregular verbs, with their principal parts. Having learned them, the pupil will also know the principal parts of the remaining verbs, for these are regular. He must not infer, however, from the word *irregular*, that the verbs so called are a mere straggling offshoot from the language; for they are really the very core or pith of it.

The Two Past Forms Different.*

Present.	*Past, or Pret.*	*Perf. Participle.*
Arise,	arose,	arisen.†
Awake,	awoke, R.,	awaked, awoke.*
Be *or* am,	was,	been.
Bear (*bring forth*),	bore, bare,	born.
Bear (*carry*),	bore,	borne.
Beat,	beat,	beaten, beat.
Become,	became,	become.
Befall,	befell,	befallen.
Beget,	begot, begat,*	begotten, begot.
Begin,	began,	begun.
Bid,	bid, bade,	bid, bidden.
Bite,	bit,	bitten, bit.
Blow,	blew,	blown.
Break,	broke, brake,*	broken, broke.*
Chide,	chid,	chidden, chid.
Choose,	chose,	chosen.
Cleave (*adhere*),	cleaved, clave,*	cleaved.
Cleave (*split*),	cleft, clove, clave,*	cleft, cloven, cleaved.
Come,	came,	come.
Crow,	crowed, crew,	crowed.

* In general, only those irregular verbs are liable to be used improperly, of which the *past tense* and the *perfect participle* are *different* in form. These verbs have therefore been given first, and separate from the rest, that they may be learned perfectly. R. denotes that the regular form may also be used in stead of the other. * denotes that the form under it is seldom used, being either ancient, poetic, or of late introduction. The form supposed to be of the best present usage, is placed first. The second form of some verbs is preferable when applied in a certain way; as, "*freighted* with spices and silks," "*fraught* with mischief"; "thunder*struck*," "sorrow-*stricken*."—Commit to memory the unmarked forms only.

† The pupil may also mention the present participle just before he mentions the perfect

Present.	*Past, or Pret.*	*Perf. Participle.*
Dare (*venture*),	durst, dared,	dared.
(Dare, *to challenge;* regular.)		
Do (prin. verb.),	did,	done.
Draw,	drew,	drawn.
Drink,	drank,	drunk, drank.*
Drive,	drove,	driver
Eat,	ate, ĕat,	eaten, ĕat.*
Fall,	fell,	fallen.
Fly,	flew,	flown.
Forbear,	forbore,	forborne.
Forget,	forgot,	forgotten, forgot.
Forsake,	forsook,	forsaken.
Freeze,	froze,	frozen.
Freight,	freighted,	freighted, fraught.
Get,	got,	got, gotten.
Give,	gave,	given.
Go,	went,	gone.
Grave,	graved,	graven, R.
Grow,	grew,	grown.
Heave,	heaved, hove,	heaved, hoven.*
Hew,	hewed,	hewn, R.
Hide,	hid,	hidden, hid.
Hold,	held,	held, holden.*
Know,	knew,	known.

Present.	*Past, or Pret.*	*Perf. Participle.*
Lade (*load*),	laded,	laden, R.
Lie (*repose*),	lay,	lain.
(Lie, *to speak falsely;* regular.)		
Mow,	mowed,	mown, R.
Prove,	proved,	proved, proven.*
Rend,	rent,	rent, R.*
Ride,	rode,	rode, ridden.
Ring,	rang, rung,	rung.
Rise,	rose,	risen.
Rive,	rived,	riven, R.*
Run,	ran,	run.
Saw,	sawed,	sawn, R.
See,	saw,	seen.
Seethe,	seethed, sod,*	seethed, sodden.
Shake,	shook,	shaken.
Shape,	shaped,	shaped, shapen.*
Shave,	shaved,	shaved, shaven.
Shear,	sheared, shore,*	shorn, R.
Show,	showed,	shown, R.
Shrink,	shrunk, shrank,	shrunk, shrunken.*
Slay,	slew,	slain.
Slide,	slid, R.,	slidden, slid, R.
Smite,	smote,	smitten, smit.*

Present.	*Past, or Pret.*	*Perf. Participle.*	*Present.*	*Past, or Pret.*	*Perf. Participle.*
Sing,	sung, sang,	sung.	Strive,	strove, R.,*	striven, R.*
			Strow,	strowed,	strown, R.
Sink,	sunk, sank,	sunk.	Swear,	swore, sware,*	sworn.
Sow (*to scatter seed*),	sowed,	sown, R.	Swell,	swelled,	swollen, R.
Speak,	spoke, spake,*	spoken.	Swim,	swam, swum,	swum.
			Take,	took,	taken.
Spin,	spun, span,*	spun.	Tear,	tore,	torn.
Spit,	spit, spat,*	spit, spitten.*	Thrive,	thrived, throve,	thrived, thriven.
(Spit, *to pierce with a spit;* regular.)			Throw,	threw,	thrown.
Spring,	sprung, sprang,	sprung.	Tread,	trod,	trodden, trod.
Steal,	stole,	stolen.	Wax (*grow*),	waxed,	waxed, waxen.*
Stride,	strode, strid,	stridden, strid.	Wear,	wore,	worn.
			Weave,	wove, R.,*	woven, R.*
Strike,	struck,	struck, stricken.	Write,	wrote,	written.

The Two Past or the Three Forms Alike.

Present.	*Past, or Pret.*	*Perf. Participle.*	*Present.*	*Past, or Pret.*	*Perf. Participle.*
Abide,	abode,	abode.	Bless,	blessed, blest,	blessed, blest.
Behold,	beheld,	beheld.			
Belay,	belaid, R.,	belaid, R.	Breed,	bred,	bred.
Bend,	bent, R.,	bent, R.	Bring,	brought,	brought.
Bereave,	bereft, R.,	bereft, R.	Build,	built, R.,*	built, R.*
Beseech,	besought,	besought	Burn,	burned, burnt,	burned, burnt.
Bet,	bet, R.,	bet, R.			
Betide,	betided, betid,*	betided, betid.*	Burst,	burst,	burst.
			Buy,	bought	bought.
Bind,	bound,	bound.	Cast,	cast,	cast.
Bleed,	bled,	bled.	Catch,	caught, R.,*	caught, R.*
Blend,	blended, blent,*	blended, blent.*	Cling,	clung,	clung.

Present.	*Past, or Pret.*	*Perf. Participle.*
Clothe,	clothed, clad,	clothed, clad.
Cost,	cost,	cost.
Creep,	crept,	crept.
Cut,	cut,	cut.
Deal,	dĕalt,	dĕalt.
Dig,	dug, R.,	dug, R.
Dwell,	dwelt, R.,	dwelt, R.
Dream,	dreamed, drĕamt,	dreamed, drĕamt.
Dress,	dressed, drest,*	dressed, drest.*
Feed,	fed,	fed.
Feel,	felt,	felt.
Fight,	fought,	fought.
Find,	found,	found.
Flee,	fled,	fled.
Fling,	flung,	flung.
Gild,	gilded, gilt,	gilded, gilt.
Gird,	girt, R.,	girt, R.
Grind,	ground,	ground.
Hang,	hung, R.,	hung, R.[a]
Have (prin. verb.),	had,	had.
Hear,	heard,	heard.
Hit	hit,	hit.
Hurt,	hurt,	hurt.
Keep,	kept,	kept.
Kneel,	knelt, R.,	knelt, R.
Knit,	knit, R.,	knit, R.
Lay,	laid,	laid.
Lead,	led,	led.
Lean,	leaned, lĕant,	leaned, lĕant.
Leap,	leaped, lĕapt,*	leaped, lĕapt.*
Learn,	learned, learnt,	learned, learnt.
Leave,	left,	left.
Lend,	lent,	lent.
Let,	let,	let.
Light,	lighted, lit,	lighted, lit.
Lose,	lost,	lost.
Make,	made,	made.
Mean,	mĕant,	mĕant.
Meet,	met,	met.
Pass,	passed, past,*	passed, past.[b]
Pay,	paid,	paid.
Pen (*fence in*),	penned, pent,	penned, pent.
(Pen, *to write;* regular.)		
Plead,	pleaded, plĕad,* pled,*	pleaded, plĕad,* pled.*
Put,	put,	put.
Quit,	quit, R.,	quit, R.
Rap,	rapped, rapt,	rapped, rapt.[c]
Read,	rĕad,	rĕad.
Reave,*	reft,	reft.
Rid,	rid,	rid.
Say,	said,	said.
Seek,	sought,	sought.

(*a.*) Hang, hanged, hanged ; *to suspend by the neck with intent to kill ;* but the distinction is not always observed. (*b*) *Past* is used as an adjective or as a noun. (*c*) Rap, rapt, rapt ; *to seize with rapture.*

Present.	*Past, or Pret.*	*Perf. Participle.*
Sell,	sold,	sold.
Send,	sent,	sent.
Set,	set,	set.
Shed,	shed,	shed.
Shine,	shone, R.,*	shone, R.*
Shoe,	shod,	shod.
Shoot,	shot,	shot.
Shred,	shred,	shred.
Shut,	shut,	shut.
Sit,	sat,	sat.
Sleep,	slept,	slept.
Sling,	slung,	slung.
Slink,	slunk,	slunk.
Slit,	slit, R.,*	slit, R.
Smell,	smelt, R.,	smelt, R.
Speed,	sped, R.,*	sped, R.*
Spell,	spelled, spelt,	spelled, spelt.
Spend,	spent,	spent.
Spill,	spilt, R.,	spilt, R.
Split,	split, R.,*	split, R.
Spoil,	spoiled, spoilt,*	spoiled, spoilt.*
Spread,	spread,	spread.
Staÿ,	staid, R.,	staid, R.[d]
String,	strung,	strung, R.[e]
Stave,	stove, R.,	stove, R.
Stand,	stood,	stood.
Stick,	stuck,	stuck.
Sting,	stung,	stung.
Sweat,	swĕat, R., swet,	swĕat, R. swet.
Sweep,	swept,	swept.

Present.	*Past, or Pret.*	*Perf. Participle.*
Swing,	swung,	swung.
Teach,	taught,	taught.
Tell,	told,	told.
Think,	thought,	thought.
Thrust,	thrust,	thrust.
Wake,	waked, woke,*	waked, woke.*
Wed,	wedded, wed,*	wedded, wed.*
Weep,	wept,	wept.
Wet,	wet, R.,*	wet, R.*
Win,	won,	won.
Wind,	wound,	wound.
Work,	worked, wrought,	worked, wrought.
Wring,	wrung,	wrung.
Beware,	(*wanting*,)	(*wanting*.)
Can,	could,	"
Do (auxil'y),	did,	"
Have, "	had,	"
May,	might,	"
Must,	must,	"
Ought,	ought,	"
(*wanting*,)	quoth,	"
Shall,	should,	"
Will, "	would,	"

(Will, *wish, bequeath*; regular.)

Wit, Wot,* Wis,* Weet,*	wot,* wist,* wote.*

Most of the verbs that have no participles, are auxiliary verbs.

(*d*) Stay, stayed, stayed; *to cause to stop*. (*e*.) *Stringed* instruments.

372. A derivative verb generally forms its principal parts in the same way as the primitive verb.

Ex.—Mis*take*, mis*took*, mis*taken;* under*go*, under*went*, under*gone.*

373. A **Redundant Verb** is a verb that has more than one form for some of its principal parts.

Ex.—Kneel; *knelt, kneeled; knelt, kneeled.*

374. A **Defective Verb** is one that has not all the parts which belong to a complete verb.

The defective verbs are most of the auxiliaries, and the following:—

Beware; from *be* and *ware* (*wary*). It has no participles.

Methinks, *I think*, **methought,** *I thought;* **meseems,** *to me it seems;* **meseemed,** *to me it seemed*. These words are anomalous and poetical.

Ought is an old preterit of *owe.* It is in the present tense when it is followed by the present infinitive; as, "I *ought* to go": and in the past tense when followed by the perfect infinitive; as, "I *ought* to have gone."

Quoth is sometimes used, in quaint or humorous language, for *said;* as, "'Not I,' *quoth* Sancho."

Wit, in the sense of *know,* is yet used in the phrase *to wit* = *namely.* The other forms are nearly obsolete.

Give the principal parts; and tell whether the verb is regular or irregular:—

Flow, fly, flee, sow, grow, sin, win, spin, skim, swim, heal, steal, fling, bring, spread, dread, fold, hold, uphold, close, lose, loose, blind, find, fine, reel, feel, lend, loan, need, feed, land, stand, heat, eat, free, see, play, slay, may, call, fall, fell, bind, bound, come, welcome, hive, strive, live, give, rise, raise, tell, toll, lie, lay, seat, set, sit.

Finite and Not Finite.

375. Verbs are divided, according to their relation to subjects, into *finite* and *not finite.*

376. A **Finite Verb** is a verb that predicates the act or state of its subject.

Ex.—The plant *grows.* John *has arrived.* I *am* alone.

377. A verb that is not finite, does not predicate the act or state of its subject.

"The plant *growing.*" "John *having arrived.*" "For me *to be* alone."

Observe the difference between these phrases and the preceding sentences, ¶ 376.

378. Verbs that are not finite, may be divided into two classes; *Infinitives* and *Participles*. — See p. 158.

Transitive and Intransitive.

379. VERBS are divided, according to their relation to objects, into *transitive* and *intransitive*.

380. A **Transitive Verb** is a verb that has an object, or requires one to complete the sense.

Ex. — "The lightning *struck* the *oak*." (Struck *what?*)
"I *knew him* well, and every truant *knew*" [*him*]. — *Goldsmith.*

Transitive verbs are used in two forms. — See Voice, p. 13.

381. An **Intransitive Verb** is a verb that does not have or require an object.

Ex. — Birds *fly*. Roses *bloom*. Gamblers *cheat*.

382. An intransitive verb that does not imply action or exertion, is sometimes called a *neuter verb*.

Ex. — The ocean *is* deep. The book *lies* on the table.

383. The same word is sometimes used as a transitive verb, and sometimes as an intransitive.

"The prince *succeeds* the *king*." "In every project he *succeeds*."

384. A verb usually transitive may become intransitive, when the chief design is to set forth the act, and to leave the object unknown or indefinite.

Ex. — "She *reads* well." "He *rides* out every day."

Observe that the design is to show *how* she reads, not *what* she reads.

385. A verb usually intransitive may become transitive, —

1. When it is used in a causative sense.

Ex. — "*To march* armies"; *i. e.*, to cause them to march.

2. When the object is like the verb in meaning.

Ex. — "*To live* a righteous *life*." "*To die* a miserable *death*."

3. In certain poetical expressions.

Ex. — "And eyes *looked* | *love* to eyes that spake again." — *Byron.*
"The lightnings *flashed* a brighter *curve*." — *Thomson.*

4. In certain idiomatic expressions.

Ex. — "I *laughed* | *myself* hoarse." "He *slept* | *himself* weary."

In such expressions the verb has both a causative and a reflexive sense.

386. Sometimes the object is combined with the verb so closely as to make in sense almost a part of it.

Ex. — To *take care* of; to *lay hold* of; to *bethink oneself*.

A similar remark applies sometimes to other words used with verbs.

387. Some verbs, mostly of asking or teaching, are followed by two objects, each of which they can govern.

Ex. — "She taught *me grammar*"; *i. e.*, she taught *me*, and she taught *grammar*. In parsing, however, it is probably better to supply a preposition; as, "She taught grammar *to* me"; or, "She taught me *in* grammar."

388. Some verbs are followed by two objects, of which one is governed by the preposition *to* or *for* understood, and the other by the verb.

Ex. — "She gave *me* a *book*"; *i. e.*, she gave a book *to* me.

The object governed by the verb is called the *direct object;* the object governed by the preposition understood, is called the *indirect object*.

389. Some verbs are followed by two objects that are in apposition.

Ex. — "They made *him captain*." — See ¶ 292.

Principal and Auxiliary.

390. Verbs are divided, in regard to the chief mode of combining them, into *principal* and *auxiliary*.

391. A **Principal Verb** is a verb that expresses by itself the act or state, or the chief part of it.

"He *studies*." "He may have *studied*." *Study* is a principal verb.

392. An **Auxiliary Verb** helps other verbs to express their grammatical properties.

Ex. — "He *was* captured." (Voice.) "He *can* learn." (Mood.)

For an explanation of auxiliary verbs, see p. 148.

PROPERTIES OF VERBS.

393. VERBS have *voice*, *mood*, *tense*, *person*, and *number*.

VOICE.

394. Voice is that property of verbs which shows whether the subject does, or receives, the act.

395. There are two voices; the *active* and the *passive*.

396. A verb is in the *active voice*, when it represents its subject as acting. "He *watches*."

397. A verb is in the *passive voice*, when it represents its subject as acted upon. "He *is watched*."

Most transitive verbs imply action; but a few — as, *resemble*, *own*, and *have* — do not imply action. Such a verb is in the *active voice*, when it relates to an object; and in the *passive*, when it has the object for its subject.

398. Voice is a property that belongs to transitive verbs only.

399. A few intransitive verbs are sometimes used in the *passive form*.

This is a French idiom, and the verbs are not passive.

Ex. — "He *is fallen*." "She *is gone*." "The melancholy days *are come*." Equivalent to *has fallen*, *has gone*, *have come*.

The passive form generally differs from the active by an elegant shade of meaning: in the latter, the mind dwells on the act; in the former, on the state of things after the act.

400. A few intransitive verbs can be made passive, when combined with a preposition or other word.

The whole phrase should be called a *compound passive verb*.

Ex. — "*Had* Monmouth really *been sent for?*" — *Macaulay*.

"Colonel Butler *was* accordingly *written to*." — *Irving*.

So, "My claim *was lost sight of*"; *i. e.*, *disregarded*.

The modifying word is so closely blended in sense with the verb, that it seems to make a part of it.

401. Transitive verbs are sometimes passive, even in the active form.

Ex. — "This field *ploughs* well." "Your poem *reads* smoothly." "Wheat *sells*, *is selling*, is sold for a dollar a bushel." "The fortress *was building*." — IRVING. And probably, "An ax *to grind*."

Most such verbs denote merely the *capacity* to receive the act in the way specified; and when this is the meaning, some grammarians call them simply intransitive verbs.

402. The object of the active verb is made the subject of the passive.

We caught these *partridges*. These *partridges* were caught by us.
W. We were shown some very curious fossil remains.

A verb is generally made passive by combining the corresponding tense or part of the verb *be* with the perfect participle of a transitive verb; as, *was*, *was broken*. "The pitcher *was broken*."

403. Sometimes the object of the preposition is made the subject of the passive verb.

Ex. — "If you wear that coat, people will laugh at you."
"If you wear that coat, you *will be laughed at*."
"He *was smiled on* [*favored*] by fortune."

404. We may use, at pleasure, either the active voice or the passive. The following are the chief advantages of having both forms: —

1. To enrich language in variety of expression.

Ex. — Snow protects plants. Plants are protected by snow.

2. To avoid the confusion which is apt to arise from introducing different subjects into the same sentence.

Ex. — "I went to the river, was ferried over, and saw the procession." Make *was ferried* active by introducing another subject, and you can easily notice the bad effect.

3. In the active voice, to make the doer and the act prominent.

Ex. — *Washington defended* our country.

4. In the passive voice, to make the result and the act prominent, or to avoid mentioning the doer.

Ex.—"The *work was done*, nevertheless." "My watch *was stolen*." I may not know, or may not wish to say, who stole it. "The ship *was stranded*." It might be very tedious to give the causes: to state the result is sufficient.

MOOD.

405. Mood is that property of verbs which shows how the act or state is referred to its subject.

The act or state can be referred to the subject, as something *real*; as something merely *supposed*; as something *real* or *supposed*, and modified by a *relation*; as something *commanded*; or as something merely *assumed*, and *not predicated*.

406. There are four moods; the *indicative*, the *subjunctive*, the *potential*, and the *imperative*.

Most grammarians call the *infinitive* the *infinitive mood*, thus making five moods; and some call the *participle* the *participial mood*, thus making six moods. Infinitives and participles may be considered a mood; but it seems to us that they are sufficiently distinguished by being called *infinitives* and *participles*.

Indicative Mood.

The **Indicative Mood** denotes what is *real*.

407. A verb in the *indicative mood* expresses an actual occurrence or fact.

Ex.—I *went*. It *snows*. "Moses *was* God's first pen."—*Bacon*.

408. The indicative mood can be used interrogatively.

Ex.—"'*Is* he in the army, then?' said my uncle Toby."—*Sterne*.

Here an inquiry is made about the *fact*.

409. A doubt, condition, or inference, assumed as a fact or expressed in indicative time, must also be in the indicative mood.

Ex.—If I *am deceived*, I am ruined.
If I *was deceived*, I did not know it.
This will produce a quarrel, when he *returns*.

W. Though he *be* helpless now, he will not remain so. See p. 160.
Which phrase, if it *mean* any thing, means paper-money.—*Atlantic Monthly*.
If he *have* a rival, it is Mrs. Barbauld.—*Coleridge*.
She doubted whether this *were* not all delusion.—*Irving*.

Subjunctive Mood.

The **Subjunctive Mood** denotes what is *supposed.*

410. A verb in the *subjunctive mood* may express, —

1. A future contingency.

Ex. — "If I *go*, I shall go alone." "Beware lest thou *fail.*"

W. If any member absents himself, he shall pay a dollar.
He will maintain his suit, though it costs him his whole estate.

2. A mere wish or supposition.

"O *had* I the wings of a dove!" But I have not.

"O that I *were* as when my mother pressed me to her bosom, and sung the warlike deeds of the Mohawks!" But I am not.

"*Were* I in your condition, I would remain."

"*Had* I *been* in your condition, I would have remained."

W. O that I was at home. I wish I was at home.
He talked to me as if I was a widow.
Was there not another reason, I would object. — *P. Henry.*

3. A mere conclusion, conception, or consequence.

Ex. — "It *were* useless to resist." (Would be.)
"He *had* need all circumspection." — *Milton.*
That is, he *would have* need of all circumspection.
"If it were done when it is done, then 't *were* well
It *were done* quickly." — *Shakespeare.*
"Had more time been given, my translation *had been* better." — *Dryden.*

Colloquialism: "I *had* much rather *be* myself the slave." — *Cowper.*

To the pure subjunctives of conclusion, good writers now generally prefer the subjunctive potential forms; as, *would be, would have been, should be,* etc.

411. The subjunctive mood, being mental, is generally applied to the suppositions and conclusions in reasoning and wishing.

"*Were* half the wealth bestowed on camps and courts
Given to redeem the human mind from error,
There *were* no need of arsenals and forts." — *Longfellow.*

Since reasoning always implies two parts, a premise and a conclusion, —

A clause with a subjunctive verb either has or implies another clause; and hence the mood is called *subjunctive*, which means *joined dependently to something else.*

412. When the subjunctive mood refers to present or past time, it generally implies a denial of the fact; when to future time, that the fact is uncertain or contingent.

This is obvious: we can not do a past act; we may do a future; and a present supposition, developed into reality, becomes indicative.

413. The subjunctive mood uses *be* in stead of *am*, *are*, and *is; were* in stead of *was;* and generally undergoes no change of form throughout the same tense.

To a verb in the subjunctive mood, *should* or some other auxiliary verb can generally be understood; as, "If thou ever return, thou shouldst be thankful" = If thou *shouldst* ever return, thou shouldst be thankful.

414. *If*, *though*, *lest*, *unless*, *except*, *whether*, *that*, *till*, or a similar word, generally precedes and indicates the subjunctive mood.

Ex. — *If* I *were*. *If* I *had been.*

415. By placing the verb or its auxiliary before the subject, the conditional word can generally be omitted.

Ex. — *Were I*, for *If I were*. *Had I been*, for *If I had been.*

416. The subjunctive mood has three tenses: the present, the past, and the past-perfect; which are generally equivalent in time to a future tense, a present tense, and a past tense.

Present (**Future**, in time): "If he *be* at home, I shall speak to him."
Past (**Present**, in time): "If he *were* at home, I would speak to him."
Past-perfect (**Past**, in time): "*Had* he *been* at home, I would have spoken to him."

These tenses are sufficient, yet needed, for all the purposes of this mood. Most grammarians reject the past-perfect tense: but this tense is *subjunctive*, not indicative, in time; *subjunctive* in origin, and *subjunctive* in syntax.

The past subjunctive may sometimes be called the *indefinite* subjunctive; and the past-perfect, the *pluperfect*.

The outer or real world impresses itself so vividly and with such distinctness upon the mind, that the indicative mood has *two* tenses for each great period of time; but the subjunctive mood, being applied to what is more vague and less important, has and needs but *one* tense for each period. Sometimes other tenses, especially the perfect, are found in this mood; but such forms are antiquated, and not considered necessary to modern English.

There is one thing about the subjunctive mood that is remarkable. Obliged to borrow the tenses of the indicative mood, and unable to vary them sufficiently in form, it adopts for each period of time the tense of the prior period, in order to avoid expressing the matter-of-fact sense denoted by the indicative mood; because we can not now, for instance, do a past act. Thus the past-perfect tense becomes simply a past tense; the past, a present; and the present, a future.

Potential Mood.

The **Potential Mood** expresses our chief relations to acts or states, either indicatively or subjunctively.

Ex.—"I *could* not *go* yesterday"; *indicative*, in time.
"I *would go* now or to-morrow"; *subjunctive*, in time.

That is, the tenses of this mood, especially in time, correspond sometimes with the *indicative* mood, and sometimes with the *subjunctive*.

417. A verb in the *potential mood* may express,—

1. Power. "I *can go*." "I *could go*."
2. Possibility. "It *may rain*." "It *might rain*."
3. Liberty or permission. "You *may go*."
4. Inclination. "I *would go*."
5. Duty. "I *should go*."
6. Necessity. "I *must go*."
7. A wish. "*May* you *prosper*."

Occasionally, this mood expresses other relations, as *tendency*, *adaptation*, *consequence*, *contingence*, etc.; and in some expressions the relational sense is so nearly lost that the mood is almost indicative or subjunctive.

418. The potential mood can be used interrogatively.

Ex.—"*Must* I *endure* all this?"

419. The signs of the potential mood are *may*, *can*, *must*, *might*, *could*, *would*, and *should*.

Shall in the sense of *must*, and *will* when it expresses volition, belong rather to the potential mood than to the indicative; but, to avoid troublesome distinctions, they are always considered as belonging to the indicative mood.

Imperative Mood.

The **Imperative Mood** expresses our volitions, generally as commands.

420. A verb in the *imperative mood* may express, —

1. Command. "John, *sit* up."
2. Entreaty. "*Forgive* our trespasses."
3. Exhortation. "*Believe*, *reform*, and *be saved*."
4. Permission. "*Go* in peace."

We *command* inferiors, *entreat* superiors, *exhort* equals, and *permit* in compliance with the wishes of others.

421. The imperative mood is generally used only in the present tense and the second person.

Ex. — "*Charge*, Chester, *charge!*" — *Scott.*

422. The subject of a verb in the imperative mood is *thou*, *you*, or *ye*, generally understood.

Ex. — "Know thyself" = Know *thou* thyself.

Sometimes the imperative mood is found in the perfect tense; as, "*Have done* thy charms, thou hateful, withered hag." — *Shakespeare.*

423. Sometimes the imperative mood is used in the first or the third person.

Ex. — "*Somebody call* my wife." — *Shakespeare.*
"'And *rest we* here,' Matilda said." — *Scott.*
"*Laugh those* who can, *weep those* who may." — *Id.*
"*Whoever* comes this way, *behold* and *tremble*." — *Pollok.*

Such expressions are generally poetical forms, preferred to the common imperative *let*.

The imperative *let* is often used with little or no reference to a person addressed; simply as a form of expression, to make known the will of the speaker; as, "*Let* it rain." To let this be done evidently does not depend on the power of the person addressed.

TENSE.

424. Tense is that property of verbs which shows the distinctions of time.

TIME may be divided into *present, past,* and *future.* PRESENT TIME, strictly speaking, can denote but a moment of duration; yet longer periods, extending into both the future and the past, are often considered present; as when we say, *this day, this week, this year, this century, in our lifetime.* PAST TIME begins from the present, and goes back as far as our thoughts can wander. FUTURE TIME begins from the same point, and goes forward to a similar extent. In each of these periods, an act may be considered either as merely taking place or as completed, thus making the *six tenses.*

Read the following both down the page and across it:—

Present.	**Past.**	**Future.**
I write	I wrote	I shall write
I have written	I had written	I shall have written.

425. There are six tenses: the *present,* the *present-perfect;* the *past,* the *past-perfect;* the *future,* and the *future-perfect.*

The terms *perfect* and *pluperfect* may also be used in stead of *present-perfect* and *past-perfect.*

It seems better to define the tenses according to their forms, and in every mood, than according to the time which they denote.

Present Tense.

426. Present Indicative. A verb in the *present tense* of the indicative mood may denote,—

1. A present act or state.

Ex.—The grass *is growing.* This *is* a warm day.

2. A present habit or custom.

Ex.—He *chews* tobacco. People *go* to church on Sunday.

3. An unchangeable truth.

Ex.—Heat *melts* snow. Virtue *produces* happiness.

W. The Doctor said that fever always produced thirst.
He said it was forty miles from Baltimore to Washington.

Such acts or states are truths inherent in the nature of things, and therefore belong not only to present time, but to all time. Since we live, however, only in present time and are mostly concerned with this period, the present tense is preferred.

4. A past or future transaction, which is thus presented with greater vividness or certainty.

Ex. — "On Linden, when the sun was low, ...
The combat *deepens*. On, ye brave!" — *Campbell.*
"The Guard never *surrenders*: it *dies!*" *i. e.*, will never, etc.

By this species of present tense, the reader is made, as it were, a spectator of the scene.

5. Some characteristic of an author, as observed in his works now existing.

Ex. — Seneca *reasons* and *moralizes* well. Milton *is* sublime.

427. The **present subjunctive** implies future time.

Ex. — If it *rain*, our flowers will live.
It is necessary that the messenger *be sent* as soon as possible.

428. The **present potential** is present or future in regard to both the mood and the act or state.

Ex. — He *may be coming*. I *can pay* you next Christmas.

429. The **present imperative** is present in regard to the mood, and future in regard to the act or state.

Ex. — "*Return* soon." "I said, *Go*; and he went."

The imperative mood has the *form* of the *present tense*; in other respects, however, it has little or nothing to do with time, but expresses merely the will of the speaker in regard to the person addressed.

Present-perfect Tense.

430. Present-perfect Indicative. A verb in the *present-perfect tense* of the indicative mood may represent something, —

1. As completed in present time.

Ex. — I *have finished* the work.

2. As connected with present time.

Ex. — "They *have been married* twenty years." And still remain so.
W. They continue with us now three days.

431. An act may be connected with present time, —

1. By the present existence of the doer.

Ex. — "I *have* often *read* Virgil." And I still live, and may read him again.

2. By the present continuance of the act or state.

Ex. — "Thus *has* it [the Mississippi] *flowed* for ages." And it still flows and flows.

3. By the present existence of the result.

Ex. — "Cicero *has written* orations." Cicero is dead, and the writing is past, but the orations still exist.

4. By the presence of some important circumstance.

Ex. — "Many important events *have happened* | *during this year.*" "*On this island* several duels *have been fought.*" Time and place yet remaining.

432. The **present-perfect potential** is present or future in regard to the mood, and presents the act or state as relatively past.

Ex. — "The child *may have fallen* into the well." "By that time he *may have gone* ahead of you."

Past Tense.

433. Past Indicative. A verb in the *past tense* of the indicative mood denotes, —

1. Simply a past act or state.

Ex. — "He *was fishing* when I *saw* him." "If he ever *was* rich."

2. Sometimes a past habit or custom.

Ex. — "The good times when the farmer *entertained* the traveler without pay, when he *invited* him to tarry, and join in the chase, and when Christmas and Fourth of July *were* seasons of festivity, have passed away." — *Benton.*

434. The **past subjunctive** denotes present or indefinite time, and it generally denies the act or state.

Ex. — If I *were* rich, I would give freely.

W. He runs as if he was running for life.

This tense sometimes becomes definitely past or future from its syntax.

435. The **past potential** may be present, past, or future, in regard to both the mood and the act or state. It represents the act or state as real, contingent, or denied.

"He *would go* yesterday." "He *would go* now or to-morrow, if he *could.*"

Sometimes it denotes a past habit or custom.

Ex. — "There *would* she *sit* and *weep* for hours."

Past-perfect Tense.

436. Past-perfect Indicative. A verb in the *past-perfect tense* of the indicative mood represents something as completed or ended in past time.

Ex. — "Here a small cabin *had been erected*."

W. And he that was dead, sat up, and began to speak.

437. The **past-perfect subjunctive** or **potential** denotes simply past time, and denies the act or state.

Ex. — "If I *had been* at home, I *should have gone*."

Future Tense.

438. A verb in the *future tense* denotes, —

1. Simply a future act or state.

Ex. — "The snow *will melt*." "I *shall be* busy this evening."

2. Sometimes a future habit or custom.

Ex. — "The steer and lion at one crib *shall meet*."

Future-perfect Tense.

439. A verb in the *future-perfect tense* represents something as completed in future time.

Ex. — The house, when finished, *will have cost* a fortune.

W. This was four years ago next August. — *School Report.*
Next Christmas I shall be at school a year.

General Remarks.

440. The tenses of the *subjunctive mood*, in order to be distinguished better from the tenses of the indicative, move forward in time.

Indicative: "If I *am*" — now. "If I *was*" — in past time. "I *had been* there" — *before* a certain past time.

Subjunctive: "If I *be*" — hereafter. "If I *were*" — now. "*Had* I *been* there" — *at* a certain past time, etc.

441. The tenses of the *potential mood*, when used subjunctively, also move forward in time.

Ex. — "I *should think* you *might risk* it"; *i. e.*, *now* or *hereafter*.

442. Sometimes *when*, *till*, *before*, *as soon as*, *whoever*, *whatever*, or a similar term, carries the present or the present-perfect tense into future time.

Ex. — "When he *comes*, I shall go." "Catch whatever *comes*."
"When he *has finished* the work, I shall pay him."

A tense is sometimes used to deny the same act or state of the subject in a neighboring tense; as, "He *has been* rich"; *i. e.*, he is *not* so *now*.

The present, the past, and the future, are called the *absolute tenses;* and the present-perfect, the past-perfect, and the future-perfect, the *relative tenses*, for these relate from one point of time to another. Sometimes the prominent idea in the absolute tenses is simply that a certain act or state exists; in the relative tenses, that it is completed.

Since the perfect passive participle generally implies completion, a passive verb in the absolute tenses is frequently equivalent in time to the corresponding relative tenses of the active voice.

"My rose-bush *is destroyed*"; "Some one *has destroyed* my rose-bush."
"The coat *will* then *be finished*"; "The tailor *will* then *have finished* the coat."

Observe also the kindred analogy in the following passive forms: —

"The house *is building*"; present. "The house *is built*"; completed. } So, "The house *was building*"; imperfect. "The house *was built*"; completed.

FORMS OF THE TENSES.

443. The **Forms** of a **Tense** are the different ways in which it can be expressed.

Ex. — He *strikes*, *does strike*, *is striking*, *is struck*, *striketh*.

444. There are five forms; the *common*, the *emphatic*, the *passive*, the *progressive*, and the *ancient*, or the *solemn style*.

445. The **Common Form** is the verb expressed in the most simple and ordinary manner.

Ex. — Time *flies*. He *went* home.

446. The **Emphatic Form** denotes emphasis, expressed by *do* or *did* as a part of the verb.

Ex.—I *did say* so. Really, it *does move.*

Do and *did* do not make negative propositions emphatic, but simply give a better position to the negative by helping to enclose it within the verb; as, "I *did n o t see* him."

Do and *did* do not make interrogative propositions emphatic, but simply give the interrogative form by preceding the subject; as, "*Did* ye not *hear* it?"

447. The **Passive Form** is that which is generally used to express the passive voice; and it is made by combining the verb *be*, or some variation of it, with the perfect participle.

Ex.— The oak *was shattered* by lightning.
"The melancholy days *are come.*" — *Bryant.*

448. The **Progressive Form** is that which expresses continuance of the act or state; and it is made by combining the verb *be*, or some variation of it, with the present participle.

This form, by spreading out, as it were, the act before the mind, is sometimes highly vivid and expressive.

Active: I wrote; I *was writing.* She *is dancing.* (*Dances*—trait.)
Passive: "I guessed that some mischief *was contriving.*" —*Swift.*
"Where a new church *is* now *building.*" — *Everett.*
"While these affairs *were transacting* in Europe." — *Bancroft.*
"Our chains *are forging.*" — *Wirt,* as *Patrick Henry.*
"Yankee Doodle *was playing* as I came in." — *M. C.*
"Where the new rifle-practice *was being introduced.*"—*Atl. Monthly.*
"Your friend *is being buried.*" — *Harper's Magazine.*
"The shocking neologism, 'The ship *is being calked.*'" — *Marsh.*

"The participial form [infin. and part.] is, in most languages, a stumbling-block. (Query for the purists: Ought I rather to say, A block-that-is-being-stumbled-at?)" — *Marsh.*
For additional remarks on this subject, see pp. 307 and 316.

The progressive form can generally be applied only to those acts or states which admit of intermissions and renewals. Permanent mental acts or states, and unchangeable truths, can therefore be seldom expressed in it. We can not say, "I *am respecting* him," "I *am understanding* you," "The air *is having* weight"; but we must say, "I *respect* him," "I *understand* you," "The air *has* weight."

449. The **Ancient Form** is an old common form that is still retained in the solemn style.

It has the ending *t*, *st*, or *est*, for the second person singular; *th* or *eth* in stead of *s* or *es*, for the third person singular; and generally uses *thou* or *ye* in stead of *you*.

This form occurs in the Bible, in prayer, in sermons, and in poetry.

Ex. — "Thou *barb'dst* the dart." "Adversity *flattereth* no man."

Doth is used for the auxiliary *does*, and *doeth* for the verb *does*. *Hath* and *saith* are contractions of *haveth* and *sayeth*.

450. Interrogative. A proposition is made *interrogative*, generally by placing the verb, or some part of it, before the nominative.

Ex. — "*Know ye* the land?" "*Have you seen* him?"

451. Negative. A proposition is made negative by placing *not* after the verb or after the first auxiliary.

Ex. — "I *know not*." "It *could* not *have* been known."

A participle or an infinitive is expressed negatively, generally by placing *not* before it; as, "*Not to know* some things is an honor." "*Not hearing* of him, we returned."

Some propositions are both interrogative and negative. Negative questions generally imply something contrary to the speaker's belief, or ask for confirmation. Both affirmative and negative questions are answered by *no* or *yes* alike. "Did you go? — No." "Did you not go. — No."

"And did they not catch you, then? — No, thank Heaven!" — *Garrick*.

PERSON AND NUMBER.

452. The **Person** and **Number** of a verb are its form to suit the person and number of its subject.

Ex. — I *am*. Thou *art*. He *is*. We *are*.

Verbs have, like their subjects, three persons and two numbers.

453. A finite verb must agree with its subject, in person and number.

That is, it must be expressed according to the Conjugation, pp. 160-170, which shows how the best writers and speakers express the verb in regard to its subject.

454. *I*, *thou*, *you*, *he*, *she*, *it*, *we*, and *they*, either are the subjects of finite verbs, or they can represent all other subjects in person and number.

455. Thou generally requires the verb, or the first auxiliary, to end with *est*, *st*, or *t*.

"Thou *knowest* that thou *didst* the deed." "Thou *art* the man."

When the termination required by *thou* would be harsh, it is sometimes omitted, especially in poetry.

"O Thou my voice inspire,
Who *touched* Isaiah's hallowed lips with fire." — *Pope.*
"Perhaps thou *noticed* on thy way a little orb." — *Pollok.*

In the imperative mood, *thou* does not require any variation in the form of the verb.

456. He, **she**, or **it**, requires that the verb, in the present indicative, shall end with *s* or *es*, *th* or *eth*.

Ex. — He *has*, or *hath*. She *teaches*, or *teacheth*.

The verb *ought*, which is never varied, is the only exception.

457. In the plural number the verb has the same form for all the persons.

Ex. — We *write*. You *write*. They *write*.

The agreement of the verb with its subject, and the agreement of the pronoun with its antecedent, make the chief syntax of the English language; let us therefore consider, —

1. The person of the subject or antecedent.
2. The number of the subject or antecedent.
3. The terms relating to the subject or antecedent, which do not affect the form of the verb or pronoun.

1. Person.

458. When two or more nominatives or antecedents, differing in person, are taken together, or are connected merely by *and*, the verb or pronoun prefers the first person to the second, and the second to the third.

Ex. — "*You* and *I*," or, "*You*, *he*, and *I*" = *We*; "*You* and *he*" = *You*.
"James and I *have recited* | *our* lessons."

459. When two or more nominatives, differing in person, are taken separately, or connected by *or* or *nor*, the verb prefers the nominative next to it.

Ex. — "You or I *am* to blame"; better, Either you *are* to blame, or I *am*. "Thou or thy friends *are* to make reparation."

W. He or you is the cause of my trouble.

2. Singular Subject or Antecedent.

460. The following subjects or antecedents are *singular*: —

1. A singular noun or pronoun denoting a single object.

Ex. — The fire *burns*. John *is* at home.

2. A singular collective noun denoting a group of objects as one thing.

Ex. — "His family *is* large, yet he supports *it*."

W. The army of Xerxes were vanquished by the Greeks.

3. A plural noun denoting but one thing.

Ex. — The "Pleasures of Hope" *was written* by Campbell.

W. Young's "Night Thoughts" are a gloomy but instructive poem.

4. Two or more nouns joined by *and*, yet denoting but one person or thing.

Ex. — Yonder *lives* a great scholar and statesman.
"Why *is* dust and ashes [man] proud?"
Goldsmith's "Edwin and Angelina" *is* a beautiful poem.

5. Sometimes two or more singular substantives, joined by *and* and denoting different things, but taken as one whole.

Ex. — "*Wooing, wedding, and repenting,* | *is* a Scotch jig, a measure, and a cinque pace." — *Shakespeare.* Here *is* seems to be proper, as referring to the three things taken in a certain order as one whole.

"*Descent and fall* to us *is* adverse." — *Milton.*

So, "*To turn and flee* | *was* now impossible." — *Irving.*

6. A singular substantive, or a phrase of two or more, modified by *each*, *every*, *either*, *neither*, *many a*, or *no*.

Ex.—"Every house *was burned;* and every man, woman, and child, *was killed*."—*Burke.*

"No rank, no fortune, no honor, *makes* the guilty happy."—*Blair.*

"Full many a flower *is born* to blush unseen."—*Gray.*

W. No crop, no house, and no fence, were left.—*Newspaper.*
Every heart and eye were filled with pity.—*Croly.*

7. Two or more singular substantives joined by *or* or *nor*.

"Tuesday, Wednesday, or Thursday, *was* the appointed day."

"To forsake a friend, or to divulge his secrets, *is* mean."

"Neither precept nor discipline *is* so forcible as example."

"Nor eye nor listening ear an object *finds*."—*Young.*

W. Neither poetry nor criticism have emerged from pedantry.
Edinburgh Review.

8. A series of substantives placed after a verb, when the verb, for the sake of emphasis, agrees only with the first, and is understood to each of the rest.

"Thine *is* the kingdom, and the power, and the glory."—*Bible.*

"There *is* Concord, and Lexington, and Bunker Hill, and there they will remain forever."—*Webster.*

The pronoun *they*, in this last example, seems to afford, in regard to pronouns, an exception to the general principle; but it is obvious that this apparent exception arises simply from a different view that is taken of the sense.

3. Plural Subject or Antecedent.

461. The following subjects or antecedents are *plural:*—

1. A plural substantive that denotes two or more objects, or that is plural in sense.

Ex.—The fires *burn.* The ashes *have lost* | *their* heat.

W. Here is five or six barrels that you may take.
There was not more than ten or fifteen persons present.

2. A collective noun that is singular in form, but plural in idea.

Ex.—"The council *were divided* in *their* opinions."

Such a noun is plural in idea when we must think of the persons or things separately, in order to make the assertion.

Ex.—"The majority are handsome, and of large stature."

That is, the individual islanders of this majority are so.—See Ellis's *Polynesian Res.*

W. The public is respectfully invited.
The multitude eagerly pursues pleasure.

3. A singular noun, used, by synecdoche, for a plural.

Ex. —Forty *head* of cattle *were grazing* on the meadow.

4. Two or more substantives connected by *and*, and denoting different persons or things.

Ex.—"John, James, and William, [= the boys,] *are studying.*"
"You, he, and I, [= we,] *are allowed* to go."

"To love our enemies, to mind our own business, and to relieve the distressed, *are* things oftener praised than practised."

W. Where is your slate and pencil?
Is your father and mother at home?
There was at least he and I, who did not recite.

5. A singular and a plural substantive, or two or more plurals, joined by *or* or *nor*.

"The king or his advisers *were opposed* to that course; while neither the prince nor his friends *were prepared* to defend it."—*Hume.*

Sometimes the verb agrees with the nearest nominative; as, "Where there *is* an *infant* or *infants who are* yet," etc.—*Mo. Statutes.*

4. Terms that do Not Affect the Form of the Verb or Pronoun.

462. The following terms do not affect the form of the verb or pronoun:—

1. An adjunct to the nominative.

Ex.—"The long *row* of elms *was* magnificent."
So, "Six months' *interest is* due."

W. The chief portion of the exports consist of silks.—*Newspaper.*

2. A term in apposition.

Ex.—"*Love*, and love only, *is* the loan for love."

W. The Bible, or Holy Scriptures, are the best book.

3. A predicate-nominative.

Ex.—"*I was* eyes to the blind, and feet *was I* to the lame."—*Bible.*
"His *meat* [food] *was* locusts and wild honey."—*Ib.*
"The *people are* a many-headed beast."—*Pope.*

W. The crown of virtue are peace and honor.

It is sometimes difficult to determine which of the nominatives is the subject, or to which nominative a relative clause should be referred. The sense is the best guide. "The wages of sin *is* death." Here *wages* is the nominative to *is*. "I am the general, *who command you*"; *i. e.*, I am the general. "I am the general *who commands you*"; *i. e.*, I am *your* general.

4. A term set off parenthetically or emphatically.

"This *man* (and, indeed, all such men) *deserves* death."
"Our *statesmen*, especially John Adams, *have reached* a good old age."
"The *carriage*, as well as the horses, *was* much *injured*."

The subjects belong to different propositions, and the verb agrees with the first subject.

W. Our taxes, especially the military tax, is enormous.
The house, as well as the furniture, were destroyed.

5. An excepted or excluded term, or a term that is apparently set aside for a more important or expressive one.

Ex.—"*Pleasure*, and not books, *is* his delight."
"*Books*, and not pleasure, *are* his delight."
"Since *none* but thou *can end* it."—*Milton.*
"Not only rage, but even *murmurs cease*."—*Pope, abridged.*
"What black despair, what *horror fills* his heart!"—*Thomson.*
"Honor and virtue, nay, even *interest demands* a different course."

W. Industry, and not mean savings, produce wealth.
Nothing but wailings were heard.

---

463. Words must sometimes be supplied, to complete the subject.

Ex.—"Little and often fills the purse" = *To put in* little and often, etc. "Dear and far-fetched is for ladies" = *What is* dear, etc.

It would probably be quite as well to parse the whole phrase as a noun, without supplying words.

464. A few verbs denote such acts or states that the language has no nouns suitable to be their subjects; and these verbs are therefore accommodated in syntax with the pronoun *it*.

Ex. — "It *rains*." "It *snows*." "It *thunders*."

Verbs of this kind are *impersonal* in some languages; they are logically so in ours, but not grammatically so; for the difficulty is in the meaning of *it*, and not in the agreement of the verb. The word *it* seems to be needed in syntax; for without it such words as *rains* and *thunders* might sometimes appear as the plurals of the nouns *rain* and *thunder*, and not as verbs.*

465. An **Impersonal Verb** is a verb that has person and number, without having a subject; being generally a mere modifying form of expression.

Ex. — *Methinks*, *meseems*, frequently the imperative *let*, and sometimes other imperatives; as, "There are, *say*, a thousand languages and dialects;" *i. e.*, *probably* a thousand, etc.

It is worthy of notice that independent infinitive and participial phrases also fall into the foregoing analogy; as, "*To speak frankly*, he will probably not succeed." "*Generally speaking*, the people are in good circumstances."

Let us next notice by what means all the foregoing properties of verbs are expressed.

AUXILIARY VERBS.

466. The auxiliary verbs express voice, mood, tense, person, and number.

They also contribute to what is called, in syntax, *position* (as in negative or interrogative propositions); and they are used as the *pronouns* or *pro-verbs* to other verbs.

467. The auxiliary verbs are *be* and its variations; *do*, *did*; *can*, *could*; *have*, *had*; *may*, *might*; *must*; *shall*, *should*; *will*, and *would*.

Be is used to express the verb in the passive and the progressive form; as, "The house *is built*." "The leaves *are falling*." It shows when or how the person or thing *exists* in the state denoted by the rest of the verb.

Do and **Did**, except in negative or interrogative propositions, are generally used to give emphasis to the verb; as, "But when I *do go*, I choose to go as a lady." — *Mrs. Caudle*. They denote action indefinitely, which is made specific by the rest of the verb.

Can and **Could** are used to express, —

1. Ability. "I *can carry* the basket."
2. Possibility. "It *can* not *be*." It is impossible.

Have and **Had** are used to express the *perfect* tenses.

Ex. — I *have seen.* I *had seen.* I *shall have seen.*

May and **Might** are used to express, —

1. Ability or probability. "I *might have done* it."
2. Possibility or probability. "It *might have been.*" "It *may rain.*"
3. Permission. "You *may go.*"
4. Wishing. "*May* you *prosper.*"

Must is used to express necessity. "*Die* I *must.*" — *H. K. White.*

Shall and **Should** are used to set forth the act or state, —

1. As a duty, as something commanded or authorized, or as something determined or resolved upon.

Ex. — "Thou *shalt love* thy neighbor as thyself." "You *should obey.*"
"He *shall stay* at home." "They said, 'It *shall be done.*'"
"*Shall* I *be left,* forgotten in the dust,
When Fate, relenting, lets the flower revive?" — *Beattie.*

W. Will I be allowed to occupy this seat?

2. As something compelled by circumstances, especially when the subject is of the first person.

Ex. — "I *shall be drowned;* for nobody will help me."

W. I will suffer, if I do not take my overcoat.
We would then be obliged to retreat.

3. As something future or contingent, but without reference to the will of the subject, and especially when the subject is of the first person.

Ex. — "I *shall call* to see you this evening."
"*Should* you *meet* any of my friends, remember me to them."
"Do you think the book will sell? — I *should think* so."
"Whoever *shall violate* this rule, shall [¶ 1] be punished."
"Yes, my son; you *shall* often *find* the richest men the meanest." — *Tattler.* That is, this fact will often force itself upon your notice. An obsolescent but good use of the word.

W. Will I find you here when I return? — See also ¶ 1.
Would we hear a good sermon if we would go?
Isabella promised a pension to the first seaman who would discover [land.

The various meanings of *shall* tend to make it very expressive in prophecy.

Ex. — "Earth *shall* by angel feet *be trod,*
One great garden of her God!" — *Croly* (on the Millennium).
"Beware of the day when the Lowlands *shall meet* thee." — *Campbell.*

Will and **Would** are used to set forth the act or state,—

1. As something proceeding from the will or nature of the subject.

Ex.—"We *will drain* our dearest veins, but they shall be free."

"I *would* not *live* always; I ask not to stay."

"This *will do.*" "It *will rain* soon." "The cause *will raise* up armies."

W. I shall go home, in spite of all opposition."

2. As something repeated from a steadfast inclination to do it.

Ex.—"There *would* she *sit* and *weep* for hours."

3. Simply as something future, wherever *shall* or *should* would imply compulsion; and hence especially when the subject is of the second or third person.

Ex. —"You *will be ridiculed* for your eccentricity."

"If he should go to church, he *would hear* a good sermon."

W. I believe that all these volunteers shall be sent away.

In conditional propositions, *shall* or *should* must nearly always be used to express simple futurity or contingence; for *will* and *would* in such propositions generally refer to the will of the subject.

Ex.—"If I *shall have been.*" "If you *shall have been.*" "When he *shall go.*" "Whoever *shall say* so."

468. Auxiliary verbs are often convenient when we wish to express the verb interrogatively, negatively, or elliptically.

Ex.—"Do you know Lydia Flare?" Placed before the nominative.

"Can you go?" "I do not want his company." (See page 141.)

"If man will not do justice, God *will*" [do justice].

"They herd cattle, and raise corn, just as we used *to do; i. e.*, to herd cattle and raise corn. *Do* is sometimes thus used as a sort of *pro-verb* to represent an active verb or a phrase.

469. *Be*, *do*, and *have*, and sometimes other auxiliaries, are used also as principal verbs. They are thus used when not combined with a principal verb expressed or understood.

PRINCIPAL.	AUXILIARY.
"I *was* sick."	"I *was made* sick."
"He *does* well."	"He *does write* well."
"She *has* nothing."	"She *has learned* nothing."

470. The auxiliaries *do*, *have*, *may*, *can*, *must*, *will*, and *shall*, generally accord best with one another, and with the present tenses; the auxiliaries *did*, *had*, *might*, *could*, *would*, and *should*, generally accord best with one another, and with the past tenses.

Ex. — "What Nature *has* denied, fools *will* pursue." — *Young.*
What Nature *had* denied, he *would pursue.*

W. If I lend you my horse, I should have to borrow one myself.

To the foregoing paragraph there are many exceptions.

INFINITIVES.

471. An **Infinitive** is a form of the verb that generally begins with *to*, and that expresses the act or state without predicating it.

Ex. — To lead, to have led, to be led, to have been led.

472. There are two infinitives; the *present* and the *perfect.*

A transitive verb has both in each voice; thus making *four* forms, as above.

Present Infinitive.

473. The **Present Infinitive** denotes, —

1. Simply the act or state.

Ex. — "*To love* is *to serve.*"

2. The act or state as present in regard to the word on which the infinitive depends.

Ex. — "She *seems* | *to study.*"

3. The act or state as future in regard to the word on which the infinitive depends.

Ex. — "Man never is, but always *to be*, blest." — *Pope.*

W. I hoped to have heard from you.
I intended to have said less.
It was still in his power to have refused. — *Dryden.*

474. The present infinitive consists of *to*, combined with the simplest form of the verb; or of *to be*, with a simple participle.

Ex. — To write, to be writing, to be written.

Perfect Infinitive.

475. The **Perfect Infinitive** represents the act or state as completed at the time referred to.

Ex. — "You *seem* | *to have come* through the rain."

476. The perfect infinitive consists of *to have*, or *to have been*, combined with a simple participle.

To have written, to have been writing, to have been written.

The perfect infinitive is so combined with the verb *ought*, and sometimes with the verb *have* or *was*, that the whole expression is equivalent in time to the past-perfect potential; as, "I *ought to have gone*." And in the idiom, "I *had* like *to have fallen* overboard."— *Swift*. And, probably, "I *was to have gone*," implying, "I did not go," and considered incorrect by most grammarians, is allowable as belonging to the same analogy. — See p. 307.

It is remarkable that, in combination with most of the auxiliary verbs, the perfect infinitive does not imply antecedent time; and all the foregoing verbs seem have fallen into the same analogy.

Syntax of Infinitives.

477. An *infinitive* may express something, —

As the *cause*. "I grieve *to hear* of your bad conduct."
As the *purpose*. "And fools, who came *to scoff*, remained *to pray*."
As simply a *future* or *subsequent event*. "He fell *to rise* no more."
As the *respect wherein*. "Willing *to wound*, and yet afraid *to strike*."
As a *determination* or *obligation*. "I am *to go*." "It is *to be deplored*, that," etc.
As the *manner*. "All things went *to suit* me."
As the *supplement of a comparison*. "Good enough *to sell*." "So mean as *to be despised*."

478. An *infinitive* may be used, —

Chiefly as a *verb*. "He is supposed *to have gone*."
Partially as an *adverb*. "I came *to see* you." (Came *why*?)
Partially as an *adjective*. "An opportunity *to study*."
Partially as a *noun*. "*To have learned* the art, will be a pleasure."
In *combination* with all the auxiliary verbs except *have* and *be*. "I did [*to*] *write*." "I can [*to*] *study*."
Independently, for a clause or a sentence. "But, *to proceed*," etc.

479. In its substantive sense, the infinitive may be used, —

As the *subject* of a verb. "*To retreat* was impossible."
As the *object* of a *verb*. "He wished *to retreat*."

An infinitive becomes thus the object of a verb when that verb is *transitive*.

As the *object* of *about, except,* or *but.* "He is about *to retreat.*"
As a *predicate-nominative.* "To sin is *to suffer.*"
As an *appositive.* "Delightful task! *to rear* the tender thought."

480. An *infinitive* may be construed with, —

A *noun.* "He has the *courage* to venture."
A *pronoun.* "Hear *him* speak."
An *adjective.* "He is *anxious* to start."
A *verb.* "He *seems* to prosper." "I *came* to remain."
An *adverb.* "He knows *when* to purchase."

Strictly speaking, the whole phrase, *when to purchase*, depends on *knows.*

A *preposition.* "He is *about* to sell his farm."
A *conjunction.* "He is wiser *than* to believe it."
An *interjection,* elliptically. "*O,* to be in such a condition!"

Strictly speaking, the infinitive phrase is here used as a nominative independent, by exclamation.

Be is often combined with *about* and the infinitive, to express something as future and impending at the time referred to; as, "We *were* | *about to start.*"

Be, in some of the tenses, may be combined with the infinitive, to express determination or design; as, "They *are* | *to be sold.*"

Have is often combined with the infinitive, to express obligation or necessity; as, "I *shall have* | *to pay* it."

The verbs *seem, appear, suppose,* etc., are often combined with the infinitive, to modify or soften the assertion; as, "She *seems to know* but little."

481. To is omitted when the infinitive is combined with an auxiliary verb.

Ex. — "He *does* [*to*] *study.*" "I *can* [*to*] *study*" = I am able to study.

482. To is omitted after the active verbs *bid, make, need, hear,* | *let, see, feel,* and *dare;* after *let* in the passive voice; sometimes after *have, help, please, find,* and equivalents of *see;* and sometimes after a conjunction, or in colloquial expressions.

Ex. — "Let us [*to*] *sing.*" "I heard him [*to*] *say* it."
[It is] "Better [to] lose than [to] be disgraced."

About seven hundred years ago the infinitive had the ending *en* or *an* in stead of the prefix *to.* The combinations of the infinitive with auxiliaries, and with most of the foregoing verbs, were then or previously made; and it would therefore be more appropriate to say that these verbs are followed *by the* OLD *infinitive, which had not* TO; as, "Heo conne speken" = They can speak.

PARTICIPLES.

483. A **Participle** is a form of the verb that expresses the act or state without predicating it, and generally resembles an adjective.

Ex. — "A tree, *bending* with fruit, fell to the ground."

Observe that *fell*, and not *bending*, predicates something of *tree*; also that the phrase, *bending with fruit*, is, like an adjective, descriptive of the tree.

484. There are two participles; the *present* and the *perfect*, each of which is either simple or compound.

Present Participle.

485. The **Present Participle** represents the act or state as present and continuing at the time referred to.

Ex. — "We saw the moon *rising*."
"*Being* thus *wounded*, he can not return to his regiment."

486. The simple present participle is made by annexing *ing* to the simplest form of the verb.

Ex. — Catch, *catching*; hide, *hiding*; dig, *digging*.

487. The simple present participle, of a transitive verb, is nearly always in the active voice.

Ex. — "The bee, *stinging* the boy, soon set itself free."

488. In some connections this participle can be used in the passive voice.

Ex. — "Virgil describes some spirits as *bleaching* in the winds, others as *cleansing* [*i. e.*, *being cleansed*] under great falls of water, and others as *purging* in fire, to recover the primitive beauty and purity of their nature." — *Addison.* "I could easily see what *was doing* on the other side of the river." — *Bulwer.*

Perfect Participle.

489. The **Perfect Participle** represents the act or state as completed at the time referred to.

Ex. — "A fox, *caught* in a trap."
"A fox, *having caught* a hen, met the owner," etc.

490. The simple perfect participle is made by annexing *ed* to the simplest form of the verb; or it is an irregular form, given in the list of irregular verbs.

Ex. — Pitch, *pitched;* give, *given;* see, *seen;* teach, *taught.*

491. The simple perfect participle of a transitive verb is either active or passive.

492. It is in the *active voice*, when *have* in any of its forms is combined with it.

Ex. — Having *given.* To have *given.* I have *given.* I had *given.* I shall have *given.*

493. It is in the *passive voice*, —

1. When it stands by itself.

Ex. — "The apple *eaten* by Eve was the first temptation."

2. When *be* in any of its forms, is combined with it.

Ex. — "The apple was *given* to Eve to be *eaten* by her."

494. The simple perfect participle of some verbs can be used as a present participle.

Ex. — "He lives *loved* by all."

Compound Participle.

495. A **Compound Participle** is one that consists of *being*, *having*, or *having been*, combined with some other participle.

Being, *having*, and *having been*, thus become *auxiliary* participles to other participles.

Ex. — Written; *being written, having written, having been written.*

496. Being is used chiefly to express the present passive participle.

Ex. — "The soldier, *being wounded*, was carried to the hospital.

The act of wounding is past; but he still remains in the wounded state.

The compound participle, thus formed, generally expresses the present continuance of a completed act, rather than the present receiving of the act.

497. Having is used chiefly to express the perfect active participle of transitive verbs, or to express the participle in time that corresponds to some perfect tense.

Ex. — Loved, *having loved.* "*Having said* this, he withdrew" = When he *had said* this, he withdrew. "*Having learned* the lesson, you may play" = Since or when you *have learned* the lesson, etc.

498. Having been is used chiefly to express the perfect participle corresponding to the compound present passive participle, or to the simple perfect passive participle that is present in time.

"The soldier, *having been wounded,* was recognized by the scar."

Loved, *having been loved;* occupied, *having been occupied.*

Occasionally, the auxiliary participles are used for other purposes, of which the principal are, to exclude predication, to distinguish voice, to distinguish cause from condition, to show more distinctly the participial sense, and to give more distinctly the sense of a clause to the participial phrase.

"This *being proved,* the conclusion is irresistible." *Proved,* without *being,* would seem to be a finite verb, and in the active voice. "The army did not march, *being* ill *provided,*" implies cause; "The army did not march ill *provided,*" implies condition. "*Being admired* and *applauded,* she became vain," is simply a little more forcible or formal than, "*Admired* and *applauded,* she became vain." It is thus that simple and compound participles approach so nearly in meaning that they are sometimes almost equivalent.

A compound participle that consists of *been* placed between two participles that end each with *ing,* is frequently found; as, "*having* been *standing.*" But a compound participle that consists of *being* combined with some other participle that also ends with *ing,* is seldom found; as, "*being standing.*" Good writers generally prefer to change the form of expression; as, "The inhabitants, *being starving,* surrendered"; better, "The inhabitants, *being in a starving condition,* surrendered."

From what has thus far been said of participles, we may infer, —

1. That *intransitive* verbs have *three* participles, or participial forms, — the present, the perfect, and the compound; as, *Rising, risen, having risen.*

Risen is used chiefly in combination, *having risen* is used alone.

2. That *transitive* verbs have *six* participles, three in each voice, — the present, the perfect, and the compound; but that of these six the perfect active can be used only in combination with *have,* thus leaving but *five* participles that can be used alone. We may also observe that the compound participle has three forms.

Ex. — ACTIVE: *Building, built, having built.*
PASSIVE: *Being built, built, having been built.*
COMPOUND: *Being built, having built, having been built.*

Observe here that *being built* is not only a somewhat clumsy form, but that it does not strictly express the progressive passive sense; therefore *building* is sometimes compelled to serve in its place. Observe also that the active *built* has the same form as the passive; but as the passive was more needed, the active *built* left the field to the passive, and *having built* came in to supply the place of the former.

Syntax of Participles.

499. A *participle* may express something subordinate,—

As the *cause*. "John, *being tired*, went to bed."

As the *means*. "The horse charged upon the wolves, *striking* them with his fore feet."

As the *manner*. "The cars came *rattling*." — See Southey's Lodore.

As the *time*. "*Having taken* shelter here, he saw an ant," etc.

As the *state*. "He became *attached* to us."

As the *accompaniment*. "She sat near, *reading* a book."

As the *condition*. "*Circling* round, you may approach on the other side."

As the *respect wherein*. "I consider him as *having lost* his right."

500. A participle may be used,—

Chiefly as a *verb*. "*Seeing* me, he approached."

Chiefly as an *adjective*. "States *severed*, discordant, belligerent."

Wholly as an *adjective*. "*Interesting* stories." "*Farming* utensils."

Chiefly as an *adverb*. "The horse stands *sleeping*." (How?)

Wholly as an *adverb*. "*Scalding* hot."

Partially as a *noun*. "By *sending* those books immediately."

Wholly as a *noun*. "By the immediate *sending* of those books."

In *combination* with the auxiliary *be*, to express the passive form. "They *were shot*."

In *combination* with the auxiliary *be*, to express the progressive form. "They *were shooting*."

In *combination* with the auxiliary *have*, to express the perfect tenses. "I have *seen*." "I had *seen*." "I shall have *seen*."

Absolutely with a substantive. "The bells *having rung*, we went to church."

Absolutely after an infinitive. "To go *prepared*, is necessary."

Independently, in the sense of a clause. "Generally *speaking*, few men," etc.

501. In its substantive sense the participle may be used,—

As the *subject* of a verb. "*Reading* is taught daily."

As the *object* of a verb. "He teaches *reading* and *writing*."

As the *object* of a preposition. "By *reading* the book."

As a *predicate-nominative*. "To die for her is *serving* thee." — *Holmes*.

This last construction occurs so frequently in good writers that it must be allowed when the sense is obvious, especially in verse; though the infinitive would be better, for *is serving* might in some constructions appear to be a verb.

Participles and Infinitives.

Agreements.

502. Participles and infinitives have voice, something of tense, but neither person nor number.

503. Participles and infinitives are annexed to auxiliary verbs, to express all those parts of the verb which it can not express by itself.

504. Participles and infinitives partake of the nature of nouns, adjectives, and adverbs.

505. Participles and infinitives lose the idea of time as they become nouns or adjectives.

506. Participles and infinitives become verbal nouns when they assume case; and they may then be used in any case except the possessive.

"*To be despised* is the consequence of *meddling*." What is? and of what?

Mr. Gould Brown repudiates this extension of case. But case, in English, is a relation as well as a form of words; and had he been better acquainted with foreign languages, especially the Greek, in which the article is even declined before the infinitive, he would probably have come to a different conclusion.

Only participles that end with *ing*, and compound participles, can be used as nouns.

507. By virtue of their verbal sense, verbal nouns may govern other substantives in the objective case, or be modified adverbially.

Ex.—"*To consider* | *sometimes* the *consequences* of our actions, is our duty."

Such participles and infinitives may be parsed first as participles and infinitives, and then they may be disposed of substantively in syntax.

Differences.

508. *Participles* are combined with the auxiliaries *be* and *have; infinitives,* with all other auxiliaries.

Participles.	*Infinitives.*
I am *writing.*	I can [*to*] *study.*
I was *struck.*	I did [*to*] *study.*
I had been *writing.*	I might [*to*] *have studied.*
I have *written.*	I shall [*to*] *study.*

To is used here simply to show the infinitives; for the infinitives of these old syntactical combinations never had *to*, but an ending in the place of it.

W. The ground is froze. The sun has rose.
My horse was stole. The coat is wore out.
The slate is broke. I might have went.

So, on the contrary, participles should not be used for the past tense.
I seen him. (See p. 122.) He done it. He begun well.
We drunk but little. I knowed it. — See ¶ 369.

509. *Participles* are used after prepositions; *infinitives* are generally required in connection with finite verbs.

Ex. — "You will lose nothing by *helping* him."
"*To defer* the matter is *to give* it up."

510. *Participles* may become concrete, and even assume number; *infinitives* never do, but remain strictly abstract.

Ex. — "*To lodge* in comfortable *lodgings*."

511. A *participle*, by virtue of its substantive sense, may govern the possessive case; an *infinitive*, never.

Ex. — "He made no secret of *my* | *having written* the review." — IRVING.

Such possessives are condemned by Mr. Brown; but they are abundantly authorized by good writers. It is sometimes better, however, to use, in stead of the participle, an ordinary noun, or a clause beginning with *that*.

512. A participial noun may become so nearly a full noun, as to require an adjective rather than an adverb.

Ex. — "By *carefully reading* the book." "By a *careful reading* of the book." "By *slow marching*." But, "To march *slowly*."

Only participles that end with *ing*, can be used as such nouns.

All participles thus deprived of their verbal syntax should be parsed simply as participial nouns.

513. A *participle* sometimes becomes an adjective; an *infinitive*, never.

Ex. — PARTICIPIAL ADJECTIVES: "A *broken* pitcher"; "Life's *fleeting* moments." Sometimes the participle becomes a mere adjective; as, "This is *surprising*" = *wonderful*. — See p. 221.

Only the simple participles can be used as adjectives.

514. *Infinitives* lean more to predicates and substantives; *participles*, to modifiers.

Participles and infinitives form a very important circuit of expressions between finite verbs and other parts of speech.

CONJUGATION.

515. The **Conjugation** of a verb is the proper combination and arrangement of its parts, in their full order.

"In their full order," — that is, in all the persons and numbers of each mood, tense, etc. *Conjugation* embraces *all* the persons and numbers; *synopsis*, only *one* person and number.

516. A **Synopsis** of a verb is only an outline of it, which shows its parts in a single person and number, through the moods and tenses.

SYNOPSIS of *write*, with *I*, through the indicative mood: —

Present,	*I write.*	Present-Perfect,	*I have written.*
Past,	*I wrote.*	Past-Perfect,	*I had written.*
Future,	*I shall write.*	Future-Perfect,	*I shall have written.*

517. Most forms of the verb consist of auxiliaries combined with participles or infinitives; and such forms may be called *composite.*

The present and the past are the forms mostly used without auxiliary verbs.

In general, verbs branch out thus: They have *moods;* moods have *tenses;* tenses have *forms;* and forms have *persons* and *numbers.*

518. The irregular verb *BE* is conjugated thus: —

PRINCIPAL PARTS.

Present.	*Past.*	*Present Participle.*	*Perfect Participle*
Be *or* am,	was,	being,	been.

INDICATIVE MOOD.

Present Tense.

SINGULAR.		PLURAL.
First Person.	I am,	1. We are,
Second Person.	You are,	2. You are,
Third Person.	He, she, or it, is;	3. They are.

Formerly, *be* was used in stead of *am, are, is,* etc.

Present-Perfect Tense.

SINGULAR.	PLURAL.
1. I have been,	1. We have been,
2. You have been,	2. You have been,
3. He has been;	3. They have been.

Past Tense.

1. I was,	1. We were,
2. You were,	2. You were,
3. He was;	3. They were.

Past-Perfect Tense.

1. I had been,	1. We had been,
2. You had been,	2. You had been,
3. He had been;	3. They had been.

Future Tense.

Simple futurity; foretelling.

1. I shall be,	1. We shall be,
2. You will be,	2. You will be,
3. He will be;	3. They will be.

Promise, threat, or determination.

1. I will be,	1. We will be,
2. You shall be,	2. You shall be,
3. He shall be;	3. They shall be.

Future-Perfect Tense.

Simple futurity; foretelling.

1. I shall have been,	1. We shall have been,
2. You will have been,	2. You will have been,
3. He will have been;	3. They will have been.

SUBJUNCTIVE MOOD.

Present Tense.

1. If I be,	1. If we be,
2. If you be,	2. If you be,
3. If he be;	3. If they be.

Past Tense.

SINGULAR.		PLURAL.	
1. If I were,	Were I,	1. If we were,	Were we,
2. If you were,	Were you,	2. If you were,	Were you,
3. If he were; or,	Were he;	3. If they were; or,	Were they.

Past-Perfect Tense.

1. If I had been,	1. If we had been,
2. If you had been,	2. If you had been,
3. If he had been;	3. If they had been.

Or thus: —

1. Had I been,	1. Had we been,
2. Had you been,	2. Had you been,
3. Had he been;	3. Had they been.

POTENTIAL MOOD.

Present Tense.

1. I may be,	1. We may be,
2. You may be,	2. You may be,
3. He may be;	3. They may be.

In the same way conjugate *can be* and *must be.*

Present-Perfect Tense.

1. I may have been,	1. We may have been,
2. You may have been,	2. You may have been,
3. He may have been;	3. They may have been.

In the same way conjugate *must have been* and "Can I have been?"

Past Tense.

1. I might be,	1. We might be,
2. You might be,	2. You might be,
3. He might be;	3. They might be.

In the same way conjugate *could be, would be,* and *should be.*

Past-Perfect Tense.

1. I might have been,	1. We might have been,
2. You might have been,	2. You might have been,
3. He might have been;	3. They might have been.

In the same way conjugate *could have been, would have been,* and *should have been.*

IMPERATIVE MOOD.

Present Tense.

Singular.	Plural.
2. Be thou ; or, Do thou be.	2. Be ye ; or, Do ye be.

	Present.	Perfect.	Compound.
INFINITIVES.	— To be.	To have been.	
PARTICIPLES.	— Being.	Been.	Having been.

Synopsis of the verb *be*, with *thou*.

INDICATIVE MOOD.

Present Tense, Thou art.
Present-Perfect Tense, Thou hast been.
Past Tense, Thou wast, or wert.
Past-Perfect Tense, Thou hadst been.
Future Tense, Thou shalt or wilt be.
Future-Perfect Tense, Thou shalt or wilt have been.

"Thou *wert*, thou art, the cherished madness of my heart." — *Byron*.

SUBJUNCTIVE MOOD.

Present Tense, If thou be.
Past Tense, If thou wert ; or, Wert thou.
Past-Perfect Tense, If thou hadst been ; or, Hadst thou been.

"If thou *were*," and "If thou *had been*," are sometimes used by good writers.

POTENTIAL MOOD.

Present Tense, Thou mayst, canst, or must be.
Present-Perfect Tense, Thou mayst, canst, or must have been.
Past Tense, Thou mightst, couldst, wouldst, or shouldst be.
Past-Perfect Tense, Thou mightst, couldst, wouldst, or shouldst have been.

IMPERATIVE MOOD.

Present Tense, Be thou ; or, Do thou be.

519. The regular verb *RŌW* is conjugated thus: —

PRINCIPAL PARTS.

Present.	*Past.*	*Present Participle.*	*Perfect Participle.*
Row,	rowed,	rowing,	rowed.

INDICATIVE MOOD.

Present Tense.

SINGULAR.	PLURAL.
1. I rōw,	1. We row,
2. You row,	2. You row,
3. He row**s**;	3. They row.

☞ Let the verbs *love*, *rule*, *permit*, *carry*, *strike*, and *see*, be now conjugated in the same way by other members of the class. So, in each following tense.

Emphatic Form.

Do, combined with the present infinitive.*

1. I do row,	1. We do row,
2. You do row,	2. You do row,
3. He do**es** row;	3. They do row.

Present-Perfect Tense.

Have, combined with the perfect participle.

1. I have rowed,	1. We have rowed,
2. You have rowed,	2. You have rowed,
3. He ha**s** rowed;	3. They have rowed.

In the solemn style, *hath*, *roweth*, and *doth row* are used for *has*, *rows*, and *does row*.

Past Tense.

1. I rowed,	1. We rowed,
2. You rowed,	2. You rowed,
3. He rowed;	3. They rowed.

* The infinitive, in combining with auxiliary verbs, drops the sign *to*; and these composite forms tend to show that the *present* should be considered the *present infinitive* rather than the *present indicative*; but since the latter is also needed as a principal part, it may be well to call the present either.

The English infinitive, as we have already said, formerly had the ending *an* or *en* instead of the prefix *to*; and hence such primitive combinations of verbs as must have been made with auxiliaries, are without the sign *to*.

Emphatic Form.

Did, combined with the present infinitive.

SINGULAR.	PLURAL.
1. I did row,	1. We did row,
2. You did row,	2. You did row,
3. He did row;	3. They did row.

Past-Perfect Tense.

Had, combined with the perfect participle.

1. I had rowed,	1. We had rowed,
2. You had rowed,	2. You had rowed,
3. He had rowed;	3. They had rowed.

Future Tense.

Shall or *will*, combined with the present infinitive.

Simple futurity; foretelling.

1. I shall row,	1. We shall row,
2. You will row,	2. You will row,
3. He will row;	3. They will row.

Promise, threat, or determination.

1. I will row,	1. We will row,
2. You shall row,	2. You shall row,
3. He shall row;	3. They shall row.

Future-Perfect Tense.

Shall or *will*, combined with the perfect infinitive.

Simple futurity; foretelling.

1. I shall have rowed,	1. We shall have rowed.
2. You will have rowed,	2. You will have rowed,
3. He will have rowed;	3. They will have rowed.

SUBJUNCTIVE MOOD.

The tenses of the subjunctive mood are formed like those of the indicative.

Present Tense.

1. If I row,	1. If we row,
2. If you row,	2. If you row,
3. If he row;	3. If they row.

Emphatic Form.

SINGULAR.	PLURAL.
1. If I do row,	1. If we do row,
2. If you do row,	2. If you do row,
3. If he do row;	3. If they do row.

Past Tense.

1. If I rowed,	1. If we rowed,
2. If you rowed,	2. If you rowed,
3. If he rowed;	3. If they rowed.

Emphatic Form.

1. If I did row,	1. If we did row,
2. If you did row,	2. If you did row,
3. If he did row;	3. If they did row.

Past-Perfect Tense.

1. If I had rowed,	1. If we had rowed,
2. If you had rowed,	2. If you had rowed,
3. If he had rowed;	3 If they had rowed.

Or thus:—

1. Had I rowed,	1. Had we rowed,
2. Had you rowed,	2. Had you rowed,
3. Had he rowed;	3. Had they rowed.

POTENTIAL MOOD.

Present Tense.

May, *can*, or *must*, combined with the present infinitive.

1. I may row,	1. We may row,
2. You may row,	2. You may row,
3. He may row;	3. They may row.

Present-Perfect Tense.

May, *can*, or *must*, combined with the perfect infinitive.

1. I may have rowed,	1. We may have rowed,
2. You may have rowed,	2. You may have rowed,
3. He may have rowed;	3. They may have rowed.

In the same way conjugate *must have rowed.*

Past Tense.

Might, could, would, or *should*, combined with the present infinitive.

SINGULAR.	PLURAL.
1. I might row,	1. We might row,
2. You might row,	2. You might row,
3. He might row;	3. They might row.

In the same way conjugate *could row, would row,* and *should row.*

Past-Perfect Tense.

Might, could, would, or *should*, combined with the perfect infinitive.

1. I might have rowed,	1. We might have rowed,
2. You might have rowed,	2. You might have rowed,
3. He might have rowed;	3. They might have rowed.

In the same way conjugate *could have rowed, would have rowed,* and *should have rowed.*

IMPERATIVE MOOD.

Present Tense.

2. Row thou; or, Do thou row. 2. Row ye; or, Do ye row.

	Present.	Perfect.	Compound.
INFINITIVES.	— To row.	To have rowed.	
PARTICIPLES.	— Rowing.	*Rowed.	Having rowed.

Synopsis of the verb *row,* with *thou.*

INDICATIVE MOOD.

Present Tense, Thou rowest, or dost row.
Present-Perfect Tense, Thou hast rowed.
Past Tense, Thou rowedst, or didst row.
Past-Perfect Tense, Thou hadst rowed.
Future Tense, Thou shalt or wilt row.
Future-Perfect Tense, Thou shalt or wilt have rowed.

SUBJUNCTIVE MOOD.

Present Tense, If thou row, or do row.
Past Tense, If thou rowed, didst row, or did row.
Past-Perfect Tense, If thou hadst rowed.

* The simple perfect participle of a transitive verb, in the active voice, is used only in combination with the auxiliary verb *have.*

POTENTIAL MOOD.

Present Tense, Thou mayst, canst, or must row.
Present-Perfect Tense, Thou mayst, canst, or must have rowed.
Past Tense, Thou mightst, couldst, wouldst, or shouldst row.
Past-Perfect Tense, Thou mightst, couldst, wouldst, or shouldst have rowed.

IMPERATIVE MOOD.

Present Tense, Row thou; or, Do thou row.

The Passive Form and the Progressive Form of the Verb Row.

The passive or the progressive form of any tense consists of the corresponding tense of the verb *be*, combined with the simple perfect or present participle.

INDICATIVE MOOD.

Present Tense.

SINGULAR.

Person	Neuter.	Passive.	Progressive.
	1. I am	*rowed,*	*rowing,*
	2. You are	*rowed,*	*rowing,*
	3. He is	*rowed;*	*rowing;*

PLURAL.

1. We are	*rowed,*	*rowing,*
2. You are	*rowed,*	*rowing,*
3. They are	*rowed.*	*rowing.*

The pupil should first conjugate through each three persons the verb *be*, then the passive verb, then the verb in the progressive form.

Present-Perfect Tense.

SINGULAR.

1. I have been	*rowed,*	*rowing,*
2. You have been	*rowed,*	*rowing,*
3. He has been	*rowed;*	*rowing;*

PLURAL.

1. We have been	*rowed,*	*rowing,*
2. You have been	*rowed,*	*rowing,*
3. They have been	*rowed.*	*rowing.*

Past Tense.

SINGULAR.

1. I was	*rowed,*	*rowing,*
2. You was	*rowed,*	*rowing,*
3. He was	*rowed;*	*rowing;*

PLURAL.

1. We were	*rowed,*	*rowing,*
2. You were	*rowed,*	*rowing,*
3. They were	*rowed.*	*rowing.*

Past-Perfect Tense.

SINGULAR.

1. I had been	*rowed,*	*rowing,*
2. You had been	*rowed,*	*rowing,*
3. He had been	*rowed;*	*rowing;*

PLURAL.

1. We had been	*rowed,*	*rowing,*
2. You had been	*rowed,*	*rowing,*
3. They had been	*rowed.*	*rowing.*

Future Tense.

Simple futurity; foretelling.

SINGULAR.

1. I shall be	*rowed,*	*rowing,*
2. You will be	*rowed,*	*rowing,*
3. He will be	*rowed;*	*rowing;*

PLURAL.

1. He shall be *rowed*, *rowing*,
2. You will be *rowed*, *rowing*,
3. They will be *rowed*. *rowing*.

Promise, threat, or determination.

SINGULAR.

1. I will be *rowed*, *rowing*,
2. You shall be *rowed*, *rowing*,
3. They shall be *rowed*; *rowing*;

PLURAL.

1. We will be *rowed*, *rowing*,
2. You shall be *rowed*, *rowing*,
3. They shall be *rowed*. *rowing*.

Future-Perfect Tense.

Simple futurity ; foretelling.

SINGULAR.

1. I shall have been *rowed*, *rowing*,
2. You will have been *rowed*, *rowing*,
3. He will have been *rowed* ; *rowing*;

PLURAL.

1. We shall have been *rowed*, *rowing*,
2. You will have been *rowed*, *rowing*,
3. They will have been *rowed*. *rowing*.

SUBJUNCTIVE MOOD.

Present Tense.

SINGULAR.

1. If I be *rowed*, *rowing*,
2. If you be *rowed*, *rowing*,
3. If he be *rowed*; *rowing*;

PLURAL.

1. If we be *rowed*, *rowing*,
2. If you be *rowed*, *rowing*,
3. If they be *rowed*. *rowing*.

Past Tense.

SINGULAR.

1. If I were *rowed*, *rowing*,
2. If you were *rowed*, *rowing*,
3. If he were *rowed*; *rowing*;

PLURAL.

1. If we were *rowed*, *rowing*,
2. If you were *rowed*, *rowing*,
3. If they were *rowed*. *rowing*.

Or thus : —

SINGULAR.

1. Were I *rowed*, *rowing*,
2. Were you *rowed*, *rowing*,
3. Were he *rowed*; *rowing*;

PLURAL.

1. Were we *rowed*, *rowing*,
2. Were you *rowed*, *rowing*,
3. Were they *rowed*. *rowing*.

Past-Perfect Tense.

SINGULAR.

1. If I had been *rowed*, *rowing*,
2. If you had been *rowed*, *rowing*,
3. If he had been *rowed*; *rowing*;

PLURAL.

1. If we had been *rowed*, *rowing*,
2. If you had been *rowed*, *rowing*,
3. If they had been *rowed*. *rowing*.

Or thus : —

SINGULAR.

1. Had I been *rowed*, *rowing*,
2. Had you been *rowed*, *rowing*,
3. Had he been *rowed*; *rowing*;

PLURAL.

1. Had we been *rowed*, *rowing*,
2. Had you been *rowed*, *rowing*,
3. Had they been *rowed*. *rowing*.

POTENTIAL MOOD.

Present Tense.

SINGULAR.

1. I may be *rowed*, *rowing*
2. You may be *rowed*, *rowing*,
3. He may be *rowed*; *rowing*;

PLURAL.

1. We may be *rowed, rowing,*
2. You may be *rowed, rowing,*
3. They may be *rowed. rowing.*

In like manner conjugate ***can be*** and ***must be.***

Present-Perfect Tense.

SINGULAR.

1. I may have been *rowed, rowing,*
2. You may have been *rowed, rowing,*
3. He may have been *rowed; rowing;*

PLURAL.

1. We may have been *rowed, rowing,*
2. You may have been *rowed, rowing,*
3. They may have been *rowed. rowing.*

In like manner conjugate ***must have been.***

Past Tense.

SINGULAR.

1. I might be *rowed, rowing,*
2. You might be *rowed, rowing,*
3. He might be *rowed; rowing;*

PLURAL.

1. We might be *rowed, rowing,*
2. You might be *rowed, rowing,*
3. They might be *rowed. rowing.*

In like manner conjugate ***could be, would be,*** and ***should be.***

Past-Perfect Tense.

SINGULAR.

1. I might have been *rowed, rowing,*
2. You might have been *rowed, rowing,*
3. He might have been *rowed; rowing;*

PLURAL.

1. We might have been *rowed, rowing,*
2. You might have been *rowed, rowing,*
3. They might have been *rowed. rowing.*

In like manner conjugate ***could have been, would have been,*** and ***should have been.***

IMPERATIVE MOOD.

Present Tense.

SINGULAR.

2. Be thou *rowed; rowing,*

PLURAL.

2. Be ye *rowed. rowing.*

INFINITIVES.

Present. To be *rowed. rowing.*
Perfect. To have been *rowed. rowing.*

PARTICIPLES.

Present. Being *rowed.*
Perfect. Rowed.
Compound. Having been *rowed, rowing.*

The synopsis with *thou* is similar to the synopsis given on p. 163.

When neither of the foregoing forms of the verb can express the *progressive* passive sense, the compound present passive participle is sometimes joined to the verb *be* in stead of the simple perfect or present participle ; in other words, *being* is put into the common passive verb, between the auxiliary and the participle. These clumsy forms, however, are usually tolerated only in the present and the past indicative and the past subjunctive. — See p. 307.

	SINGULAR.	PLURAL.
Present Indicative.	1. I am being educated, 2. You are being educated, 3. He is being educated;	1. We are being educated, 2. You are being educated, 3. They are being educated.
Past Indicative.	1. I was being educated, 2. You were being educated, 3. He was being educated;	1. We were being educated, 2. You were being educated, 3. They were being educated.
Past Subjunctive.	1. If I were being educated, 2. If you were being educated, 3. If he were being educated;	1. If we were being educated, 2. If you were being educated, 3. If they were being educated.

Exercises.

How many and what tenses has the *indicative* mood? — the *subjunctive?* — the *potential?* — the *imperative?* What *infinitives* are there? — what *participles?*

In what mood and tense do you find *do?* — *did?* — *have?* — *had?* — *shall* or *will?* — *shall* or *will have?* — *may, can,* or *must?* — *may, can,* or *must have?* — *might, could, would,* or *should?* — *might, could, would,* or *should have?*

What is the sign of the present indicative? — the past? — the future? — the present-perfect? — the past-perfect? — the future? — the future-perfect? — the present subjunctive? — the past? — the past-perfect? — the present potential? — the present-perfect? — the past? — the past-perfect?

Change the following verbs into the other tenses of the same mood: — I write. I may write. If I write. If I be writing.

Change into the other forms of the same tense: — He strikes. He struck. He has struck. You rule. You ruled. You have ruled.

Give, in the order of the Conjugation, the infinitives, then the participles; first in the active voice, and then in the passive, if the verb can have the passive voice: — Move, rise, spring, degrade, drown, invigorate, overwhelm, bleed.

Give the synopsis of the verb *be* with *I*, through each tense of all the moods; first affirmatively throughout, then interrogatively, then negatively; — with *thou;* — with *he;* — with *they;* — with *you.* Now of *I* and *he* together, or in pairs, through all the tenses; — of *he* and *they;* — of *you* and *thou.*

Give in like manner the synopsis of *see,* through both voices; of *love, bind, carry,* and *permit;* — of *rise,* in the progressive form.

Give *thou* with each auxiliary except *be;* — give *he;* — give *they.*

How do the indicative and the subjunctive mood agree and differ in form?

Conjugate each of the following verbs, beginning with the first person singular, and stopping with the subject: — The boy learns. (Thus: SINGULAR, 1st person, *I learn;* 2d person, *You learn;* 3d person, *He,* or *the boy, learns.*) The leaves are falling. Flowers must fade. Jane reads. Jane and Eliza read. Jane or Eliza reads.

Tell of what mood and tense, then conjugate throughout the tense, beginning with the first person singular: — I imagine. He suffered. We have lost it. I had been ploughing. I will visit. Were I. Had I been. If he were. Were I invited. Had I been invited. If I be invited. They shall have written. I lay. We read. It may pass. You should have come. We may have been robbed. I was speaking. It is rising. You might be preparing. Had you been studying. Do you hope? Did she smile? If I do fail. If thou rely. Thou art. Art thou? He forgiveth. Dost thou not forgive? It must have happened. They are gone. Thou art going.

Predicate each of the following verbs correctly of *thou;* then of *he,* and of *they:* — Am, was, have been, would have been, are deceived, had been, do say, did maintain, gave, touched, cast, amass, recommend, be discouraged, shall have been, will pardon, may have been rejoicing, was elected, should have been elected.

The verbs, and why: —
Regular or irregular, and why: —
Transitive or intransitive, and why; with voice, and why: —
Mood and tense, and why; with emphatic or progressive form, and why: —
Person and number, and why: —

He is reading the Bible. We have slept. She died. Were we surpassed. You had sent him. Take care, lest you lose it. My time might have been improved better. The corn was ripening. The wind has risen.

For additional exercises, if needed, use the examples on p. 104. The best mode of drilling pupils on verbs is simply this: Whenever the pupil parses a verb, let him give the synopsis of it through all the preceding moods, or only through the mood in which it is, to the tense in which it is found; then let him conjugate it to the person and number of its subject. By this process he will soon become master of all parts of the verb.

ADVERBS.

520. An **Adverb** is a word used to modify the meaning, —

1. Of a *verb*. "She sings *well*." Sings *how?*
2. Of an *adjective*. "*Very* deep." How deep?
3. Of another *adverb*. "To run *very* fast." How fast?
4. Of a *phrase*. "He sailed *nearly* | *round the world*."
5. Of a *clause*. "*Even* | *as a miser counts his gold,*
   Those hours the ancient time-piece told."

Even emphasizes the adverbial clause after it; and this clause modifies ***told***.

A phrase or a clause sometimes has the meaning of an adjective or an adverb; and therefore an adverb can modify such a phrase or clause.

521. Words from other parts of speech, especially when imitative, are sometimes used as adverbs.

"*Smack* went the whip, *round* went the wheels." — *Cowper*.

522. Some idiomatic phrases are commonly used as adverbs, and are therefore called *adverbial phrases*.

In general = generally.	In vain,	as yet,
By and by = soon.	at least,	in short,
At present = now.	at last,	out and out.

Most adverbial phrases are adjuncts from which the noun has been dropped.

523. Most adverbs modify other words by expressing *manner*, *place*, *time*, or *degree*.

Frequently, an adverb denotes manner when it modifies a verb, and degree when it modifies an adjective or an adverb.

"He thinks *so*"; *manner*. "He writes *so* awkwardly"; *degree*.
"*How* did you do it?" *manner*. "I know *how* deep it is"; *degree*.

524. A **Conjunctive Adverb** is an adverb that usually connects two clauses, by relating to a word in one and forming a part of the other.

When,	while,	as,	before,	till,	ere,
where,	why,	how,	after,	since,	whereby, etc.

"The seed grew up *where* it fell."

Where relates to *grew* and *fell*, or it joins to the word *grew* a clause denoting place. "The seed grew up *from the place* | *on which* it fell." *Where* is thus resolved into two phrases, which attach themselves respectively to each of the clauses, and the latter of which has a relative pronoun.

Sometimes a conjunctive adverb joins a phrase to some word or clause, in stead of uniting two clauses.

525. The clause which has the conjunctive adverb, is used in the sense of an adverb, an adjective, or a noun.

"You speak of it *as you understand it*." How?
"In the grave *where our hero was buried*." What grave?
"I saw *how a pin is made*." I saw what?

A conjunctive adverb shows merely whether its clause expresses *manner*, *time*, *place*, or *identity*; and it is sometimes essentially a preposition or a conjunction.

526. Sometimes the antecedent or correlative adverb is expressed, and then the latter adverb modifies its own clause, or annexes an *identifying* explanation.

Ex.—"I was *there* | *where* it happened." *Where it happened*, is explanatory of *there*, somewhat like an appositive. So, "*Now*, *while it is cool*, let us work." "*As the mother is*, *so* will the daughter be."

527. Some adverbs of addition, exclusion, emphasis, or quantity, may relate to any part of a sentence.

Ex.—"But *chiefly Thou*, O Spirit, ... instruct me."—*Milton*.
"Take, O boatman, *thrice* thy *fee*."
"Can *not you* go?" "Can you *not go?*" are different.

Such a word is sometimes best parsed as an adjective, and sometimes as a conjunction, or as a correlative or auxiliary conjunction.

528. Some adverbs are the equivalents of independent propositions, and some appear as remnants and representatives of such propositions. Such adverbs are said to be used *independently*.

Ex.—Yes, no, amen, well, why, secondly, nay, thus.

"*Yes;* there is a remedy." "*So, so;* and this is the way," etc.

"*Well*, I hardly know what to say." "*Why*, you must be crazy."

"*Thus*, in France common carriers are not liable for robbery."

Such an adverb may sometimes be parsed as modifying the entire sentence or the preceding sentence or discourse, or else something understood; and sometimes perhaps better as a conjunction or an interjection, for most such adverbs have more or less the nature of conjunctions or interjections.

529. Adverbs are short equivalents for phrases or propositions.

Now = at this time.	Thus = in this manner.
There = in that place.	In vain = in a vain manner.
Where = in what place.	Occasionally = as occasion requires.

A conjunctive adverb generally supplies the place of *two* phrases; as, "She was buried *when* [*at the time* | *in which time*] the sun was setting."

530. Many adverbs are compound words.

Ex.—Indeed, forever, hereafter, whithersoever, afoot.

531. Most adverbs are formed from adjectives, by annexing *ly*, sometimes *s*, to the adjective.

Ex.—Brave, *bravely;* easy, *easily;* upward, *upwards.*

Many of the most common modifying words can be used in the same form either as adjectives or as adverbs.

Ex.—No, well, better, best, very, more, most, hard, long, like, less, least, worse, worst, ill, yonder, fast, late, early.

"He is *no* fool"; *adjective.* "He is *no* better"; *adverb.*

"Few men, *like* him, fight"; *adj.* "Few men fight *like* him"; *adv.*

532. In poetry and in compound words, the adjective form or comparison is allowed to a greater extent than elsewhere.

"The swallow sings *sweet* from her nest in the wall."—*Dimond.*

Here *sweet* is an adverb, used by poetic license for the adverb *sweetly*.

"Drink *deep*, or taste not the Pierian spring." — *Pope.*

Here *deep* is an adverb, used, by ellipsis, for the objective phrase *deep draughts.*

"Though thou wert *firmlier* fastened than a rock." — *Milton.*

"By the verdurous banks of a *smooth*-gliding stream." — *Moore.*

It is sometimes difficult to tell whether a given word is or should be an adjective or an adverb.

533. To express manner or describe the act, the adverb should be used; to describe the object, the adjective.

"Things look [are] *favorable* this morning"; *adj.*

"He looks *skillfully* at the moon, through his telescope." How?

"We arrived *safe*"; *i. e.*, we were *safe* when we arrived.

W. She looks beautifully in her new silk dress.

534. When the verb *be* or *become* can be joined to the verb, or put in its place, the modifying word is or should be an *adjective.*

"The waves dashed *high*"; *i. e.*, they *were high*, and *dashed.*

"*Soft* blows the breeze"; *i. e.*, it *is soft*, and *blows.*

"He spoke *better*"; *adv.* "He seemed *better*, felt *better*"; *adj.*

535. A word may remain an adjective, and qualify a substantive, when the adjoining verb shows merely how the quality is acquired or made known.

"The clay burns *white.*" "The milk tastes *sour.*"

"The glass was colored *blue.*" "Magnesia feels *smooth.*"

"Amid her smiles her blushes *lovelier* glow."

"How much *nearer* he approaches to this end!"

The verbs *look*, *appear*, *taste*, *feel*, *smell*, *make*, and other verbs that imply transformation of the subject, are most commonly associated with such adjectives.

In the sentence, "*Previous to* the next draft, an enrollment of all the men will be made," — NEWSPAPER, — *previous* relates to the entire following proposition; or, rather, *previous to* has fallen into the analogy of the prepositions *according to* and *contrary to.* — See p. 300.

536. Sometimes an adverb becomes a noun.

Ex. — "For *once.*" "By *far* the best." "We have *enough.*"

Much, *little*, and *enough*, are generally nouns after transitive verbs; adverbs, after intransitive.

COMPARISON OF ADVERBS.

537. Adverbs are compared like adjectives; except that a smaller number can be compared, and that these are more commonly compared by *more* and *most*.

Regular.

Soon,	*sooner,*	*soonest.*	Wisely,	*more wisely,*	*most wisely.*
Long,	*longer,*	*longest.*	Wisely,	*less wisely,*	*least wisely.*
Early,	*earlier,*	*earliest.*	Foolishly,	*more foolishly,*	*most foolishly.*

Irregular.

Well,	*better, best.*	Little,	*less, least.*
Badly or ill,	*worse, worst.*	Forth,	*further, furthest.*
Much,	*more, most.*	Far,	*farther, farthest.*

Compare the foregoing adverbs with the adjectives on p. 113.

CLASSES OF ADVERBS.

1. Adverbs of Manner.

So,	well,	otherwise,	separately,	aloud,	in vain,
as,	ill,	headlong,	together,	apart,	in brief,
thus,	like,	fast,	somehow,	asunder,	happily,
how,	else,	slowly,	however,	amiss,	trippingly.

Most words that end with *ly*, are adverbs of manner.

Adverbs of manner answer to the question *How?*

2. Adverbs of Place.

Here,	thence,	whither,	nowhere,	away,	in, out,
there,	whence,	herein,	everywhere,	aside,	back,
where,	hither,	therein,	yonder,	aloof,	forth,
hence,	thither,	wherein,	far, off,	up, down,	forwards.

Adverbs of place answer to the question *Where? Whence?* or *Whither?* and hence imply position or direction.

3. Adverbs of Time.

Now,	always,	after,	sometimes,	to-morrow,	since,
when,	already,	lately,	seldom,	yesterday,	till,
then,	as,	early,	daily,	immediately,	yet,
ever,	while,	again,	forever,	hitherto,	just,
never,	before,	often,	to-day,	hereafter,	anon.

Adverbs of time answer to the question *When? How long? How often? How soon?* or *How long ago?* and hence they denote present time, future time, relative time, duration, or repetition.

Adverbs of Number. — Once, twice, thrice. These denote time.

Adverbs of Order. — First, secondly, thirdly, etc. These denote either place or time.

4. Adverbs of Degree, Extent, or Quantity.

Much,	less,	so,	wholly,	even,	chiefly,
more,	least,	just,	partly,	how,	nearly,
most,	very,	fully,	all,	however,	well-nigh,
mostly,	too,	full,	quite,	enough,	ever so,
little,	as,	generally,	scarcely,	nevertheless,	somewhat.

Adverbs of this class answer to the question, *In what degree? To what extent?* or *How much?*

Adverbs from other classes can be frequently used as adverbs of degree.

The following adverbs of the foregoing class are worthy of separate notice.

Adverbs of Addition, Exclusion, or Emphasis. — Too, only, merely, but, especially, also, besides, else, still, likewise, even, not, particularly, moreover, withal, eke.

5. Modal Adverbs.

These show how the statement is made or regarded.

Of Affirmation or Approval. — Yes, yea, ay, verily, surely, certainly, forsooth, indeed, truly, really, amen, of course, to be sure.

Of Negation. — Not, nay, no, nowise, by no means.

Of Doubt. — Perhaps, probably, perchance, may-be, haply.

Of Cause or Means. — Why, therefore, wherefore, hereby, thereby, whereby, wherewith, whereof, accordingly, consequently, hence, thence, whence, etc. Some of these adverbs, as *whereby*, consist of a *pronominal adverb* and a *preposition*, and may therefore be called *adjunctive adverbs*.

Of Position. — There. "*There* was no one there."

There, as used in such sentences, is a word that has withdrawn from the common vocabulary of significant words, and become simply a word of *syntax*; having been appropriated by Language as something necessary "to run the machinery." *There*, thus used, simply serves to give the sentence another form, by allowing the words to assume a more emphatic arrangement. A similar remark is applicable to *it*, and some other words.

Exercises.

Mention six adverbs of manner; — six of place; — six of time;— six of degree; — five different modal adverbs; — six conjunctive adverbs.

Compare late, soon, early, much, little, well, ill, long, far, heroically.

An adverb, and why; of what kind, and what it modifies: —

Wisely, now, here, very. The horse runs swiftly. God is everywhere. Never before did I see her look so pale. These things have always been so. I have been too idle heretofore; but henceforth I will study more diligently. Your book is more beautiful. He was lately here. The hall was brilliantly illuminated, and densely crowded with hearers.

PREPOSITIONS.

538. A **Preposition** is a word used to show the relation between a following noun or pronoun and some other word.

"The rabbit *in* the hollow tree was caught." What in what?

The substantive after the preposition must be in the *objective case.*

539. Two prepositions are sometimes combined, and used as one; and some phrases are generally used as prepositions.

Ex. — Upon, according to, as to, as for.

"The river flowed *from under* the palaces."

Such phrases are sometimes called *complex* or *compound prepositions.*

540. An **Adjunct**, or *Prepositional Phrase*, is a preposition with its object, or with the words required after it to complete the sense.

Ex. — "The wind swept *in waves* | *over the bristling barley.*"

An adjunct generally shows *where*, *when*, *how*, *how long*, *of what kind*, *by whom*, *by what means*, etc.

Ex. — "A fox | *of the largest size* | was caught { *under the bluff*, *before sunrise*, *by our dogs.*"

541. Some adjuncts may be inverted or parted, especially in poetry.

Ex. — "*Whom* was it given *to?*" better, "*To whom* was it given?"

"From peak to peak, *the rattling crags among.*" — *Byron.*

That is, "From peak to peak, *among the rattling crags.*"

542. An adjunct may relate to, —

1. A substantive.

Ex. — "The *caves* | *of Kentucky* are wonderful." What caves?

2. A verb.

Ex. — "The river *rises* | *in the mountains.*" Rises where?

3. An adjective.

Ex. — "The river is *clear* | *in the mountains.*" Clear where?

4. An adverb.

Ex. — "You have acted *inconsistently* | *with your professions.*"

But when the adverb relates to the adjunct, then the adjunct relates to some other word; as, "You were far before us." *Before us* relates to *were*, and *far* modifies *before us*.

Sometimes an adjunct relates to a phrase; as, "You study grammar for your improvement in language." Here *for* relates rather to *study grammar* than to *study* only.

543. The substantive which follows the preposition, or is governed by it, may be, —

1. A noun.

Ex. — "The fox ran under the *bluff*." Under **what?**

2. A pronoun.

Ex. — "Come to *me*." To whom?

3. An infinitive.

Ex. — "None knew thee but *to love* thee." Except what?

4. A participial noun.

Ex. — "*In* the *selling* of their estate, a mistake was made."

5. A participle that has case, yet retains the syntax of the verb.

Ex. — "*By* carefully *removing* the difficulties, you may succeed."

6. A clause.

Ex. — "This will depend ON *who the commissioners are*."

"Reason and justice have been jurymen ever *since* | *before Noah was a sailor*." — *Shakespeare*.

544. Two or more prepositions may govern the same substantive.

Ex. — "He walked *up* and *down* the *hill*."

545. Two or more substantives may be governed by the same preposition.

Ex. — "A battle *between Mexicans* and *Indians*."

"He left his estate TO his *wife*, *children*, and *friends*."

Two or more adjuncts may be combined. "*The gold in a piece of quartz*."

The modified term, which commonly precedes the adjunct, is called the *antecedent term;* and the governed substantive the *subsequent term*.

546. Frequently, the adjunct precedes the word to which it relates, or is considerably removed from it.

"*On the next day*, while we retreated, the enemy *approached*."

547. An adjunct is generally equivalent to an adverb or an adjective.

Ex. — "He acted *with wisdom*" = He acted *wisely*.
"A man *of wisdom*" = A *wise* man.
"He is *in misery*" = He is *miserable*.

Adjuncts can supply the place of the possessive case; as, "*Absalom's* beauty" = The beauty *of Absalom*. (See p. 97.) Sometimes an adjunct is equivalent to a participle or a verb; as, "He is *in trouble*" = He *is troubled*. Finally, adjuncts supply the deficiency of all other descriptive expressions, and often relieve them.

548. A preposition that has no word to govern, becomes an adverb; sometimes, a noun or an adjective.

Ex. — "The eagle flew *up*, then *round*, then *down* again."
"It fell *from above*." "It came *from within*."

Above is a noun, or *from above* can be parsed as an adverbial phrase.

"The forest overlooked the shaded plain *below*." — *Dryden*.

Below is equivalent to the adjective adjunct *below it*, or the adjective clause *which was below*; and it is therefore a *definitive* adjective. *Below* is a preposition or an adverb in regard to the omitted words; and it becomes an adjective only as having assumed the office of an adjective phrase or clause, which it represents.

549. Sometimes the object is merely omitted.

"The man you spoke *of*; *i. e.*, *of whom* you spoke."
"I have nothing to tie it *with*; *i. e.*, *with which* to tie it."

550. The antecedent term is sometimes omitted, or there is none.

"Industrious all, from the youngest to the oldest"; *reckoning* from, etc.

"Sold at the rate *of from* fifty cents to a dollar;" *i. e.*, of *prices varying* from, etc. It seems to us that it would not be improper to parse the whole phrase after *of* as a noun.

"*As to* riches, they are not worth so much care."

551. The preposition itself is sometimes omitted; especially *to*, *unto*, or *for*, after *like*, *unlike*, *near*, *nigh*, *worth*, *opposite*, and verbs of giving or imparting.

Ex. — "The house was near [*to*] the river, nearer [*to*] the river, next to ours." "The son is like [*to* or *unto*] his father." "Opposite [*to*] the market." "Lend him your knife" = Lend your knife *to* him. "Give [*to*] us our daily bread." "Who departed [*from*] this life," etc.

The adjective or adverb has essentially absorbed the preposition; and it might therefore be called a *prepositional adjective* or *adverb*, governing the object.

552. Prepositions are much used as parts of compound words; and when thus used, they are generally adverbial.

Ex.—*Over*shoot, *under*mine, *up*hold, *in*come, *after*thought.

LIST OF PREPOSITIONS.

Learn the List, and tell between what words each preposition shows the relation.

A. "We went *a* fishing." "This set people *a* thinking."—*Swift.*
Aboard. "To go or be *aboard* a ship."
About. "To run *about* the house." "To dine *about* noon."
Above. "The stars *above* us." "To be *above* meanness."
Across. "A tree lying *across* the road."
After. "To start *after* dinner."
Against. "We rowed *against* the stream."
Along. "The cloud is gilded *along* the border."
Amid, amidst. "The rogues escaped *amidst* the confusion."
Among, amongst. "Flowers perish *among* weeds."
Around, round. "The ring *around* his finger." "To sail *round* the world."
At. "She lives *at* home." "The sun sets *at* six o'clock."
Athwart. "Why advance thy miscreated front *athwart* my way?"
Before. "The tree *before* the house." "To rise *before* day."
Behind. "The squirrel hid *behind* the tree."
Below. "The James River is very crooked *below* Richmond."
Beneath. "The chasm *beneath* us." "He is *beneath* contempt."
Beside, besides. "A large sycamore grew *beside* the river."
Between. "The river flows *between* two hills."
Betwixt. "He was crushed to death *betwixt* two cars."
Beyond. "The life *beyond* the grave is a mystery."
But. "Whence all *but* him had fled."
By. "A lily *by* a brook." "Demolished *by* soldiers."
Concerning. "He spoke *concerning* virtue."
Down. "The boat went *down* the river."
During. "He remained abroad *during* the war."
Ere. "He came *ere* noon."
Except, excepting. "All *except* him were set free."
For. "To sell *for* money." "A collection *for* the poor.
From. "A branch *from* the tree." "To judge *from* the description."
In. "A pond *in* a meadow." "To play *in* the afternoon."
Into. "To step *into* a carriage, and then ride *in* it."
Notwithstanding. "He succeeded, *notwithstanding* the opposition."
Of. "The house *of* a friend." "To die *of* a disease."

Off. "Juan Fernandez lies *off* the coast of Chili."
On. "The picture *on* the wall." "To start *on* Tuesday."
Over. "The bridge *over* the river." "To rule *over* a nation."
Past. "They drove *past* the house."
Respecting. "*Respecting* his conduct, there is but one opinion."
Save. "All *save* him remained."
Since. "He has not been here *since* last Christmas."
Till, until. "He will remain here *till* next Christmas."
To, unto. "To go *to* the river." "Verily, I say *unto* you."
Toward, towards. "He came *towards* me."
Through. "To travel *through* woods and swamps."
Throughout. "There was commotion *throughout* the whole land."
Under. "The earth *under* our feet." "To be *under* age."
Underneath. "*Underneath* this sable hearse lies the subject of all verse."
Up. "He climbed *up* the tree."
Upon. "The people stood *upon* the house-tops."
With. "Girls *with* sparkling eyes." "Enameled *with* flowers."
Within. "The war will end *within* the next six months."
Without. "A purse *without* money." "To live *without* company."
According to. "It was done *according to* law."
Contrary to. "He has acted *contrary to* orders."
As to. "*As to* your case, nothing was said."
From beyond. "They came *from beyond* Jordan."
From out. "*From out* thy slime the monsters of the deep are made."
In stead of. "This *in stead of* that." Better, *in stead of*, as "*in place of*," "*in lieu of*," "*in my stead*," "*but this in stead*." *Stead* is a noun.
Out of. "Drawn *out of* a well." "A piano *out of* tune."

To the foregoing prepositions may be added the following, which are less common: *Abaft, adown, afore, aloft, alongside, aloof, aneath, aslant, atween, atwixt, bating, despite, despite of, inside, maugre, minus, outside, pending, per, plus, sans, saving, than, thorough, touching, versus, via, withal, withinside; aboard of, as for, along with, from among, from before, from betwixt, from off, from under, off of, over against, round about, but for.*

CONJUNCTIONS.

553. A **Conjunction** is a word used to connect words, phrases, or propositions.

Ex.—"The mossy fountains *and* the sylvan shades."—*Pope.*
"John *and* James are happy, *because* they are good."

554. Conjunctions not only connect parts of a sentence, but they also show how the connected parts are related or regarded.

"Dear, *because* worthless." "Read *and* write"; "Read *or* write."

555. Two conjunctions are sometimes combined, and used as one; and sometimes a common phrase is used as a conjunction.

"*And yet* I would not get riches thus, *even if* I were a beggar."

"John, *as well as* Arthur, must be punished, *inasmuch as* they have both been disobedient."

Such phrases are sometimes called *complex* or *compound conjunctions.*

Sometimes an adverb is added to a conjunction simply to strengthen or vary the connecting sense, and the two words may then be called a *conjunctive phrase*, or simply a *conjunction;* but such adverbs as *even*, *too*, and *also*, should probably rather be referred to our Note VII, under the Rules of Syntax.

556. A **Corresponding Conjunction,** or *Correlative Connective,* is one of a separated pair that connect the same parts.

Ex. — "*Neither* flattery *nor* threats could prevail."

Neither is a corresponding conjunction answering or relating to *nor*, and helping it to connect the words *flattery* and *threats*. The two connectives give greater completeness to the connection, by *enfolding* the terms; while one connective would appear as a *mere tie*. It is sometimes probably best to say that the subordinate connective is an *auxiliary* connective that helps the other to unite two words, phrases, or clauses, by giving emphasis or greater completeness to the connection.

Sometimes the connectives, as *so* and *as*, or *rather* and *than*, stand next to each other; but they still belong to different clauses or phrases.

557. *And*, *or*, and *nor*, are the chief conjunctions; and they are mostly used for connecting words or phrases.

Ex. — "Bees *and* blossoms." "Bees *or* blossoms." "Neither bees *nor* blossoms."

558. *But*, *if*, and *that*, are the next most important conjunctions; and they are mostly used for connecting clauses.

Ex. — "She tries a thousand arts, *but* none succeed." — *Young.*

In language, the simple succession of parts implies connection. Hence,—

559. For the sake of brevity, conjunctions are sometimes omitted.

"'Twas certain [*that*] he could write, and cipher too."

"Had I been at home, you should have staid;" *i. e.*, *If* I, etc.

"The way was long, [*and*] the wind was cold."

When *and*, *or*, or *nor*, is used before the last term of a series, it probably shows simply that the end is reached; and it is therefore hardly proper to consider it as being understood before each preceding term.

560. A conjunction is sometimes used where it is not absolutely needed.

1. At the beginning of a sentence, to make its introduction less abrupt.

"*And* tell me, I charge you, ye clan of my spouse,
Why fold ye your mantles, why cloud ye your brows?"

2. In the body of a sentence, when the speaker means to dwell on particulars, in order that the hearer may duly appreciate what he says.

Ex. — "Italy teems with recollections of every kind; for courage, *and* wisdom, *and* power, *and* arts, *and* science, *and* beauty, *and* music, *and* desolation, have all made it their dwelling-place."

561. When a conjunction connects words or phrases, they are nearly always in the same construction.

Ex. — "Mary, Jane, and Alice, | *went* into the garden, and *brought* some *large*, *ripe*, and *juicy* peaches."

Here the connected nouns are nominatives to the same verbs, the connected verbs or predicates have the same subject; and the connected adjectives qualify the same noun.

562. Most conjunctions are emigrants from other parts of speech.

Ex. — Both, either, that, *adj.*; then, yet, as, *adv.*; except, provided, if (probably from *give*), *verbs.*

LIST OF CONJUNCTIONS.

Learn the List, and show what terms are connected by each conjunction.

And; *copulative*; *co-ordinate.* "The winds *and* the waves are absent there."

As; *causal*; *subordinate.* "*As* you request it, I will go."

As; *comparative*; *subordinate*, sometimes *co-ordinate.* "You did as well *as* I."

As, implying comparison, is generally rather a conjunctive adverb than a pure conjunction.

As well as; *copulative; co-ordinate.* "He, *as well as* I, was deceived."
Because; *causal; subordinate.* "Success is difficult, *because* many strive."
But; *adversative; co-ordinate.* "I go, *but* I return."
Except; *restrictive; subordinate.* "He is sane, *except* when he talks of politics."
Except; *conditional; subordinate.* "*Except* a man be born again," etc.
For; *causal; subordinate,* sometimes *co-ordinate.* "Rise, *for* it is day."
Furthermore; *copulative; co-ordinate.* It sometimes begins a paragraph.
If; *conditional; subordinate.* "*If* the advice is good, take it."
Lest; *cautionary* or *causal; subordinate.* "Touch it not, *lest* ye die."
Notwithstanding; *adversative* and *co-ordinate,* or *concessive* and *subordinate.*

Notwithstanding, when used in the sense of "*still, however,*" is co-ordinate; when used in the sense of "*even if,*" subordinate.

Moreover; *copulative; co-ordinate.* It sometimes begins a paragraph.
Nor; *disjunctive; co-ordinate.* "He said nothing more, *nor* did I."
Or; *disjunctive; co-ordinate.* "We must educate, *or* we must perish."
Provided; *conditional; subordinate.* "I will go, *provided* you go."
Since; *causal; subordinate.* "*Since* you have come, I will go."
Still; *adversative; co-ordinate.* "He has often failed, *still* he strives."
Than; *comparative; subordinate.* "Performance is better *than* promising."
That; *final; subordinate.* "He studies, *that* he may," etc. For what *end?*
That; *demonstrative; subordinate.* *That,* in this sense, is a sort of pronoun, with which the rest of the clause is put in apposition; or it forms a kind of handle to the clause, by pointing out a group of words that must be referred as a whole to something else. "*That* | *the war is a calamity,* is admitted." "It is admitted *that* | *the war is a calamity.*" "We all know *that* | *the war is a calamity.*"
Then; *illative; co-ordinate.* "The cotton is yours? *then* defend it."
Though, although, sometimes **what though**; *concessive, subordinate.* "*Though* he owns but little, he owes nothing."
Unless; *conditional; subordinate.* "*Unless* you study, you will not learn."
Unless; *adversative; co-ordinate.* "Remain, *unless* you must go."
Whether; *indeterminate; subordinate.* "I will see *whether* he has come."
Whether, and not *if,* should begin an indeterminate clause used as a noun.
W. Nobody knows if the war will end soon. I will see if he has come.
Whereas; *causal; subordinate.* "*Whereas* it doth appear," etc.
Whereas; *adversative; co-ordinate.* "Reason errs; *whereas* instinct," etc.
Yet; *adversative; co-ordinate.* "All dread death, *yet* few are pious."

The principal co-ordinate conjunctions are *and, or, nor,* and *but.*
The principal subordinate conjunctions are *that, than, as, if,* and *because.*

The left or first column of meanings will serve for *parsing;* and the right or second, for *analysis.* CO-ORDINATE

CONJUNCTIONS *join the parts of* COMPOUND *phrases or sentences;* SUBORDINATE, *of* COMPLEX.

There are some exceptions to what has been said in the List; but these we refer to the judgment of the teacher, for it would be too tedious to mention them.

Correlative Conjunctions or Connectives.

Both — and. "It is *both* mine *and* yours."
Either — or. "It is *either* mine *or* yours."
Neither — nor. "It is *neither* mine *nor* yours."
Whether — or. "I know not *whether* it is mine *or* yours."
Though, although — yet, nevertheless. "*Though* deep, *yet* clear."
If — then. "*If* you have no confidence, *then* do not venture."
As — as; *equality.* "Time is *as* precious *as* gold."
As — so; *equality.* "*As* the one dies, *so* dies the other."
So — as; *consequence.* "It is *so* plain *as* to require no explanation."
So — that; *consequence.* "The road was *so* muddy *that* we returned."
Not only — but also. "He is *not only* bold, *but* he is *also* cautious."
Or — or; sometimes used by poets in stead of *either — or.*
Nor — nor; sometimes used by poets in stead of *neither — nor.*

To these correlative connectives may be added *such* and *as*, *same* and *as*, *such* and *that*, *not* and *nor*, *other* and *than*, *rather* and *than*, *else* and *than*, the comparative degree followed by *than*, *the* and *the* followed each by the comparative degree, and a few similar expressions. Correlative connectives are sometimes not conjunctions. The antecedent correlative is frequently an adverb or an adjective. Such a correlative connective should be first parsed as the part of speech to which it belongs; and then its conjunctive character may be stated, with the Rule for conjunctions.

To the conjunctions already given may be added *as if, even if, even though, except that, provided that, save, saving that, seeing that, inasmuch as, forasmuch as, so that, in order that, so as, on the contrary, on the other hand, the moment that,* etc. Some of these may be more appropriately called *conjunctive phrases.*

Again, also, however, now, nay, even, further, besides, therefore, wherefore, namely, nevertheless, otherwise, likewise, so, thus, else, accordingly, consequently, and a few other such words, though originally adverbs, may be considered conjunctions when they stand near the beginning of a clause or sentence, and serve to introduce it. Most such words have acquired their conjunctive sense by ellipsis.

It is sometimes difficult to determine whether a given word should be considered an adverb, a preposition, or a conjunction. The chief characteristic of adverbs is, *to modify;* of conjunctions, *to connect;* and of prepositions, *to govern substantives in the objective case.* It is generally not so much a matter of importance to know precisely to what class a given word should be referred, as to understand clearly the meaning and force of the word in the sentence.

INTERJECTIONS.

563. An **Interjection** is a word that expresses an emotion, and is not connected in construction with any other word.

Ex. — "'O, stay!' the maiden said, 'and rest.'" — *Longfellow.*

Omit *O*, and the sentence will still make good sense without it.

564. Words from almost every other part of speech, and sometimes entire phrases, when abruptly uttered to express emotion, may become interjections.

Ex. — Strange! behold! what! why! indeed! mercy!
"Why, *there, there, there!*"
"*Fire and brimstone!* what have you been doing?"

But when it is not the chief purpose of such a word to express emotion, and when the omitted words are obvious, the word should be parsed as usual; as, "*Patience*, good lady! *comfort*, gentle Constance!" = *Have patience*, good lady! receive comfort, gentle Constance.

565. Words used in speaking to the inferior animals, and imitative words or syllables that are uttered with emotion, are generally interjections.

Ex. — Haw! gee! whoh! scat! whist! 'st, 'st!
"The words are fine; but as to the sense — *b-a-h!*"
"Up comes a man on a sudden, *slap! dash!*"
"Be sure that you blow out the candle, —
Ri fol de rol tol de rol lol." — *Horace Smith.*

566. A substantive after an interjection is independent, or else its case depends on some word understood.

Ex. — "O *thou!*" "Ah *me!*" = Ah! *pity me;* or, Ah! what has happened *to me!* or, Ah! wo is *to me!* or, Ah! it *grieves me.*

"O, happy *we!*" = O, happy *are we!* Or else apply Rule II.

LIST OF INTERJECTIONS.

1. Of Earnestness in Address. — O!

2. Of Surprise, Wonder, or Horror. — Hah! ha! what! h'm! heigh! indeed! hey-day! la! whew! zounds! eh! ah! oh! hoity-toity!

3. Of Sorrow or Pity. — Oh! alas! ah! alack! welladay!

4. Of Joy, Exultation, or Approbation. — Aha! ah! oh! hey! eh! eigh! huzzah! hurrah! good! bravo!

5. Of Contempt or Aversion. — Pshaw! pish! tut! tush! poh! fie! bah! humph! faugh! whew! off! begone! avaunt!

6. Of Attention or Calling. — Ho! lo! behold! look! see! hark! la! heigh-ho! soho! hollo! halloo! hoy! whoh! 'st!

7. Of Silence. — Hush! hist! whist! 'st! aw! mum!

8. Of Interrogating. — Eh? hem, or h'm? (The opposite of the preceding class.)

9. Of Detection. — Aha! oho! ay-ay!

10. Of Laughter. — Ha, ha, ha! he, he, he!

11. Of Saluting or Parting. — Welcome! hail! all-hail! adieu! good-by! *and perhaps* good-day! good-morning! etc.

Can you mention two interjections of grief? — two of joy? etc.

QUESTIONS FOR REVIEW.

1. What is a **Verb**? . . . ¶ 361
2. Give the Classification of Verbs.
3. What is a *regular verb?* . . . 365
4. What is an *irregular verb?* . 366
5. Which are the *principal parts* of a verb? and why are they called such? 367
6. What is a *redundant verb?* . . 373
7. What is a *defective verb?* . . 374
8. What is a *finite verb?* . . . 375
9. What parts of the verb are not finite? 378
10. What is a *transitive verb?* . . 380
11. What is an *intransitive verb?* . 381
12. What is a neuter verb? . . . 382
13. When may a transitive verb become intransitive? 384
14. When may an intransitive verb become transitive? 385
15. What is a *principal verb?* . . 391
16. What is an *auxiliary verb?* . . 392
17. What properties have verbs? . 393
18. What is **Voice**, in grammar? . 394
19. How many voices are there, and what are they called? . . 395
20. When is a verb in the *active voice?* 396
21. When is a verb in the *passive voice?* 397
22. To what verbs does voice belong? . 398
23. What is said of such verbs as *are come, is gone?* . . . 399
24. How is a verb in the active voice changed into the passive? . . 402
25. What is **Mood**? . . . 405
26. How many moods are there, and what are they called? . . . 406
27. What does a verb in the *indicative mood* express? . . . 407
28. A verb in the *subjunctive mood?* . 410
29. A verb in the *potential mood?* . 417
30. A verb in the *imperative mood?* . 420
31. What is **Tense**? . . . 424
32. How many tenses are there, and what are they called? . . . 425
33. What is said of the *present indicative?* 426
34. Of the present subjunctive? . . 427
35. Of the present potential? . . 428
36. Of the present imperative? . . 429
37. Of the *present-perfect indicative?* 430
38. Of the present-perfect potential? . 432
39. Of the *past indicative?* . . 433
40. Of the past subjunctive? . . 434
41. Of the past potential? . . 435
42. Of the *past-perfect indicative?* . 436
43. Of the past-perfect subjunctive and potential? 437
44. Of the *future tense?* . . . 438
45. Of the *future-perfect tense?* . 439
46. What is said of the tenses of the subjunctive mood? . . . 440
47. Of the tenses of the potential? . 441
48. Of *when, till, as soon as,* etc.? . 442
49. What are the Forms *of a* Tense? 443
50. How many forms are there, and what are they called? . . 444
51. What is said of the *common form?* 445
52. Of the *emphatic form?* . . 446
53. Of the *passive form?* . . . 447
54. Of the *progressive form?* . . 448
55. Of the *ancient form?* . . . 449
56. How is a proposition made interrogative? 450
57. How is it made negative? . . 451

58. What are the **Person** and **Number** of a verb? 452
59. What ending to the verb does *thou* generally require? 455
60. *He*, *she*, or *it*, in the present indicative? 456
61. When a subject or antecedent consists of words that differ in person, how do you determine the *person* of the verb or pronoun? . 458, 459
62. What kinds of subjects or antecedents are *singular* in construction? 460
63. What kinds of subjects or antecedents are *plural* in construction? 461
64. What terms do not affect the form of the verb or pronoun? . . . 462
65. What is an *impersonal verb?* . 465
66. What do the **Auxiliary Verbs** express? 466
67. Which are the auxiliary verbs? 467
68. In what instances is it proper to use *shall* and *should?*
69. In what instances is it proper to use *will* and *would?*
70. In what other ways than that of expressing grammatical properties, are auxiliary verbs useful? . . 468
71. When are *be*, *do*, and *have* principal verbs? 469
72. What is an **Infinitive?** . . 471
73. How many infinitives are there, and what are they called? . 472
74. What is said of the *present infinitive?* 473
75. How is it formed? 474
76. What is said of the *perfect infinitive?* 475
77. How is it formed? 476
78. When is *to*, the sign of the infinitive, omitted? . . . 481, 482
79. What is a **Participle?** . . 483
80. How many participles are there, and what are they called? . 484
81. What is said of the *present participle?* 485
82. How is the simple present participle made? 486
83. What is said of it in regard to voice? 487
84. What is said of the *perfect participle?* 489
85. How is the simple perfect participle made? 490
86. When is it in the *active voice?* 492
87. When is it in the passive voice? . 493
88. What is a *compound participle?* 495
89. For what purpose is the auxiliary participle *being* used? . . 496
90. For what purpose is the auxiliary participle *having* used? . 497
91. For what purpose is the auxiliary participle *having been* used? . 498
92. How many and what infinitives in both voices?
93. How many and what participles in both voices?
94. Mention the chief particulars in which participles and infinitives agree? . . . . . P. 158
95. Mention the chief particulars in which they differ?
96. What is **Conjugation?** . ¶ 515
97. What is *synopsis?* . . . 516
98. What is an **Adverb?** . . . 520
99. What is a *conjunctive adverb?* 524
100. From what are most adverbs formed? 531
101. When should the adverb be used? and when the adjective? . 533
102. How are adverbs compared? . 537
103. Into what classes are adverbs divided?
104. What is a **Preposition?** 538
105. What is an *adjunct?* . . . 540
106. What may the antecedent term be? 541
107. What may the subsequent term be? 543
108. Repeat the list of prepositions.
109. What is a **Conjunction?** . 553
110. What is a *corresponding conjunction?* 556
111. Repeat the list of conjunctions.
112. What is an **Interjection?** . 563
113. Mention some interjections.

Write a sentence that has a proper noun.
Write a sentence that has a common noun.
Write a sentence that has a collective noun.
Write a sentence that has a personal pronoun.
Write a sentence that has a compound personal pronoun.
Write a sentence in which the relative *who* is properly used.
Write a sentence in which the relative *which* is properly used.
Write six sentences to illustrate different constructions of the relative *that.*
Write a sentence that has your name properly used in the possessive case.

(The teacher should extend these exercises so far as to draw out all the important points of the book.)

RULES OF SYNTAX.

567. Syntax comprises *relation* and *position.*

568. The **Relation** of words is their reference to one another according to the sense.

RELATION frequently implies *government* and *agreement.*

Government is the power which one word has over another, in determining its case, person, number, or some other property.

Agreement is the correspondence of one word with another, in case, person, number, or some other property.

569. Position refers to the place which a word occupies in reference to other words of the sentence.

570. A **Rule**, in grammar, is generally a brief statement that teaches the proper form or use of words.

RULE I.—Nominatives.

A **Noun** or **Pronoun**, used as the subject of a finite verb, must be in the nominative case.

John studies. *I* study. *They* study.

EXPLANATION. — Since John does the studying, there is plainly a relation between *John* and *studies*. Observe also that we can not use objective forms, and say, "*Me* study," "*Them* study"; but we must use the nominatives *I* and *they*. Hence the Rule.

W. I have tasted no better apples than *them* are.
Were you and *him* at the party?
Whom, would you suppose, stands head in our class?
He is taller than *me*, but I am as tall as *her*.

RULE II.—Nominatives.

A **Noun** or **Pronoun**, used independently or absolutely, must be in the nominative case.

Mary, your lilies are in bloom.
The *rain* having ceased, we departed.

EXPLANATION. — Mary is simply addressed, and something else is said; or the sentence would make sense without the word *Mary*, which is therefore said to be used *independently* of the rest of the sentence.

The noun *rain* is so used with a participle that it does not relate to any other word; and it is therefore said to be used absolutely, with the participle.

NOMINATIVE INDEPENDENT.

By direct Address: "Auspicious *Hope!* in thy sweet garden grow
Wreaths for each toil, a charm for every woe."
By Exclamation: "*Scotland!* there is magic in the sound."
By Pleonasm or **Specification:** "*He* that hath, to him shall be given."

NOMINATIVE ABSOLUTE.

Before a Participle: "*Peace* being established, commerce revived."
"The *steed* [being] at hand, why longer tarry?"
After a Participle: "Such is the folly of becoming a *politician.*"
After an Infinitive: "To be a good *Christian* was his highest ambition."

W. *Him* who had led them to battle being killed, they retreated.
Whose gray top shall tremble, *Him* descending.
There is no doubt of its being *him.*

RULE III.—Possessives.

A **Noun** or **Pronoun** that limits the meaning of another by denoting possession, must be in the possessive case.

John's horse is in *our* pasture.

EXPLANATION.—Since John owns the horse, there is plainly a relation between *John* and *horse*; and it is also evident that not any horse is meant, but only the one which belongs to John. A similar remark is applicable to *our* and *pasture.*

W. Do you use *Webster* or Worcester's Dictionary?

RULE IV.—Objectives.

A **Noun** or **Pronoun**, used as the object of a transitive verb, must be in the objective case.

I shot a *deer.* We caught *them.*

EXPLANATION.—Since I shot the deer, there is a relation between my shooting and the deer, or between the words *shot* and *deer.* In the second example, there is as plainly a relation between *caught* and *them;* and notice also that the objective form, *them,* and not the nominative form, *they,* will make good sense after *caught.* Hence the Rule.

The foregoing Rule is also applicable to infinitives and participles.

W. *She* that is idle and mischievous, reprove sharply.
Who do you mean? *Who* did you see?
Who should I meet the other day but my old friend!

RULE V.—Objectives.

A **Noun** or **Pronoun**, used as the object of a preposition, must be in the objective case.

The money was sent by *me* to *him*.

EXPLANATION. — Sent *by* some one, sent *to* some one; hence there is evidently a relation between *by* and *me*, and between *to* and *him*. Observe also that the objective forms, *me* and *him*, and not the nominative forms, *I* and *he*, will make good sense after the prepositions. Hence the Rule.

W. Between you and *I* there is little difference of opinion.
I do not know *who* she went with.
I gave it to somebody; I have forgotten *who*.

RULE VI.—Objectives.

A **Noun** or **Pronoun** that limits the meaning of a verb, an adjective, or an adverb, is sometimes used in the objective case without a preposition expressed.

Sometimes a substantive is thus used in the objective case, to limit a *noun*.

This Rule is designed to reach all those objective nouns and pronouns, which, by the idiom of our language, are commonly used to limit other words adverbially, or in the sense of adjuncts, without having a governing word expressed. It is therefore applicable to some nouns that show the *time*, *extent*, *direction*, *manner*, *value*, or *quantity*; to the indirect objects after such verbs as *give*, *lend*, *offer*, *present*, etc.; and to the objects which follow the words *like*, *near*, *worth*, *opposite*, etc. By supplying a preposition, the Rule can be dispensed with. — See § 284 and p. 222.

We sailed *north*, a hundred *miles*, the first *day*.
We sailed *toward* the north, *over* a hundred miles of space, *during* the first day.
It is [by] a *ton* heavier. It happened five *times*. Ice a *foot* thick.
He wears his coat cloak *fashion*. It is worth *nothing*.
Give [to] *me* the reins. Oranges grow, like *apples*, on small trees.

W. My landlady had a daughter *of* nine years old. — *Swift.*
Just beyond the church is a lot *of* sixty feet square.

RULE VII.—Same Case.

A **Noun** or **Pronoun** used for explanation or emphasis, by being predicated of another, or put in apposition with another, must be in the same case.

Jones is a *lawyer*. The lawyer is *Jones*.

It is *Jones* the *lawyer*. He *himself* is *Jones* the *lawyer*.

EXPLANATION. — Since Jones is a lawyer, there must be a relation between the words *Jones* and *lawyer*; and since each word can be used as the nominative to *is*, both must be in the same case.

For an explanation of *predication* and *apposition*, see pp. 99 and 100.

Words in apposition are sometimes connected by *as*, *or*, *and*, or *than*.

W. I knew it was *him*. I knew it to be *he*. Is it *me*?

Remark. — A substantive put in apposition with a clause, phrase, or word that has not case, must be in the nominative case; as, "He resolved to rely on himself, — a *resolution* which he kept."

RULE VIII. — Two Cases.

The pronoun **what**, when it comprises a simple relative and its antecedent, has a double construction in regard to case.

I remember *what* was said.

What is here used as the object of *remember*, and also as the subject of *was said*. Rule VIII is given merely as a convenience; for this Rule can be dispensed with, by applying two other Rules.

W. Give *that* what you can spare, to the poor.

Note I. — A Compound Relative, or a similar expression, may furnish two cases, when its form allows them.

Whoever sins, must suffer. Take *whichever horse* you like.

Whoever is used as the nominative to *sins*, and also as the nominative to *must suffer*.

I will employ *whomsoever* you recommend.

What money he brought with him, was soon spent.

OBSERVATION 1. — When the form of the relative does not allow the two cases required, it must take the form needed for its own clause, and an antecedent must be supplied in parsing.

RULE IX. — Pronouns.

A **Pronoun** must agree with its antecedent, in gender, person, and number.

Mary has lost *her* bonnet.

EXPLANATION. — *Her* must be of the same gender, person, and number as *Mary*; for if it were different in any of these respects, it is evident that it could not denote Mary.

For an explanation of antecedents, see pp. 73 and 143.

W. Each of our party carried a knapsack with *them*.

Not one of the boys should come without *their* books.

You and your playmates must learn *their* lessons.

The earth is my mother; and I will recline upon *its* bosom.

RULE X. — Articles, Adjectives, and Participles.

An **Article,** an **Adjective,** or a **Participle,** belongs to the noun or pronoun to which it relates.

The girl brought *a large rose* just *refreshed* by *a* shower.

Explanation. — *The* what? *a* what? *What kind* of rose? Observe that both *large* and *refreshed* describe the rose.

Note II. — An Adjective that implies number, must agree in this respect with the substantive to which it relates.

For the sake of greater definiteness, this Note, which is applicable to the adjectives *this*, *these*, *that*, *those*, *two*, *three*, *four*, etc., may be used in parsing; though the Rule can also be used in place of it.

W. You have been playing *this* two hours.
How do you like *those* kind of apples?
The room is eighteen *foot* long, and sixteen *foot* wide.

Note III. — An Adjective or a Participle is sometimes used absolutely, after a participle or an infinitive.

The way to be *happy* is to be *good*. The dread of being *poor*.
To appear *discouraged* is the surest way to invite an attack.

Observe that *happy*, *good*, *poor*, and *discouraged*, are not used with the names of the persons described. It does not seem to us that it would be improper to parse the entire phrase simply as a noun, according to Note IV; thus dispensing with this Note altogether.

Obs. 2. — When the article stands only before the first of two or more connected nouns, it belongs to them jointly if they denote but one person or thing, or more viewed as one; if not, it belongs to the first noun, and is understood before each of the others.

I saw Webster, *the* great *statesman* and *orator*.
A man and *horse* passed by *the house* and *lot*.
The man, [the] woman, and [the] child, were drowned.

Obs. 3. — When two or more adjectives come between an article and a plural noun, they sometimes qualify each only a part of what the noun denotes.

"The *New* and *Old* Testaments" = The New Testament and the Old Testament; not, The New Testaments and the Old Testaments.

RULE XI.—Finite Verbs.

A **Finite Verb** must agree with its subject, in person and number.

John *studies*. I *study*. I *am*. He *is*. They *are*.

EXPLANATION. — Since John does the studying, there is obviously a relation between *John* and *studies*. Observe also that we can not say, when speaking properly, "John *study*," 'I *is*," "He *am*"; but we must use with each subject that form of the verb which will agree with it in person and number according to the Conjugation, pp. 162–169.

For an explanation of the different kinds of subjects, see p. 143.

W. I always *learns* my lessons before I goes to school.
My outlays *is* greater than my income.
Five *is* too many to ride in the canoe at once.
There *is* six cords of wood in the pile.
That which you yourself *has asked.*
What *signifies* fair words without good deeds?
He *dare* not say it to my face.
I called, but you *was* not at home.

A finite verb is sometimes used without a subject.

"*Meseems.*" "*Methinks.*" "God said, *Let* us make man in our image."

There are but few instances in which verbs are used so; and probably the simplest way to parse these few is, to supply *it*, *thou*, or *ye*, even when the sense must be strained a little. The two or three anomalous expressions of this kind, as *methinks*, *methought*, can be easily disposed of by the figure *enallagè*.

RULE XII.—Infinitives.

An **Infinitive** depends on the word which it limits, or which leads to its use.

We were anxious *to return* that night.
The Passions oft, *to hear* her shell,
Thronged around her magic cell.

The definitions are so arranged as *to be* easily *learned*.

To return limits *anxious*, by showing as to what we were anxious; and it therefore depends on *anxious*, according to Rule XII. *To hear* limits *thronged*, by showing for what purpose; and it therefore depends on *thronged*, according to Rule XII. *To be learned* depends on *as*, according to the last clause of Rule XII. (See pp. 153 and 216.) An infinitive depends on the word *with which it makes syntax*.

Note IV. — An Infinitive, a Participle, a Phrase, or a Clause, may be used as a noun in any case except the possessive.

To be without wants is the prerogative of God only.
His being bloody was the cause of suspicion.
It is best *not to have any thing to do with him.*

He knows *when to purchase.* He knows *what to say.*

He knows *when it is best not to purchase.*

"*Lazy wire!*" exclaimed the dial-plate. "*Very good,*" replied the pendulum. (Next parse the separate words as usual.)

This Note can be dispensed with by applying the Rule of Syntax which is applicable to the case in which the word, phrase, or clause is used. When an infinitive or a participle assumes case, it may be treated as a noun would be in the same situation. But sometimes the infinitive or participle is so intimately blended with other words, that it seems absolutely necessary to take the whole phrase as one thing; and in such cases the Note is preferable to any of the Rules.

Note V. — A Participle or an Infinitive is sometimes used independently, in the sense of a clause.

Generally *speaking,* young men are best for business.

We, generally speaking, would say, that young men are best for business.

But to proceed: it has been frequently remarked, that, etc.

But it is time to proceed, and therefore let us renew the subject thus:
Supplied words often vary the meaning, or make the sentence clumsy. Hence the Note.

RULE XIII. — Adverbs.

An **Adverb** modifies the meaning of a verb, an adjective, or another adverb.

"The horse runs *rapidly.*" Runs *how?*

"The horse runs *very* rapidly." *How* rapidly?

"The horse is *very* strong." *How* strong?

W. He spoke *clear* and *correct.* A *remarkable* fine country.
She dresses *suitable* to her means and station.

Note VI. — A Conjunctive Adverb joins a modifying clause or phrase to some other word.

See p. 173, for examples; and pp. 210 - 226, for remarks.

Note VII. — Sometimes an Adverb modifies a phrase or a clause; and some adverbs of addition, exclusion, emphasis, or quantity, may relate to any part of a sentence.

"Dryden wrote *merely* | *for the people.*" — *Johnson.*

"*Just* | *as I approached the jungle,* the panther made a spring."

"NOT *even* | *a philosopher* can endure the toothache patiently."

Even relates to the subject of the sentence; and *not* relates to the subject as modified by *even.* Some of these adverbs are a species of conjunctive adverbs. — See p. 186.

Note VIII. — An Adverb is sometimes used independently.

"*Yes,* my lord." "*No;* I was not there." — See p. 174.

RULE XIV.—Prepositions.

A **Preposition** shows the relation of an object to some other word on which the adjunct depends.

A *man* OF *wisdom* spoke. The man *spoke* OF *wisdom.*

RULE XV.—Conjunctions.

A **Conjunction** connects words, phrases, clauses, or sentences.

Words or phrases, connected by conjunctions, are generally in the same construction.

"Weeds *and* briers grow in the field, *because* it is not cultivated."

Note IX.—*As* or *than* sometimes joins a word or phrase to a clause, in stead of connecting two clauses.

Words can sometimes be supplied after the infinitive, so as to make two clauses; as, "Be so kind as *to write to me*" [*would be kind*]. But in most instances words can not be thus supplied without varying or destroying the sense.

RULE XVI.—Interjections.

An **Interjection** has no grammatical connection with other words.—See § 563 and 566.

Can you repeat Rule 1*st*?—2*d*?—3*d*?—4*th*?—5*th*?—6*th*?—7*th*?—8*th*?—9*th*?—10*th*?—11*th*?—12*th*?—13*th*?—14*th*?—15*th*?—16*th*?—*Note* 1*st*?—2*d*?—3*d*?—4*th*?—5*th*?—6*th*?—7*th*?—8*th*?—9*th*?

POSITION.

Articles generally precede their substantives.

Adjectives precede or follow their substantives.

Participles precede or follow their substantives.

Pronouns generally follow their antecedents.

Infinitives generally follow the words on which they depend.

Finite verbs generally follow their subjects.

Adverbs generally follow their verbs or the auxiliaries, and precede the adjectives or adverbs modified.

Possessive words precede the names of the things owned.

Objective words generally follow their governing words.

Explanatory words generally follow the words explained.

In regard to the arrangement of words logically and rhetorically considered, see p. 260.

PARSING.

General Formula. — The part of speech, and why; the kind, and why; the properties, and why; the relation to other words, and according to what Rule.

ARTICLES.

Formula. — An *article*, and why; *definite*, / *indefinite*, } and why; to what it belongs, and according to what Rule.

The river.

ANALYSIS. — *The river* is a phrase. The principal word is *river*, modified by the article *the*. (All the following exercises may be first analyzed, and then parsed, if the teacher deems it best to do so.)

PARSING. — **The** is an *article*, it is placed before a noun to limit its meaning; *definite*, it shows that some particular river is meant; and it belongs to *river*, according to Rule X: *An article belongs to the noun to which it relates.*

It is not necessary, in parsing, to repeat more of a Rule than the example requires.

ABRIDGED. — *The* is the definite article; and it belongs to *river*, etc.

River is a noun, it is a name; *common*, it is a name that can be applied to all objects of the same kind; *neuter gender*, it denotes neither a male nor a female; *third person*, it represents an object as spoken of; *singular number*, it means but one.

In like manner parse the following phrases: —

The man.	The men.	A rose.	An arrow.
The horse.	The horses.	A melon.	An island.
The child.	The children.	A university.	An uncle.

A man's hat.

ANALYSIS. — *A man's hat* is a phrase. The principal word is *hat*, which is modified by *man's*, showing what hat; and *man's* is modified by *a*, showing that no particular man is meant.

PARSING. — **A** is an *article*, it is placed before a noun to limit its meaning; *indefinite*, it shows that no particular man is meant; and it belongs to *man's*, according to Rule X. (Repeat it.)

ABRIDGED. — *A* is the indefinite article; and it belongs to *man's*, etc.

Man's is a *noun*, it is a name; *common*, it is a name common to all persons of the same kind; *masculine gender*, it denotes a male; *third person*, it denotes the man as spoken of; *singular number*, it means but one; and in the *possessive case*, it limits the meaning of *hat*, according to Rule III.

Hat is parsed like *river*.

ABRIDGED. — *Man's* is a common noun, of the masculine gender, third person, singular number; and in the possessive case, governed by *hat*.

A neighbor's farm.	The boy's book.
An Indian's hatchet.	The boys' books.
The sun's splendor.	Women's fancies.

ADJECTIVES.

Formula. — An *adjective*, and why; *descriptive*, / *definitive*, and why; whether *compared* or not, and how; the *degree*, and why; to what it belongs, and according to what Rule.

Descriptive Adjectives.

A beautiful morning, with a refreshing breeze.

ANALYSIS. — *A beautiful morning, with a refreshing breeze*, is a phrase. (Give definition.) The principal word is *morning*, which is modified by the article *a*, the adjective *beautiful*, and the adjunct *with a refreshing breeze*. *Breeze* is modified by the article *a*, the adjective *refreshing*, and joined to *morning* by the preposition *with*.

Beautiful is an *adjective*, — a word used to qualify or limit the meaning of a noun; *descriptive*, it describes or qualifies the morning; *compared* — pos. *beautiful*, comp. *more beautiful*, superl. *most beautiful;* in the *positive degree*, it expresses simply the quality; and it belongs to *morning*, according to Rule X.

ABRIDGED. — *Beautiful* is a descriptive adjective, (compare it,) in the positive degree, and belongs to *morning*.

Refreshing is a *participial adjective*, from the verb *refresh*. As a *participle*, it is present, and in the active voice. As an *adjective*, it is placed before *breeze* to describe it; and belongs to it, according to Rule X.

ABRIDGED. — *Refreshing* is a participial adjective, from the verb *refresh;* and it belongs to *breeze*, according to Rule X.

A ripe melon.	An upper room.	The black-winged redbird.
The fairest lady.	Purling streams.	The red-winged blackbird.
A gold cup.	The best gift.	A good boy's mother.

Definitive Adjectives.

Formula. — An *adjective*, and why; the *kind*, and why; to what it belongs, and according to what Rule.

All men.	Five dollars.

All is an *adjective*, it is used to limit the meaning of a noun; *defini-*

tive, it specifies how many men are meant; and it belongs to *men,* according to Rule X.

ABRIDGED. — *All* is a pronominal definitive adjective; and belongs to *men,* according to Rule X.

Five is an adjective, a word, etc. * * * *numeral,* and of the *cardinal* kind, because it expresses number and tells how many; and it belongs to *dollars,* according to Rule X.

Or say, — "and it agrees with men, in the plural number, according to Note I."

ABRIDGED. — *Five* is a numeral definitive adjective, of the cardinal kind; and belongs to *dollars,* according to Rule X.

Yonder house.	That barn.	Every fourth man.
This tree.	Each pupil.	Those two benches.
These trees.	Such a person.	The lawyer's own case.

NOUNS.

Formula. — A *noun,* and why; *proper,* / *common,* } and why; *collective,* and why; *gender,* and why; *person,* and why; *number,* and why; declension; *case,* and Rule.

Snow is falling.

ANALYSIS. — *Snow is falling,* is a simple declarative sentence. *Snow* is the subject, and *is falling* is the predicate.

Snow is a *noun,* it is a name; *common,* it is a name common to all substance of the same kind; *neuter gender,* etc. (see *river,* p. 198); and in the *nominative case* — it is the subject of the verb *is falling* — according to Rule I.

ABRIDGED. — *Snow* is a common noun, of the neuter gender, third person, singular number; and in the nominative case to *is falling.* Rule I.

Parsing is usually abridged, by simply omitting the reasons.

Parse the articles, the adjectives, and the nouns: —

Galile'o invented the telescope.
Henry Johnson's cattle have eaten our grass.
James the coachman is sick. George is a gentleman.
Alice, bring your books, slate, and paper.
My mother being sick, I remained at home.

PRONOUNS.

Formula. — A *pronoun*, and why; { *personal*, *relative*, *interrogative*, *adjective*, } and why; *gender*, and why; *person*, and why; *number*, and why; declension; *case*, and Rule.

Personal Pronouns.

I myself saw John and his brother.

Analysis. — This is a simple declarative sentence. The subject is *I myself; I* is the subject-nominative, which is modified by the emphatic appositive *myself*. *Saw John and his brother*, is the predicate; *saw* is the predicate-verb, which is limited by the objects *John* and *brother*, which are connected by *and*, and the latter of which is limited by *his*.

I is a *pronoun*, it is a word used in stead of a noun; *personal*, it is one of those pronouns which distinguish the grammatical persons; of the *common gender*, it may denote either a male or a female; *first person*, it denotes the speaker; *singular number*, it means but one; nom. *I;* and in the *nominative case* — it is the subject of the verb *saw* — according to Rule I.

Abridged. — *I* is a personal pronoun of the common gender, first person, singular number; and in the nom. case to the verb *saw*. Rule I.

Myself is a *pronoun*, — a word used in stead of a noun; *compound*, it is compounded of *my* and *self; personal*, etc. * * * and in the *nominative case*, to agree with *I*, according to Rule VII.

Abridged. — *Myself* is a compound personal pronoun, etc.

His is a *pronoun*, — a word used in stead of a noun; *personal*, it is one of those pronouns which distinguish the grammatical persons; of the masculine gender, third person, and singular number, to agree with *John*, according to Rule IX; (repeat it;) nom. *he*, poss. *his;* and in the *possessive case* — it limits the meaning of *brother* — according to Rule III.

Abridged. — *His* is a personal pronoun, of the masculine gender, 3d pers., s. n., to agree with *John*, according to Rule IX; (repeat it;) and in the possessive case, governed by *brother*, according to Rule III.

Parse the articles, the adjectives, the nouns, and the pronouns: —

We caught him. He came with me.
Albert hurt himself. John, you are wanted.
Art thou the man? Thou[2] majestic Ocean[7].
Martha and Mary have recited their lessons.
A dutiful son is the delight[7] of his parents.
Your horse trots well, but mine paces.

Say, *Mine* is used for *my* and *horse*. (Now parse each word.)

Relative Pronouns.

Read thy doom in the flowers, which fade and die.

Which is a *pronoun*,— a word used in stead of a noun; *relative*, it stands in close relation to an antecedent, and joins to it a descriptive clause; of the neuter gender, third person, and plural number, to agree with *flowers*, according to Rule IX; (repeat it;) and in the *nominative case* — it is the subject of the verbs *fade* and *die* — according to Rule I.

ABRIDGED. — *Which* is a relative pronoun, of the neuter gender, third person, and singular number, to agree with *flowers*, according to Rule IX; and in the nominative case to the verbs *fade* and *die*. Rule I.

James reads what pleases him.

What is a *pronoun*, — a word used in stead of a noun; *relative*, it makes its clause dependent on another; of the *neuter gender*, it denotes neither a male nor a female; *third person*, it represents an object as spoken of; *singular number*, it means but one; and it is here used as the object of *reads* and the subject of *pleases*, — because it takes the place of *that which* or *thing which*, — according to Rule VIII.

ABRIDGED. — *What* is a relative pronoun, of the neuter gender, third person, singular number, etc.

(She who studies her glass, neglects her heart.)
It was I that went. I am His who created me.
He was such a talker as could delight us all.
Take whatever you like. What is dear, few buy.
Whoever gives to the poor, lends to the Lord.

Interrogative Pronouns.

Whom did you see?

Whom is a *pronoun*, — a word used in stead of a noun; *interrogative*, it is used to ask a question; of the *common gender*, it may denote either a male or a female; *third person*, it represents an object as spoken of; *singular number*, it means but one; and in the *objective case* — it is the object of the verb *did see* — according to Rule IV.

ABRIDGED. — *Whom* is an interrogative pronoun, of the com. gen., 3d pers., s. n.; and in the obj. case, governed by *did see*, etc.

I do not know what he is doing.

What he is doing, is a clause used in the sense of a noun; of the neuter gender, third person, singular number; and in the objective case — it is the object of *do know* — according to Rule IV.

What is a *pronoun*, — a word used in stead of a noun; *responsive*, it is used as if in answer to a question; of the *neuter gender*, it denotes neither a male nor a female; *third person*, it represents an object as spoken of; *singular number*, it means but one; and in the *objective case* — it is the object of the verb *is doing* — according to Rule IV.

ABRIDGED. — *What* is a responsive relative pronoun, of the n. g., 3d p., s. n.; and in the obj. case, governed by *is doing*, according to Rule IV.

Who was Blennerhasset? Who is my neighbor? Which is it? Who can tell what democracy is?

Adjective Pronouns.

The old bird feeds her young ones.

Ones is an adjective pronoun, it is a common specifying adjective used as a pronoun; it is here used in place of *birds*, and is therefore of the common gender, third person, and plural number; and in the objective case — being the object of the verb *feeds* — according to Rule IV.

ABRIDGED. — *Ones* is an indefinite adjective pronoun, of the c. g., 3d p., and pl. n.; and in the objective case — governed by the verb *feeds* — according to Rule IV.

Others may be wiser, but none are more amiable. Some were for this, and some for that.

VERBS.

Finite Verbs.

Formula. — A *verb*, and why; *principal parts*; { *regular*, *irregular*, } and why; { *transitive*, with *voice*, *intransitive* or *neuter*, } and why; the *mood*, and why; the *tense*, and why, — with *form*, and why; conjugation; the *person* and *number*, to agree with its subject ——, according to Rule XI.

Mention *Form* only when it is progressive, or emphatic, or passive without being passive in sense.

He is ploughing the field which was bought last year.

Is ploughing is a *verb*, it expresses the act of a subject; *principal parts* — pres. *plough*, past, *ploughed*, pres. part. *ploughing*, perf. part. *ploughed*; *regular*, it takes the ending *ed*; *transitive*, it has an object (*field*), — and in the *active voice*, because it represents its subject as acting; *indicative mood*, it expresses an actual occurrence or fact; *present tense,* it denotes a present act, — and in the progressive form, it represents it as continuing; (singular number — First person, I *am ploughing;* 2d p., You *are ploughing;* 3d p., He *is ploughing;*) and in the *third person, singular number,* to agree with its subject *father,* according to Rule XI.

ABRIDGED. — *Is ploughing* is a regular transitive verb, from the verb *plough;* (principal parts, — pres. *plough,* past *ploughed,* perf. part. *ploughed;*) in the indicative mood, present tense, progressive form; and in the 3d p. and s. n., to agree with its subject *father,* according to Rule XI.

Was bought is a verb, it affirms something of a subject; *principal parts,* pres. *buy,* past *bought,* pres. part. *buying,* perf. part. *bought; irregular,* it does not assume the ending *ed; transitive* — but in the *passive voice,* because it affirms the act of the object acted upon; *indicative mood,* it asserts something as an actual occurrence or fact; *past tense,* it refers the act simply to past time; *third person* and *singular number,* to agree with its subject *which,* according to Rule XI.

ABRIDGED. — *Was bought* is an irr. pass. verb, from the verb *buy,* etc.

Parse the articles, adjectives, nouns, pronouns, and verbs: —

Regular and Irregular, Transitive and Intransitive.

The sun warms the earth. They struck me.
Birds fly. Rivers flow. It was I.
The rose is beautiful. Fierce was the conflict.

Voices.

She broke the pitcher. The pitcher was broken.
They named her Mary. She was named Mary.

Moods.

Robert sold his horse. Can you spell *phthisic?*
Were he rich, he would be lazy. Be sincere.

Tenses.

The distant hills look blue. The robber was caught.
The soldiers will be attacked. Had I known it.
The day will have passed. Do not venture yourself.
The apples might have been eaten. Tall pines are rustling.
She may have been handsome. She has been teaching.
I do object. Thou hast a heart of adamant.

Persons and Numbers.

Bees collect honey. Reckless youth makes rueful age. Time and tide wait for no man. You and I are invited. Monday or Tuesday was the day on which it happened. His family is large. The multitude pursue pleasure. Every house has a garden. Who are they?

Wait is of the 3d p., pl. n., to agree with *time* and *tide* — a plural subject — according to Rule XI. — See pp. 144, 145, 146.

INFINITIVES AND PARTICIPLES.

<table>
<tr><td rowspan="2">Formula. —</td><td>An infinitive,</td><td rowspan="2">} and why;</td><td>present,</td><td rowspan="2">} and why;</td></tr>
<tr><td>A participle,</td><td>perfect,</td></tr>
<tr><td colspan="2">transitive, with voice,</td><td rowspan="2">} and why; {</td><td colspan="2">on what it depends, Rule XII.</td></tr>
<tr><td colspan="2">intransitive or neuter,</td><td colspan="2">to what it belongs, Rule X.</td></tr>
</table>

The sun having set, we were obliged to return home.

Having set is a *participle,* — a form of the verb that expresses the act or state without predicating it, and generally resembles an adjective; *compound,* it consists of *having,* combined with another participle; *perfect,* it expresses the act or state as completed at the time referred to; *intransitive,* it does not have an object; and it belongs to *sun,* according to Rule X.

The forms of the participle, in each voice, may also be mentioned in parsing.

Abridged. — *Having set* is a compound perfect participle, from the irregular, intransitive verb *set, set, setting, set;* and it belongs to *sun,* according to Rule X.

To return is an *infinitive,* — a form of the verb that generally begins with *to,* and that expresses the act or state without predicating it; *present,* it denotes simply the act; *intransitive,* it does not have an object; and it depends on *was obliged,* according to Rule XII.

Abridged. — *To return* is a present infinitive, from the regular, intransitive verb *return, returned, returning, returned;* and it depends on *was obliged,* according to Rule XII.

The forms of the infinitive, in each voice, may also be mentioned in parsing.

Not to be sometimes deceived is impossible.

To be deceived is an infinitive used as a noun. As an *infinitive,* it is present, transitive, in the passive voice, and modified adverbially. As a *noun,* it is of the neuter gender, third person, singular number; and with the rest of the phrase of which it is the chief word, it is used as the subject of the verb *is,* according to Note IV.

I insist on writing the letter.

Writing is a *participial noun*, from the irregular verb *write, wrote, writing, written*. As a *participle*, it is present, transitive, and in the active voice. As a *noun*, it is of the neuter gender, third person, singular number; and in the objective case, governed by the preposition *on*, according to Rule V.

Participles.

The Indians fled, leaving their mules tied to the bushes.
The machinery, being oiled, runs well.
Time and thinking tame the strongest grief.
Of making many books, there is no end.

Infinitives.

We had a great curiosity to see the battle-field.
I ordered him to be brought. We are glad to see you.
He ought to have written. Let no one pass.
She is wiser than to believe his flattery.
Not to love is unnatural. I forgot to mention it.
It is reasonable to suppose[7] that he will try to escape.

ADVERBS.

Formula. — An *adverb*, and why; of *what kind;* whether *compared*, and how; what it modifies; Rule or Note.

CONJUNCTIVE ADVERB. — As an *adverb*, it modifies the verb ——, in its own clause, by expressing ——, (Rule XIII); as a *conjunctive* adverb, it refers its clause to ——, (Note VI).

The trees are waving beautifully.

Beautifully is an *adverb*, it modifies the meaning of a verb (*are waving*); it is an adverb of **manner**; and it modifies the verb *are waving*, according to Rule XIII.

ABRIDGED. — *Beautifully* is an adverb of manner, can be compared, and modifies the verb *are waving*, according to Rule XIII.

Since but few adverbs can be compared, it is not necessary, in parsing adverbs, to compare them, except when the adverb happens to be in the comparative or superlative degree.

1. *Adverbs Modifying Verbs.*

The horse galloped gracefully. Our roses must soon fade.
Then blue and lofty mountains successively appeared.
Mary sews and knits well. Here will I stand.

2. *Adverbs Modifying Adjectives.*

Her child was very young. He is perfectly honest. The music rose softly sweet. My hat is almost new. John is most studious. The wound was intensely painful.

3. *Adverbs Modifying Adverbs.*

The horse ran very fast. Thomas is not very industrious. He stutters nearly always. The field is not entirely planted. You did as well as I. She is now writing more carefully. These scenes, once so delightful, no longer please him.

PREPOSITIONS.

Formula. — A *preposition*, and why; between what it shows the relation; Rule.

The water flows over the dam.

Over is a *preposition*, — a word used to show the relation between a following noun or pronoun and some other word; it here shows the relation of *dam* to *flows*, or between *flows* and *dam*, according to Rule XIV.

Abridged. — *Over* is a preposition, showing the relation, etc.

I found a dollar in the road.
In spring the leaves come forth.
We should not live beyond our means.
From virtue to vice the progress is gradual.
The river is washing the soil from under the tree.
He struggled, like a hero, against the evils of fortune.
We went from New York to Washington City, by railroad, in eight hours.

CONJUNCTIONS.

Formula. — A *conjunction*, and why; its peculiar nature; what it connects. Rule.

The meadow produces grass and flowers.

And is a *conjunction*, — a word used to connect words, phrases, or propositions; *copulative*, it implies addition; *co-ordinate*, it is used to connect parts of equal rank; and it here joins *flowers* to *grass*, according to Rule XV: *A conjunction connects words or phrases in the same construction.*

Abridged. — *And* is a copulative co-ordinate conjunction; connecting *grass* and *flowers*, according to Rule XV.

You must either buy mine or sell yours.

Either is a conjunction, a word, etc. * * * it corresponds to *or*, and assists it in connecting two phrases according to Rule XV.

Or is a conjunction, etc. * * * *disjunctive*, it disjoins the words in sense, notwithstanding it joins them in form; *co-ordinate*, it unites parts of equal rank; it here corresponds to *either*, and connects two phrases according to Rule XV.

Words Connected.

Learning refines and elevates the mind.
We should cultivate our hearts and minds.
She is amiable, intelligent, and industrious.
Neither flatter nor despise the rich or great.

Phrases Connected.

Through floods and through forests he bounded away.
Death saw the floweret to the desert given,
Plucked it from earth, and planted it in heaven.

Clauses or Sentences Connected.

Eagles generally go alone, but little birds go in flocks.
Italian music 's sweet because 't is dear.
If it rain to-morrow, we shall have to remain at home.
Though he is poor, yet he is honest.
He was always courteous to wise and gifted men; for he knew that talents are more glorious than birth or riches [are].

INTERJECTIONS.

Formula. — An *interjection*, and why; of what kind; Rule.

Alas! no hope for me remains.

Alas is an interjection of grief; and it is used independently. Rule XVI.

Ah! few shall part where many meet.
O, young Lochinvar is come out of the West!
O Desdemona! Desdemona! dead? Dead! Oh! oh! oh!

OBSERVATIONS.

Parts of Speech. — Some grammarians include the articles with the adjectives, and thus make but eight parts of speech; others set off the participles as a distinct class, and thus make ten parts of speech. The classification of words adopted in this book seems to us not only the best, but is also that which most generally prevails.

Inflections. — INFLECTIONS may be divided into three classes; *declension, comparison,* and *conjugation.* Nouns and pronouns are said to be *declined;* adjectives and adverbs, *compared;* and verbs, *conjugated.* Inflections abound most about the core, or most ancient part, of a language. Hence our irregular verbs, especially the verb *be,* our pronouns, and some of our most common adjectives and nouns, are the most irregular words in our language. In the course of time, most inflections are dropped, or they are superseded by certain little words — such as prepositions, conjunctions, and auxiliary verbs — which are simpler and more obvious signs, and therefore better suited to express the relations of words.

Inflections, particularly ancient ones, consist sometimes of a vowel change in the word; as, man, *men;* goose, *geese;* cling, *clung:* sometimes of a different ending; as, ox, *oxen;* fox, *foxes;* great, *greater;* give, *given:* sometimes of a syllable or word prefixed; as, go, *ago(ne);* beautiful, *more beautiful;* write, *may write, to write:* and sometimes of two or more of these combined; as, weave, *woven;* break, *having been broken.*

AIDS TO PARSING AND ANALYSIS.

Designed only for Reference.

The following selections comprise the most important *idioms.*

Many words can be used as different parts of speech.

It is simply the manner in which a word is used, that determines the part of speech.

A. "*A* MAN's duties"; "*A* summer's DAY"; *article.* "To go *a* hunting"; *preposition.* "*A* few men"; *a* belongs to *few men* as denoting one aggregate. — See *Few.*

Abed, *ablaze, abroach, abroad, adrift, afoot, aloft,* etc. When these words are used with active verbs, so as to imply manner, they are adverbs. When they are used with neuter verbs, so as to denote mainly the condition of the subject, they have very much the meaning of adjectives; but they are still considered adverbs, *because they must be construed with verbs.* When such words, however, are construed with nouns rather than with verbs, they become adjectives. — See *Asleep.*

About. "What are you *about?*" prep. "He wanders *about*"; adv.

Above. "He sits *above* me"; prep. "He sits *above*"; adv.

"Amounted to *above a dozen.*" — *Swift.* Supply *number,* or call *above a dozen* a noun. Adjuncts are sometimes used for *nouns,* as well as for *adjectives* or *adverbs.*

Absolutely. "He is a friend." "*He* being a friend"; "To be a *friend*."
"He is friendly." "To be *friendly*"; "His being a *friend*."

By thus changing an intransitive verb into an infinitive or a participle, the substantive or adjective, joined to it, is frequently set free, or *absolved*, from its chief syntactical relation; though it still remains connected with the infinitive or participle by a relation that is within the reach of Analysis, and that should be mentioned in analyzing.

Adjectives. An adjective may imply quality, as *good;* quantity, as *much;* number, as *five;* time, as *eternal;* place, as *near;* position, as *perpendicular;* shape or form, as *round;* activity, as *studious*, etc. Most of the definitive adjectives imply number, place, or relative distinction.

Adieu. "*Adieu! adieu!* my native land." — *Byron.* Interjection.
"Wept a last *adieu.*" "Bid him *adieu*"; *i. e.*, say *adieu* to him. Noun.

After. "He came *after* me"; prep. "He came soon *after*"; adv.
"He came *after* I left"; conjunctive adverb.

Before, after, since, and *till,* are usually parsed as conjunctive adverbs when they stand before clauses; though they are in reality prepositions that govern the clauses in the sense of nouns.

Again. "Call *again*"; adv. "Again and again"; *i. e., repeatedly;* adv. phr. "*Again*, it has been frequently observed, that," etc.; conj.

In general, a phrase should be parsed as one word, when its meaning is different from that which the separated words give; hence, *again and again, through and through, ever and anon, now and then, here and there, over and over,* should be considered adverbial phrases. So *at all, at first, at once, at last, at least, at most,* etc.; adv. phrases, rather than adjuncts. "Not at all" = not in any degree; *at all,* adv. of degree, modified by *not.*

Ago. "It happened a hundred years *ago*"; adv. or adj.
Long ago; adv. phr., or make *long* modify *ago*, as in *long before.*

Ago is an adverb, limiting *happened*, and limited itself by *years* according to Rule VI. Or it is an adjective, meaning *past*, and belonging to *years*. "Twenty years *agone.*" — *Tillotson;* adj., or old participle. "It happened a *year before*," and similar expressions, confirm the first solution.

Alike. "They are *alike*"; adj. "They please *alike*"; adv.

All; ADJ. "*All* places." "*All* this." "*All* ye." "Ye *all*."
PRON. "*All* are but parts of one stupendous whole."
"Wealth, pleasure, and honors, must *all* be given up."
NOUN. "Our little *all*." "*All* of which." "He is *all* in *all*."
ADV. "I am *all* alone"; *i. e., wholly.*
"*All* heart they live, *all* head, *all* eye, *all* ear." — *Milton.*

A word is sometimes so used that it has not the meaning of one part of speech only, but of two or three; and if we may borrow a beautiful and expressive term from the florists, we would say that a word so used is a *variegated* part of speech. *All* is sometimes so used, and especially in the last example above. In the sentence, "They live all heart," *all* modifies adverbially neither *live* nor *heart*, but the predicate *live heart.* Note VII.

All or *both*, when it limits the plurality of a noun or pronoun, is an adjective; when it emphatically repeats the idea, an appositive. Some teachers call these words adjectives whenever they precede the substantives, and appositives when they follow them; but they should generally be considered adjectives, simply when they are joined to substantives or can be joined to them. "This is *all* that is done"; noun. "The sheep are *all* here"; adj. "The sheep are *all* of them here"; pron., appositive. "I was *all* attention"; adv., or adj. belonging to *I*. "It is *all* one to me"; adv. or noun, according to the sense; *one*, descriptive adjective. "He is *all* right," *i. e.*, in all respects; adv. *For all in all*, *all over*, *all along*, and *all hollow*, are generally adverbial phrases.

Alas. "*Alas* for us!" "*Fie* upon your law!" interj. or noun.

Alas is rather an interjection, and *fie* a noun. "Alas, *I sigh* for us!" "*I say* fie upon your law!" Compare with, "To bid welcome."

Alone; ADV. "The boy studies *alone*." Manner of studying.
ADJ. "The boy *alone* studies." "Let it [be] *alone*."

Also. "He is *also* blind"; adv. "The spring, *and also* the autumn, has its pleasures"; conj. phr. Or, *and*, conj.; *also*, adv., Note VII.

Antecedent. The antecedent of a pronoun is not the word which can be put in place of the pronoun, but the word elsewhere used in reference to which the pronoun was chosen as a substitute.

Therefore, when a pronoun is applied directly to the object itself, when the speaker can not be thought to have the supposed antecedent in his mind, and when the supposed antecedent does not first present, in the order of the sense, the object meant, Rule IX should not be applied.

Any. "*Any* person"; adj. "*Any* of them"; pron. or adj. "Are you *any* better"; adverb, analogous to the adverb *much*.

Apposition. "*Ye men* of Altorf." "*It* is known *that he is here*." Either term can be considered the appositive; but it is generally better to consider the pronoun the leading or principal term, and the other the appositive. "So, "In her *brother Absalom's* house." *Absalom's* is the explanatory and appositive word. "At *Smith's*, the *bookseller*"; *bookseller*, appositive, or else supply *who is*.

Apposition, or *identification* in language, is a much more comprehensive idea than grammars represent it to be. It reaches not only substantives, but adjectives, adverbs, phrases, clauses, and other parts. (See § 526; also *Both*, *As*, and *Such*.) When substantives are put in apposition, they must agree in case. But sometimes, in accordance with the foregoing comprehensive idea of apposition, a substantive is put in apposition with a clause or an adjective that has not case; and then the substantive is in the *nominative* case, simply because a noun naturally prefers the nominative case, or comes into the world in the nominative case, when there is nothing to make it vary or *decline* from this case.

As; ADV. "*As* cold as ice"; *degree*. Conjunctive Adverb: "Skate *as* I skate"; *manner*. "It fell *as* I entered"; *time*. And probably, "As cold *as* ice"; *degree*.
CONJ. "*As* [*since*] we all must die, why not be charitable?"
"*As* it regards this, I have nothing to say."
"Such characters are called letters; *as*, a, b, c," etc.
"Appoint him *as* clerk"; *him* and *clerk* are in apposition.
PRON. "Let such *as* hear, take heed"; *i. e.*, those *who*.
PREP. "I object to his appointment *as* clerk."

Here it seems rather better to call *as* a preposition than to say that *his* and *clerk* in apposition; but in sentences implying comparison, *as* should not be considered a preposition.

As follows and *as appears* are generally best parsed as adverbial phrases, equivalent to *thus* and *apparently:* sometimes the pronoun *it* may be supplied. In parsing *as regards* and *as concerns*, it is probably best to supply *it*. *As yet*, adv. phr.; *as if*, conj. phr. "They, *as well as* I, have written"; conj. phr. "He has done *as well as* he could"; first *as*, adv. of degree, modifying the adverb *well*.

"He concealed his good luck from everybody, *as* is usual in money dreams"; *i. e.* as it is usual for people to do, etc. *As*, in this construction, is partially a relative pronoun; because *which* could be substituted for it. So, "Then the dust shall return to the earth, *as* it was." "I bought *such as* were new," *i. e.*, *those which;* identity; *as*, relative. "I bought *such as* you have," *i. e.*, as those are which, etc.; similarity; *as*, rather conjunction, but considered a relative, to avoid troublesome distinctions. "They seek out some particular herb, which they do not use *as* food"; *food* is in apposition with *which*. So, "The wood of the silver fir is not much used *as* timber." In both these sentences, it would be hardly improper to call *as* a preposition, equivalent to *for*. "I consider him *as* responsible"; conj. adv. of manner. "Be so kind *as* to write to me"; conj., or conj. adv. of degree. "*As* the tree falls, so it lies." Here the clause, *as the tree falls*, and the adverb *so*, can both be regarded as modifying *lies;* or else the clause can be considered a modifier of *so*, by being related to it as a noun is related to the pronoun with which it is put in apposition. — See *That*.

Asleep. "He fell *asleep*"; adv. "I found him *asleep*"; adj. *Asleep* is strongly drawn into the analogy of *awake* and *alive*, and is therefore generally an adjective.

Auxiliary Verbs. Some grammarians parse auxiliaries as independent verbs, and the rest of the verb as a participle or an infinitive.

Ay. "*Ay*, so let it be"; adv. "The *ays* have it"; noun.

Before. "He stood *before* me"; prep. "I knew him *before*"; adv.
"He came *before* I returned"; conj. adv. — See *After*.

Below. "Fields *below* us"; prep. "He went *below*"; adv. "The shining fields *below*"; adj. "From *below*"; noun. So, *beneath*.

"From the supporting myrtles *round*, [adj.,]
They snatched her instruments of sound." — *Collins*.

By supplying words, *round* can be parsed as a preposition or an adverb. But the phrase or clause will still be an adjective element relating to *myrtles;* and it would seem that the same analogy of syntax should be allowed to run through word, phrase, and clause. Considered as an adjective, *round* is not a descriptive one; but it still shows what myrtles are meant, and this specifying sense comes within the province of local *definitive* adjectives.

Beside. "I stood *beside* him"; prep. "What do you know *besides*"; adv. "To all *beside* it is an empty shade," *i e.*, to all *others*. "O'er all the world *beside*," *i. e.*, all the *remaining* world; adj., or else adverb under Note VII, analogous to *also* and *too*.

Best; ADJ. "Do what is *best*."
ADV. "He *best* can tell." "Tones he loved *the best*"; adv. phr.
NOUN. "To do one's *best*." "Every creature's *best*."

At best and *at worst* are generally adjuncts rather than adverbial phrases.

Better. "I could have *better* [adv.] spared a *better* [adj.] man."
"To get the *better* of"; "Take her for *better* or *worse*"; noun.

Blame. "He is *to blame*" = *to be blamed;* passive. — See § 401.

Blow. "To blow *up, out, away, off, down, back, in*"; adverbs.

Both; ADJ. "*Both* men." "*Both* these." And probably, "We *both*."

Both and *all* are about as much *definite* or *demonstrative* adjectives as they are *indefinite* adjectives; though they are usually classed with the *indefinite*.

PRON. "The bee and the butterfly are *both* busybodies."

CONJ. "She is *both* young *and* handsome."

It is remarkable that *both*, as a representative word, can relate to two nouns, or two pronouns, or two adjectives, or two adverbs, or two prepositions. At bottom, it has always a pronominal or adjective meaning, or implies apposition; but it is usually considered a conjunction whenever it corresponds to *and*.

Either and *neither* are used as *both* is used, with this additional peculiarity, that, when they are corresponding conjunctions, they can be applied to more than two.

Burden. "A ship of two thousand *tons burden*"; apposition.

But; CONJ. "Sin may gratify, *but* repentance stings."

"No creature is so helpless, *but* it can protect itself."

PREP. "Whence all *but* him had fled"; *i. e.*, *except* him.

"None knew thee *but* to love thee."

"What rests *but* that the mortal sentence pass?" — *Milton.*

"Man *but for* [without] this were active to no end."

ADV. "Words are *but* leaves"; *i. e.*, are *only* leaves.

It is worthy of notice that the second conjunctive sense of *but*, as given above, is somewhat prepositional, for it suggests the meaning of *except*; and that more or less of this meaning lies at the bottom of all the difficult constructions of *but*. "I can *but* go" = I can *only* go. "I can not *but* go" = I can not do any thing *except* to go = I must go. It is probably best to consider *but* in the latter sentence a *modal* adverb, equivalent to *otherwise than*, and modifying the assertion (see p. 177); though different from *but*, *only*, which is an adverb of extent or quantity. So, "It can not *but* be obvious to you, that this state of things can not last." — *A. Lincoln.* "Who *but* would deem their bosoms burned anew." — *Byron.* That is, who *is there*, *but he* would, etc. By thus supplying words, *but* becomes a conjunction. Sometimes, however, *but* is used in this sense where words can not be thus supplied; and it is certainly a more sensible mode of analysis to dispose of what the writer actually said, than of what we suppose he might have said. Besides, the quoted sentence has become a condensed, idiomatic form of expression. "Who hears him, *but* [he is] is converted by him?" conj. In the sentence, "Should none be left *but he* and *I*," supply *should be left*, and parse *but* as a conjunction. This form of expression, however, is obsolescent; *but* being now generally regarded, in this construction, a preposition, and therefore followed by the objective case.

By. "He passed *by* me"; prep. "He passed *by*"; "He lives near *by*"; adv. "*By the bye*, there is a little debt behind"; conj. phrase.

Cheap. "To sell *cheap* goods"; adj. "To sell goods *cheap*"; adv.

The second *cheap* is used for the *adverbial* adjunct, *at cheap prices*; and it shows the manner of selling. — See *Make.*

Case. The possessive sign was originally *is* or *es*. "*Kingis* crowne"; "*Christes* gospel." — *Chaucer.* By putting an apostrophe in place of *e* or *i*, a double advantage was gained, — the possessive sign was distinguished from the plural sign, and language became in general one syllable shorter.

Close. "*To close* the eyes"; v. "At the *close* of the day"; n. "A *close* fit"; "To lie *close*"; adj. "Some dire misfortune lingers *close* behind"; adj. or adv.

Clown. "To play the *clown*"; "To act the *fool*"; nom. or obj.

Nominative, if the meaning is, *to be a clown*; objective, *to act the part of*.

Come. "To come to" (revive). It is probably best to supply *life*.

Comparison. Formerly, adjectives were more generally compared by *er* and *est* than at present. In Milton we find *beautifullest, virtuousest,* etc.

Superior, inferior, junior, interior, inner, etc., are adjectives in which the idea of comparison is also a part of the fundamental meaning; and they are therefore partly in the comparative degree, and partly in the positive. Hence they generally require *to* after them where pure comparatives would require *than;* and occasionally some of them may even be compared; as, "This is still *more inferior* to the other." — *Swift.*

Daggers. "To look or speak *daggers,*" *i. e., fierceness, threats;* n. obj.

Dear. "He sells *dear,*" *i. e., at dear prices;* adv., used for adv. adjunct. "To pay *dear* for," *i. e., a dear price;* adv., used for objective phrase.

Dispense. "I can *dispense with* luxuries"; "He *disposed of* his property." "Luxuries *are dispensed with*"; "The property *was disposed of.*"

Here it seems necessary to parse the verb and the preposition as one verb, a compound verb; for the words lose their meaning when they are separated. — See § 386.

Do. "This *does away with* [*removes*] my objections"; probably best parsed as a compound verb, for the meaning of the phrase is lost when the words are separated. "He has directions what *to do.*" *To do* depends on *directions,* and governs *what.* "I have more than I know what to do with" = I have more than *that is* with *which* I know what to do. *To do,* with the remaining words of its phrase, is the object of *know* (Note IV); and *what* is used as the object of *to do,* § 203. "I *am done for*"; v., passive. "I *am done,*" *i. e., I have finished my work;* passive in form, but active in sense. *Do,* thus used, is an excellent specimen of what would be called, in Latin grammars, a deponent verb.

Draw. "To draw *up, down, on, off, out, away, over, in, back*"; adverbs. "To draw *near, nigh, close, tight*"; adjectives.

Drink. "To drink *the cup dry*"; phrase, object of *drink.*

Say, in parsing *cup,* that it is in the objective case, being, with the remainder of the phrase, of which it is the chief word, the object of the verb *drink,* according to Note IV. Then parse *dry* as an adjective.

Each. "*Each* man"; adj. "They took one *each,*" pron., Rule VII.

"They help *each other.*" "They help *one another.*" Here *each* can be parsed as being in apposition with *they,* or else *each other* can be parsed as one word (see § 209). "They deemed *each other* oracles of law." — *Pope.* In this sentence, *oracles* can not be put in apposition with either *each* or *other,* but must be put in apposition with both considered as one expression. It is true, as Mr. Brown says, that the Latin *alii alios* proves that the words should be parsed separately; but it is just as true that the Greek ἀλλήλων and the German *einander* prove that they should be parsed together.

Ellipsis. The following are the most common kinds of ellipsis: —

ARTICLE: "A noun or [*a*] pronoun." "The first and [*the*] last."

ADJECTIVE: "He is wiser than you are" [*wise*].

NOUN: "At St. Paul's" [*Church*]. "Peter the Great" [*Emperor*].

PRONOUN: "Be [*ye*] seated." "Take all [*that*] there is."

VERB: "To whom thus Michael" [*spoke*]. [*Rise*] "Up, Glenarkin."
"And [*am*] I to be a corporal in his field!" "Dark [*is*] the day."
"Myself [*being*] a refugee." "Let me [*to be*] alone." [etc.
"With here and there a pearl"; *i. e.,* with a pearl *placed* here,

PREPOSITION: "Bring [*to*] me your slate."
CONJUNCTION: "Proud, stern, [*and*] inflexible." "I believe [*that*] he is [at home."
PHRASE: "Few are more resolute than he" [*is resolute*].
"O [*how much I wish*] that those lips had language!"
CLAUSE: "He returned; I know not why" [*he returned*].

The words most commonly omitted are those little ones which help to make syntax rather than to express thought.

Else. "Any one *else*," *i. e.*, any *other* one; adj. *Else* usually follows the word which it modifies. "How *else* [*otherwise*] can I do it?" adv. "He has not returned yet, *else* [*or*] he would write"; conj.

Enough. "Good *enough*"; adv. "Money *enough*"; adj. "To have *enough*"; noun.

Even. "Thy charms taught *even* toil to please." "I, *even* I, was there."

It is customary to call *even*, in the first of these sentences, an adverb; and in the second, a conjunction. But it has the same meaning in both; and it plainly relates, in the first, to the object, and in the second to the appositive. (Note VII.) It is better to say that such a word relates to the subject, the object, the predicate, or some other syntactical element, than to say that it relates to a noun or pronoun; for it affects the syntax, or the train of thought, rather than describes an object.

In the syntax of all languages are used certain little words that are promissory or reiterative; or that are designed to produce some identifying, intensifying, amplifying, or attenuating effect upon the flow of thought or the train of ideas These little words are generally adverbial or conjunctive in sense; but sometimes they defy classification.

Every. "*Every* one"; adj. "Each and *every* of them"; pron., obsolete. "Every now and then"; adv. phr. Or call *now* and *then* nouns; Rule [VI.

Fair. "To bid *fair*"; *i. e.*, *to be fair* in appearance, hence adj.

Fall. "We *fell out*, — my wife and I."— *Tennyson*. "To *fall foul of*."

Fall out does not have the meaning of *fall* and *out*; for it means *to quarrel*, and therefore the whole phrase should probably be parsed as a compound verb. (See § 386.)

Far. "A *far* country"; adj. "*Far* away"; "*Far* up the hill"; adv., modifying the word or phrase which follows it. "He went *thus* | *far*"; advs. "From *far*"; "*Thus far* is right"; noun. "He went *as far as* Richmond, *i. e.*, *to* Richmond, not, as far as Richmond is; prep.

Farewell. "*Farewell*, my friends!" interj. "A long *farewell*"; "To bid [say] *farewell*" [to]; noun. "A *farewell* address"; adj.

Fast. "A *long fast*"; adj. and n. "To *fast long*"; v. and adv. "To walk *fast*"; "*Fast* asleep"; adv. "To tie him *fast*"; adj. "Siloa's brook that flowed *fast* by the oracle of God"; adv., showing *where*.

Few. "A *few* men"; "A *dozen* men"; "A *thousand* men"; adj. "A *few* of us; "The *few* and the *many*"; "*Two* and *two*"; "By *tens*"; n.

A, in the first example, belongs to the rest of the phrase considered as denoting but one aggregate. Strictly speaking, the words *few*, *dozen*, *many*, *thousand*, etc., are *variegated* parts of speech, — partly noun and partly adjective; the substantive sense allowing the article before them, and the adjective sense enabling them to coalesce adjectively with the nouns after them. Sometimes they are nouns; and sometimes it is best to make them nouns in parsing, by supplying *of*.

Few, and some words like it, though usually called nouns, are very nearly pronouns.

"Truths would you teach, or save a sinking land?
All fear, none aid you, and *few* understand."— *Pope*.

First; ADJ. "Glenara came *first*"; *i. e.*, was first in coming.
ADV. "To write *first*, then send." "At first"; adv. phrase.

For. "Send *for* him"; prep. "I sent, *for* it was necessary"; conj. "Taken *for* granted"; *i. e.*, for a *thing* granted. "We live *for good or evil*"; "I deem it [to be] *for good* to do so"; "Taken *for perfect*"; rather, adjuncts.

"*For* him to speak would be injudicious" = To speak, for him, would be injudicious; *i. e.*, on his part. But if *to speak* is referred to *him*, then the whole phrase must be parsed as a noun. — See *Above*.

Full. "Bring it *full*"; adj. "*Full* many a flower"; adv.

Gender; the *meaning* of a word in regard to sex. A word can mean a male, a female, either, or neither; hence there can be *four* genders while there are but two sexes; and to have four genders is a great convenience in speaking of words.

Hail. "*Hail*, horrors!" interj. "He bade the stranger *hail*"; noun.

Half. "A *half* section of land"; adj. "*Half* the men," *i. e.*, half of, etc.; n. "To go *halves* with"; n., Rule VI. "*Half* dead"; adv. "He returns *half* fiddler, groom, and cook." — *Jenyns, abridged.*

Half, in the last sentence, seems to be an adverb, modifying the whole of the following appositive phrase, which has the descriptive force of an adjective; Note VII. If parsed as an adjective, it should be referred to all the following nouns as one whole.

Hand. "To go *hand in hand*"; adv. phr., or supply *being*.

Hard. "It is *hard*"; adj. "To study *hard*"; adv. Observe that *hardly* is a different word. "*Hard* by a forest's side"; adv. of place, modifying the adjunct after it.

Have. "I have *to let* a house"; active, depending on *have*. "I have a house *to let*"; passive, depending on house. (See § 401.) "Have it done to-day." "The witnesses testified that they saw him *buried*"; *i. e.*, they saw *his burial*; or, they saw *that he was buried*. *Done* is probably the perfect passive participle; but *buried* is rather the present passive infinitive, *to be* being understood.

"I *had* as lief not *be*, as be the thing I am." — *Shak.*

"He *had* better *have taken* cold than taken our umbrella." — *Mrs. Caudle.*

Had; verb, subjunctive mood, implying conclusion; past tense in form, but, like *were*, present in sense. [*To*] *be*; infinitive, depending on *had*. So, *to have taken*. §§ 410, 482.

High. "The spacious firmament *on high*"; adjunct.
"The day-spring from *on high*"; phrase used as a noun, Note IV.
"They fired too soon, and too *high*." — *Bancroft.* Adv.

How. "*How* deep"; adv. of degree. "I know not *how* to do it"; conj. adv. "*How* much is it?" "I was glad to get even *so* much."

"*How*, in the phrase *how to do it*, modifies *to do*; and joins the phrase to the verb *know*. *To do*, with the remaining words of the phrase of which it is the chief word, is used as the object of *know*; Note IV.

In parsing each of the remaining examples, supply a noun; or it is still better to parse all such mixed constructions in this way: *So* is an adverb modifying *much* as an adjective; *much* is an adjective modified by *so*; and it is also a noun, the object of *to get*.

However. "*However* great"; adv. "Great, *however*, as he is," etc.; conj.

I. "Love of fame makes *I* the little hero of each tale"; n., 3d p., obj.

"When Frog took possession of any thing, it was always said to be foi *us;* and why may not John Bull be *us,* as well as Nic. Frog was *us?*" — *Swift.* The first *us* is a pronoun; but the others are nouns, in the 3d person, and nominative case.

"Said I to myself, and myself said to me,
'Take care of thyself; for none care for thee.'"

Separate *myself* in parsing; *self,* — noun, 3d pers.; *thyself,* pron.

"Poor, guiltless *I!* and can I choose but smile?" Rule II.

"*Me* miserable!" *i. e.,* woe is to me. "Ah *me!*" "Oh *me!*"

The supplied words are not satisfactory. In truth, notwithstanding what grammars teach, there is in the English language an exclamatory *objective* independent as well as an exclamatory *nominative* independent; the former being used when the speaker is in a passive or suffering condition, and the latter in other cases.

Ill. "To fare *ill*"; adv. "He was taken *ill,*" *i. e.,* became *sick;* adj.

Impersonal. An inappropriate word, for the verbs have person. *Unipersonal* is also inappropriate, for all verbs not applicable to persons must be *unipersonal. Unsubjective* would be a better expression.

Infinitives. "The infinitive is no mode at all." — *Prof. Gibbs of Yale Col.*

"The infinitive has no claim to be considered a mood." — *Barnard.*

"The infinitives." — *Dr. Whately.* "The participials." — *G. P. Marsh.*

Dr. Whately calls both the infinitive and the participle *infinitives;* because both are not finite, or have not person and number. Mr. Marsh calls both *participials;* because they have the meaning of verbs, and also partake of the nature of other parts of speech. But neither calls either of these forms of the verb a mood. We might add much argument and authority in favor of our classification, as given on p. 119; but we have not room. Every act or state must belong to some person or thing; and, in the parsing of participles and finite verbs, this fact is made the basis of the Rule. Therefore it seems to us not altogether proper to disregard this truth wholly in parsing the infinitive; but most teachers prefer such a Rule as we have given on p. 195. Were we teaching, however, we should prefer the following Rule: —

RULE XII. — *An Infinitive relates to an expressed or indefinite subject, and generally depends on some other word.*

"He was anxious to return." *To return* relates to *he,* and depends on *anxious,* according to Rule XII. "The wagons were so arranged as to protect the camp." *To protect* relates to *wagons,* and depends on *as.* "Here was an opportunity to grow rich." *To grow* relates to an indefinite subject, and depends on *opportunity.* The subject of an infinitive is the noun or pronoun denoting the object to which the act or state belongs; and such a subject may be in the objective case, as well as in the nominative. But our language does not, like the Latin, allow a Rule for the subject of the infinitive, as being put in the objective case because the infinitive depends on it; for such an object, in English, has always a verb or preposition before it by which it is governed.

In order. "We were now obliged to gallop, *in order* to reach the boat."

In order is not so much an adjunct that modifies the verb before it, as it is an adverbial phrase that modifies the infinitive after it by strengthening the idea of purpose. In fact, while *to* is the common sign of the infinitive, *in order to* is the formal or strengthened sign, which is generally preferred when the infinitive is considerably removed from the verb on which it depends, or when it depends on another infinitive immediately before it.

Inversion. The following are the principal kinds of inversion: —

Rhetorically arranged: "My native shore with sighs and tears I leave."
Grammatically arranged: I leave my native shore with sighs and tears.

Logical or *grammatical arrangement* is that which the sense requires in parsing.

Rhetorical arrangement is some deviation from grammatical arrangement, for the sake of rhythm or effect.

"Through glades and glooms the mingled measure stole."

The mingled measure stole through glades and glooms.

"Mute was his tongue, and upright stood his hair."

His tongue was mute, and his hair stood upright.

"O Time! than gold more precious"; *i. e.*, more precious than gold.

"Oh, what a situation I am placed in!" *i. e.*, in what a situation, etc.

"When first thy sire to send on earth
Virtue, his darling child, designed."

When first thy sire designed to send Virtue, his darling child, on earth.

Irregular Verbs, in the course of time, sometimes become regular; but regular verbs never become irregular, except that *ed* is sometimes changed to *t*.

In old writers and in poets, we sometimes find *loaden*, *molten*, and *bounden*, used for the participles *loaded*, *melted*, and *bound;* also *clomb*, for *climbed;* *rid*, for *rode;* *hĕat*, for *heated;* and *writ*, for *wrote* or *written*.

It. "*It* was I" = *That person* was I. Almost demonstrative.

"*It* is easy to do so" = *This thing*, to do so, is easy.

"*It* is 12 o'clock" = *The time* is twelve o'clock.

"*It* rains." "*It* thunders." See §§ 465 and 184.

"Come, and trip *it*, as you go, on the light, fantastic toe." — *Milton.*

It here vaguely denotes doing or action.

Known. "Some men employ their time — an ugly *trick* —
In making *known* how oft they have been sick." — *Cowper.*

Trick; noun, nom. case, in apposition with the clause before it. (See *Apposition.*) [*To be*] *known* is a passive infinitive, depending on the clause that follows it, which is used as a noun.

Large. "To go *at large*," adv. phr. "The statutes *at large*"; adjunct.

Late. "He is *late*"; adj. "He came *late*"; adv. or adj. "He worked *late*"; adv. "He came *lately*"; adv. (See *Short.*) "Of *late*"; n.

Perhaps better: *Late* is an adjective relating to *he;* and an adverb, modifying *came*. (He was late in coming.) So, "He worked late"; *i. e.*, to a late hour.

Lay. "To lay *waste*"; Rule VI. "He *was laid hold of*"; verb.

Let. "Let *out*, let *off*, let *on*, let *in*, let *down*"; adverbs, modifying generally some verb understood, as *go* or *come*, "Let *loose*" = Let it be or go *loose;* adj. "Let *go*"; verb, depending on *it* and *let*.

Let is essentially the auxiliary verb which serves to express the imperative mood in the first or third person. It is unlike other auxiliaries, however, in being transitive; and therefore it prevents the intervening substantive, by governing it in the objective case, from becoming the subject.

Like. Adv. or adj., § 531. "I *like* this"; v. "I never saw the *like*"; n. "John began to chuckle and laugh, till he was like to burst his sides." — *Swift.* "He had like to have knocked John's hat into the fire." — *Id.* "I had like to have fallen." — *Cowper.*

Dr. Worcester calls *like* here a noun; and several passages in Gulliver's Travels give plausibility to this disposal of the word: but it seems to us that *like* is rather an adverb in all these cases, and modifies the following infinitive, which depends on the preceding *was* or *had*. "*Like* enough" is an obsolescent expression for *likely enough*.

"The Assyrian came down *like* the wolf on the fold." There is a peculiarity in this sentence. *On* can not be parsed without supplying a verb. When a finite verb, however, is supplied, *like* becomes a conjunctive adverb; but at the same time it ceases to be proper, and must give place to *as*. Supply *coming* after *wolf*, and you avoid the difficulty.

Little. "*Little* better"; adv. "A *little* better"; noun, Rule VI.

Long. "I *long* for rest"; v. "A *long* rest"; adj. "To rest *long*"; adv.

Look. "To look *big*," *i. e., with insolence;* adv., manner of looking.

Loose. "To break *loose*," *i. e., become* suddenly *loose*; adj. — See *Let*.

Loud. "A *loud* noise"; adj. "To talk *loud*"; adv.

Low. "To be *low*"; "To sink *low*"; adj. "To lie *low*"; adj., sometimes adv. "To aim *low*"; "To speak *low*"; "To sell *low*"; adv.

When the lowness is in the subject, *low* is an adj.; when in the verb, an adv.

Make. "To make *bold* with"; "To make *free* with"; *i. e., to be bold* with, etc.; adj. "To make *sure* of," *i. e.*, to make one's *self sure* of, or, to make [a] *sure* [*thing*] of; adj. "To make *away* with"; adv., or compound verb. "To make *much* of"; n. "He *was made much of*"; compound passive verb, § 400. "By selling all, he will *make out* to pay his debts"; compound verb. "To make *light* of," *i. e.*, a *light matter* of, — to regard *lightly*; adv.

Perhaps better: *Bold* is an adjective, relating to the subject; and it is also a noun, the object of *make*. *Light* is an adjective, relating to some noun understood; and it is also a noun, the object of *make*. So, "To pay *dear*." — See *Dear*.

Methinks. "*Methinks* I see a noble and puissant nation." — *Milton.*

Methinks is a defective irregular verb, of the indic. mood, pres. tense, 3d pers., and s. n.; but used without a subject. Or else say, *Methinks* is an anomalous expression, used, by the figure *enallagè*, for *I think*.

Thinks is used in the sense of *seems*; an old meaning still retained in this expression, though not generally understood so. "Where it *thinks* best unto your royal self."—*Shak.*

Mistake. "I *was mistaken* for my brother"; passive verb. "I thought I saw you; but I *was mistaken*." Deponent verb; see *Do*.

Mood. If our excluding the infinitive and the participle from moods be approved, then we would offer the following definition of mood in preference to the one given on p. 131: *Mood* is that property of verbs which shows how the act or state is predicated or regarded with reference to its subject.

More. "*More* work"; adj. "*More* entertaining"; adv. "To get *more*"; n. "Say no more"; *no*, adj.; *more*, noun. "Your parents are *no more*"; [adv. phr. "I will not do so *any more*," *i. e., again;* adv. phr. "He becomes *more and more* angry"; adv. phr. — See *Again*. "*The more* we urged him, *the more* he resisted"; adv. phr.

Parse *the more* first as an adverbial phrase, and apply Rule XIII; then say that it is used also as a correlative connective, relating to *the more* of the other clause, and helping it to unite the two clauses according to Rule XV.

Much. "*Much* money"; adj. "To have *much*"; n. "He reads *much*"; n. or adv. "He sleeps *much*"; adv. "*Much* the stronger"; n., Rule VI.

Must sometimes belongs to the past or the past-perfect tense of the potential mood, as well as to the present tense or the perfect. "I knew he *must rise*." — *Byron.* "But for this, the ship *must have sunk*." — *Arnot.*

Names. "He called me *names*." Rule VI.

Nay. "*Nay*, do not weep"; adv. "To say *nay*"; "The *nays* have [it"; n.

Nay and *yea* are sometimes used as amplifiers, to indicate an emphatic addition of something more. When thus used, it is generally best to call them conjunctions.

Near. *Near* is generally considered an adjective; though it has sometimes partly the nature of a preposition, and sometimes partly that of an adverb. It is not called a preposition, because it can be compared, and sometimes has *to* after it; and it is not called an adverb, because it has the adverb *nearly*.

No. "*No* place"; adj. "*No* farther"; adv. "*No*, never!" independent adverb, Note VIII.

None. "*None* sorrowed more"; pron. "*None* the better"; Rule VI. "Silver and gold have I *none*"; adj., belonging to *silver* and *gold*, § 183.

Nouns. A noun may denote a person, as *man*; a spiritual being, as *angel*; an animal inferior to man, as *dog*; a thing, as *house*; a place, as *Boston*; time, as *day*; a quality, as *goodness*; action, as *toil*, etc.

Collective nouns do not include such words as *jewelry*, *furniture*, etc.

Complex Nouns. — Some grammarians call such words as *John Smith*, *Charles XII*, and *Duke of Wellington*, complex nouns.

Most of the older grammarians teach that each word of such a name should be parsed; and some of them say that *John*, of the name *John Smith*, is an adjective, because it shows what Smith is meant; while others insist as strenuously that *Smith* is in apposition with *John*, because it shows what John is meant! It is probably best to parse the whole name as one noun.

Concrete Nouns, the names of objects with their qualities; as, *snow*.

Abstract Nouns, the names of qualities without their objects; as, *whiteness*.

Diminutive Nouns, the names of small objects as distinguished from large ones of the same kind; as, *hillock* from *hill*.

Material Nouns, the names of substance in mass; as, *water*.

Nouns, Proper and Common. — The same word is sometimes a proper and sometimes a common noun. "The planets are Mercury, Venus, *Earth*," etc. "The sun shines upon the *earth*." "*Sunday* precedes Monday"; "Preaching on every *Sunday*."

It is not necessary, and perhaps hardly proper, to apply the distinction of proper and common, to participles, infinitives, or clauses, that are used as nouns; but gender, person, and number, should be mentioned, on account of the relations which such expressions have to pronouns and verbs.

Now. "*Now* is the time to repent"; adv. "*Now* is the time to repent in"; n. "*Now* Barabbas was a robber"; conjunction, implying transition. "*Now* — *now*"; advs., and also correlative connectives.

Number. *En* was a plural termination in the Saxon language; hence we have *oxen*, *children*, and even *kine* is a contraction of *cowen*, and the poetic *eyne* (eyes) of *eyen*. In old writers, we also find verbs with this plural ending. (See p. 58.) Formerly, nouns had the ending *ie* in stead of *y*; as, "A gentle *Ladie*." — *Spenser*. Hence, according to some writers, the change of *y* to *ie* in the plural; as, *ladies*.

Off. Adv. or prep. "He is *well off*," i. e., rich; adj. "*Off* with his head!" imper. adv.; Note VIII, for no suitable verb can be supplied.

Old. "*Old* men"; adj. "Days of *old*"; "The young and the *old*"; n.

Once. "*At once* came forth whatever creeps"; adv. phr. "Now, just this *once*, we must go on the same as ever"; noun, Rule VI.

Only. "The *only* man"; adj. "I propose my thoughts *only* as conjectures"; adv., relating to the appositive phrase, *as conjectures*. See § 527.

Opposed. "I *am opposed* to this"; deponent verb. — See *Mistake*.

Ours, *yours*, *hers*, etc., are either personal pronouns in the possessive case, or else adjective pronouns of the third person and in the nominative or the objective case.

These words occupy a middle position between personal pronouns and adjective pronouns. *Ours*, for instance, may be equivalent to *our books;* and hence it may be regarded either as having the gender, person, number, and case of *our*, or as having the gender, person, number, and case of *books*. The former view is the one generally taken in English grammars; but the latter is strongly sustained by the analogy of some foreign languages. In the English language, relative pronouns are used to suit either part of the composite word; and this is rather a conclusive argument that the words should be parsed as we have shown on p. 74. "A weary life is *theirs*, *who* have no work to do." "My umbrella being torn, I will take *yours*, *which* is better."

"'T was *thine* to lead our warrior bands"; *i. e.*, *thy part*. But in parsing the phrase, "This poor self of mine," for instance, why may we not simply say that the adjective adjunct *of mine* is used as a definitive adjective belonging to *self?* — See p. 98.

Out. "To put *out;* to branch *out;* to break *out;* to draw *out;* to run *out;* to cut *out;* to make *out;* to look *out;* to play *out*," etc.; adverbs.

Over. "We passed *over* the bridge"; prep. "*Over against* the church stands a hospital"; prep. "We passed *over*"; "I turned *over* a leaf"; "It ran *over*"; "It is *over*," *i. e.*, gone over; "There were twenty dollars *over*," *i. e.*, in excess; adv. "Over and above"; adv. phr.

Participial Adjectives. — A participial adjective is derived from a verb, has little or no reference to time, and generally precedes the noun which it qualifies, and which would be the subject if the participle were a finite verb.

The following are also participial adjectives: "God's presence is *renewing*, *sanctifying*, and *lightening* to the soul." — *Bunyan*. "The office was *unsolicited* and *undesired* by me." — *McCulloch*. "Boughs *unshaken* by the wind." — *Bryant* As a general rule, prefixes do not change the part of speech; and suffixes do. When *un* is prefixed to a participle, but can not be prefixed to the verb, some grammarians call the word thus formed an adjective; others, a participle. It seems to us that such words should be called *participial adjectives*. The word *undesired*, for instance, as given above, can not make a passive verb with *was*, and therefore it is not a pure participle; but it takes after it the preposition *by*, as required by participles, and not *to*, as required by adjectives, and therefore it is not strictly an adjective.

Such words as *talented*, *double-barreled*, *unepitaphed*, etc., which are formed from nouns, and take the ending *ed* simply to give them something of an adjective form, are adjectives. Also such words as *parsing*, in the phrase *parsing exercises*.

Compound participles, as treated in this book, are to simple participles, somewhat as compound pronouns are to simple pronouns.

Participial Nouns. Whenever a participle is used with a verb or preposition in such a way that it assumes case, it may be called a participial noun; and it may then have the modifiers of either a verb or a noun, but not always a part of each class.

A participial noun that has the modifiers of a verb, should be parsed first as a participle and then as a noun. — See p. 206.

Peas, number; *pease*, quantity; — a frivolous and pedantic distinction.

Pleonasm. "*It* curled not Tweed alone, that *breeze*." — *Scott.*
"My *banks they* are furnished with bees." — *Shenstone.*

It seems to us that it would be better to apply to such examples the Rule for apposition than the Rule for nominatives independent: for, in general, no extraordinary principle should be applied where an ordinary one will do as well; and the examples are analogous to such as "Ye mountains," "I myself," in which the pronoun merely strengthens the expression. But when the words are plainly different in case, or when the mode of expression is different, Rule II may be preferable.

Possessive. "As Eden's garden bird." — *Halleck.* "Houghton's Æsop's Fables." "The Duke of Wellington's forces." "Jones the saddler's wife." "At her brother Absalom's house." "Turner and Mason's store." "Turner's and Mason's store."

Eden's is governed by *garden*, and *Eden's garden* is an adjective belonging to *bird*. *Houghton's* is governed by the phrase *Æsop's Fables*. *Duke*, *Jones*, and *brother*, should be considered the possessive words on which the names of the possessed objects depend. *Turner* is governed by *store* expressed; and *Turner's*, by *store* understood. — See *Ours*.

Post. "He rides *post*"; adv.; or noun, under Rule VI or VII, according to the sense.

"He is the post, and rides"; or, "He rides like the post, or by post." The sentence seems to be analogous to "She walks a *queen*"; "He struts a *dandy*"; and, if so, the same Rule should be applied to it, though most teachers call *post* simply an adverb.

Prithee. "I prithee" = I pray thee. "*Prithee*, say no more"; interj.

Put. "To *put up* with it"; *i. e.*, *to bear*. "To *put up* at an hotel."
Probably each phrase should be parsed as a compound verb.

Pronouns. Pronouns were probably the first of names, and afterwards adopted as general substitutes for nouns; hence pronouns sometimes have no antecedents.

Adjective Pronouns. — By supplying suitable nouns after them, most adjective pronouns can be parsed as adjectives; and those few which can not, might be parsed as personal pronouns, for they are always of the third person. Since pronouns represent nouns with their modifications, most adjective pronouns represent themselves, and the nouns understood.

Responsive or *Indirect Interrogative Pronouns.* "*Who* he was, is the question." Here no antecedent can be supplied before *who;* nor is *who* a direct interrogative. Such a pronoun resembles a relative pronoun, because it makes its clause dependent; and it resembles also an adjective pronoun, because it is equivalent to the same phrase, and implies uncertainty. Some grammarians call such pronouns *indefinite*. Sometimes an antecedent can be supplied, and the pronoun can then be parsed as a relative.

Quite. "She is *quite* a beauty." "He is *almost* a poet."
Quite and *almost* are adverbs, modifying the predicates. Note VII.

Right. "Our *rights*"; n. "It is *right*"; adj. "All is going on *right*"; adj., § 534. "You did *right*," *i. e.*, what is *right;* adj. or n. (See *Make.*) "*Right* Reverend"; "*Right* noble prince"; adv. "Right away"; "Right off"; adv. phr.

Rule VI. — *Nouns that signify which way, how far, how much, how long,* *or time when, are sometimes put in the objective case, without a preposition expressed*

We insert this Rule here, because some teachers may prefer it to Rule VI, on p. 192; though we ourselves prefer that Rule, which is more comprehensive.

Rule VII. — 1. *A Noun or Pronoun, added to another for explanation or emphasis, is put, by apposition, in the same case.*

2. *A Noun or Pronoun, after an intransitive or a passive verb, is put in the same case as the subject, when it denotes the same person or thing.*

We insert this Rule here, because some teachers may prefer it to Rule VII, on p. 192; though we ourselves prefer that Rule.

Run. "To *run riot*"; *i. e.*, in or into riot. Rule VI.

"The brooks *ran nectar*." "The streams *ran blood*."

"Forthwith on all sides to his aid *was run*
By angels many and strong." — *Milton.*

It is customary to say that *ran* is transitive, and governs *nectar* and *blood*; but the meaning in the first example plainly seems to be, that the brooks *were nectar*, and hence *nectar* is a predicate-nominative. The next example is doubtful; for it may mean simply that the rivers carried blood, or flowed with blood; and if this is the sense, Rule IV or VI should be applied. In the last example, *was run* is an impersonal verb, and a pure Latinism. — See p. 195.

Save and *but* are prepositions when followed by the objective case, and conjunctions when followed by the nominative case. — See p. 293.

Seize. "To *seize* something." "To *seize on* something"; comp. v.

Set. "To set *up, off, out, apart, by, forth, over*," etc.; adverbs.

Short. "To be *short* of money"; adj. "To stop *short*"; adv. "To come *short* of"; "To fall *short* of"; *i. e., to be short of;* adj. "He cut him *short* with this remark"; adv. "To stop *short*" (manner), and "To stop *shortly*" (time), are very different.

Sit. "To *sit* up late"; v. intr. "I *sit* me down" (poetic); v. tr. "To *sit* the matter out"; v. tr. "She *sits* a horse well"; "He *plods* his weary way." *On* may be supplied in the last two examples, but it is not improbable that the idiomatic sense makes the verbs transitive.

Situated. "London is *situated* on the Thames"; adj.

So. "*So* frowned the combatants"; adv. of manner. "It is *so* cold"; adv. of degree. "*So* he does it, no matter when"; conj. "A wry mouth or *so* was all." — *Swift.* Noun. *So* is often used as a sort of *pro-word*, to represent a word, phrase, or clause; and to express not only manner, but frequently condition, thus having the force of an adjective; but as it must be always construed with a verb, it is still considered an adverb. "He is very *stingy*, but she is more *so*."

Something. "Of worm or serpent kind it *something* looked." Rule VII.

Such. "*Such and such* a one." — *Swift.* Adj. "I do not regard his rules as *such*," *i. e.*, as *rules;* pron., apposition. "Some flowers have beautiful names; *such as heart's-ease, daisy, honeysuckle*," etc.

Such, in this last sentence, is a pronoun, in apposition with *names*, as being included in it; and *as* is a relative pronoun, predicated of *heart's-ease*, etc., by the verb *are* understood. *Such* could also be referred to *flowers*.

Take. "To take hold of; to take care of; to take up; to take on,"

"He *takes after* his father"; *i. e., resembles.* "We *should* not *take up with* mere probabilities."—*Watts.* That is,—*should not adopt.* "They *took* to the woods"; *i. e., took themselves.*

Take is sometimes used in such close combination with its modifiers, that the words can not be parsed with any perception of their separate meanings. In such cases the whole phrase may be treated as a compound verb. — See § 386.

Than. "He is wiser *than* I" [am]; conj., connecting clauses. "Who forgets the more *than* Homer of his age?" conj., connecting words. "Beëlzebub, *than* whom, Satan except, none higher sat."—*Milton.*

Than whom is an inelegant expression; though it is somewhat analogous to the abridged phrase *but me, but him. Than,* in the foregoing example, is usually considered a preposition. It may also be parsed as a conjunction, by saying that *whom* is used for *who*, by the figure *enallagè.* "I have more trouble *than* I can bear"; *i. e.,* than *that is which* I can bear." This construction of *than* is so nearly like that of the relative *as*, that it almost makes *than* a relative or else *as* a conjunction: "I have as many *as* he"; "I have more *than* he." "This aunt Deborah had no more *than* a small life annuity." Here *annuity* is put in apposition with *more*, being included in it; for the meaning is not that she had no more than a small life annuity is, but that she actually had the small annuity; the idea of *identity* predominates over that of comparison. *As* sometimes connects words in apposition, and *than* is a similar word; besides, *than*, as used above, would became *as*, if translated into German.

That; ADJ. "*That* man."
ADJ. PRON. "No other home seems so lovely as *that* of my childhood."
REL. PRON. "It was he *that* assisted me."
CONJ. "I believe *that* all sickness is caused by improper living."

"Here is love, in *that* while we were yet ..... Christ died for us."—*Bunyan. In* governs the whole clause after it; or else, only *that*, with which the clause after it is put in apposition. "A few, *that is*, eight or ten, were saved"; conj., or supply *number.* "Fool *that* I was, no one knew it" = *Although I was plainly the great* fool that I was, no one knew it. By thus supplying words, this difficult idiom can be parsed; but the supplied words hardly preserve the sense. — So, "Young *as* he is, few are his equals." Or else treat the sentences as if *that* and *as* were *though.*

The. "*The* man"; article. "*The* more we have, *the* more we want"; article. "*The* deeper, *the* cooler"; adv., and correlative connective. "*The better* to converse"; adv. phr. "He did *the best*"; adv. phr. When *the* relates to a noun, it is an article; to an adjective, an adverb; to an adverb, it forms with it an adverbial phrase.

Then; ADV. "Did you hear it thunder *then?*"
CONJ. "If you think so, *then* do not purchase."

There. See p. 177. "The ride *there and back* was delightful"; adj., showing what ride. "To the house *thereof*"; "And the fame *hereof*"; "Time *when*"; "The place *where*"; "All things *whatsoever*"; adj.

Till. "Stay *till* to-morrow"; prep. "Stay *till* I return"; conj. adv. "Till now"; "Till then"; adv. phr.; better, adjuncts.

Times. "Three times the son's age is equal to the father's." "Five times four are twenty." "Five times one are five."

There is an inconsistency in the foregoing modes of expression. Custom, however, seems determined to uphold them all. To parse them as they are, apply Rule VI to *times* in the first example, and to *four* and *one* in the others. The son's age, *taken* three times, etc. Five times *of* four, *as to* four, or *in regard to* four, etc.

To is a preposition; also the sign of the infinitive, and a part of it.

Since the infinitive was not intended for predication, it needed not an auxiliary *verb* for its sign; and therefore it adopted *to* as being best suited to express the general idea of *tendency*.

Too. "*Too* small"; adv. of degree. "Since he went, I will go *too.* "Devotion, *too,* hath lingered round each spot of consecrated ground."

Too, in the last two examples, is rather conjunctive; and, in the last one, its construction is so nearly like that of the conjunction *however*, that it would be hardly improper to call it simply a conjunction. *Too, also, likewise, even, besides*, etc., generally relate to a part of a sentence, and at the same time refer it back conjunctively to a similar part that is either expressed or implied. To those who wish to be critically nice in parsing these words, we would say, first parse the word as an adverb, relating to some part of the sentence according to Note VII; and then say, that it is also used as a conjunction, connecting this part to, etc., according to Rule XV. — See p. 177 and § 527.

Up. "To march *up* a hill"; prep. "To rise *up; keep up; go up*"; adv. "Man's life is full of *ups* and *downs*"; nouns.

Upwards. "*Upwards of twenty houses* were burned."
"*About twenty houses* were burned."
"In a sermon there may be *from three to six heads.*"

The whole phrase, in the first and the last example, can be parsed as a noun; or supply the words *number* and *heads*. Some grammarians call *upwards* a noun; and a strange one it is. Since *about* is an adverb, modifying *twenty*, it seems to us that it would be allowable to call *upwards of* an adverbial phrase modifying *twenty*. — See *Above*.

Very. "The *very* man"; adj. "*Very* strange"; adv.

Weigh. "To *weigh* [lift] anchor"; v. tr. "It weighs a *pound*"; Rule IV or VI. "To weigh a *hog*"; Rule IV. *Weigh* is as much transitive as *cost*; but the more obvious object of *weigh* has rather pushed the other under Rule VI.

Well. "A deep *well*"; noun. "He is *well*"; adj. "*Well* advanced in years"; adv. "*Well*, I don't know what to do"; independent adv.

What; *Compound relative pronoun.* "Take *what* I offer."
Interrogative pronoun. "*What* ails you?"
Responsive pronoun. "I know *what* ails you."
Adjective. "*What* news from Genoa?"
Adverb. "*What* [*somewhat*] with entreaty, *what* with threatening, [I succeeded."
Interjection. "*What!* take my money, and my life too?"

The regular expression for the relative *what* seems to have been *that what;* for the first cousin to this expression, "*das was,*" is still alive in the German language. The disagreeable monotony of sound, in the two words *that what,* seems to have caused the rejection of one. "Eschewe *that* evil is."—*Gower.* Here the *what* is dropped; but, in the course of time, *what* gained the supremacy, and now rules in place of both words. Gradually, *what* also assumed the function of a plural.

"He demands as a favor *what* the former requires as a debt." *What* is the object of *demands* and *requires;* and *favor* and *debt* are put in apposition. "*Whatsoever* you find, take it." Pleonastic; the antecedent of *whatsoever* is in apposition with *it*. "To others do—the law is not severe—*what* to thyself thou wishest to be done." The antecedent part of *what* is governed by *do*, and *wishes* governs the relative part in connection with the infinitive. "Is it possible that he should know *what* he is, and be *what* he is?" *Know* governs the clause after it; and *what* is responsive, agreeing in case with *he*, according to Rule VII. "I tell thee *what*, corporal; I could tear her." That is, I tell thee *what* I *think* or *feel*. *What* if he should sue you?" *i. e.*, what *would you do?* "*What* if there is an old dormant law, nobody will enforce it"; *i. e.*, what *avails it*. "*What though* no real voice nor sound," etc.; conj. phr., for it seems to have become a sort of poetic *although*. "*What ho!* warder"; interj. "For all men *whatsoever*"; adj.; or supply *they are*, and apply Rule VII. — See *There* and *Do*.

When. "*When* was it?" interrog. adv. "Come *when* you can"; conj. adv. "Since *when* was it?" noun. So, *where*.

Though it is customary to teach that relative pronouns and conjunctive adverbs connect clauses, yet most words of this kind allow the clauses to which they belong to be contracted into infinitive phrases; and then the chief syntax rests sometimes on the relative word, and sometimes on the infinitive. "*I* know *how to do it*"; Note IV; *to do* is rather the object of *know*, and modified by *how*. So, "I knew not *which to choose*"; "I know *what to do*." "These precious minstrels could find no room *in which to warble*"; "He has no money *with which to begin the business*"; the infinitives rather depend on the preceding nouns or predicates, and the adjuncts on the infinitives. "Tell me *when to come*, and *where to meet you*"; Note IV, but the infinitive rather depends on the adverb. So, "The Son of man hath not *where to lay his head*." In the last two sentences, the nouns *time* and *place* can be supplied; and in the last one it would be hardly improper to parse *where* simply as a noun.

Whereby, *wherewith, whereon, whence,* imply each a relative pronoun; and they are therefore generally conjunctive adverbs.

Which. "The table on *which* I write"; rel. pron. "*Which* is he?" interrog. pron. "*Which* book?" adj. "I know not *which* it is"; "I know not *which* to choose"; responsive pronoun.

"Can you tell *which* is *which*?" "He does not know *what* is *what*?" "We shall soon see *who* is *who*." This idiom is a very curious knarl in language. The first word seems to be a common interrogative or responsive pronoun, and the subject of the verb; the word after the verb is a kind of indefinite pronoun, altogether peculiar. "Which is which?" seems to be equivalent to "Which is *the right one*"?

"Has earth a clod its Maker meant should not be trod by man, erect and free?" Supply *which*, and make *meant* govern the whole clause, *which should not be trod*," etc.

Who. "The man *who*"; rel. pron. "*Who* can tell *who* he is?" first *who*, interrog. pron.; second *who*, responsive, or indirect interrogative. "To any one *whomsoever*"; rel. pron., in apposition; analogous to "The man *himself*." — See end of *What*. [adv.

Why. "*Why* go?" interrog. adv. "The reason *why* he went"; conj.

Wit. "They are, *to wit*," etc.; adv. phr. "These men, *to wit*," etc.; conj.

Worse. "To be *worse*"; adj. "To do *worse*"; adv. "For *worse*"; noun.

Would. "I *would* go"; auxiliary verb. "I *would* I were out of the difficulty"; prin. v. "*Would* God it were done!" prin. v.; *God*, subject. The meaning seems to be, "O that God *wished* [subjunctive] it done!" implying that it would then be instantly done. But it is customary to supply *I*, and to govern *God* by *to*.

Worth. "Slow rises *worth* by poverty depressed"; noun. "My knife is *worth* a dollar," *i. e., equal in value to;* adj.; *dollar*, Rule VI. "*More worth* to men, *more joyous* to themselves." — *Young*. "Woe *worth* the day"; verb; old imperative of the verb *be;* akin to *were*, or derived from this branch.

English syntax would sustain a Rule of this kind: "Verbs, adjectives, and adverbs, that have absorbed the meaning of *to* or *for*, may govern the same case." *Like, worth*, and verbs of giving, would come under this Rule.

Yet; CONJ. "*Yet*, though destruction sweep these lovely plains,
ADV. Rise, fellow-men, our country *yet* remains!" — *Campbell.*

"*Yet a few days*, and thee the all-beholding sun shall see no more." — *Bryant*. One writer supplies *passing;* but the expression is fully in the idiom of the German language; and in this the sense is, "After a few days yet," etc., *yet* being an adverb that modifies the phrase. *Yet*, Note VII; *years*, Rule VI.

Yonder. "*Yonder* church"; adj. "He lives *yonder*"; adv.

PART IV.

WORDS LOGICALLY COMBINED.

ANALYSIS OF SENTENCES.

"A mighty maze! but not without a plan."

Analysis is the resolving of a whole into its parts.

Synthesis is the combining of parts into a whole.

571. Analysis, in grammar, is the resolving of a sentence into its principal and subordinate parts.

Analysis is simply *graded* syntax; and the most important principal parts are *subjects* and *predicates*. Analysis treats of thought and its elements; parsing treats of words and of those properties which sometimes cause changes in the forms of words.

572. Parsing is the resolving of a sentence into its parts of speech, and mentioning their properties and syntax.

DISCOURSE.

573. Discourse is any train of thought embodied in language; and it may be, —

1. *Description*, which depends chiefly on place.

Description is an account of persons, places, and things.

2. *Narration*, which depends chiefly on time.

Narration is a rehearsal of events.

3. *Science* or *Philosophy*, which aims to unfold the nature or plan of things.

On this division is based *didactic* literature, which inculcates moral truth.

4. *Illustration*, which is any foreign matter introduced for the sake of making the speaker's meaning more intelligible or impressive.

Illustration is generally rhetorical matter, comprised under the head of *Rhetorical Figures*.

Any one of the first three kinds may predominate in a piece of composition; but the four are frequently combined and mixed.

574. **Discourse**, or **Literature**, is usually divided into *prose* and *poetry*.

575. The chief divisions of *prose* are science, philosophy, history, travels, novels, essays, addresses, critiques, and letters.

576. The chief divisions of *poetry* are epic poetry, dramatic poetry, lyric poetry, satires, epistles, epigrams, and epitaphs.

Dramatic poetry is divided into tragedies and comedies; and lyric poetry is divided into odes, songs, and sonnets.

PARAGRAPHS.

577. The division of his discourse into volumes, books, parts, cantos, verses, chapters, sections, paragraphs, and sentences, is left chiefly to every writer's own taste and judgment.

578. All discourse can usually be divided into *paragraphs*.

It is generally more convenient to divide poetry into *stanzas*.

579. A **Paragraph** is a sentence, or a combination of sentences, distinguished by a break and a new beginning; and it should comprise all that relates to a distinct part of the subject. It may also serve to make prominent an important thought, or to give a needed rest.

Most writers seem to know but little of the nice uses of the paragraph; and they abuse it even more than they abuse capital letters and punctuation-marks. That acute writer, Dean Swift, must have well understood the emphasizing force of the paragraph and the dash, when he wrote, —

"All modern trash is
Set forth with numerous *breaks* and *dashes*."

580. All paragraphs can be divided into sentences.

SENTENCES.

581. A **Sentence** is a thought expressed by a proposition, or a union of propositions, followed by a full pause.

Sometimes a sentence consists merely of a word or phrase, that is equivalent, however, to a proposition; as, "And still her former self lay there, unaltered in change. *Yes.* The old fireside had smiled on that same sweet face," etc. — *Dickens* (on the Death of little Nell). Sometimes, though very seldom, a complete sentence reaches beyond a full pause. (See a piece called "The Forgiven Debt," by L. M. Sargent.)

582. A **Proposition** is a subject combined with its predicate.

583. A **Clause** is a proposition that makes but a part of a sentence.

Ex. — "The morning was pure and sunny, | the fields were white with daisies, | and bees hummed about every bank." — *Irving.*

The foregoing expression is a sentence, consisting of three clauses.

584. A clause or sentence is, —

1. *Declarative*, when it expresses a declaration.

Ex. — John rides that wild horse.

2. *Interrogative*, when it asks a question.

Ex. — Does John ride that wild horse?

3. *Imperative*, when it expresses command, entreaty, or permission.

Ex. — John, ride that wild horse.

4. *Exclamatory*, when it expresses an exclamation.

Ex. — Does John ride that wild horse!

An exclamatory clause or sentence is simply a declarative, an interrogative, or an imperative one, uttered chiefly to express the emotion of the speaker.

585. Any of the foregoing modes of predicating may be either *affirmative* or *negative*.

586. Sometimes a sentence is a composite of clauses differently predicated.

Ex. — "The earth is green again;
But where are they who strove upon this field?"

This is a compound sentence, consisting of a declarative and an interrogative clause.

587. Sentences are divided into three classes; *simple*, *complex*, and *compound*.

Before we explain these classes, it will be necessary to show the chief relations of words in sentences, and to investigate the elements of sentences.

THE THREE RELATIONS.

588. Almost the whole of what is usually called Analysis, is based simply on three common relations of syntax, generalized and extended.

589. These are the predicate relation, the adjective relation, and the adverbial relation.

Predicate Relation.

1. Trees | grow.
2. Young trees | grow rapidly.
3. The young trees along the river | have grown rapidly this year.

Observe that the relation between *trees* and *grow*, in the first example, is the common syntax relation between nominative and verb. In analysis, we simply *extend this relation over the entire phrase, so as to take in the whole sense.* Hence, while *trees* remains the nominative in parsing, in analysis we make *trees*, *young trees*, and *the young trees along the river*, respectively the subjects. So, while *grow* remains the verb in parsing, in analysis we make *grow*, *grow rapidly*, *have grown rapidly this year*, respectively the predicates.

Adjective Relation.	**Adverbial Relation.**
Black HORSES.	They BUILD *wonderfully.*
These HORSES.	They BUILD *ships.*
The HORSES.	They BUILD *now.*
John's HORSES.	They BUILD *everywhere.*
HORSES, *the property of John.*	They BUILD *concealed.*
HORSES *owned by John.*	They BUILD *to be remembered.*
HORSES *to be sold.*	They BUILD *in great splendor.*
HORSES *of strength and speed.*	They BUILD *while labor is cheap.*
HORSES *of which he boasts.*	They BUILD *that they may have homes.*
HORSES *that have been rode.*	They BUILD *because they are rich.*

Observe that not merely the adjectives *black* and *these* tell what or which horses are meant, but that also the article *the*, the possessive

John's, the appositive, the participle, the infinitive, the adjunct, and the relative clause, — indeed, all the different words, phrases, and clauses, joined to *horses*, — tell *what* or *which* horses are meant. The adjective sense is thus extended over kindred meanings and over phrases and clauses.

Observe that the adverb *wonderfully*, and the object *ship*, which limit *build*, though in very different ways, still both show what kind of building is meant; namely, *wonderful building* and *ship-building*.

Observe also that all the different words, phrases, and clauses, joined to *build*, show *how*, *when*, *where*, *why*, or *as to what* the building is done, — that is, they are used in the sense of adverbs; and the adverbial sense is thus extended over kindred meanings and over phrases and clauses.

THE ELEMENTS OF SENTENCES.

590. The **Elements** of sentences are words, phrases, and clauses.

591. All sentences can be resolved into propositions or clauses.

592. Sometimes a sentence has, besides, an independent word or phrase.

Ex. — *No, gentlemen of the jury;* this is not law.

593. All the foregoing parts of sentences can be divided into six classes of elements: —

Two Principal Parts, or Elements.
Two Modifiers, or Modifying Elements.
A Connecting Element, or Connectives.
An Independent Element.

PRINCIPAL PARTS.

594. Every proposition must have at least two principal parts; a *subject-nominative* and a *predicate-verb.*

595. The **Subject-Nominative** is a noun, a pronoun, or an equivalent expression, that is the nominative to the verb.

596. The **Predicate-Verb** is the finite verb which predicates an act or state of the subject.

Ex.—Full many a *flower* | *is born* to blush unseen.

597. Every proposition must consist of a *subject* and a *predicate.*

598. The **Subject** is a word, phrase, or clause, denoting that of which something is predicated.

599. The **Predicate** is a word or phrase denoting that which is predicated of the subject.*

Ex.— Bells | tolled.
Full many a flower | is born to blush unseen.
That our life resembles a journey, | has often been observed.

600. Every subject and every predicate is either simple or compound.

601. A subject is *simple*, when it has but one subject-nominative to the same verb.

602. A subject is *compound*, when it has two or more subject-nominatives to the same verb.

603. A predicate is *simple*, when it has but one predicate-verb belonging to the same subject.

604. A predicate is *compound*, when it has two or more predicate-verbs belonging to the same subject.

Ex.— Roses | fade.
Roses and lilies | bloom and fade.
Days, months, years, and ages, | shall circle away.
Full many a flower | is born to blush unseen,
And waste its sweetness on the desert air.

* The subject is what remains after the predicate is removed; the predicate is what remains after the subject is removed. The subject, or the entire subject, is the subject-nominative with all its modifiers; the predicate, or the entire predicate, is the predicate-verb with all its modifiers. When the subject or the predicate consists of two or more words, the teacher may let the pupil call it the *entire subject*, the *entire predicate*; simply to give the expression a little more fullness or force.

The subject-nominative is sometimes called the *grammatical subject*, and the predicate-verb the *grammatical predicate*; the entire subject is sometimes called the *logical subject*, and the entire predicate the *logical predicate*. The predicate-verb *be*, or any other neuter verb, is sometimes called the *copula*; and the adjective, noun, or kindred expression, which follows it, is sometimes called the *attribute*.

The word *subject*, in grammar, is sometimes applied to the entire expression to which a predicate refers, sometimes to the nominative only, and sometimes to a person or thing; the word *object* is sometimes applied to a governed word or expression, and sometimes to a person or thing.

Mention the subjects, the predicates, the subject-nominatives, the predicate-verbs; and tell whether the subjects and predicates are simple or compound: —

Deep rivers | flow in silent majesty.

Rome | was not built in one day.

A thing of beauty is a joy forever.

The summer breeze parts the deep mazes of the forest shades.

There is a mourner o'er the humblest grave.

To meet danger boldly is better than to wait for it.

Our feelings and actions are evidently according to our belief.

The dipping paddle echoes far,
And flashes in the moonlight gleam.

When the subject or the predicate is a long or mixed phrase, it may be better to mention first the subject-nominative or predicate-verb, and then the modifiers that make with it the entire subject or predicate.

MODIFIERS.

605. A **Modifier** is a dependent word, phrase, or clause, added to some other word or expression, to limit or vary the meaning.

Ex. — *The* PATHS *of glory* lead but to the grave.

The and *of glory* are modifiers; because they cease to make sense when the word *paths* is removed, and they serve to show what paths are meant.

A modifier generally *specifies*, *limits*, *explains*, or *describes*.

606. There are two kinds of modifiers; *adjective* and *adverbial*.

607. An **Adjective Modifier** is one that modifies a noun or pronoun, or that belongs to it or depends on it.

An adjective modifier generally describes some person or thing.

Ex. — "*Solomon's* Temple." What temple?
"David, the *king* and *psalmist*." What David?

"The land *of palms*." What land?

"A hill *crowned with majestic trees*." What kind of hill?

"A proposition *to sell the farm*." What proposition?

"The store *which is on the corner*." What store?

Omit the words *land* and *hill*, and you can see at once that the remaining words cease to make sense; therefore *land* and *hill* are *principal* words, and the others *depend* on them. To ascertain which word can not be omitted without destroying the phrase or sentence, or the sense, will generally be the easiest way in which the pupil can find the principal word and its modifiers.

It is very difficult to define modifiers in such a way as to make the definition sufficiently comprehensive, and at the same time forcible and exact. Our definition of adjective modifiers would include predicates; — and, in truth, all predicates are modifiers or attributes of their subjects; — but the definition which we have given of predicates, will enable the pupil to distinguish them from modifiers.

608. A Noun or Pronoun may be modified, —

By Words,

1. **By an Article.** "*A* SERVANT brought *the* HORSE."
2. **By an Adjective.** "A *beautiful* rose." "Money *enough*."
3. **By a Possessive.** "*John's* horse." "*My* slate."
4. **By an Appositive.** "John the *saddler*." "The poet *Milton*."
5. **By a Participle.** "Fields *ploughed*." "Birds *singing*."
6. **By an Infinitive.** "Horses *to be fed*." "A house *to let*."

Sometimes also an adverb modifies a substantive, or must be taken with it in analysis. — See § 527.

Phrases,

1. **By an Adjunct.** "A bunch *of fresh flowers*."
2. **By an Appositive Phrase.** "Greece, *the cradle of arts*."
3. **By a Participial Phrase.** "Barns, *filled with hay and grain*."
4. **By an Infinitive Phrase.** "Ties *never to be thus broken*."
5. **By an Adjective Phrase.** "Days, *short and very cold*."

Sometimes, though very seldom, a substantive is modified by an absolute phrase that is used for a relative clause.

Clauses.

1. **By a Relative Clause.** "The winds *which bring perfume*."
2. **By an Appositive Clause.** "It was lucky *that I found it*."
3. **By an Adverbial Clause.** "The place *where he fell*."
4. **By a Conjunctive Clause.** "A request *that you will come*."

Exercises.

Mention the nouns and pronouns, and by what they are limited or modified: —

A house. Faithful friends. The river Hudson.
An orange. Lurking Indians. Mary the cook.

The ship. Twenty-five dollars. They themselves.
Warm weather. California bears. Time misspent.
Rainy weather. Virtue's reward. I, having escaped.
Large rooms. Our country's welfare. Visitors much delighted.
The President's proclamation. The songs of birds.
A path through the woods. A man without money.
An order to retreat. A watch to be repaired.
Scouts to watch the enemy. Indians lurking near.
Indians that lurk near. The sun's bright beams.
Lakes fringed with cedars. Two pillars of marble.
The armaments which thunder-strike the walls of rock-built cities.

609. An **Adverbial Modifier** is one that modifies a verb, an adjective, or an adverb; or that belongs to it or depends on it.

An adverbial modifier generally specifies the kind, limits the action, adds a circumstance, or expresses degree. — See below.

A modified verb is a finite verb, an infinitive, or a participle.

By *adverbial modifier* we mean whatever is *added* to a *verb* to make with it a predicate; or whatever modifies an adjective, an adverb, a participle, or an infinitive. A comprehensive term is needed; so that we are compelled either to enlarge the meaning of *adverbial*, or to coin a new expression. Perhaps it would be better to call these modifiers *predicate modifiers*, because they are mostly used in making predicates; and all adjective modifiers *substantive modifiers*, because they modify substantives.

Predicate or Adverbial Modifiers.

610. A VERB may be modified, —

By Words,
1. **By an Object.** "Men build *houses.*"
2. **By a Predicate Substantive.** "He became a *farmer.*"
3. **By a Predicate Adjective.** "The milk turned *sour.*"
4. **By an Adverb.** "The horse ran *fast.*"
5. **By a Participle.** "The ball went *whizzing.*"
6. **By an Infinitive.** "I have come *to be instructed.*"

"James is idle." — Owing to a slight radical difference in the modes of classifying, there is sometimes an apparent incongruity between Parsing and Analysis. Thus, in parsing, *idle* is referred to *James*, because *James* denotes the object to which the quality belongs; but, in analyzing, it is referred to *is*, because it makes with *is* the predicate.

Phrases,
1. **By an Adjunct.** "Apples grow *on trees.*"
2. **By an Objective Phrase.** "He knew *when to sell.*"
3. **By an Explanatory Phrase.** "To be good is *to be happy.*"
4. **By an Adverbial Phrase.** "He will come *by and by.*"
5. **By a Participial Phrase.** "He fell, *grasping his sword.*"
6. **By an Infinitive Phrase.** "He fell *to rise no more.*"
7. **By an Absolute Phrase.** "*He being sick*, I returned."

A modifying phrase that begins with an adverb, as well as a phrase that has the sense of an adverb, is sometimes best called an *adverbial phrase.*

Clauses.
1. **By an Objective Clause.** "I believe *that he is honest.*"
2. **By an Explanatory Clause.** "My wish is, *that you remain.*"
3. **By an Adverbial Clause.** "Study *while you are young.*"
4. **By a Conjunctive Clause.** "I am convinced *that you are right.*"

611. An Adjective or an Adverb can have the same modifiers as a verb, except those modifiers which are substantive or adjective.

Modifiers of adjectives or adverbs generally express degree or circumstance.

Exercises.

Mention the finite verbs, the infinitives, and the participles; and by what they are limited or modified:—

Exercises produce health.	Cast not pearls before swine.
He sold a variety of goods.	Columbus did not become disheartened.
She thinks he is rich.	I fully intended to go.
Time is money.	Concealing himself in a thicket.
He is considered an honest man.	Act wisely that you may win.
She was there yesterday.	The horse has become lame.
To write with neatness.	To write neatly and rapidly.

Nature from the storm shines out afresh.
I believe he will succeed when he makes the effort.
The sun having set, we returned to the camp, and made a fire.

The adjectives and the adverbs, and by what they are limited or modified:—

Uncommonly beautiful.	How dear to my heart.
Too beautiful to last.	It is very badly done.
Rich in knowledge.	She studies most diligently.

General Remarks.

612. A modified word may have two or more modifiers at the same time.

613. A word or part that modifies another, may itself be modified.

Ex. — "The boy who studied most diligently, gained the prize."

Boy is modified by the article *the* and the relative clause *who studied most diligently*; *diligently* modifies *studied*, and is itself modified by *most*.

Articles, *prepositions*, *conjunctions*, and *interjections*, are never modified.

For convenience, all modifiers of subject-nominatives and predicate-verbs may be called *primary modifiers*; and all modifiers of these may be called *secondary modifiers*.

614. A modified word may be called *principal*, in regard to that which modifies it.

615. An infinitive, used as a noun, takes only the modifiers of a verb.

616. A participial noun takes the modifiers of either a verb or a noun.

617. An adverbial modifier sometimes modifies a whole phrase or clause, rather than some word in it.

For examples, see Note VII, p. 196; see also pp. 172 and 210.

618. *Modify* we use as the most comprehensive word; but *limit*, *explain*, and *describe* can also be used, especially when more appropriate or expressive.

It is said that modifiers *always* limit. This is not true. "I study"; "I do not study." *Not* modifies or reverses *do study*, but does not limit it.

619. The predicate-verb *be*, when followed by an adjective, a noun, or a kindred expression, is simply *combined* with it, rather than modified by it; and the latter term can generally be called an *attribute* of the subject.

It is an attribute when it *describes*; it is simply an explanatory or identifying term when it *explains* or *identifies*. "Thou art a *man*"; attribute. "Thou art the *man*"; identity. "It was the *wind*"; *wind* is no attribute of *it*.

All other neuter or intransitive verbs, and also passive verbs, can be be treated in the same way as the verb *be*; though it is seldom necessary to do so, because the word *modify* can generally be applied to them.

620. All adverbial modifiers can be divided into three classes: —

1. **Objective Elements**; objects, — words, phrases, and clauses.
2. **Attributive Elements**; predicate adjectives or substantives, — words, phrases, and clauses.
3. **Adverbial Elements**; adverbs, adjuncts, etc., — words, phrases, and clauses.

Though this classification is obvious and instructive in the gross, in practical detail it can never be carried far without endless perplexity: because participles, infinitives, and clauses, belong to all these classes; adjuncts belong to at least two; and all these parts range and intertwist through the classes by many and almost imperceptible shades of difference. To a certain extent, the classification can be made profitable in schools.

CONNECTIVES.

621. The **Connectives** are the conjunctions, the prepositions, the relative pronouns, the responsive pronouns, and the conjunctive adverbs.

See pp. 75, 181, 182, 185.

622. A connective that is not a conjunction, performs also the office of the part of speech to which it belongs.

Connectives may consist of words or phrases.

Also the clauses "*that is*" and "*that is to say*" are sometimes used simply as coordinate conjunctions. Such phrases as, *the moment that*, *the instant that*, *as far as*, *as soon as*, etc., are frequently used in the sense of conjunctive adverbs.

Connectives are generally used singly, but sometimes in pairs.

Connectives are generally expressed, but sometimes they are omitted.

Parts are sometimes connected by simple succession or mere dependence.

Complex sentences have most connectives; and the parts of compound sentences are the ones most frequently connected by simple succession.

INDEPENDENT ELEMENT.

623. An **Independent Element** may be, —

1. An interjection.
2. An adverb.
3. An independent nominative, or a phrase with such a nominative.

Ex. — *O, yes, my Lord;* the rallying hosts advance.

Sometimes an independent substantive may be taken as a part of a logical subject. Sometimes an independent substantive has a relative clause joined to it, and the whole expression then forms an independent propositional phrase. See Gray's Ode to Adversity.

4. Occasionally an absolute, a participial, an infinitive, or a prepositional phrase.

See Note V and Rule II.

Sometimes a sentence has a loose participial, infinitive, absolute, or prepositional phrase, which is still, however, so related to the proposition that it can generally be taken as a part of the subject or the predicate. Such a phrase is sometimes grammatically independent, or does not modify the matter contained in the proposition, when it still modifies the mode of assertion, or shows as to what, or under what restriction, the statement is made. The phrase then modifies the proposition in the sense of a *modal adverb.* "Generally speaking" = *probably;* "Upon the whole" = "*hence, probably.*" (See p. 176.) But when such a phrase has no perceptible connection with the remaining words, it must be called *independent.*

624. An independent element may accompany any kind of sentence; and sometimes it stands by itself, like a sentence.

PHRASES AND CLAUSES.

625. A phrase or clause is generally named from its leading or introducing word, from its principal word, from its form, or from its use in the sentence.

The different systems of grammar have run the nomenclature and distinctions of phrases and clauses into such a maze, that no scientific classification can now be made without revolution and a new nomenclature. The following seems to us the best classification that can be made without a radical change.

626. In its *form*, a phrase may be, —

1. **Simple.** "On the ground." "To be there." "A large tree."
2. **Complex.** "At the close of the day." One phrase modifying another.
3. **Compound.** "At night and in the morning." Two co-ordinate phrases joined.
4. **Propositional,** or **Clausal.** "This depends *on who the commissioners are.*" "Between him and the man whom he had employed." A phrase, comprising a clause.
5. **Mixed.** See the beginning of *Paradise Lost,* down to the word *sing.*

627. In its *grammatical* nature, a phrase may be substantive, — nominative, possessive, objective, appositive; adjective; participial; infinitive; prepositional (the adjunct); adverbial; absolute; independent; idiomatic.

For examples of phrases and clauses, see pp. 234, 235, and 236.

628. In its *logical* nature, a phrase is substantive, adjective, adverbial, or independent.

629. In its *form*, a clause is, —

1. **Simple,** when it has but one predicate.
2. **Complex,** when it comprises a principal clause with a dependent clause.
3. **Compound,** when it comprises two co-ordinate clauses.

A proposition is either simple or complex. A complex proposition or clause is one that has an incorporated clause, or a clause that is folded in.

A combination of two or more clauses that makes but a part of a sentence, is sometimes called a *member;* but the term *complex* or *compound clause* is probably more convenient.

630. In its *grammatical* nature, a clause may be substantive, — nominative, objective, appositive, or explanatory; relative; adverbial; conjunctive.

To avoid the ambiguity of the word *adverbial*, it would be well to call clauses that begin with conjunctive adverbs, *conjunctive.*

631. In its *logical* nature, a clause is substantive, adjective, or adverbial.

632. By a farther remove, a clause may be considered, —

Independent; when it depends on no other clause. And then it is *principal,* when another clause depends on it or is incorporated into it.

Dependent, or **subordinate;** when it depends on some word or phrase.

Co-ordinate; when it is a companion, of equal rank, to some other independent or dependent clause.

SIMPLE SENTENCES.

633. A **Simple Sentence** is a sentence that has but one proposition.

It may have, besides, an independent word or phrase.

The subject of a simple sentence has no clause.

The predicate of a simple sentence has no clause.

634. The core of syntax, in all sentences, is *predication.*

1. Simplest Combination of Subject and Predicate.

Soldiers fight. Dogs bark. Time flies. Wolves howl. Doves coo. Jewels glitter. Sin degrades. Bees were humming. Mary was chosen. We shall return. Clouds are gathering.

ANALYSIS. — This is a simple declarative sentence. The subject is *soldiers*, and the predicate is *fight*.

2. Object added to the Predicate-Verb.

Dogs bite *strangers*. Wolves catch *lambs*. Lightning strikes *trees*. Misers love *gold*. Merchants sell *goods*. Horses draw *carriages*. Wealth produces *pride*. I shall see *him*.

ANALYSIS. — This is a simple declarative sentence. The subject is *dogs*. The entire predicate is *bite strangers*. The predicate-verb is *bite*, which is limited by its object *dogs*.

3. Article or Adjective added to the Subject or the Object.

The vessel was wrecked. John found *a* knife. Leaves cover *the* ground. *Sweet* music rose. She wrote *a good* composition. *Tall* and *beautiful* poplars fringe *the* river.

ANALYSIS. — This is a simple declarative sentence. The entire subject is *the vessel;* the subject-nominative is *vessel*, which is modified by the article *the*. *Was wrecked* is the predicate.

4. Adjective or Nominative added to the Predicate-Verb.

Lead is *heavy*. Most people are *ambitious*. A bad companion is *dangerous*. The wind blew *cold*. Flies are *insects*. The rose is a famous *flower*. It was *you*.

ANALYSIS. — This is a simple declarative sentence. *Lead* is the subject. *Is heavy* is the predicate. *Is* is the predicate-verb; and it is combined with *heavy*, an attribute of the subject. *Flies are insects*, is a simple declarative sentence. *Flies* is the subject, *are insects* is the predicate. *Are* is the predicate-verb; and it is combined with *insects*, an attribute of the subject.

5. Adverb added to the Predicate-Verb.

John comes *frequently*. Good pupils study *diligently*. The procession moved *slowly*. The eagle flew *round* and *upwards*. Flowers are peeping *out* | *everywhere*. I was *there*.

6. Adjunct added to the Predicate-Verb.

The mountain is clothed *with evergreens*. The wind glided *over the grass*. Our troubles are aggravated *by imaginary evils*. My cousin went *to your house*, | *at noon*, | *in a carriage*.

ANALYSIS. — This is a simple declarative sentence. The subject is *the mountain;* the subject-nominative is *mountain*, which is modified by the article *the*. *Is clothed with evergreens* is the predicate; *is clothed* is the predicate-verb, which is modified by the adjunct *with evergreens.*

7. Adjunct added to the Subject or the Object.

A wreath *of rose-buds* encircled her head. She brought a basket *of fruit.* The old oak is loaded *with a flock* | *of singing blackbirds.* The path *through the woods* is cool and pleasant.

ANALYSIS. — This is a simple declarative sentence. The entire subject is *a wreath of rose-buds;* the subject-nominative is *wreath*, which is modified by the article *a* and the adjunct *of rose-buds. Encircled her head* is the entire predicate; *encircled* is the predicate-verb, which is modified by the object *head*, and *head* is modified by the possessive *her*.

8. Possessive or Appositive added to Subject or Object.

My hat is new. *Mary's* eyes are blue. *Our* | *neighbor's* bees left *their* hive. Rogers *the poet* was a banker. Lake *Erie* is a beautiful sheet of water. We visited Rome, *the capital of Italy.*

Simple Sentences with Adjuncts.

Twilight is weeping *o'er the pensive rose.*

The world is bright *before thee.*

The hatred *of brothers* is the hatred *of devils.*

The violet has mourned *above their graves* | *a hundred years.*

A hundred years is an abridged adjunct, modifying *mourned.*

In darkness dissolves the gay frost-work *of bliss.*

Rhetorically arranged; grammatically arranged, it would be, The gay frost-work of bliss dissolves in darkness.

Like the leaves | *of the forest* they all passed away.

Like the leaves of the forest is an adverbial adjunct, modifying *passed.* Name phrases beginning with *like*, *near*, or *worth*, from the leading word. Say that verbs of giving are modified by ——, the direct object; and by ——, the indirect object.

Tell *me* the story. I gave *him* some wholesome advice.

I insist *on sending* | *him* | *the horse immediately.*

None knew thee *but to love thee.*

Upon the whole, I am pleased *with the terms.*

Looking upon the whole, etc. But it is probably better to say, that *upon the whole* modifies *am pleased,* in the sense of a modal adverb. (See p. 176.)

Simple Sentences with Participial or Absolute Phrases.

The poor fellow, *baffled so often*, became at last disheartened.

I saw him *returning home*. They fled, *pursued by our cavalry*.

The money being furnished, he purchased the estate.

The absolute phrase relates to *purchased*, and modifies it.

She sits *inclining forward as to speak*, |
Her lips half open, and her finger up. — ROGERS.

The compound absolute phrase tells how she sits. Sometimes such phrases are independent. Supply *being*.

Meanwhile the neighboring fields, *trampled and beaten down*, become barren and dry, *affording nothing but clouds of dust*.

That is, — "and afford," etc. This last participial phrase relates to *fields*, in the sense of a partial predicate; for it modifies neither the subject nor the predicate. Sometimes a participial or an infinitive phrase is almost a predicate or clause.

Simple Sentences with Infinitive Phrases.

I went to the river *to find a skiff*.

A path *to guide us* could not be found.

To protect persons and property is the duty of government.

It is the duty of government *to protect persons and property*.

The best way to thrive is *to keep out of debt*.

She has learned *to do nothing* but | *dress and visit*.

Surely we are not destined *to live always in war and discord*.

He is very well able *to bear the loss*.

The rain makes the grass *grow rapidly*.

The grass grow rapidly is the entire object of *makes*, and grass is the grammatical object. Such infinitive phrases are almost clauses, and such sentences are nearly complex; but they are still simple sentences.

I ordered him *to be brought*. Let no one *pass by*.

To speak plainly, he was a pedant puffed up with conceits.

The last infinitive phrase is grammatically independent, but logically it modifies the following proposition in the sense of a modal adverb. Page 176.

Simple Sentences with Compound Subjects.

There *health* and *plenty* cheered the laboring swain.

FORMULA. — A simple sentence with a compound subject; the subject-nominatives are ——, connected by ——, and modified by ——.

Around the post hung *helmets*, *swords*, and *spears*.

The breezy *call* of incense-breathing Morn,
 The *swallow* twittering from the straw-built shed,
The cock's shrill *clarion*, or the echoing *horn*,
 No more shall rouse them from their lowly bed.

Simple Sentences with Compound Predicates.

They softly *lie*, and sweetly *sleep*, low in the ground.
He *tried* each art, *reproved* each dull delay,
Allured to brighter worlds, and *led* the way.

Here and there a lark, scared from his feeding-place in the grass, *soars* up, bubbling forth his melody in globules of silvery sound, and *settles* upon some tall tree, and *waves* his wings, and *sings* to the swaying twigs.

Simple Sentences with Compound Modifiers.

The water ran | around the bridge and over the bridge.
A proverb is the *wit* of one and the *wisdom* of many.
LET | not Ambition mock their useful toil,
 Their homely joys, and destiny obscure;
Nor Grandeur hear, with a disdainful smile,
 The short and simple annals of the poor.

See, in Gray's Elegy, stanzas 16, 17, and 18; all of which make but one simple sentence.

Simple Sentences with Independent Parts.

Why, no, my lord; he has not failed.

But the daughter — alas! poor creature — she is accomplished, and cannot do household work.

Flag of the brave! thy folds shall fly
The sign of hope and triumph high. — *Drake.*
Ah! then how sweetly closed those boyhood days!
The minutes parting one by one like rays. — *Allston.*

☞ In general, any part of all the foregoing simple sentences can be made *compound*, by adding *similar* words or phrases, and thus making a *series;* and any part can be made *complex*, by adding *modifiers*, which are generally *different* words or phrases. It is thus that *long* simple sentences are produced.

2. COMPLEX SENTENCES.

635. A Complex Sentence is a sentence that has but one independent or principal clause, with one or more dependent clauses.

It is a sentence in which the parts are connected, at their widest or greatest joint, by a subordinate relation.

There runs through discourse, more or less, a serial sense, and also a modified sense. The former gives us *compound* structure; and the latter, *complex* structure.

1. A sentence that consists of two clauses connected by a relative pronoun, is *complex*.

2. A sentence that consists of two clauses connected by a conjunctive adverb, is *complex*.

3. A sentence that consists of two clauses connected by a subordinate conjunction, is *complex*.

4. A sentence that consists of two clauses, of which one is used in the sense of a noun, an adjective, or an adverb, is *complex*.

This class includes the three classes before it; and it is itself included in the general class, § 635.

In stead of having but two clauses, a complex sentence may also have several distinct clauses, or else a cluster of clauses, depending thus on the principal clause, or incorporated into it; and it can also have two or more independent clauses, provided the dependent clause relates to them jointly.

Almost every sentence must have at least one clause that is independent; and its clauses may all be so. When a sentence has two or more independent clauses, it is generally *compound*.

636. A subordinate clause may be used as a noun in any case except the possessive.

Substantive Clauses.

Nominative Clauses.

That the soul is immortal, is believed by all nations.

This is a complex declarative sentence, of which the subject is a subordinate or incorporated clause. *That the soul is immortal*, is the principal subject; and *is believed by all nations* is the principal predicate. *Is believed* is the predicate-verb; and it is modified by the adjunct *by all nations*. *That* is the connective, showing the dependence of the subordinate clause on something else. *The soul*, of the dependent clause, is the subject, etc.

Why he did not go, is obvious.

When Æneas landed in Italy, is not known.

Whether he can finish the work, is doubtful.

How an oak becomes an acorn, is a mystery.

Where Warren fell, is not precisely known.

By what means he succeeded, has never been explained.

Can he hold his position? is the question.

Appositive Explanatory Clauses.

It is universally believed *that the soul is immortal.*

This is a complex declarative sentence, of which the dependent clause is in apposition with the subject. *It*, with the clause *that the soul is immortal*, is the entire principal subject. *It* is the subject-nominative, which is modified by the explanatory clause. *Is universally believed* is the principal predicate; *is believed* is the predicate-verb, which is modified by the adverb *universally*. (Dispose of the dependent clause as heretofore.)

It is obvious *why he did not go.*

It is not known *when Æneas landed in Italy.*

It is doubtful *whether he can finish the work.*

It is mysterious *how an acorn becomes an oak.*

It is not precisely known *where Warren fell.*

It has never been ascertained *by what means he succeeded.*

The question, *Can he succeed?* is now discussed in the papers.

They did not seem to know the fact *that all parties must obey the laws.*

One truth is clear: *Whatever is, is right.*

Objective Clauses.

All nations believe *that the soul is immortal.*

This is a complex declarative sentence, of which the object is a dependent clause. *All nations* is the principal subject: *nations* is the subject-nominative, modified by *all*. *Believe that the soul is immortal*, is the entire principal predicate; *believe* is the predicate-verb, and it is limited by the objective clause *that the soul is immortal.*

You now see *why he did not go.*

No one knows *when Æneas landed in Italy.*

We doubt *whether he can finish the work.*

I have been considering *how an acorn becomes an oak.*

Our guide showed us *where Warren is supposed to have fallen.*

I have never ascertained *by what means he succeeded.*

He said, "*How can I ever forget your favors to me?*"

The laws, he thought, *should be more rigidly enforced.*

Teach me to know myself, and feel *what others are.*

Predicate Explanatory Clauses.

The universal belief is, *that the soul is immortal.*

This is a complex declarative sentence, into which a dependent clause is incorporated as a predicate-nominative, explanatory of the subject. (Analyze the principal subject.) *Is that the soul is immortal*, is the principal predicate; *is* is the predicate-verb, and it is combined with the predicate clause after it, which is explanatory of the subject.

The only wonder is, *that one head can contain it all.*

The cause of anxiety was, *why he did not write.*

One of the greatest mysteries is, *how an acorn becomes an oak.*

The question is, "*What is it best to do, under the circumstances?*"

Adjective Clauses.

The following sentences are complex because each has a clause that is used as an adjective, and is therefore dependent. The adjective clause is usually *folded in* or *appended.*

Relative Clauses with Expressed Antecedents.

The man *who escapes censure*, is fortunate.

This is a complex declarative sentence, with a dependent clause used as an adjective. The entire principal subject is, *the man who escapes censure;* the subject-nominative is *man*, and it is modified by the article *the* and the relative clause *who escapes censure*. *Is fortunate* is the principal predicate. *Is* is the predicate-verb; and it is combined with the predicate adjective *fortunate*, an attribute of the subject. *Who* joins the dependent clause to *man*, and is also the subject of the dependent clause. *Escapes censure* is the predicate; *escapes* is the predicate-verb, and it is modified by its object *censure.*

He *who is intelligent*, will be intelligible.

Mary has brought a beautiful rose, *which grew in the garden.*

The man *whose conscience is pure*, needs fear no accusation.

They met with such disasters *as reduced them to poverty.*

Who *that loves independence*, would ever become a politician?

Yonder is the plain *on which the battle was fought.*

The man *on whose fidelity I relied most*, was absent.

He owned several lots, *from the sale of which he became rich.*

There never yet were hearts or skies *clouds might not wander through.*

That is, — "through *which* clouds might not wander." — See § 176.

All questions, *of whatever*[10] *nature they may be*, are referred to the council.

Here the preceding noun is not an antecedent; but the clause, folded in, still describes it.

All questions, *whatever*[7] *they may be*, are decided by the council.

Relative Clauses without Antecedents.

Such an antecedent is, in reality, usually included or comprehended in the relative.

What can not be prevented, must be endured.

This is a complex declarative sentence, comprising a principal and an incorporated clause. The entire principal subject is, *what can not be prevented;* the subject-nominative is *what*, which is modified by the subordinate predicate, to which it is also the subject. (Now analyze the principal predicate, and then the subordinate predicate.)

The foregoing is a simplified though somewhat anomalous mode of analyzing; but it is logical, and can be easily explained to the pupil. A double relative is modified by the rest of the subordinate clause, because this remainder represents a simple relative clause that is partly included in the double relative. — See p. 193.

What is thoroughly understood, is easily described.

Whoever plants trees, must love others besides himself.

You can easily explain *what you thoroughly understand.*

Can easily explain what, etc., is the entire principal predicate; *can explain* is limited by *what you thoroughly understand* as the entire object, and by *what* as the grammatical object, which is modified by the rest of the subordinate clause, because this represents a relative clause partly comprised in *what*. *You* is the subordinate subject; *understand* is the predicate-verb, which is modified by the adverb *thoroughly* and the relative part of *what*.

Most politicians advocate *whatever seems popular.*

By indolence he lost *what ability he once had.*

Whomsoever the bishop appoints, the church will receive.

I will not object to *what is reasonable.*

To what is reasonable is the entire adjunct; *to what* is the grammatical adjunct. *What* is the grammatical object; and it is modified by the subordinate predicate, to which it is also the subject.

You know what you can do, by *what you have done.*

It is the tree which in *I know not what far country* grows.

Adverbial and Conjunctive Clauses used as Adjectives.

Not a soldier discharged his farewell shot
O'er the grave *where our hero was buried.— Wolfe.*

There are times *when the soul becomes tired of its earthly pilgrimage.*

A presentiment *that he would be killed*, made him sad.

Where and *when* are used in place of *in which*.
What kind of presentiment? Here the conjunctive clause is rather adjective than appositive; for it rather *describes* than *identifies*.

Adverbial Clauses.

The following sentences are complex because each has a clause that is used as an adverb, and is therefore dependent. The dependent clause generally *precedes* or *follows* the principal clause.

Adverbs of Time.

When the sun rises, the birds begin to sing.

This is a complex declarative sentence. *The birds begin to sing*, is the principal clause. (Analyze it.) *When the sun rises*, is the dependent clause, modifying the predicate of the principal clause in the sense of an adverb of time. *When* is a conjunctive adverb, connecting the two clauses.

While the robbers were plundering, she set fire to the house.

He locked the door *after the horse was stolen*.

Before reinforcements could be sent, the battle was lost.

He has become a citizen of this place *since you were here*.

I will take care of your horse *until you return*.

As we approached the top of the hill, we saw the Indians.

As soon as my money was gone, I no longer had friends.

Then, *when I am thy captive*, talk of chains.

Adverbs of Place.

We sowed the seed *where the soil was moist and loamy*.

Where the soil was moist and loamy, is the dependent clause, modifying *sowed* in the sense of an adverb of place.

He will be respected *wherever he may be*.

As far as we went, the country was well cultivated. Page 250.

Our language has no variety of clauses to express place. The farther any field of expression lies from the common track of thinking, the more it tends to circumlocution; and *vice versa*. Place is something that presses so closely and variously into us, and its ideas are so obvious, that they have been favored in language with the simpler garb of words and phrases (adjuncts).

Adverbs of Manner.

Forgive us *as we forgive our enemies*.

This is a complex imperative sentence. *Forgive (thou) us*, is the principal clause. *As we forgive our enemies*, is a dependent clause of manner, modifying *forgive*.

As he understands it, so he talks about it. Page 212.

As blossoms in spring, so are hopes in youth.

You will please to speak so *that we can hear you*.

The dependent clause is explanatory of *so*, and *so* expresses manner; but the clause also implies consequence.

Degree or Extent.

I am as tall *as he*.

This is a complex declarative sentence. The principal clause is, *I am as tall*. The dependent clause is *as he (is tall)*, which is an adverbial clause, modifying in an explanatory or limiting sense the phrase *as tall*, or more directly the adverb *as*. It determines the degree.

She sings as sweetly *as a nightingale.*

This construction expresses sometimes mere manner; but the idea of degree generally predominates.

He is as kind to me *as he can be.*

I was as much instructed *as I was excelled.*

We were so fatigued *that we could not sleep.*

They had advanced as far *as they could with safety.*

I have gone so far *that I can not turn back.*

There was such a noise *that I could not write.*

In this construction the dependent clause generally implies more or less of degree; but it may also have, partly or wholly, the sense of an identifying clause explanatory of *such.* A similar remark is applicable to other clauses.

After *as* and *than,* words are generelly understood.

Contentment is better *than wealth.*

He has more *than I.* He has more money *than brains.*

I had more fear *than it was prudent to confess.*

The more I use the book, the better I like it.

This is a complex declarative sentence, consisting of two clauses that are mutually dependent. (Those who insist on having one independent clause in every sentence, can call the second clause the independent one. "When I have used the book more, I shall like it better.")

The deeper the well, the cooler the water.

Degree is an abstract idea, but a very comprehensive and multifarious one, with which our judgments are much concerned; hence language is both rich and complicated in regard to it.

Cause, Purpose, Doubt, Concession, etc.

The connectives in the following sentences are subordinate conjunctions; but most of the dependent clauses answer to the adverb *why,* or imply doubt; and hence the clauses fall into the general analogy of *modal adverbs.*

The corn will grow, *because it rained last night.*

This is a complex declarative sentence. The principal clause is, *the corn will grow;* the dependent clause is the conjunctive clause *because it rained last night,* which is used adverbially, to modify *will grow,* of the principal clause, by showing *why.*

It rained last night, *because the ground is wet.*

Observe that the cause, in this sentence, is *logical,* and not *physical.* The wet ground did not cause the rain, but the speaker's belief; and therefore we incline to think words should be supplied. Thus: "I *know* that it rained last night, *because* the ground is wet." A similar remark is applicable to some other sentences that have conjunctive clauses.

Since the soil has been enriched, the corn will grow.

As he is quite young yet, he should rather go to school.

I will not sell the horse, *for I can not spare him.*

Say that the dependent clause modifies *will not sell.* It is often better to say that a modifier relates to a phrase or clause, than to try to make every modifier relate to a single word. Analysis aims to take in the whole thought or the complete ideas, and it is therefore in accordance with its principles to dispose of phrases and clauses as if they were single words. Such a mode of analyzing will also often remove the perplexity when a word seems to relate to each of several words; for in such cases it generally relates to the whole expression rather than to any one word in it.

When *for* joins two members of a sentence so loosely that they can be separated into two sentences, it is sometimes better to call the sentence compound.

I am sorry *that you did not come.*

I have written to you, *that you may know how we are.*

"These lofty trees wave not less proudly
That their ancestors moulder beneath them." — BRYANT.

If both the vowels are sounded, the diphthong is proper.

If spring have no blossoms, autumn will have no fruit.

Were I a lawyer, I should not like to plead a rogue's case.

Unless you do better, you will lose your situation.

Unsheathe not the sword, *except it be for self-defense.*

However much I may regret it, I can not do otherwise.

He hesitated,‸ *whether he should do this.* (As to.)

If Virgil was the better artist, Homer was the greater genius.

This is a logical condition, not a physical. (See p. 250.) "If you maintain that Virgil was the better artist, I shall maintain that Homer was the greater genius."

Though the whole race of man is doomed to dissolution, and we are all hastening to our long home; yet, at each successive moment, life and death seem to divide between them the dominion of mankind, and life seems to have the larger share.

All the sentences of the foregoing class are allied to compound sentences; and there are some grammarians who call them such. Sometimes it is better to call a sentence of this general class compound; and it seems to us, upon reflection, that it would be better to call such sentences as the last on p. 250, and the one above relating to Homer and Virgil, compound, than to supply words.

☞ In general, any part of all such complex sentences as we have shown, can be made *compound*, by adding *similar* words, phrases, or clauses, and thus making a *series;* and any part can be made *complex*, by adding *modifiers*, which are generally *different* words, phrases, or clauses. It is thus that *long* complex sentences are produced.

637. Most of the *long* complex sentences are made so, —

1. By a **series** of clauses.

That is, some clausal element is expanded into a series.

"I call that MIND free *which protects itself against animal appetites,* | *which resists the usurpations of society,* | *which recognizes its own greatness and immortality,* | *and which ever delights to pour itself forth in fresh and higher exertions.*" — CHANNING, *abridged.*

"We can not help KNOWING
That skies are clear and grass is growing,
That the breeze comes whispering in our ear,
That dandelions are blossoming near,
That maize has sprouted, that streams are flowing," *etc.* — LOWELL.

2. By a **gradation** of clauses.

"There is strong reason to suspect that some able Whig politicians, who thought it dangerous to relax, at that moment, the laws against political offenses, but who could not, without incurring the charge of inconsistency, declare themselves adverse to relaxation, had conceived a hope that they might, by fomenting the dispute about the court of the lord high steward, defer for at least a year the passing of a bill which they disliked, and yet could not decently oppose."

There is strong reason to suspect.
That some able Whig politicians had conceived a hope.
(*Who thought it dangerous to relax the laws against political offenses.*
But who could not declare themselves averse to relaxation.)
That they might defer for at least a year the passing of a bill.
Which they disliked, and yet could not decently oppose.

For the complete analysis of this sentence, see Kerl's Comprehensive English Grammar.

"He was a man | who never swerved from the path | which duty pointed out."

"Come | as the winds come | when navies are stranded."

"'No,' | said he; | 'for I never wished | that it might be so.'"

"I knew a man | who had it for a by-word, | when he saw men hasten to a conclusion, | 'Stay a little, | that we may make an end the sooner.'" — *Bacon.*

We have now shown the different modes of forming nearly all complex sentences. There are, besides, a few peculiar sentences of this general class that lie in the unfrequented nooks and around the borders of the empire; but we must leave them to the judgment of the teacher, for we have not room for them, and they can easily be referred to the general definition, § 635.

COMPOUND SENTENCES.

638. A **Compound Sentence** is a sentence that has two or more independent clauses.

It is a sentence in which the parts are connected, at their widest or greatest joint, by a co-ordinate relation.

1. A sentence that consists of two clauses, connected by a co-ordinate conjunction, is *compound*.

Ex. — The way was long, and the wind was cold.

2. A sentence, consisting of two clauses that have no connective, is generally *compound*.

Ex. — Some ran into the woods; others plunged into the river.

639. A compound sentence may consist, —

1. Of two or more simple sentences.

Ex. — Life is short, | and art is long.

"The curfew tolls the knell of parting day;
The lowing herd wind slowly o'er the lea;
The ploughman homeward plods his weary way,
And leaves the world to darkness and to me." — *Gray.*

2. Of two or more complex sentences.

"He lived as mothers wish their sons to live;
He died as fathers wish their sons to die." — *Halleck.*

"What in me is dark, illumine; what is low, raise and support."

"The character of General Washington, which his contemporaries reverence and admire, will be transmitted to posterity; and the memory of his virtues, while patriotism and virtue are held sacred among men, will remain undiminished."

3. Of two or more compound sentences.

Ex. — "Talent is power, tact is skill; talent is wealth, tact is ready money."

"There 's the marble, there 's the chisel;
Take them, work them to thy will:
Thou alone must shape thy future, —
Heaven give thee strength and skill."

A compound sentence, consisting of two members; and the first member, of two compound clauses.

4. Of a mixture of simple, complex, and compound sentences.

Ex. — "Life is short, and art is long; therefore it is almost impossible to reach perfection in any thing." — *Goethe.*

"Though the world smile on you blandly,
Let your friends be choice and few;
Choose your course, pursue it grandly,
And achieve what you pursue." — *Read.*

A compound sentence, consisting of two members; and the second member, of two simple clauses and a complex clause.

5. Of an independent clausal phrase, and a clause.

"Triumphal arch! that fill'st the sky when storms prepare to part,
I ask not proud philosophy to teach me what thou art."

The independent clausal phrase here ranks with an independent clause.

640. Compound sentences may be divided into the following classes: —

Copulative. Parts united in Meaning.

Times change, *and* we change with them.
The house was sold; ^ *also* the furniture. (And.)
Alice has been studious, *as well as* James.
The way is beset by enemies; *besides*, we have no provisions.
I believe it is so; *nay*, I am sure it can not be otherwise.
The people demand peace; *yea*, the army itself demands it.

Since mere succession implies addition or connection, copulative conjunctions are often omitted.

"The way was long, the wind was cold,
The minstrel was infirm and old." — *Scott.*
"It burst; it fell; and, lo! a skeleton." — *Rogers.*

Disjunctive. Parts united in Form but separated in Meaning.

You may study your lessons, *or* you may write a composition.
We can not assist him, *nor* can you.
Strong proofs, (*and*) *not* a loud voice, produce conviction.

Also clauses joined by *or else* or *neither* make compound sentences.

Adversative. Parts opposed in Meaning.

The world is made for happiness; *but* many people make themselves miserable.

There is much wealth in England, *yet* there are many poor people.
He has acted unwisely; *nevertheless* I will help him.
The wounded man died; *notwithstanding* several surgeons attended [him.
The dictionary is not perfect; *still* it is the best we have.
The prospect is not good; I will do, *however*, the best I can.
He is a sensible man; *though* he is not a genius.

Illative. Parts related in the Sense of Consequence or Inference.

The three angles are equal; *therefore* the three sides are equal.

Observe that the equality of the sides does not show how the angles are equal; and although the first clause is the basis of the truth in the second, yet this meaning is taken up by the substitute *therefore*, which modifies the second predicate, being equivalent to the phrase *from this cause*. *And*, understood, is the real connective.

The ground is wet; *therefore* it rained.
He is not at home; *hence* I have not written to him.
Corn is very cheap; *so* I concluded not to sell mine.
You see I am busy; *then* why do you trouble me?

The relation of consequence or inference is a very common and forcible one; and hence the connective in many such sentences may also be omitted, the meaning being sufficiently obvious without it. By reversing the propositions, the sentences would come under the head of *cause;* and hence many sentences of this kind also dispense with the connective, and are then generally compound sentences rather than complex.

He is a mean boy: let him alone.
Let him alone: he is a mean boy.

Such a sentence may be considered compound, chiefly because it could be divided into two sentences.

He is poor: deal liberally with him.
Deal liberally with him: he is poor.
Live not in suspense: it is the life of a spider.

To the foregoing sentences may be added a few others that are somewhat different; but of which the second clause is still in some way explanatory of the first, or is suggested by it.

You know the man; do you not?

"Each rising art by just gradation moves:
Toil builds on toil; and age on age improves."— *Collins.*

"Ambition often puts men upon performing the meanest offices: so climbing and creeping are performed in the same posture."—*Swift.*

"That which we have acquired with most difficulty, we retain the longest; as those who have earned a fortune, are generally more careful in keeping it than those who have inherited one." — *Colton.*

Parenthetic. An Extraneous Clause between Related Parts.

A parenthetic clause that is not used in the sense of a part of speech, and that has not the remainder of the sentence for its object, generally makes the sentence compound.

"A rose — I know not how it came there — lay on my book."

A rose lay on my book: I know not how it came there.

"They call us angels — though I am proud to say no man ever so insulted my understanding — that they may make us slaves."—*Jerrold.*

When you meet with a long sentence, glance through it, and notice the joints between clauses. If the sense at the greatest or widest of these joints is a subordinate relation, the sentence is *complex;* if a co-ordinate relation, the sentence is *compound.*

The general construction of sentences is this: Words make phrases; words or phrases make simple sentences; simple sentences make complex or compound sentences; and simple, complex, or compound sentences make compound sentences. Complex sentences are sometimes said to be *compact* in structure; and compound, *loose.*

A sentence is sometimes compound in form, but complex in sense; and sometimes complex in form, but compound in sense. When these characteristics are strongly developed, the sentence may be analyzed accordingly. (See Kerl's Comprehensive Grammar, p. 85.) For the sake of greater effect, conditional or dependent clauses are sometimes expressed in the form of independent interrogative or imperative clauses.

Having now shown the general construction of sentences, let us next notice some of the modifying laws, which may be explained under two heads,—*Contraction* and *Arrangement.*

CONTRACTION.

641. Brevity, in the construction of sentences, is obtained either by *ellipsis* or by *abridgment.*

Sometimes, by substituting a different expression.

642. Compound constructions are generally shortened by ellipsis.

643. Complex constructions are generally shortened by abridgment.

644. Compound Elements. When the clauses of a compound sentence have the same predicate, the sentence can be changed to a simple one with a compound subject.

"Wheat grows well on these hills, and barley grows well on these hills."
Wheat and barley grow well on these hills.

645. When the clauses of a compound sentence have the same subject, the sentence can be changed to a simple one with a compound predicate.

"The hurricane tore down trees, and the hurricane overturned houses."
The hurricane tore down trees, and overturned houses.

646. When the clauses of a compound sentence have the same subject and predicate-verb, all the repeated parts can be omitted.

"He is a wise man; *he is a* good *man;* and *he is a* patriotic man."
He is a wise, good, and patriotic man.

647. A compound modifier is contracted by referring the common part to the rest of the phrase as a compound.

Ex. — "*In* peace and *in* war" = *In* peace and war.
"To *the house* and from *the house*" = To and from *the house.*
"To speak *prudently* and act *prudently*" = To speak and act *prudently.*

648. Simple Sentences are often contracted by retaining only the most important part, or that which necessarily implies the rest.

"Bread."	"Order!"	"Arm!"
Give me some bread.	Let us have order.	Arm ye yourselves.

In accordance with this analogy, language has single words that are permanently used as equivalents or representatives of sentences; as, *yes, no, well, why.*

649. The verb *be*, in all its forms, is frequently omitted.

"Where now her glittering towers?" Where *are* now, etc.
"This done, we instantly departed." This *being* done, etc.
[*To be*] "Everybody's friend, [*is to be*] everybody's fool."

The subject of the imperative mood is generally omitted; and an imperative verb may be omitted with its subject when there remains a forcible adverb to represent the entire expression.

650. Language frequently affords us the choice of either a word, a phrase, or a clause; especially in regard to modifiers.

"*Pleasant* scenes." "Scenes *of pleasure.*" "Scenes *that please.*"

651. A word or phrase that remains as the result of abridgment, generally retains the logical construction of the phrase or clause which it represents, or from which it is abridged.

Ex.—"I BELIEVE *that he is honest*" = I BELIEVE *him to be honest.*

To ascertain the syntax of a difficult word or phrase, it is often best to consider the term the result of contraction, and to pass thence to the original expression; yet it must not be supposed that there ever was a perfect and ponderous language from which all the parts thus supplied have fallen away by ellipsis or abridgment.

There are many exceptions to what is usually taught about equivalent expressions. The constructions which we are obliged to call equivalents, frequently differ from each other, at least rhetorically, by a shade of meaning. "I believe *that he is honest*," and "I believe *him to be honest*," are equivalent; but "I will see *that he does it*," and "I will see *him do it*," are different. "A purse *of silk*" is the same as "a *silken* purse"; but "a purse *of gold*" is not "a *golden* purse."

652. Complex Sentences can often be abridged into simple sentences.

Ex.—"*As we approached the house*, we saw *that the enemy were retreating*" = *On approaching the house*, we saw *the enemy retreating*.

The abridged part is usually the dependent clause.

653. The abridged form of a *substantive clause* is generally an infinitive phrase.

"*That I may go alone*, is my wish" = *To go alone* is my wish.

"It is my wish *that I may go alone*" = It is my wish *to go alone*.

"I wish *that he may go alone*" = I wish *him to go alone*.

Sometimes the dependent clause is abridged into a *participial phrase*.

654. The abridged form of an *adjective clause* is,—

1. An adjunct or an adjective.

Ex.—"Our house *which is in the country*" = Our house *in the country* = Our *country* house.

2. A participial phrase.

"The book *which contains the story*" = The book *containing the story*.

3. An infinitive phrase.

"A day *that may suit you*" = A day *to suit you*.

4. Sometimes an absolute phrase.

For an example, see p. 269.

655. The abridged form of an *adverbial clause* is, —

1. An adjunct.

Ex. — "You will suffer from cold, *if you remain here.*"
You will suffer from cold, *by remaining here.*

2. A participial phrase.

Ex. — "*When I had eaten my dinner,* I returned to the store."
Having eaten my dinner, I returned to the store.

3. An infinitive phrase.

Ex. — "I have come *that I may assist you.*"
I have come *to assist you.*

4. An absolute phrase.

"*When Cæsar had crossed the Rubicon,* Pompey prepared for battle."
Cæsar having crossed the Rubicon, Pompey prepared for battle.

Sometimes there remains, by abridgment, simply a participle, an infinitive, or a single word of some other kind.

656. Sometimes only the prominent part of the dependent clause is retained.

"*When young,* life's journey I began" = When *I was* young, etc.
"*If so,* you need not remain longer" = If *it is* so, etc.
"It is more easily imagined *than described*"; *i. e.,* than *it is* described.

The pronoun, and the verb *be,* are thus often omitted together.

657. When the principal and the subordinate clause have both the same subject, the subordinate clause generally loses its subject by abridgment.

"When *I* had done this, *I* returned" = Having done this, *I* returned.
"*I* came that *I* might assist you" = *I* came to assist you.

658. When the principal and the subordinate clause have different subjects, the subject of the subordinate clause usually remains; but it is generally changed in its case, to suit the syntax of the new arrangement.

"I expect that *he* will come" = I expect *him* to come.
"There is no doubt that *he* wrote it" = There is no doubt of *his* having written it. "*When he was caught,* we returned" = *He being caught,* we returned.

The subject of the dependent clause generally becomes, by contraction, an objective word, a possessive word, or a nominative absolute.

659. A modifying phrase can often be abridged into a compound word.

Ex. — "Boots *with red tops*" = *red-topped boots.* "Having a sharp edge" = *sharp-edged.*

660. Connectives can often be omitted.

See §§ 176, 551, 559.

ARRANGEMENT.

661. The place most important in a sentence is the beginning; and the next most important is the end.

Hence the subject, which is the germ of the whole sentence, naturally stands first; as, "*Rome* was an ocean of flame." — *Croly.*

662. When a subordinate word, phrase, or clause, denotes what is most striking, or what is uppermost in the speaker's mind, it may occupy the chief place.

Adjective: "*Great* is Diana of the Ephesians."
Verb: "*Out-flew* millions of flaming swords." — *Milton.*
Object: "*Silver* and *gold* have I none."
Adverb: "*Down* I set him, and *away* he ran."
Adjuncts: "*By these* [*swords*], we acquired our liberty; and *with these,*" etc.
Infinitive or **Participle:** "*To do this,* men and money are needed."

663. Frequently, an adjunct, a participial phrase, or an infinitive phrase, may be transposed.

Ex. — "*In proportion to the increase of luxury,* the Roman state evidently declined" = The Roman state, *in proportion to the increase of luxury,* evidently declined = The Roman state evidently declined *in proportion to the increase of luxury.*

664. Frequently, the clauses may change places, or one may be placed within another.

Ex. — "*If you desire it,* I will accompany you" = I will accompany you, *if you desire it* = I will, *if you desire it,* accompany you.

665. Some regard should be paid to the relative importance of the parts, and to the natural order of things.

666. A sentence so constructed that the meaning is suspended till the close, is called a *period.*

See the beginning of the Declaration of Independence.

SENTENCES FOR PARSING.

☞ The following sentences comprise the general circuit of principles involved in Parsing.

1.

A fisherman's boat carried the passengers to a small island. Mexico lies between the Pacific Ocean and the Gulf of Mexico. I have John's book, not Mary's. He, being a mere boy, was spared. He being a mere boy, the Indians spared him. Friends, Romans, countrymen, lend me your ears. Hail, Sabbath, thee I hail, — the poor man's day.

2.

I will never forsake you. The party reposed themselves on the shady lawn. John and James know their lessons. Neither John nor James knows his lesson. It is wicked to scoff at religion. It is too early for flowers. It was he. My heart beats yet, but hers I can not feel.

3.

That man is enslaved who can not govern himself. Assist such as need thy assistance. Whatsoever he doeth, shall prosper. I see you what you are. Whom do you take him to be? "Who is there to mourn for Logan? — Not one." The profit is hardly worth the trouble. The Atlantic Ocean is three thousand miles wide.

4.

On the grassy bank stood a tall waving ash sound to the very top. There are two larger pear-trees in the second row. The cedars highest on the mountain are the smallest. It is well to be temperate in all things whatsoever. You are yet young enough to learn the French language very easily. She gazed long upon the clouds in the west, while they were slowly passing away. The pipers loud[13] and louder blew; the dancers quick[10] and quicker flew.

5.

Respect yourself. I would I were at home. You or he is to blame. You behave too badly to go into company. James ran fast, pursuing John, and pursued by us. Considering his age, he is far advanced. To speak plainly, I do not like her. To escape was impossible. It is easier to be a great historian than a great poet. The sailors, in wandering over the island, found several trees bearing delicious fruit. That he should think so, is strange.

6.

A troop of girls are searching for flowers on yonder hill. The Rhone flows out from among the Alps. Washington died at his residence, on the 19th of December, 1797; and was buried near the Potomac, among his relatives. However, if they do not come, I shall neither wait nor return. Such, alas! is the fate of ambition.

CONDENSED ORDER OF ANALYSIS AND PARSING.

Sentence; simple, complex, or compound; declarative, interrogative, imperative, exclamatory, or a composite of.

Independent Phrase, if any; principal word, modifiers.

Simple Sentence; subject, subject-nominative, modifiers; predicate, predicate-verb, modifiers.

Complex Sentence; independent or principal clause; analysis. Dependent clause or clauses; analysis.

Compound Sentence; consisting of, § 639. Analyze the clauses.

Article: kind; disposal; Rule.

Adjective; kind; sub-class; comparison; degree; disposal; Rule.

Noun; kind; gender; person; number; declension; case; disposal; Rule.

Pronoun; kind; sub-class; antecedent and Rule IX, or gender, person, number; declension; case; disposal; Rule.

Finite Verb; principal parts; kind in regard to form; kind in regard to objects, — with voice; mood; tense; form; synopsis; conjugation; person and number; disposal; Rule.

Omit synopsis, conjugation, and declension, when familiar to the student.

Infinitive; its forms; kind in regard to time; kind in regard to objects, — with voice; disposal; Rule. (So, Participles.)

Infinitive, used as a noun; its nature as an infinitive; its nature as a noun; disposal; Rule for nouns. (In a similar way dispose of participial nouns and participial adjectives.)

Adverb; kind; comparison; degree; disposal; Rule.

Preposition; relation; Rule.

Conjunction; kind; connection; Rule.

Interjection; kind; Rule. (See Kerl's "First Lessons," p. 121.)

SENTENCES FOR ANALYSIS AND PARSING.

The following collection of sentences is of such a nature, and has been so classified, as to exhibit the types of all sentences, and the general construction of language according to the principles of Analysis.

PRINCIPAL PARTS.

Simple Subjects and Predicates.

Unmodified.

1. Banners waved. 2. Lights were shining. 3. He should have been rewarded. 4. Could they have gone? 5. To whisper is forbidden. 6. Whispering is forbidden.

Modified by Words and Phrases.

1. Manners make fortunes. 2. These roses are very beautiful. 3. Too much fear is an enemy to good deliberation. 4. Virtuous youth brings forth accomplished and flourishing manhood. 5. Milton, the author of Paradise Lost, was deeply versed[10] in ancient learning.

Modified by Clauses.

SUBJECT. — 1. They who are set to rule over others, must be just. 2. There was one clear, shining star, that used to come out into the sky before the rest, near the church spire, above the graves. 3. The disputes between the majority which supported the mayor, and the minority headed by the magistrates, had repeatedly run so high that bloodshed seemed inevitable.

PREDICATE. — 1. Heaven has imprinted, in the mother's face, something that claims kindred with the skies. 2. I was assured that he would return. 3. We found, in our rambles, several pieces of flint which the Indians had once used for arrow-heads.

Inverted and Elliptical Constructions.

1. In every grove warbles the voice of love and pleasure. 2. Bursts the wild cry of terror and dismay. 3. How wonderfully are we made!

1. Write. 2. Sweet the pleasure. 3. Here the wigwam blaze beamed on the tender and helpless.

4. "Where 's thy true treasure?" Gold says, "Not in me";
And, "Not in me," the Diamond. Gold is poor!

3. Supply *children*. Or say, *Tender* and *helpless* are adjectives, relating to some noun understood that denotes persons; and they are also used as a noun, because they represent the noun understood, — and hence of the com. g., 3d p., pl. n., etc.

Infinitive Phrases used as Subjects.

1. To relieve the poor is our duty. 2. To pay as you go, is the safest way to fortune. 3. To have advanced much farther without supplies, would have been dangerous.

Sometimes we find also participial phrases used as subjects; but clauses or infinitive phrases are generally preferable to such constructions.

Inverted and Elliptical.

Unknown to them, when sensual pleasures cloy,
To fill the languid pause with finer joy.

Clauses used as Subjects.

1. That the earth is round, is now well known. 2. How the soul is connected with the body, is a great mystery. 3. "Dust thou art, to dust returnest," was not written of the soul.

Compound Subjects and Predicates.

Compound Subjects.

1. Patience and perseverance can remove mountains. 2. Either James or Henry is talking. 3. His magnificence, his taste, his classical learning, his high spirit, and the suavity of his manners, were admitted even by his enemies.

2. A sentence of this kind can be considered compound, by supplying another predicate; but it is more common to say simply that the subject is compound. When in parsing, however, a distinct predicate must be furnished to each nominative, then the sentence, not the subject, should be considered compound; as, "You or he is to be blamed." "The best books, not the cheapest, should be our object."

1. To remain and to advance were equally dangerous. 2. To fight that night, or to retreat, was the only alternative left. 3. To hope and strive is the way to thrive.

3. *To hope and strive* is the entire subject and the subject-nominative. *To hope* is in part the subject of *is*. *Is* agrees with *to hope* and *to strive* conjointly, taken as one thing.

Clauses.

That he should take offense at such a trifle, that he

should write an article about it, and that he should then publish it, surprised us all.

Clausal Phrases.

The wit whose vivacity condemns slower tongues to silence, the scholar whose knowledge allows no man to fancy that he instructs him, the critic who suffers no fallacy to pass undetected, and the reasoner who condemns the idle to thought and the negligent to attention, are generally praised and feared, reverenced and avoided.

Compound Predicates.

1. He rose, reigned, and fell. 2. Slowly and sadly they climb the distant mountains, and read their doom in the setting sun.

3. The rose had been washed, just washed in a shower,
    Which Mary to Anna conveyed;
  A delicate moisture encumbered the flower,
    And weighed down its beautiful head.

4. Glass is impermeable to water, admits the light and excludes the wind, is capable of receiving and retaining the most lustrous colors, is susceptible of the finest polish, can be carved or sculptured like stone or metal, never loses a fraction of its substance by constant use, and is so insensible to the action of acids that it is employed by chemists for purposes to which no other substance could be applied.

ADJECTIVE MODIFIERS.

(SUBSTANTIVE MODIFIERS.)

1. Articles.

1. A church stands on the adjoining hill. 2. A statesman's character should be an honor to his country.

Elliptical and Peculiar Constructions.

1. A man and woman were drowned. 2. He bought a house and lot. 3. A river runs between the old and the new mansion. 4. A great many adjectives are derived from nouns. 5. Peter the Great is the pride of Russia.

2. Adjectives.

1. This little twig bore that large red apple. 2. Green fields and forests were before us. 3. A swift and limpid rivulet purled over the pebbles. 4. He used very forcible but courteous language. 5. Two plum-trees, radiant with white blossoms on every bough, overtop the garden wall. 6. The whole world swarms with life, animal and vegetable.

1. *Apple* is modified by *red*; *red apple*, by *large*; and *large red apple*, by *that*.
2. *Green* belongs to both *fields* and *forests*.

Inverted and Elliptical.

1. It was a bright morning, soft and balmy. 2. Calm, attentive, and cheerful, he confutes more gracefully than others compliment. 3. Then followed a long, a strange, a glorious conflict of genius against power. 4. Violets meek and jonquils sweet she chose.

2. The dependent clause, *than others compliment*, limits, determines, or completes the comparison; or it modifies the phrase *more gracefully*, by showing the manner and degree. 3. Supply *conflict*; and put each *conflict*, after the first, in apposition with the first.

3. Possessives.

1. John's horse is in our garden. 2. Gen. George Washington's residence was on the Potomac. 3. Soft blows the breeze o'er India's coral strand.

Elliptical and Peculiar Constructions.

1. I will wait at Smith's, the bookseller.[7] 2. I will wait at Smith[3] the bookseller's.[7] 3. Lewis[3] and Raymond's[3] factory was burned. 4. This is a discovery of Sir Isaac Newton's. 5. That head of yours has many strange fancies in it. 6. The bard of Lomond's lay is done.

5. *Yours*, an idiom; equivalent to *your possession*. — See p. 221.
6. *Bard* (*'s*) is governed by *lay*, and *Lomond* (*'s*) by *of*.

4. Appositive or Explanatory Expressions.

Nouns and Pronouns.

1. Thou, thou,[7] art the man. 2. I myself was present. 3. The nurse, that ancient lady, preached decorum.

4. There is but one God, the author, the creator, and the governor of the world; almighty, eternal, and incomprehensible. 5. Thou sun, both eye and soul of the world.

6. A cove, or inlet, divides the island. 7. As a writer, he has few equals. 8. Madame de Stael calls beautiful architecture frozen music. 9. Messrs. William and Robert Bailey were conversing with the Misses Barnes. 10. Two things a man should never fret about; what he can help, and what he can not help. 11. The saint, the father, and the husband prays. 12. You are too humane and considerate; things few people can be charged with.

8. *Calls* is modified by *beautiful architecture frozen music*, as the entire object; and by *architecture* as the simple object. *Music* is put in apposition with *architecture*, and is partially governed by *calls*.

9. *William* (*Bailey*) and *Robert Bailey* are put in apposition with *Messrs.*; but *Misses Barnes* is best parsed as one noun.

12. *Things*, nominative, in apposition with the adjectives *humane* and *considerate*; Remark under Rule VII. Supply *which* as the object of *with*.

Infinitive Phrases.

1. It is foolish to lay out money in a purchase of repentance. 2. It is our duty to be friendly toward mankind, as much as it is our interest that mankind should be friendly toward us.

1. *It*, with the explanatory infinitive phrase, *to lay out money*, etc., is the entire subject; and *it* is the subject-nominative. *It* is modified by the phrase *to lay out money*, etc., as the entire appositive or explanatory phrase; and by the infinitive *to lay*, as the simple appositive.

Clauses.

1. It is through inward health, that we enjoy all outward things. 2. It is scarcely to be imagined, how soon the mind sinks to a level with its condition. 3. Study is at least valuable for this — that it makes man his own companion.

Inverted and Elliptical.

1. Child of the Sun[7], refulgent Summer comes. 2. Thyself shalt see the act. 3. This monument is itself[7] the orator of this occasion. 4. I sold them for a dollar a pair.[7] 5. One by one the moments fly. 6. They had one each.

7. He thought it an honor to do so. 8. Strange that a harp of thousand strings should keep in tune so long.

2. Thou thyself. 4. I sold them, each pair for a dollar. 5. *One by one* might also be considered an adverbial phrase. 7. He thought it, to do so, an honor. *To do so* is in apposition with *it*. *Honor* is also in apposition with *it*; but it is, besides, partially governed by *thought*. 8. It is strange, etc.

5. Participles.

1. Truth, crushed to earth, shall rise again. 2. The deer, seeing me, fled. 3. The wolf, being much exasperated by the wound, sprang upon the horse. 4. There are twenty-six senators, distinguished for their wisdom, not elevated by popular favor, but chosen by a select body of men. 5. The blast seemed to bear away the sound of the voice, permitting nothing to be heard but[14] its own wild howling, mingled with the creaking and the rattling of the cordage, and the hoarse thunder of the surges, striving like savage beasts for our destruction.

Inverted.

6. Close beside her, faintly moaning, fair and young, a soldier lay,
Torn with shot and pierced with lances, bleeding slow his life away.

6. This is one of the sentences in which it is difficult to determine what makes the subject, and what makes the predicate. Perhaps the division is properly made thus: *A soldier, fair and young, torn with shot and pierced with lances,* | *lay close beside her, faintly moaning, and slowly bleeding away his life.* It is sometimes difficult to determine whether an adjunct, an adjective phrase, a participial phrase, or an infinitive phrase, should be referred to the subject or to the predicate. — See p. 232.

6. Infinitives.

1. Contributions to relieve the sufferers were sent in. 2. The book to be adopted by us should be compared with others of the same kind. 3. Persuade Mary to let him have his books. 4. Let us have some of these clams cooked for supper.

4. *Cooked* is rather the present passive infinitive than the perfect passive participle. If the clams were already cooked, then it would be the participle.

7. Adjuncts.

Simple.

1. The roar of the lion was heard. 2. She bought a house with its furniture. 3. The promises of Hope are sweeter than roses in the bud, and far more flattering to

expectation. 4. The sailors did not like the idea of being treated so. 5. There is a flower about to bloom. 6. The question of who is to lead them, was next discussed.

Complex.

1. A Gothic cathedral is a blossoming in stone, subdued by the insatiable desire of harmony in man. 2. The gold in a piece of quartz from the mines of California, weighed several pounds.

Compound.

1. The large elm between the house and the river seems to be the king of the forest. 2. Brazil is regarded as a land of mighty rivers and virgin forests, palm-trees and jaguars, anacondas and alligators, howling monkeys and screaming parrots, diamond-mines, revolutions, and earthquakes.

8. Clauses.

1. The man who sows his field, trusts in God. 2. Self-denial is the sacrifice which virtue must make. 3. We encamped by a limpid rivulet, that purled over the pebbles. 4. He paid more for the flowers and gems which he brought, than they are worth. 5. 'T is the land where the orange and citron grow. 6. There is plain proof that[15] he is guilty. 7. The man with whom love is a sentiment, ever yearns for a home of his own. 8. Get what is needed.

Inverted and Elliptical.

1. Whom ye ignorantly worship, him declare I unto you. 2. We have no such laws as those by which he was tried in the State from which he came. 3. 'T is the land I love.

Abridged.

She turned, — a reddening rose[7] in bud,
  Its calyx half withdrawn, —
Her cheek on fire with damasked blood
  Of girlhood's glowing dawn! — *Holmes.*

Its calyx half withdrawn is an absolute phrase, used here in the sense of a relative clause describing *rose*. *Her cheek [being] on fire*, etc., is an absolute phrase, used here for an adverbial clause of manner or cause, and modifying *turned*.

ADVERBIAL MODIFIERS.

(PREDICATE MODIFIERS.)

1. Objectives.

Nouns and Pronouns.

1. Birds build nests. 2. The soil produces corn, hemp, tobacco, wheat, and grass. 3. Here we saw green fields, groves of ancient oak, and happy homes embowered in tufts of shade. 4. The hurricane even tore down enclosures that had been lately made, trees that had stood for ages, and mansions that had been built of stone. 5. She gave what she could not sell.

Infinitives and Participles.

1. I like to study. 2. We preferred to remain at home, and learn our lessons. 3. He intended to move to the West, to purchase him a farm, and to end his days on it in peace and quiet. 4. He knew not what to say. 5. After such a hint, I could not avoid offering her my assistance, and regretting my apparent want of gallantry.

Clauses.

1. I believe that he is honest and industrious. 2. Every one must have noticed how much more amiable some children are than others. 3. She saw that we were tired, and needed some refreshment. 4. Tell us not, sir, that we are weak, unable to cope with so formidable an adversary. 5. They said that Halifax loved the dignity and emolument of office, that while he continued to be president it would be impossible for him to put forth his whole strength against the government, and that to dismiss him would be to set him free from all restraint. 6. Who can tell who he is?

Inverted and Elliptical.

1. Me glory summons to the martial scene. 2. Him well I knew, and every truant knew. 3. I have nothing to say. 4. "Trifles," said Sir Joshua Reynolds "make

perfection; but perfection is no trifle." 5. O that those lips had language! 6. Heaven hides from brutes what men, from men what spirits, know. 7. Teach me my own defects to scan; what others are, to feel; and know myself a man.

3. Supply *that I wish*, or *which I am able*, or *which it is proper for me*; or else parse *to say* according to § 401.

2. Predicate Substantives.

Nouns and Pronouns.

1. He is a farmer. 2. She was appointed governess. 3. Man is a bundle of habits and relations. 4. His daily teachers had been woods and rills. 5. This aunt Betsy[7] was the neatest and most efficient piece of human machinery that ever operated in forty places at once. 6. A poor relation is the most irrelevant thing in nature, an odious approximation, a haunting conscience, a perpetually recurring mortification, a drawback on your rising, a stain in your blood, a drain on your purse, and a more intolerable drain on your pride. 7. It is we who are Hamlet. 8. I shall be all anxiety, till I know what his plans are. 9. "Shall we not wait for Decius? — No; were he ten times Decius." 10. I knew it to be him. 11. He, being a partner[7], was called in as a witness. 12. He is tired of being a loafer[2].

13. She looks a goddess, and she walks a queen.—*Dryden.*

12. When a governing word cuts off one substantive from the other, Rule VII can not be applied.

Infinitives and Participles.

1. To venture in was to die. 2. The best way to preserve health is to be careful about diet and exercise. 3. The great object of all knowledge is to enlarge and purify the soul. 4. There is nothing like facts; seeing is believing. 5. It was being idle that made me miserable.

Clauses.

1. My impression is, that you will succeed. 2. The law should be, that he who can not read should not vote.

3. The excuse was, that the army had not been well enough equipped, and that the roads were too bad.

4. It is not that my lot is low,
That bids the silent tear to flow;
It is not grief that bids me moan,
It is that I am all alone.

4. The relative *that*, of the second line, relates to the clause *that my lot is low*, as its antecedent, or to *it*. — See p. 298.

Inverted and Elliptical.

1. A joy thou art, and a wealth, to all. 2. We stand the latest, and, if we fall, the last, experiment of self-government.

3. The moss his bed, the cave his humble cell;
His food the fruits, his drink the crystal well.

3. Predicate Adjectives.

1. You are studious. 2. Her countenance looked mild and gentle. 3. The question now before Congress is practical as death, enduring as time, and high as human destiny. 4. Blennerhasset is described as having been amiable and refined, and a passionate lover[7] of music. 5. To bleach is to make white. 6. Correct the heart, and all will go right. 7. To be poor is more honorable than to be dishonorably rich. 8. There is no way of being loved but by being amiable.

4. When a participle is thus construed with an adjective, call the participle a participial adjective. 8. *Except to be loved* by being amiable.

Inverted and Elliptical.

1. Lovely art thou, O Peace! 2. Deep in the sea is a coral grove. 3. Large, glossy, and black hung the beautiful fruit. 4. Green 's the sod, and cold the clay. 5. O vain to seek delight in earthly things.

4. Adverbs.

Veros Modified. — 1. He spoke eloquently. 2. The net was curiously woven. 3. The bird flew rapidly away. 4. What he did, he did patiently, accurately, and thoroughly. 5. His heart went pit-a-pat. 6. Do not aim low.

Adjectives Modified. — 1. The work is very useful. 2. The well is deep enough. 3. How various, how animated, how full of interest, is the survey! 4. I had never seen any thing quite so beautiful before.

Adverbs Modified.—1. We marched rather slowly. 2. You have come altogether too soon. 3. The car runs not quite fast enough.

Adverbial Clauses.

1. The child seemed to recline on its mother's bosom, as some infant blossom on its parent stem. 2. The cottage stood where the mountain shadows fell when the sun was declining. 3. Remember, while you are deliberating, the season now so favorable may pass away, never to return. 5. When misfortunes overtake you, when sickness assails you, and when friends forsake you, religion will be your greatest comfort. 5. The farther we went, the worse we fared. 6. As you sow, so you shall reap.

6. Observe that not the sowing, but the reaping, is described. *As* is a conjunctive adverb that joins its clause to *shall reap* to express manner, according to Note VI. Or say, *As* is an adverb of manner, modifying *sow* according to Rule XIII; and it is also a corresponding conjunction relating to *so*, and connecting two clauses according to Rule XV. Parse *so* in a similar manner.

Inverted and Elliptical.

1. Up soars the lark, the lyrical poet of the sky. 2. Here, all is confusion; there, all is order and beauty. 3. When young, life's journey I began.

4. The blessed to-day is as completely so,
As who began three thousand years ago.

The man blessed to-day . . . . . as he who, etc.

5. Participles.

1. He walks limping. 2. They lay concealed. 3. He went on his way rejoicing. 4. Now the bright morning star, day's harbinger, comes dancing from the east.

5. The scythe lies glittering in the dewy wreath
Of tedded grass, mingled with fading flowers,
That yester-morn bloomed waving in the breeze.

6. Infinitives.

Verbs Modified. — 1. The child seemed to sleep. 2. She was supposed to be rich. 3. He was known to have assisted the editor. 4. To curb him, to stand up against him, we want arms of the same kind.

Adjectives Modified. — 1. She is rather young to go to school. 2. It is a thing not easy to be done. 3. Pope was not content to please; he desired to excel, and therefore always did his best.

Adverbs Modified. — 1. It is too badly done to last. 2. It was so bright as to dazzle our eyes. 3. He proceeded too cautiously to fall into such a trap.

It is probably best to say, that *as to dazzle our eyes* modifies *so bright.*

NOTE V. — To say truth, Jack heard these discources with some compunction.

7. Adjuncts.

Verbs Modified. — 1. I am in trouble. 2. Deliver us from evil. 3. Religion dwells not in the tongue, but in the heart. 4. You are suspected of having been negligent. 5. This will depend on who he is.

Adjectives Modified. — 1. Let us be watchful of our liberties. 2. He is indolent about every thing. 3. They were invincible in arms.

Inverted and Elliptical.

1. By fairy hands their knell is rung. 2. Come, go with me the jungle through. 3. On that plain, in rosy youth, they had fed their father's flocks. 4. According to some ancient philosophers, the sun quenches his flames in the ocean.

5. Like the leaves of the forest when summer is green,
   That host, with their banners, at sunset were seen.

4. Supply *To believe*, etc.; for the sun does not quench his flames according to these ancient philosophers.

8. Clauses.

1. We came that we might assist you. 2. He is afraid that you will not return. 3. I am convinced that he is right.

This class comprises a few clauses that can not be referred to any preceding class, and that are *adjunctive* in sense.

QUESTIONS FOR REVIEW.

1. Repeat the Rules of Syntax.
2. Repeat the Notes.
3. Give the general formula for parsing.
4. What is Analysis? . . . ¶ 571
5. What is Parsing? . . . 572
6. How do they differ?
7. What is said of discourse? . . 573
8. What other division of discourse? 574
9. What are the chief kinds of prose? 575
10. Of poetry? 576
11. What else is said of discourse? 577, 578
12. What is a paragraph? . . . 579
13. What is a sentence? . . . 581
14. What is a proposition? . . . 582
15. What is a clause? . . . 583
16. When is a clause or sentence declarative? — interrogative? — imperative? — exclamatory? . . 584
17. Into what classes are sentences divided? 587
18. On what three syntactical relations is Analysis chiefly based? . 589
19. What are the elements of sentences? 590
20. Into what six classes can these be divided? 593
21. Into what can all sentences be resolved? 591
22. What else may a sentence have? . 592
23. What two chief words or terms must be in every proposition? 594
24. What is the subject-nominative? . 595
25. What is the predicate-verb? . 596
26. Of what two parts must every clause or proposition consist? . 597
27. What is the subject? . . 598
28. What is the predicate? . . . 599
29. How are subjects and predicates classified? 600
30. Define these classes? . . 601 - 604
31. What is a modifier? . . . 605
32. What kinds of modifiers are there? 606
33. What is an adjective or substantive modifier? 607
34. Tell, so far as you can, by what a noun or pronoun may be modified. 608
35. What is an adverbial or predicate modifier? 609
36. Tell, so far as you can, by what a finite verb, an infinitive, or a participle can be modified? . . 610
37. What modifiers can adjectives and adverbs have? . . . 611
38. What more is said of modifiers? . . . . . 612 - 614
39. What parts of speech are never modified?
40. What parts of speech, then, can have modifiers?
41. What is said of primary and of secondary modifiers?
42. An infinitive, used as a noun, can have what kind of modifiers? . 615
43. A participial noun? . . . 616
44. What is said of modified phrases and clauses? 617
45. What is said of *modify?*
46. What is said of the predicate-verb *be?* 619
47. Into what classes can the predicate modifiers be divided? . . . 620
48. What kinds of words are connectives? 621
49. What words or phrases are used independently? 623
50. What more is said of them? . 624
51. From what does a phrase or clause usually take its name? . . 625
52. What is said of phrases, in regard to form, parsing, and analysis? 626 - 628
53. What is said of clauses, in regard to form, parsing, and analysis? 629 - 631
54. What is said of propositions?
55. What is a member of a sentence?
56. What is an independent clause? — a principal clause? — a dependent or subordinate clause? — a coordinate clause? 632
57. What is said of simple sentences? . 633
58 What is said of complex sentences? 635
59. Of compound sentences? . 638, 639
60. What is said of brevity? . . 641
61. Of ellipsis? 642
62. Of abridgment? 643
63. How are compound sentences contracted? . . . 644, 645, 646
64. How are compound modifiers contracted? 647
65. How are simple sentences abridged? 648
66. What is said of the verb *be*, and of imperative propositions? . 649
67. What is said of equivalent expressions? 650
68. What is said of the syntax of abridged expressions? . . 651
69. How can the syntax of a difficult word or phrase be frequently most readily ascertained?
70. Into what are complex sentences abridged? 652
71. Which part is usually abridged?
72. Into what is an abridged substantive clause usually converted? . 653
73. An abridged adjective clause? . 654
74. An abridged adverbial clause? . 655
75. When a complex sentence is abridged, what is the effect on the subject of the dependent clause? . 657, 658
76. Into what can modifying phrases frequently be abridged? . 659
77. What place in a sentence is considered the most important? . . 661
78. When may a subordinate element occupy the chief place? . . 662
79. What is said of transposing phrases and clauses? . . 663, 664, 665
80. What is a period? 666
81. State how sentences should be analyzed. Page 262.
82. State how each part of speech should be parsed.
83. Which of the five parts of grammar are used in Analysis and Parsing?

PART V.

WORDS IMPROPERLY COMBINED.

FALSE SYNTAX.

All the errors, in the use of language, can be reduced to four heads: —

1. Too Many Words.
2. Too Few Words.
3. Improper Word or Expression.
4. Improper Arrangement of Words.

1. TOO MANY WORDS.

General Rule I. — No needless word should be used.

This here is my seat.* That there is your place.
I have got to go. You have got to stay.
She is a poor widow woman. He died in less than two hours time.
You had n't ought to do it. He had n't ought to go.
Had I have been there, I would have gone with them.
Had I have known it, I could have sent yesterday.
His two sisters were both of them well educated.
I bought it of the bookseller, *him* who lives opposite.
The neck connects the head and trunk together.
He went away about the latter end of the week.
You will never have another such a chance.

* We shall not encumber the following exercises with formulas. Surely the teacher, if at all competent, can show the student how to correct the sentences in a clear and sensible manner. As a general rule, the pupil should first say that the sentence is incorrect; he should then state in what respect it is wrong, make the necessary correction, and give his reasons for the change. Lastly, he may read the corrected sentence.

Formerly, arithmetic was taught chiefly by arbitrary rules committed to memory. Since the introduction of mental arithmetic into schools, pupils have been taught to reason out problems by relying rather on themselves for logic and language. Can not a similar mode of instruction be applied to false syntax?

There are but a few *other* similar places in the city.

What is used for *that* and *which*. (Omit *and*.)

It is equally as good as the other. Mine is equally as good as yours.

The correlatives *as* and *as* themselves imply equality. — See p. 186.

Who *first* discovered America? When the world was first created, etc.

For *his* avoiding that disaster, he is indebted to you.

In *their* discussing *of* the subject, they became angry.

He knows the lesson, but you do not *know the lesson*.

Perseverance in laudable pursuits will reward all our toils, and *will* produce effects beyond our calculation.

This is taught by Plato; but it is taught still better by Solomon *than by him*. *Most* is annexed to the end of these words.

Our flowers are covered over. I was not able for to do it.

I borrowed the knife for to sharpen my pencil.

For was formerly used before the infinitive; but it should not be used so now.

Where is William at? Their situation can hardly be conceived of.

My father presented me with a new knife.

A very common error. — He did not present me, but the knife. Omit *with*.

Mr. C. S. Bushnell, of New Haven, has presented the divinity school *with* five thousand dollars. — *N. Y. Times.*

Say, — "has presented five thousand dollars to the divinity school."

The emotion is at last awakened by the accidental in stead of by the necessary antecedent. — *Wayland.*

Omit the second *by*. "In a horizontal in stead of a perpendicular direction." — *Everett.*

It is *to* you to whom I am indebted for this favor.

The pronoun *it* needs *you* for its predicate-nominative; and therefore *to* should be rejected.

It is to this last feature of the game laws, to which we intend to confine our notice. — *Sidney Smith.*

Our debts and our sins are generally greater than we think *for*.

At about what time will you come?

The performance was approved of by all who saw it.

From thence we sailed to Liverpool. From whence it came I know not.

Hence, *thence*, and *whence*, imply *from*, which therefore becomes superfluous when inserted before any of these words.

Whenever he sees me, he always inquires after my health.

He then told us how that he had always been a Union man.

> The carol they began that hour,
> How that a life was [is] but a flower. — *Shakespeare.*

The carol, that a life is but a flower, etc.

I have no doubt *but* that he will come.
He never doubts but that he knows their intention. — *Trench.*
This barbarous custom, and which prevailed everywhere, the missionaries have abolished.

A relative pronoun is a connecting word, and therefore does not allow *and* between itself and the antecedent, except when the *and* is needed to join one relative clause to another.

The distinguishing excellence of Virgil, and which he possessed above all others [other poets], is tenderness. — *Blair.*
If I mistake not, I think I have seen you before.
Her tears dropped and fell upon the face of her dying and expiring babe. A little flowing rivulet. Mr. Henry Felton, Esq.

A name should not stand between two titles, when the greater title implies the less; but a name can have two or more titles, when one does not necessarily imply the other; as, *Rev. Dr. Lothrop.*

UNDER PARAGRAPH 482. We made her to believe it.
If I bid you to study, dare you to be idle.
To go I could not. You need not to have staid.
Make me to understand the way of thy precepts.

Special Rules.

1. A pronoun should not be added to its antecedent, when the antecedent alone would express the meaning better.

John he went, and Mary she went; but the rest they all staid at home. Henry Barton his book. (Apply also Rule III.) Mary Johnson her book. These lots, if they had been sold sooner, they would have brought a better price. These wild horses having been once captured, they were soon tamed. It is indisputably true, his assertion; though it seems erroneous.

2. When two negatives are equivalent to an affirmative, only one of them should be used to express denial.

I will never do so no more. We did n't find nobody at home.

Change also any word of the sentence, when it is necessary to do so.

I don't know nothing about your affairs; and I don't want to know.
I never said nothing about it to nobody.
Death never spared no one. She will never grow no taller.
I sha'n't go, I don't think. (Change the sentence.)

This England never did, nor never shall,
Lie at the proud foot of a conqueror. — *Shakespeare.*

Neither you nor nobody else can walk ten miles in one hour.
No banker, brewer, nor merchant, wanted a partner. — *Newspaper.*

3. Double comparatives and superlatives should be avoided.

The office could not have been given to a more worthier man.
A farmer's life is the most happiest.
She is the most loveliest one of the sisters.
She seemed more lovelier to me than ever before. — *Croly.*
The less*er* quantity I remove to the other side.

The ending *er*, of the comparative degree, is equivalent to the word *more.*

Nothing can be more worse — worser.
These were the least happiest years of my life.
This was the most unwisest thing you could have done.

4. The article is commonly omitted, —

1. When a word is used merely as a title.
2. When a word is spoken of merely as a word or name.
3. When we refer to the kind generally, or to only a part indefinitely.

Santa Anna now assumed the title of a Dictator.
The original signification of knave was a boy.
The ancients supposed the air, the earth, the water, and the fire, to be the elements of all material things.
What kind of a man is he? What sort of a thing is it?

A kind or sort is comprised in the general class, rather than in a single object.

I have had a dull *sort of a* headache all day.
The Tennessee and the Mississippi are names from the Indian tongues.
The whites of America are the descendants of the Europeans.

5. When connected descriptive words refer to the same person or thing, the article can generally be used only before the first of the words.

A white and a black calf is one calf with two colors.
There is another and a better world.
My friend was married to a sensible and an amiable woman.

She is not so good a cook as a washerwoman.
Fire is a better servant than a master.
I am a better arithmetician than a grammarian.
Everett, the patriot, the statesman, and the orator, should be invited.
The earth is a sphere, a globe, or a ball.
The Old and the New Testaments make the Bible.

Better: "The Old Testament and the New make the Bible"; or, "The Old and the New Testament make the Bible."

The first and the second pages were our first lesson.
The terror of the Spanish and the French monarchies. — *Bolingbroke.*

6. Do not make transitive verbs intransitive, by inserting a needless preposition.

Pharaoh and his host pursued after them.
We had just entered into the house. Follow on after us.
His estate will not allow of such extravagance.
If you can wait till to-morrow, I will consider of it.
We entreat of thee to hear us. I do not recollect of such an instance.
Many talented men have deserted from the party.

7. Do not let the same word, sound, or expression recur too frequently, nor in close proximity to itself.

The fault is still worse when the word is used in different senses.

Too much of the same sound frequently produces harshness, and is always so unpleasant to the ear that the word *monotony* has become a common term for whatever is disagreeable from excessive sameness.

The subject of which I shall now treat, is not a subject of general interest; but no other subject is of greater importance to the subjects of this kingdom.

Pronouns, auxiliary verbs, and the word *so*, are often convenient substitutes.

Avarice and cunning may gain an estate, but avarice and cunning can not gain friends. (Substitute *they.*)

A catalogue of the children *of* the public schools of this city has been published. (Substitute *in.*)

John's friend's horse ran away. § 278.

I believe that he is the man *that* I saw. (Substitute *whom.*)

One can not imagine what a monotonous being one becomes if one constantly remains turning one's self in the circle of one's favorite notions. *A person* . . . . . *he*, etc.

Observe that the irregularities in the declension of pronouns give beauty to language.

2. TOO FEW WORDS.

General Rule II. — No necessary word should be omitted.

White sheep are much more common than black.
He does not know you better than John. (Ambiguous.)
Lovest thou me more than these? You suppose him younger than I.
A squirrel can climb a tree quicker than a boy. — *Webster.*
He did it for your and my friend's welfare.
Ignorance is the mother of fear as well as admiration.
He had fled his native land. He was expelled the college.
What prevents us going? What use is it to me?
The remark is worthy the man that made it.
My business prevented me attending the last meeting.
She could not refrain shedding tears.
San Francisco is the other side the Rocky Mountains.
Out of these modifications have sprung most complex modes.

Say, — "most *of the*," etc.; for otherwise *most* apparently modifies *complex*.

The court of France or England was to be the umpire.
The valley of the Amazon is perhaps as large as the Mississippi.
Let us consider the works of nature and art, with proper attention.
The word depends on what precedes and follows. (Supply *what.*)
She praises who praise her. (Object wanting; supply *those.*)
We speak that we do know.
The privileges to which he was entitled, and had long enjoyed, were taken from him. (Supply *which* and *he.*)
An officer on European and on Indian service are in very different situations. — *S. Smith.* (Supply *service* and *one.*)
Though virtue borrows no assistance from, yet it may often be accompanied by, the advantages of fortune. — *Blair.*

So great a separation between two prepositions or other words that govern the same object, always produces a disagreeable hiatus in the sense; therefore place the noun after the first preposition, and the corresponding pronoun after the second.

He first spoke for, and then voted against, the measure.
The freight was added to, and very much increased, my expenses.
He is not now in the condition he was. (Supply *in which.*)

The omission of a relative adjunct generally produces a disagreeable gap in the sense.

Yonder is the place I saw it. This is the way it was done.
The money has not been used for the purpose it was appropriated.
I shall persuade others to take the same measures for their cure that I have. No man can be more wretched than I. (Supply *am.*)

I never have and never will assist such a man.

They either have or will write to us about the matter.

Money is scarce, and times hard. (Supply *are.*)

Allowable, by zeugma (p. 300); yet when a verb or an auxiliary is omitted near a different form of the same verb or auxiliary, the attraction between the expressed verb and the nominative of the omitted verb generally produces a disagreeable hiatus in the sense. In other words, it is generally improper to omit the verb when a different form of it is required.

The winter is departing, and the wild-geese flying northward.

The ground was covered with forests, and the ravines hidden.

A dollar was offered for it, but five asked.

I can not go, but I want to. I have not subscribed, nor do I intend to.

Allowable in the most colloquial style; though it is generally inelegant to let a sentence end with a word so insignificant. Supply *go* and *subscribe.*

This must be my excuse for seeing a letter which neither inclination nor time prompted me to. — *Washington.*

We ought not speak evil of others, unless it is necessary. § 482.

It is better live on a little than outlive one's income.

This old miser was never seen give a cent to any charitable under-[taking.

Please excuse my son for absence yesterday.

Allowable in the familiar style; though it is generally better to insert *to.*

How do you like up here? We like right well up here.

This is an error common in New England. Supply *to live* or some other words.

Surely no man is so infatuated to wish for a different government from that which we have. Page 186.

He is a man of visionary notions, unacquainted with the world, unfit to live in it.

Special Rules.

1. The article *the* is frequently needed to show that all of a class are meant; and when connected descriptive words refer to different persons or things, an article is generally needed before each of the words.

The Indians are descendants of the aborigines of this country.

Men who are indolent, generally complain of hard times.

A black and white calf were the only two I saw.

The white and black inhabitants amount to several thousands.

A beautiful stream flowed between the old and new mansion.

The sick and wounded were left at this place.

2. In comparison, *other*, *else*, or a similar word, must sometimes be inserted to prevent the leading term from being compared with itself.

That tree overtops all the trees in the forest.
He thinks he knows more than anybody.
Nothing is so good for a sprain as cold water.
There is no situation so good anywhere.
No magazine is so well written as the *Atlantic Monthly*.
Jacob loved Joseph more than all his children.
Noah and his family outlived all the people who lived before the flood.
In no case are writers so apt to err as in the position of the word *only*. — *Maunder*.

3. Parts emphatically distinguished, or to be kept distinct in thought, should be expressed with equal fullness.

Neither my house nor orchard was injured. (Supply *my*.)
Both the principal and interest were paid.
Neither the principal nor interest was paid.
The principal, as well as interest, was paid.
Not the use, but abuse, of worldly things, is sinful.
The hum of bees, and songs of birds, fell sweetly on the ear.
I would rather hear the whippoorwill than katydid.
You must either be quiet, or must leave the room.
God punishes the vices of parents, either in themselves or children.
Such a relation as ought to subsist between a principal and accessory.
They were rich once, but are poor now.
A man may be rich by chance, but can not be good or wise without effort.
He may be said to have saved the life of a citizen, and consequently entitled to reward.
He is distinguished both as a teacher and scholar.

Serial parts must generally be expressed with equal fullness or with uniformity.

Such a law would be injurious to the farmer, mechanic, and the merchant.

Either use the article but once, and place it before the first word, or else use it before each word.

She possesses more sense, more accomplishments, and beauty than the other.
My duty, my interest, and inclinations, all urged me forward.
He is a man of sagacity, experience, and of honesty.
By industry, by economy, and good luck, he soon acquired a fortune.
While the earth remaineth, seed-time and harvest, cold, heat, summer, winter, day and night, shall not cease.

4. It is generally improper to omit the subject-nominative, unless the verb is in the imperative mood, or closely connected with another verb relating to the same subject.

He was a man had no influence. (Supply *who.*)
There is no man knows better how to make money.
It was this induced me to send for you.
If there are any have been omitted, they must say so.
She saw at once what was best to do. This is what became us to do.
Am sorry to hear of your misfortune; but hope you will recover.
This is a position I condemn, and must be better established to gain the faith of any one.

> Whose own example strengthens all his laws,
> And is himself the great sublime he draws.
>
> Will martial flames forever fire thy mind,
> And never, never, be to heaven resigned?

5. A participial noun generally requires an article before it, and *of* after it; or else the omission of both the article and the preposition.

Keeping of one day in seven as a day of rest, is required by the Bible.
By the exercising our judgment it is improved.
This is a betraying the trust reposed in him.
A wise man will avoid the showing any excellence in trifles.
A wise man will avoid showing of any excellence in trifles.
Great benefit may be derived from reading of good books.

There is sometimes a difference in sense; as, "He expressed his pleasure in hearing the philosopher." He heard. "He expressed his pleasure in the hearing of the philosopher." The philosopher heard. — In the use of a few verbs, when the antecedent term denotes the doer, both *the* and *of* should be omitted; when the subsequent term denotes the doer, *the* and *of* should be used.

3. IMPROPER WORD OR EXPRESSION.

General Rule III. — In the use of words, great care should be taken to select the most appropriate.

To lay; to make lie, to place. *To lie;* to rest in a reclining position. *To set;* to place. *To sit;* to rest. *To seat;* to place in a sitting position, to furnish with a seat. *To learn;* to acquire knowledge. *To teach;* to impart knowledge. *To like;* to be pleased with, to desire moderately. *To love;* to feel affectionate or very kind towards. *To raise;* to lift. *To rise;* to erect one's self, to ascend. *To affect;* to impress. *To effect;* to accomplish. *To elude;* to escape. *To illude;* to deceive. *To suspect;* to mistrust. *To expect;* to await, to regard as something that is to be. *Stinted;* insufficiently fed, restrained. *Stunted;* checked in growth, dwarfish. *Go* is estimated from the starting-point; and *come,* from the point to be reached. *Less* implies size or number; *fewer,* number only. *Whole,* the entire object; *all,* the entire number. *Either, neither,* or *each other,* should be used in speaking of two only; *any one, no one, none,* or *one another,* in speaking of more.

Into, from outside to inside; *in,* inside only; *at,* indefinitely in or about; *in,* definitely within; *at,* border, no surroundings; *in,* enclosure, surroundings; *between* or *betwixt,* two only; *among,* three or more; frequently, *by,* the agent, and *with,* the means or manner; a taste *of* what is enjoyed, a taste *for* what we wish to enjoy; disappointed *of* what is not obtained, disappointed *in* what fails to answer our expectations after it is obtained; die *of* disease, *by* an instrument; compare *with,* for ascertaining merits, — *to,* for illustration; attended *by* persons, *with* consequences; agree *with* a person, *to* something proposed, and *upon* some settlement of affairs; change *for* by substitution, and *to* or *into* by alteration; concur *with* a person, *in* a measure, and *to* an effect; a thing consists *of* what it is composed of, and consists *in* what it is comprised in; conversant *with* men, and *in* things; what corresponds *with,* is consistent with, — and what corresponds *to,* answers to; defend or protect ourselves *against,* and others *from;* disagree *with* a person, *as to* what is proposed; usually, expert or skillful *in,* before an ordinary noun, — and *at,* when immediately before a participial noun; we are familiar *with* things, and they are familiar *to* us; indulge *with* occasionally, and indulge *in* habitually; we introduce a person *to* another, and a person or thing *into* a place; intrude *upon* a person or thing, and *into* something enclosed; we usually look *for* what is sought, and *after* what is entrusted to us; prevail *with, on,* or *upon,* by persuasion, — and *over* or *against* all opposition; reconcile one friend *to* another, and apparent inconsistencies *with* one another; reduce *under* implies subjugation, and reduce *to* implies simply a change of state; to have regard *for*, and to pay regard *to*; *to unite to* means *to join to*, and frequently as an appendage, — *to unite with* means *to combine with*, and generally as a colleague or an equal; to vest authority *in* a person, and to invest a person *with* authority.

Abhorrence *of*; abhorrent *to*, *from*; access *to*; accord *with*; accuse *of*; adapted *to*; adequate *to*; agreeable *to*; aspire *to*; brag *of*; capacity *for*; comply *with*; confide *in*; conformable *to*, *with*; congenial *to*, *with*; consonant *with*; contiguous *to*; cured *of*; deficient *in*; dependent *on*; independent *of*; derogate *from*; derogatory *to*; destined *to*; differ *from*, seldom *with*; difficulty *in*; diminish *from*; diminution *of*; discourage *from*; discouragement *to*; disgusted *at*, *with*; disparagement *to*; dissent *from*; in distinction *from*; eager *in*, *for*, *after*; embark *in*, *for*; enamored *of*, *with*; enter, entrance, *on*, *upon*, *into*; exception *from*, *to*, *against*; exclude *from*; exclusive *of*; extracted *from*; followed *by*; fond *of*; fondness *for*; foreign *to*, *from*; founded *on*, *upon*, sometimes *in*; free *from*; glad *of*, sometimes *at*; guard *against*; hanker *after*; inaccessible *to*; incentive *to*; incorporate *into*, *with*, sometimes *in*; indulgent *to*; influence *over*, *with*, *on*; initiate *into*, sometimes *in*; inroad *into*; intermediate *between*; intervene *between*; inured *to*; invested *with*, *in*; involve *in*; join *with*, *to*; lame *of*; land *at*; level *with*; long *for*, *after*; made *of*; marry *to*; intermarry *with*; meddle *with*; martyr *for*; militate *against*; mingle *with*; mistrustful *of*; necessary *to*, *for*; need *of*; neglectful *of*; object *to*, *against*; occasion *for*; offend *against*; offensive *to*; omitted *from*; overwhelmed *with*, *by*; peculiar *to*; penetrate *into*; pertinent *to*; pleasant *to*; pleased *with*; preferable *to*; preference *to*, *over*, *above*; prejudice *against*; prejudicial *to*; preserve *from*; productive *of*; profit *by*; profitable *to*; provide *with*, *for*, *against*; pursuant *to*; pursuance *of*; refrain *from*; relation *to*; release *from*; relieve *of*, *from*; rely *on*, *upon*; replete *with*; resemblance *to*, *between*; *in* or *with* respect *to*; *in* or *with* regard *to*; rise *above*; rid *of*; similar *to*; strip *of*; subtract *from*; swerve *from*; sympathize *with*; sympathy *for*, *with*; unison *with*; weary *of*; worthy *of*.

Upon is to *on* as *into* is to *in*; but it can often be used for *on*, and is then simply a little more forcible.

The same preposition that follows a primitive word, naturally follows the derivative; but there are many exceptions.

Verbs and Nouns. He laid abed till breakfast. Lay down and rest.
We had laid on the ground all night. — *Newspaper*.
After laying awhile in this position, he raised up.
We were all setting round the fire. We set up late.
Set down a little bit. Are you going to go? I ain't going yet.
I didn't go to do it. I calculate to invest my money in something else.

She is as peevish as a setting hen. The nurse sat him in a chair.

The sun *sets*; and a current may *set* in a certain direction: but a hen rather *sits* than *sets* on eggs; and a garment *sits* or fits well, though it may have a good *set*.

I love bread and butter. Can you learn me to write?
The business will suit any one who enjoys bad health.
He was raised in the South. Carry the horse to water.

Cattle and agricultural productions are *raised*; but a child or a family is *reared* in a certain style of life.

I expect it rained here yesterday. The garment was neatly sown.
We suspect the trip will afford us great pleasure.
All the bottom-lands along the Mississippi were overflown.
They shall fly from the wrath to come. — *flee* —
Very many rivers empty into the Mississippi. — *flow* —
The thief illuded the police. He was much effected by the news.
A verb ought to agree with its subject, in person and number.

Say *should agree*, for *ought* usually implies moral obligation.

Write for me no more, for I will certainly ——.
If I can absent myself, I will —— to see him.
He has made a fine crop of wheat. I am necessitated to go.

To make a crop is perhaps as proper an expression as *to make money*; still, crops are not manufactured. Why not prefer *obliged* or *compelled* to *necessitated?* for the latter is a long, clumsy word, almost as uncouth as *necessitude*.

Four goes in thirty, seven times, and two over.

CORRECTED: Four *is contained* seven times in thirty, with two *remainder*.

Be that as it will, I cannot give my consent.

As it will implies certainty; *as it may* implies uncertainty.

He throwed the ball. I seed him. He knowed better.

Only those verbs, or forms of verbs, should be used, which are authorized by good present usage.

I drawed the line. I writ the name. He shoed the horse.
We be all of us from York State. John alit from his horse.
He was drownded. They were attackted. That is no preventative.
The goods were shipt yesterday. Want of money has checkt trade.
"Dipt, stript, dropt, perplext, elapst, absorpt, linkt, distrest."

> Rather than thus be overtopt,
> Would you not wish their laurels cropt? — *Swift.*

Thou didd'st weep for him. Thou mightest return. He try'd in vain.
Spirit of Freedom! once on Phyle's brow thou satt'st. — *Byron.*

The simpler forms, *didst*, *mightst*, *tried*, and *satst*, are preferable.

Wast thou chopping wood? Learns he the lesson?

In the familiar style, grave or poetic forms of expression are not becoming.

A drive into the country delighteth and invigorates us.
The eve was fair, but the morn was cloudy and darksome.
It was not taken notice of. — *was not noticed.*
It was made use of for this purpose.
She said our noise and romping must be put a stop to.
He was found fault with, and taken hold of. — *censured and seized.*
Weights and measures were now attempted to be established.

From Carlyle. Better: "An attempt was now made to establish," etc.

She is getting the better of her sickness. — *recovering from* —
I have *done* written the letter. He is done gone. — *already* —
Since you have made the first, you may *do* the rest. — *make* —
No one ever sustained such mortifications as I have done to-day.
I did not say, as some have done. — *Bolingbroke.*
A poet can rise higher . . . than a public speaker can do. — *Blair.*
She is administrator. He married a Jew. She is a good songster.

She is a good *singer;* for *songster* is now generally applied to birds.

A cruel tyrant, and her name is Death. § 224.
Her stupidness soon appeared. I thought she treated me with negligence.

Pronouns and Adjectives.

Take either of the five. Each one of the dozen is injured.
Any one of the two roads will take you to town. § 210.
Neither one of these three hats is large enough for my head.
Jack and Peg called one another nicknames. — *Swift.* § 210.
Mankind resemble each other most in the beginnings of society.
Verse and prose run into one another like light and shade. — *Blair.*
You may take e'er a one or ne'er a one, just as you please.
That very point which we are now discussing, was lately decided in the supreme court. § 211.
These very men with whom you traveled yesterday, are now in jail.
There is a right road, and there is a wrong road, before every person: this leads to happiness; and that, to misery.
It all tends to show that our whole plans had been discovered.
A proper fraction is less than one, because it expresses less parts than it takes to make a unit. — *Colburn.*
I am willing to pay a hundred or two dollars.
We have not the least right to your protection. The least distinct part.
These evils were caused by Catiline, who, if he had been punished, the republic would not have been exposed to such great dangers.

Who is used here as a mere connective, or it is deprived of its chief syntax. (§ 622.) Say, — "the punishment *of whom* would have prevented the republic from being exposed to dangers so great."

He reached Charleston about the same time that we did.

Perhaps allowable, as being an idiom; but *that*, in this construction, is a dubious word for parsing. Say, — "about the time *in which* we *arrived there*."

At the same time that men are giving their orders, God is also giving his. *While men*, etc.

He has never preached, that I have heard of.

No man is so poor, *who* has not something to enjoy.

Say, — "*that he* has not," etc.; for the idea of consequence predominates.—See p. 186.

Adverbs and Conjunctions.

A wicked man is not happy, be he never so prosperous.

Home is home, be it never so homely.

He is seldom or ever here.

He said nothing farther. I can go no further.

Further; additional, more; applied to quantity. *Farther*, more distant; applied to space.

Such cloaks were in fashion five years since.

Ago, from present time back; *since*, from some past time forward. (Dictionaries do not make this distinction; but it is nevertheless well founded.)

I saw him about five weeks since. I have not seen him ——.

Do like I did. You are not studious, like he is. — *not so . . . as* —

As, and not *like*, should be used as a conjunctive adverb, between two clauses.

A diphthong is where two vowels are united.

A diphthong is when two vowels are united.

Say, "A diphthong is the *union of*," etc.; for a diphthong is neither place nor time.

Fusion is while a solid is converted into a liquid by heat.

He drew up a petition where he represented his grievances.

Say, — "a petition *in which*," etc.; for *where* might seem to be conjunctive adverb relating to *drew*.

She is such a good woman. — *so good a woman.*

Such expresses quality; and *so*, degree.

I have seldom seen such a tall man.

The letter was not as well written as I wished it to be.

He is such a great man, there is no speaking to him.

Allowable, if the meaning is, he is a great man of *such a kind* that it is impossible to speak to him. But if degree only is meant, the phrase *so great a man* should be used.

I will see if it rains or no. — *whether . . . or not.* Page 185.

Whether it can be proved or no, is not the thing. — *Butler.*

Go, and see if father has come. See if that will do.

Tell me if we are going to have but one session to-day.

Neither our position, or the plan of attack, was known. Page 186.

I demand neither place, pension, or any other reward. — *Franklin.*

By personification, things are often treated as though they were hearers.

That is, — "as (they would be) *if* they were hearers."

You look as though you have been sick.

There is no doubt but what he is mistaken.

After words of doubt, fear, or denial, *that* is preferable to *but*, *but what*, *but that*, and sometimes to *lest*. Also *how* and *as that* are sometimes used improperly for *that*.

I have no doubt but you can help him. — *Dr. Johnson.*

I am surprised how you could do such a thing.

He could not deny but what he borrowed the money.

There is no question but the universe has certain bounds to it.

I was afraid lest you would not return soon enough.

I don't know as I shall go, and I don't know but what I shall.

He is not so tired but what he can whistle. — *that ... not* — P. 186.

This is none other but the gate of Paradise.

Other, *else*, or the comparative degree, must generally be followed by *than*. Page 186.

O fairest flower, no sooner blown but blasted! — *Milton.*

It is nothing else but the people's caprice. — *Swift.*

The loafer seems to be created for no other purpose but to keep up the ancient order of idleness. — *Irving.*

Style is nothing else but that sort of expression which our thoughts most naturally assume. — *Blair.*

There is no other umbrella here but mine.

Nothing else but this will do. It was no one else but him.

It would be still better to omit *else* from the two foregoing sentences.

Scarcely had he uttered the word, *than* the fairy disappeared. (*when*)

I will not go without you go too. — *unless* —

They were all there, unless two or three.

Proportion is simple and compound. — *either ... or* —

To borrow or to lend is equally imprudent. (*Equally* requires *and.*)

Every one was dressed alike. — *Swift.*

Say, "They were all dressed alike"; for *alike* here requires plurality.

The multitude rebuked them, because they should hold their peace.

The donation was the more acceptable, that it was given without solicitation.

Prepositions. He died with a fever. He died for thirst.

Do not let the dog come in the house. He came of a sudden.

This is a very different dinner to what we had yesterday.

I have little influence with him. I live to home.

I left my book to home. His case has no resemblance with mine.

I should differ with you, in regard to that affair.

Well authorized, and therefore proper; still, *from* seems to be in better keeping with analogy. English writers generally say *differ with*, in reference to matters of opinion; and *differ from*, in all other cases. "I *differ with* the honorable gentleman on that point." — *Brougham.*

The soil is adapted for wheat and corn.

He was accused with having acted unfairly.

The sultry evening was followed with a storm.

(What is the difference between walking *in a garden* and walking *into a garden?*)

They spent the summer at the North, in a small village.

He resides —— No. 125, —— Tenth Street.

A person lives *at* a No., and *in* a street; also *on* a street, especially if it is wide, like an avenue.

Please walk in the setting-room. "His prejudice to our cause." *Dryden.*

Far preferable is a cottage with liberty, than splendor with debt.

Such were the difficulties with which the question was involved.

He always tries to profit from the errors of others.

You may rely in what I say, and confide on his honesty.

I was disappointed in the pleasure of meeting you.

There is constant hostility between the several tribes of Indians.

The space between the three lines is the area of the triangle. (*within*)

The greatest masters of critical learning differ among one another.

Say, — "among *themselves*"; for we could not say *one among another.*

A combat between twenty Texans against fifty Mexicans.

Sundries. I was thinking of the best place for an office.

This can be made an objection against one government as well as [another.

Abercrombie had still nearly four times the number of the enemy.

I am looking for reinforcements, which the enemy cannot expect.

My Christian and surname begin and end with the same letter.

Each then took hold of one end of the pole, to carry the basket.

Between grammar, logic, and rhetoric, there exists a close and happy connection; which reigns through all science, and extends to all the powers of eloquence. — *Mahan.*

Observe that *which* does not denote the identical connection mentioned before it; and therefore the word *connection* is not the proper antecedent. Say, "Grammar, logic, and rhetoric, have . . . . and such a connection reigns, indeed, through all science," etc.

The use of which accents [Greek and Roman] we have now entirely lost. — *Blair.* (We never had them to lose. Say, *is lost.*)

Our pronunciation must have appeared to them [the Greeks and the Romans] a lifeless monotony. — *Blair.* (They never heard it. Say, *would have appeared.*)

RULES OF SYNTAX.

Rule I.

Them that seek wisdom, shall find it.

INCORRECT; the pronoun *them*, in the objective case, is the subject of the verb *shall find*; and therefore it should be *they*, in the nominative case, according to Rule I.

Her and him were chosen. Thee art most in fault.

Him I accuse, has entered. *He whom*, etc.

Who made the fire? — John and me [made it].

The word containing the answer to a question must generally be in the same case as the word which asks it.

Who swept the room? — Us girls.

Who rode in the buggy? — Him and Jane.

What were you and him talking about? Whom shall I say called?

You did fully as well as me. He writes better than me.

The whole need not a physician, but them that are sick. — *Bunyan.*

We sorrow not as them that have no hope.

I do not think such persons as him competent to judge.

Truth is greater than us all. — *Horace Mann.*

The advice of those whom you think are hearty in the cause, must direct you. — *Washington.*

A reward was offered to whomsoever would point out a practicable road. — *Sir W. Scott.* Obs. I, p. 193.

Rule II.

Them refusing to comply, I withdrew. Pages 96, 191.

Her being the only daughter, no expense had been spared in her [education.

I have no wish to be him. And me, — what shall I do?

He had no doubt of its being me. — *that I was the person.*

Rule III.

I will not destroy the city for ten sake. A five days journey.

Brown, Smith, and Jones's wife, usually went shopping together.

We insist on them staying with us. I rely on you coming.

His father was opposed to him going to California.

What do you think of [*us?* or *our?*] going into partnership?

A participle that follows a noun or pronoun, becomes a participial noun, when the participle is the chief word in sense.

Rule IV.

Who did you call? Who shall I send? Who have you got?

Who can I trust in such a place, or who shall I employ?

Let him send you and I. Let thou and I the battle try.
Ye only have I known. Tell me who you mean.
Let them the state defend, and he adorn. — *Cowley.*
Him you should punish; not I, who am innocent.

Rule V.

Who did you come with? Who is it for? Who do you work for?
Who is that boy speaking to? This is between you and I.
They who much is given to, will have much to answer for.
I saw no one there except he. "Who did he send for? — We."
Who were you talking with? Who shall I direct it to?
My son is to be married to I don't know who. — *Goldsmith.*

When *but* and *save* are followed by a substantive, and not by a clause, they are now considered prepositions rather than conjunctions; as, "Whence all *but him* had fled." — *Hemans.* "All desisted, all *save him* alone." — *Wordsworth.*

Rule VI.

A lad of twelve or fifteen years old. I returned on yesterday.
Let a gallows be made of fifty cubits high. — *Bible.*
To an infant of two or three years old. — *Wayland.*
Who do I look like? She promised him and I some peaches.

Rule VII.

Let us worship God, he who created and sustains us.
It is me. It was them. Was it him, or her?
I did not know it was her. I thought it was her.
It was n't me, but him. It could not have been us.
Is it me you want? It was them that did it.
Whom do you think it was? Who do you take me to be?
Let the same be she whom thou hast appointed.
Whom do men say that I am? — *Bible.* It is him who, etc. — *S. Smith.*

Rule VIII.

I would like to have it now, what I had then.
Whatever she found, she took it with her.

Rule IX.

Nobody will ever entrust themselves to that boat again.

When the antecedent is a substantive of the common gender, denotes a person, and is of the singular number, so that it becomes necessary to choose either a masculine or a feminine pronoun, the masculine is preferred. § 221.

Every person should try to improve their mind and heart.
A person who is resolute, energetic, and watchful, is apt to succeed in their undertakings.

If there is anybody down there, let them answer.

She took out the ashes, and gave it to a servant. § 241.

If you have any victuals left, we will help you eat it.

When a bird is caught in a trap, they of course try to get out. § 222.

The regiment was much reduced in their number. §§ 245, 246.

The people can not be long deceived by its demagogues.

The army being abandoned by its leader, pursued meanwhile their miserable march.

Let the construction be either singular throughout or plural throughout, but not both.

The tongue is like a race-horse, which runs the faster, the less weight it carries. — *he carries.* Or, — *race-horse: it runs,* etc.

The pronominal construction should relate, throughout, either to the tongue or to the horse, but not to both.

An idler is a watch that wants both hands,
As useless when he goes as when he stands.

Here the second line relates more directly to the watch.

I have sowed all my oats, and it is growing finely.

Our language is not less refined than those of Italy, France, or Spain.

A pronoun must agree with its antecedent, or *with the noun which the pronoun represents.*

The peacock is fond of displaying its gorgeous plumage.

The hen looked very disconsolate when its brood rushed into the pond.

Horses is of the plural number, because they denote more than one.

Every half a dozen boys should have its own bench.

Poverty and wealth have each their own temptation.

Discontent and sorrow manifested itself in his countenance. § 461.

One or the other of us must relinquish their claim. § 460.

No man or woman ever got rid of their vices, without a struggle.

Say, — "*his or her* vices," etc. When the antecedent is of the common gender, the masculine pronoun can be used; but when the opposite sexes are distinctly mentioned, it is better to use a pronoun suitable to each antecedent than to use a pronoun suitable to one only. A different expression is sometimes still better.

If any gentleman or lady wishes to have their fortune told, etc.

Notice is hereby given to every person to pay their taxes.

(Change the antecedent; say, — "*to all persons,*" etc.)

Our teacher does not let any one of us do as they please.

Every person and thing had *its* proper place assigned to it. — *the* —

I do not know which one of the men finished their work first.

Coffee and sugar are brought from the West Indies; and large quantities of *it* are consumed annually. § 461.

More exercises, in the construction of pronouns, will be found under Rule XI.

Rule X.—Note II.

The inlet was two mile wide. I bought three ton of hay.
It weighed five pound. How do you like these kind of chairs?
I never could endure those kind of people. These sort of things.
These sort of fellows are very numerous. — *Spectator*. *Fellows of*, etc.
This twenty years have I been with thee. — *Bible*.
Plumb down he dropped ten thousand fathom deep. — *Milton*.
I measured the log with a pole ten foot long,— with a ten-feet pole.

When a compound adjective consists of a plural numeral and a noun, the noun is not made plural. — See p. 316.

The lot has twenty-five foot front, and is eight rod deep.
The work embraces every minutiæ — all the minutia — of the science.
Learn the sixth and seventh page, and review the fourth and the fifth pages.

Rule XI.

Circumstances alters cases. The molasses are excellent.
His pulse are beating too fast. Was you there?
He dare not meddle with it. She need not trouble herself.

Need and *dare*, especially the former, are sometimes used by good writers in stead of *needs* and *dares*; but it is generally better to avoid such usage.

Five dimes is half a dollar. There was only seven of us.
Peace has at last come, and with it has come many changes.
Thou heard the storm; did thou not? Thou shall go.
Oats is sowed in spring. *Tion* are pronounced *shun*.
Such is the tales his Nubians tell. Every ten tens makes a hundred.

§ 458.

You and your companions must not forget their duty.
John, you, and I, are attached to their country.

§ 459.

Neither he nor you was mentioned. Is I or he to blame for it?
On that occasion, neither he nor I were consulted.

§ 460.

2. There go a gang of deer. Generation after generation pass away.
A committee were appointed to examine the accounts.
The society hold their meetings on Fridays.
The fleet were seen sailing up the channel.
3. "Reveries of a Bachelor" were written by D. G. Mitchell,
6. Everybody are disposed to help him.
Each strove to recover their position.

Every person are hereby notified to pay their taxes.
Neither one are suitable to my purpose.
Everybody is fighting, and have been for several days. — *Newspaper.*
Every tall tree and every steeple were blown down.
Every soldier and every officer remained awake at their station.
Every leaf, every twig, and every drop of water, teem with life.
Every skiff and canoe were loaded to the water's edge.
No wife, no mother, and no child, were there to comfort him.
No thought, no word, no action, whether they be good or evil, can escape the notice of God.
Many a man looks back on the days of their youth, with melancholy [regret.
7. Either Thomas or George have to stay at home.
Neither Holmes, Forbes, nor Jenkins, *were classmates* of mine.
Neither the father nor the son had ever been distinguished for their business qualifications. If you should see my horse or mule, I wish you would have them turned into your pasture.
Riding on horseback, or rowing a skiff, are good exercise.
It is neither Osmyn nor Jane Shore that speak. — *Blair.*

§ 461.

1. Has the horses been fed? There 's two or three of us.
The victuals was cold. There is no tidings.
There seems to be no others included.
On each side of the river was ridges of hills.
There was no memoranda kept of the sales.
The book is one of the best that ever was written.
Such accommodations as was necessary, was provided.
He is one of the preachers that belongs to the church militant, and takes considerable interest in politics.
What is twenty-two poor years to the finishing a lawsuit! — *Swift.*

While ever and anon there falls
Hugè heaps of hoary mouldered walls. — *Dyer.*

2. The committee disagrees. At least half the members was present.
The higher class looks with scorn on those below them.
All the world is spectators of your conduct.
In France, the peasantry goes barefoot, while the middle sort makes use of wooden shoes.
Send the multitude away, that it may buy itself food.
3. Five pair was sold. Fifty head was drowned.

Pair and *head*, when thus plural in sense without being plural in form, resemble collective nouns.

4. Mary and her cousin was at our house last week.
Time and tide waits for no man. This and that house belongs to him.
Hill and dale doth boast Thy blessing.
In all her movements there is grace and dignity.
Two and two is four, and one [and four] is five. — *Pope.*
There seems to be war and disturbance in Kansas.
Every store and residence were pillaged.
Every merchant's store and residence was pillaged.
Enough money and time has already been expended.
Both minister and magistrate are sometimes compelled to choose between his duty and his reputation.

5. For the sake of brevity and force, one or more words is sometimes omitted. One or more persons was concerned.
Neither beauty, wealth, nor talents, was injurious to his modesty.
I borrow one peck, or eight quarts, and add —— to the upper term.

§ 462.

1. Every one of the witnesses testify to the same thing.
Each one of the vowels represent several sounds.
How are each of the relatives used? Neither of us have a dollar left.
Either one of the schools are good enough.
A variety of pleasing objects charm the eye.
Which one of these soldiers were wounded?
The sum of twenty thousand dollars have been expended.
A hundred thousand dollars of revenue is now in the treasury.
The mother, with her daughter, have spent the summer here.
The mechanism of clocks and watches were unknown. — *Hume.*
Nothing but expense and trouble have grown out of the business.
The richness of their arms and apparel were conspicuous. — *Gibbon.*
Each one of us *have* as much as *we* can do. Rule IX.
Neither of us is willing to give up our claim.
Correct, if common possession is meant; if not, *our* should be *his.*
There is more stamina in the Western men. — *more of* —
The idea of such a collection of men as make an army. — *Locke.*

2. Lafayette Place, or Gardens, occupy several acres.

3. Two parallel lines is the sign of equality.
The sign of equality are two parallel lines. — *consists of* —
My cause and theirs is one. — *Dryden.*
The few dollars which he owes me, is a matter of small consequence.

Virtue and mutual confidence is the soul of friendship.

To the Christian, the pleasures of this world is vanity.

This sentence, as it stands, means that Christians take the greatest delight in vanity.

Twelve single things, viewed as a whole, is called a dozen.

Said the burning Candle, "My use and beauty is my death."

Minced pies was regarded as a profane viand, by the sectaries.—*Hume.*

It is vanity and selfishness that ma—— a woman a coquet.

In such constructions, the genuine antecedent is *it;* but the relative clause is usually attracted into the nearer or identifying word or words, and agrees with them in grammatical properties. "It is the mental and moral *forces which govern* the world." —*Everett.*

4. and 5. Homer, as well as Virgil, were translated and studied on the banks of the Rhine. — *Gibbon.*

All the speakers, but especially the last one, was very eloquent.

He, not less than you, deserve punishment.

He, and not I, am responsible. I, and not he, is responsible.

The father, and the son too, were in the battle.

"*Ay*, and *no* too, *was* no good divinity." —*Shakespeare.*

The sons, and also the father, was in the battle.

Not his wealth, but his talents, deserves praise.

It is his wealth, and not his talents, that give him position.

It is his talents, and not his wealth, that gives him position.

There is sometimes more than one auxiliary to the verb. — *Angus.*

The comparison itself excludes one term from the other.

Special Rules.

1. The pronoun *them* should not be used for the adjective *those.*

Them boys are very lazy. Give me them books.

What do you ask for them peaches? Take away them things.

Let some of them boys sit on some of them other benches.

Them are good mackerel. Them are my sentiments.

2. Adverbs should be used to qualify verbs, adjectives, or other adverbs; and adjectives, to qualify nouns or pronouns.

She sews good and neat. Speak slow and distinct.

The work is near done. I am only tolerable well.

I never studied no grammar, but I can talk just as good as them that talk grammatical. I am exceeding busy.

I was scarce sensible of the motion. You behaved very bad.

I came there previous. He acted conformable to orders.

We ought to value our privileges higher. I can write easiest this way.

Apples are more plenty than peaches. — *Webster.*
We landed safely after all our misfortunes.
Things look much more favorably this morning.
How beautifully this whole section of country appears! [*Dryden.*
It rarely happens that a verse of monosyllables sounds harmoniously.
I can not say a word too highly in praise of his services. — *Grant.*
Now the moonlight began to prevail over the twilight, and Emma felt very poetically. — *A Novel.*

3. The comparative degree is used when but two objects are compared; and the superlative, when three or more are compared.

The eldest of her two sons is going to school. The latter of three.
John is the oldest, but James is the largest, of the two boys.
Which is the largest number, — the minuend or the subtrahend?
Which do you like best, — tea or coffee? The last of two.
Which is farthest north, — Chicago or London?
Choose the least of two evils. This hurt him worst of any thing else.
China has the greatest population of any other country on earth.

4. The leading term of a comparison should not be compared with itself, nor included in that to which it does not belong.

When the comparative degree is used, the latter term of comparison should always *exclude* the former; and when the superlative degree is used, the latter term of comparison should always *include* the former. But the term construed after the superlative degree should always express plurality; for if it does not, the leading term is also compared with itself. *Other*, or a similar word, makes two distinct parts, but comprises them in one general class.

Youth is the most important period of any in life.
These people seemed to us the most ignorant of any we had seen.
Lake Superior is the largest of any lake in the world.
That boy is the brightest of all his classmates.
That is a better-furnished room than any in the house.
That is the best-furnished room of any in the house.
China has the greatest population of any nation [country] on the globe.
This was the thing which of all others I wished most to see. — *Southey.*
Homer had the greatest invention of any writer whatever. — *Pope.*

5. Avoid all improper modes of expressing comparison or the plural number.

I think the rose is the beautifullest of flowers. § 345.
He is the awkwardest fellow I ever saw.
He lives in the fartherest house on the street.
The vallies of California are among the most beautiful in the world.
We need two astronomys. All the Lee's were officers.
They seem to have been only the tyro's, or younger scholars. — *Swift.*
The vermins were so numerous that we could raise no fowl.
We saw three deers in the wheat-field. Those are good mackerel.
His brother-in-laws were educated at the same school. § 255.

6. Words should not be compared, or made plural, when the sense does not allow or require it.

It is the most universal opinion. This is more preferable than that.
Virtue confers supremest dignity on man, and should be his chiefest desire. A more perpendicular line. (A line *more nearly*)
It is not so universally known as you think.

Say, — "not *so generally*," etc.; for *so* expresses degree, and therefore implies comparison. § 337.

I hope the people are more uncorrupt than their leaders.

Say, — "*less corrupt* than their leaders."

The farm is a long ways from market. Make a memoranda of it.

By the same analogy, *somewheres*, *nowheres*, etc., are frequently used improperly for *somewhere*, *nowhere*, etc.

Few persons are contented with their lots.
It was for our sakes that Jesus died upon the cross.
His father's and mother's names were written on the blank leaf.

Better: "His father's name and his mother's were written," etc. — See p. 316.

Both he and I were neither of us any great talkers.

7. *A* should be used before *consonant* sounds; and *an*, before *vowel* sounds. §§ 313, 314.

We encamped in a open field. Such an one said so.
It is an useful exercise. He is a honest man.
Argus is said to have had an hundred eyes.
There was not an human being on the place.
A heroic deed it was. It is an universal complaint.
An ubiquitous quack. — *Poe.* An united people. — *Jefferson.* An hundred times. — *Swift.*

8. *A* or *an* denotes an indefinite one of several; *the* denotes the only one, the class, or a particular one of several.

He does not own as much as the fifth part of what you own.

No particular fifth part was meant; and there are more fifths than one in a whole.

An oak is a tree of great durability. That noble animal, a horse.

The assertion may not be true of any one tree; but it is true of the class in general.

A lion is bold. A pink is a very common species of flower.

When a whole is put for the part, or the part for a whole, the figure is called synec′doche.

9. The object of the active verb, and not that of the preposition, should be made the subject of the passive verb.

We were shown a sweet potato that weighed fifteen pounds.

You were paid a high compliment by the young lady.

Mr. Burke was offered a very lucrative employment. — *Goodrich.*

Washington was given the command of a division. — *Irving.*

He was presented a beautiful sword by his neighbors.

10. The possessive case of a noun should always be written with an apostrophe; the possessive case of a personal pronoun should never be written with an apostrophe.

A possessive noun, in apposition with another, is sometimes written without any possessive sign. § 291.

This is the boys hat. Six months interest is due. §§ 275, 276.

A mothers tenderness and a fathers care are natures gifts for mans advantage. Mens and boys hats.

No ones ability ever went farther for others good. § 304.

The two electric fluids neutralized each others' effects. — *Harper's Magazine.*

These are our's. That is your's or their's, not her's.

Do not say *yourn*, *hern*, *hissen*, *ourn*, or *theirn*, for *yours*, *hers*, *his*, *ours*, or *theirs*.

This mans place is taken. These mens places are taken.

That officers servant is here. Those officers servants are here.

This sheeps wool is fine. These sheeps wool is fine.

11. A compound word or a complex term takes the possessive sign but once; generally at the end, or next to the name of what is owned.

I will meet you at Mason's, the apothecary's.
We used to read about Jack's the Giant-killer's wonderful exploits.
This palace had been the grand Sultan's Mohammed's.
These works are Cicero's, the most eloquent of men's.

12. A pair or series of nouns, implying common possession, take the possessive sign at the end, and but once.

Bond's and Allen's store is the next one above us.
Allen's, Thomson's, and Hardcastle's store is opposite to ours.
Peter's and Andrew's occupation was that of fishermen.
Beaumont's and Fletcher's Plays were the joint production of two men.
Bond and *Allen's store* is one store, belonging to both men.
Bond's and *Allen's store* are two stores, one belonging to each man.

That one ownership allows but one possessive sign, that each distinct ownership requires a distinct possessive sign, and that the possessive sign should be placed as near as possible to the name of what is owned, are fundamental ideas that govern the syntax of the possessive case.

13. A pair or series of nouns, not implying common possession, or emphatically distinguished, take each the possessive sign.

John and William's boots fit them well. Is it John or William's book?
Allen, Thomson, and Hardcastle's store, are the next three above us.
As well, or better, thus: "Allen's store, Thomson's, and Hardcastle's, are the next," etc.
They took the surgeon as well the physician's advice.

14. To avoid harshness or inelegance, possession is sometimes better expressed by *of;* and sometimes even the possessive *s* may be omitted.

Essex's death haunted the conscience of Queen Elizabeth.
Leonidas's soldiers were as brave as himself.
England and France's armies fought side by side in the Crime'a.
Such were Daniel Boone of Kentucky's adventures.
He thinks his own opinions better than any one else's opinions — any one's else opinions. — *than those of any one else.*

In the colloquial style, the first expression is probably allowable. "Like nobody else's children." — *Jerrold: Mrs. Caudle.*

They cast themselves down at Jesus's feet.
Archimedes's screw is an hydraulic machine

15. Pronouns should be so used that it may not be doubtful for what they stand.

Pronouns are very indefinite words, and are therefore often liable to ambiguity.

Ambiguity in the use of pronouns is generally best avoided by substituting nouns for them.

Since pronouns are substitutes for nouns, it is hardly proper to make a pronoun represent an adjective or a predicate when a better expression can be found.

When a conjunction is to be supplied, it is called asyndedon.

Say, — "*the figure* is called," etc. ("When I see many *its* on a page, I always tremble for the writer." — *Cobbett.*)

When a man kills another from malice, it is called murder.

Religion will afford us pleasure when others leave us.

The lord can not refuse to admit the heir of his tenant upon his death; nor can he remove his present tenant so long as he lives. *Blackstone.*

He wrote to that distinguished philosopher [Aristotle] in terms the most polite and flattering, begging of him to undertake his education, and to bestow upon him those useful lessons which his numerous avocations would not allow him to bestow. — *Goldsmith's Greece.*

Philip wrote .... Alexander's education .... his own numerous, etc.

John told James that his horse had run away. (Change the sentence.)

They flew to arms, and attacked Northumberland's horse, whom they put to death. — *Hume.*

The law is inoperative, which is not right.

Say, — "*and that it is so*, is not right."

The servant took away the horse, which was unnecessary.

The prisoners rebelled against the regulations of the establishment, of which we shall presently give an account.

Mr. Dana asked Mr. Gore's leave to say a few words, which he did; after which he retired from the Convention. — *Elliot's Debates.*

16. *Who* is applied to persons, *which* to all other objects, and *that* to either.

For more definite directions, see pp. 76, 77, and 78.

Those which are rich, should assist the poor and helpless.

Eve gave of the fruit to the other creatures in Eden, who all ate of it, and so became mortal, with the sole exception of the phœnix who refused to taste it, and consequently remained immortal.

The horse and rider which we saw, fell in the battle.

Of all the congregations whom I ever saw, this was the largest.

The entire collection of persons is evidently regarded as one *thing* § 191.

This was certainly the largest congregation which I ever saw.

All the people which were present, joined in the prayer.

There was a certain householder which planted a vineyard. — *Bible.*

A butterfly, which thought himself an accomplished traveler, etc.

Pitt was the pillar who upheld the state.

I am the same as I was. I gave all what I had. [Alamo.

It is the best which can be got. The heroic souls which defended the

This lubberly boy we called Falstaff, who was but another name for fat and fun. (A mere name is a *thing*.)

The most tremendous civil war which history records. — *Newspaper.*

Who ever became great, who was not ambitious?

Who of these boys has lost a knife? § 201.

With the return of spring came four martins, who were evidently the same which had been bred under those eaves the previous year.

17. It is improper to mix different kinds of pronouns in the same construction.

Know thyself, and do your duty. You have mine, and I have thine.

Ere you remark another's fault, bid thy own conscience look within.

The poor man who can read, and that has a taste for reading, can find entertainment at home.

The man who came with us, and that was dressed in black, is the preacher. Such as yours, or which you bought. — *or such as* —

But what we saw last, and which pleased us most, was the farce.

Policy keeps coining truth in her mints, — such truth as it can tolerate; and every die except its own she breaks, and casts away.

18. It is generally improper to use different forms of the verb in the same construction.

Does he not behave well, and gets his lessons well?

Did you not borrow it, and promised to return it soon?

If these remedies be applied, and the patient improves not, the case may be considered hopeless.

To profess regard, and acting differently, discovers a base mind.
Spelling is easier than to parse or cipher.
To say he is relieved, is the same as saying he is dismissed.

19. What is forced upon the speaker, or what will simply happen to him, is better expressed by *shall* or *should* than by *will* or *would*.

Will or *would* generally represents the act or state as something desired or wished by the subject. — See also pp. 148 - 150.

A foreigner, having fallen into the Thames, cried out, "I will be drowned; nobody shall help me."
I was afraid I would lose my money.
If I wished him to come, I would have to write to him.
We will then find that this confiscation bill was impolitic; and we will have to suffer for our folly, in the protraction of this war. — *Crittenden.*
Death was threatened to the first man who would rebel.

The overt act was meant; and therefore *should*, not *would*, is the proper word.

Whoever will neglect his duties, will suffer the appointed punishment.

20. The past tense, and not the perfect participle, should be used to predicate, without an auxiliary, a past act or state.

The perfect participle, and not the past tense, should be used after *be*, *have*, and their variations.

I done so. They done the best they could.
He run all the way. I never seen it. He has took my hat.
I seen him when he done it. Mary has tore her book.
I knew he had wrote it; for it was well writ.
The tree had fell, and its branches were broke.
The apples were shook off by the wind.
Toasts were [*drank?* or *drunk?*]
You have chose the worse. — *Irving.*
He had broke the ice. — *Harper's Magazine.*

21. Avoid needless passive forms, and generally the passive form of intransitive verbs.

He is possessed of great talents. We are agreed on this.
My friend is arrived. He was already come.

What is become of him? The tumult is entirely ceased.
The greater part of the forces were retired into winter-quarters.

22. The indicative mood, in conditional clauses, expresses doubt in the regular time of the tense; the subjunctive mood expresses doubt or mere supposition, and makes the tense move forward in time.

If you be now willing, I will accept the offer.
Though he excel her in knowledge, she excels him in behavior.
If I was you, I would accept the offer.
If it rains to-morrow, we shall not go. — See pp. 131 - 133.
If the book be in my library, I will send it.
If the book is found in my library, I will send it.
If the book was in my library, I would send it.
If the book were in my library, some one must have taken it.
Take care that the horse does not run away with you.

Lest and *that*, annexed to a command, require the subjunctive mood after them. *If*, with *but* following it, when futurity is denoted, also requires the subjunctive mood.

Beware lest he falls. Be it ordered that the law remains unchanged.
If he comes but by 10 o'clock, he will be in time.

23. The verbs of a sentence should correspond in tense, and also be consistent with the other words.

I have bought it, and now I have sold it. Pages 136 - 140.
I know the family more than twenty years.
By the first of next month, I shall finish this book.
I should be obliged to him, if he will grant my request.
Ye will not come unto me, that ye might have life.
The most glorious hero that ever desolated nations, might have mouldered into oblivion, did not some historian take him into favor. — *Irving.*
When the nation would have rushed again and again to war, his voice has sheathed the sword in lasting peace.

"To-morrow *will be* Saturday"; correct. "To-morrow *is* Saturday"; allowable. — See below, and also § 426. 4.

24. Present facts and unchangeable truths must be expressed in the present tense.

Our teacher told us that the air had weight.

He told me where the church was. (An existing church was meant.)
Is not that dear? — I should think it was.
What did you say his name was?
What did you say was the capital of Florida?
He seemed hardly to know that two and two made four.
No one suspected that he was a foreigner.
Plato maintained that God was the soul of the universe.

25. The perfect infinitive denotes something as past at the time referred to; and the present infinitive, as present or future.

I intended to have written to him.
It was your duty to have arrested him.
I expected to have heard from him yesterday.
I hoped to have met several of my friends there.
He is supposed to be born about a thousand years ago.
They were not able, as individuals, to have influenced the twentieth part of the population. — *Jefferson.*

26. Avoid the needless use of compound participles in stead of simple participles; and never use a compound participle as a part of a finite verb, unless it is absolutely necessary to use it.

Such a poem is worth being committed to memory. (*committing*)
Whatever is worth being done, is worth being done well.
Dram-shops are now being closed on Sundays. (Omit *being.*)
The report is being circulated everywhere.
Wheat is now being sold for a dollar a bushel. — *is selling* —
The books are being printed. § 488. The new church is being built.

27. Avoid the ambiguous or clumsy use of participles in place of infinitives, clauses, or ordinary nouns.

A participial noun is seldom the most appropriate expression, when it does not follow a preposition. § 509.

A participial noun is seldom the most appropriate expression, when it is much encumbered with modifiers.

Cyrus did not wait for the Babylonians coming to attack him. — *Rollin.*
My being sick was the cause of my being absent.

What is the reason of you not having gone to school to-day ?
Going to law is giving the matter in dispute to the lawyers.
Compromising conflicting opinions will ever be necessary in a republic.
He failed reciting his lesson. No one likes being in debt.
Her lameness was caused by a horse's running away with her.

See Kerl's Comprehensive Grammar. pp 235 and 159.

Such will ever be the consequences of youth associating with vicious companions.
Since these objects are stripped of their importance, we wonder at their ever having been the cause of hatred and bloodshed.

4. IMPROPER ARRANGEMENT OF WORDS.

General Rule IV. — All the parts of a sentence should be so arranged as to make it correct, clear, and elegant.

Any violent break or separation in the natural order of words is generally improper. except when it is needed for great rhetorical effect.

Poetry allows great liberty in the arrangement of words; but any inversion that perverts or obscures the meaning, or that is more uncouth than poetical, should be avoided.

She praised the farmer's, as she called him, excellent understanding.

Change also the kind of expression, when it is necessary to do so.

A sober and industrious life he had nothing of. — *Brougham.*
Nature mixes the elements variously and curiously sometimes, it is true.
Adversity both taught you to think and to reason. — *Steele.*

Special care should be taken to give correlatives their right place in the sentence.

I shall neither depend on you nor on him.
Not only he found her employed, but pleased and tranquil also.
Our pleasures rather seem to spring from things too low that lie.
How pleasant it is at night no follies to have to repent.
His visage to the view was only bare. — *Dryden.*

Sire, from the foot
Of that great throne these hands have raised aloft
On an Olympus, looking down on mortals
And worshiped by their awe — before the foot
Of that high throne — spurn you the gray-haired man! — *Bulwer.*

Special Rules.

1. Nouns and pronouns should be so used as not to leave the case or relation ambiguous.

The settler here the savage slew. (Which slew the other ?)

And thus the son the fervent sire addressed. — *Pope.*

If the lad should leave his father, he would die.

Substitute a noun for *he*, or change the order of the words. — See p. 303.

The king dismissed his minister without inquiry, who had never before done so unjust an action.

Relative clauses should generally be placed as near to their antecedents as possible.

He should never marry a woman in high life, that has no money.

2. Politeness usually requires that the speaker shall mention the addressed person first, and himself last.

I, Mary, and you, are to go next Sunday.

Mother said that I and you must stay at home.

Exception. — When a fault is to be confessed, or when responsibility is to be assumed, it is generally more appropriate for the speaker to mention himself first.

3. Adjectives, adverbs, and adjuncts, must generally be placed as near as possible to the parts which they are designed to modify.

The bad position of adjectives and adjuncts is improved by bringing them nearer to what they qualify; and adverbs should generally be placed before the adjectives or adverbs which they modify, after verbs in the simple form, and between the auxiliary and the rest of the verb in the compound form.

Sometimes there is a gradation of adjectives before a noun. When this is the case, the adjectives should be so arranged that each may properly qualify all the remainder of the phrase which follows it; as, "An *old* man," "A *respectable old* man," "*Three respectable old* men."

I bought a new pair of shoes. There is a fresh basket of eggs.

I only recited one lesson. (Only what ?)

He is only so when he is drunk. Some virtues are only seen in adversity.

I shall be happy always to see my friends.

He is considered generally honest. He is just such another man.

They became even grinders of knives and razors.

They all went to the party, nearly dressed alike.

Every man can *not* afford to keep a coach. — *Webster.*

I came not to call the righteous, but sinners, to repentance.

All that glitters, is not gold. All that we hear, we should not believe.

Please to sing the three first stanzas. The two last classes have not recited. Rows of silk small green buttons.

At that time I wished somebody would hang me a thousand times.

A lecture on the methods of teaching geography at ten o'clock.

Wanted — a young man to take care of some horses, of a religious turn of mind. [Eastern States.

This victory seemed to be like a resurrection from the dead, to the

There is a remakable union in his style of harmony and ease. — *Blair.*

The solar system, space, and time. The most prudent and best men.

Apparently, "solar space and time." Apparently, "most best."

4. It is generally improper to place an adverb between *to* and the rest of the infinitive.

They were not such as to fully answer my purpose.

He had men enough to strongly garrison the fort.

He knew not which to most admire. — *Harper's Magazine.*

We were to cautiously and quickly advance to the hill above.

5. When a part of a sentence refers to each of two or more other parts, it should be suitable to each.

Cedar is not so hard, but more durable, than oak.

Cedar is not so hard as oak, but more durable. Complete the construction of the first part, and leave understood that of the second.

She is fairer, but not so amiable, as her sister. [than the old.

It is *different* and superior *to the old.* It is different and much better

He *can* and ought *to give* more attention to his business.

The reward has already or will hereafter be given to him.

We have the power of *retaining*, altering, and compounding those images which we have received, *into* all the varieties of picture and vision. — *Addison.*

Frequently, a sentence has two or more different errors.

It is our duty to protect this government and that flag from every assailant, be they whom they may. — *Douglas.*

Parents are of all other people the very worst judges of their children's merits; for what they reckon such, is seldom any thing else but a repetition of their own faults. — *Addison.*

Prepositions, you recollect, connect words as well as conjunctions; how, then, can you tell the one from the other. — *R. C. Smith.*

The empire of Blefuscu is an island situated to the northeast side of Lilliput, from whence it is parted only by a channel of eight hundred yards wide. — *Swift.*

OBSERVATIONS.

There are three great causes which will always produce errors in the use of language. These causes are *logical sense, euphony* or *attraction*, and *similarity*.

Logical Sense. — We are sometimes governed, in our use of language, by the general meaning of words rather than by their grammatical form. For instance, we frequently begin a sentence with a singular grammatical term that implies, however, plurality, or a class; and before we reach the end of the sentence, we forget or disregard the singular term with which we commenced, and select words according to the general or logical sense; as, "*A person* who is energetic and vigilant, is apt to succeed in *their* undertakings."

Euphony or Attraction. — When two words approximate in meaning, yet one gives a better sound to the expression than the other, we sometimes select the more euphonious one even when it is less proper. It is probably from this cause that people are so apt to say *them* for *those*, and *done* for *did*. When two kindred expressions stand near each other, one is sometimes attracted into the form of the other, even when a difference is required; as, "He *said* it *was* forty miles from Baltimore to Washington," for, "He *said* it *is* forty miles from Baltimore to Washington." Increase the distance between the terms, and there is less attractive force; as, "He *said* that the distance from Baltimore to Washington *is* forty miles." "It was *to him* | *to whom* I was mostly indebted," for, "It was *he* | *to whom* I was mostly indebted." *To whom* being a forcible part of the unexpressed thought, it causes the utterance of *to him* in stead of *he*.

Similarity. — When words, or forms of words, are nearly alike, as *wore* and *worn*, *broke* and *broken*, we are apt to mistake one for the other. It is, indeed, chiefly this slight variety in the forms of words which has made it necessary to have the science of grammar.

It is worthy of observation that the foregoing causes of error have become to a slight degree in our language, and to a considerable degree in some foreign languages, established laws that justify the expressions which they produce.

1. Too Many Words. 2. Too Few Words.

In general, the fewer the words we use to express our meaning, the better. Many of the most admired and durable expressions in our literature are those which tell much in very few words. No one likes to read through a large volume to get what might have been told as well in a pamphlet. Tautology is one of the worst faults of bad writing. It consists in telling the same thing, or nearly the same thing, again and again, in other ways; as, "The dawn is overcast, the morning lowers, and heavily in clouds brings on the day." — *Addison.* It is generally much easier to find other ways of telling the same thing, than to add new thoughts; and hence it very often happens that persons, in order to fill up the time or paper, add new words or expressions without adding new thoughts: they string together synonymous words and phrases just as if they meant to repeat what they have learned in some dictionary. We get tired of seeing a person always in the same dress, and, as with dress, so is it with thought and language. But while such use or repetition of words as indicates poverty of thought or language is disagreeable, it should be remembered that there can be emphatic or musical repetition or fullness that is sometimes one of the greatest beauties of style; as, —

"Must I then leave you? *Must* I needs forego
So good, *so* noble, and *so* true a master?
The king shall have my service; but my prayers
Forever *and forever* shall be yours." — *Shakespeare.*

"By foreign hands thy dying eyes were closed;
By foreign hands thy decent limbs composed;
By foreign hands thy humble grave adorned;
By strangers honored, and *by* strangers mourned." — *Pope.*

The words most commonly repeated for emphasis are articles, conjunctions, prepositions, pronouns, and small adjectives or adverbs. A long series of terms is sometimes elegantly gathered into groups, and thus a compromise is made between ellipsis throughout and fullness throughout; as, "I could demonstrate to you that the whole of your political conduct has been one continued series of weakness, temerity, and despotism; of blundering ignorance and wanton negligence; and of the most notorious servility, incapacity, and corruption." — *Chatham.*

Whenever words merely encumber the sentence, or do not improve its clearness and force, they should be omitted; but great care should be taken, in the omission of words, to avoid obscurity, ambiguity, and bad syntax, for these are the chief faults of excessive ellipsis. Hence, when the omission of words would obscure the sentence, weaken its force, or be attended with impropriety, they should be inserted.

Much of what is now considered erroneous English is simply old English that was once in fashion and in good repute.

Our old writers sometimes used, in imitation of the classic languages, double comparatives or superlatives and double negatives, for the sake of greater effect. Two negatives are still sometimes used so, when one does not destroy the effect of the other; as, "I *not* only *never* said so, but *never* thought so." Sometimes two negatives are elegantly used to express an affirmation, especially when one of the negatives is a prefix; as, "He is *not un*schooled in the ways of the world"; *i. e.,* he is shrewd enough. It is sometimes very difficult to determine whether *or* or *nor* should be used. When a preceding negative adjective or adverb plainly modifies both connected parts, *or* may be preferable; but when the latter part is but faintly affected by the preceding negative, or when the parts are long, *nor* may be preferable.

A is sometimes elegantly omitted before *few* and *little*, to give a negative meaning; and inserted, to give a positive meaning; as, "He has *few* friends"; *i.e.*, almost none. "He has *a few* friends"; *i. e.*, some at least. The phrase *kind of a* or *sort of a* is generally improper; though it may sometimes be allowable because needed; as, "What kind of *paper* [the *material*] have you?" differs from "What kind of *a paper* [*document*] have you?" When connected words require different forms of the indefinite article, it is seldom necessary to repeat the article for this cause alone.

Absolute comparisons, without the needed *other* or *else*, occur so frequently in good writers that they are perhaps sometimes allowable by the figure *synecdoche* or *hyperbole*.

Objective relative pronouns can be sometimes omitted; but nominative relatives can seldom be omitted with propriety, except in verse.

It is not necessary to repeat the subject before the second of two connected verbs that differ in mood and tense, or imply contrast, unless the parts are unusually long, or the contrast is marked and emphatic. "Many of them *were* of good families, and *had held* commissions in the civil war. Their pay *was* far higher than that of the most favored regiment of our time, and *would* in that age *have been thought* a respectable provision for the son of a country gentleman." — *Macaulay*. "So large a sum was expended, but expended in vain." — *Id.*

The omission of the nominatives in hasty business letters, is generally inelegant; for it implies an affectation, on the part of the writer, of being exceedingly busy.

There are some expressions in which *to*, the sign of the infinitive, should be used after *bid*, *dare*, *feel*, *make*, *see*, etc.; as, "My horse bids fair [promises] to take the premium." "I dared [challenged] him to bet." "I feel it to be my duty." "How could you make out to get along?" "I can not see to write this letter." — See § 482.

Choice of Words.

In writers of the last century we frequently find *an* used before sounded *h* and before *u* long. *An* is still preferred before sounded *h* when the chief accent is on the second syllable of the word, for then the *h* is but faintly heard. But when the *h* is forcibly aspirated, *a* is sometimes preferred. In this country we usually say *a hotel;* but the English generally prefer *an hotel.* "A hotel." — *Noah Webster;* "An hotel." — *Russell, Kinglake,* etc.

It is sometimes very difficult to decide whether the adverbial or the adjective form of a word should be used. The adjective expresses the quality of the subject, and the adverb the manner of the act; as, "She looks *cold*" [is *cold*]; "She looks *coldly* [*in a cold manner*] on him." (See p. 175.) Sometimes language needs two adverbs from the same word; and then one usually takes the regular adverbial form, and the other retains the adjective form; as, "The lesson is *hard;* and I can *hardly* learn it, though I have been studying *hard.*" We say, "He came there *previously,*" or we choose the adverbial form when the word stands by itself; but when *to* is added, some writers say *previously to* and some *previous to.* The analogy of *contrary to* and *according to* seems to be converting this phrase into a preposition of the same class with themselves. The analogy seems to be also affecting, though in a less degree, the words *agreeable* and *conformable.* "I feel [*bad?* or *badly?*] about the matter." Analogy is in favor of *bad;* but custom is in favor of *badly.* (See Kerl's Comp. Gram., p. 248.) In discussing a subject by numerical divisions, whether we should say *first, secondly, thirdly,* or *first, second, third,* etc., depends chiefly on whether we refer to the verb or to the divisions. "*Page twenty-fifth*" is correct, and "*page twenty-five*" is also correct; for *twenty-five* is here used as a noun, which represents page by the figure synecdoche, and is therefore put in apposition with *page.*

What is taught about relative pronouns in grammars, rests perhaps on a sandy foundation; for there are good English writers who simply apply *who* to persons and *which* to all other objects, and who use *that* and *as* simply for euphony, or when *who* or *which* would be less appropriate.

When an antecedent is a figurative word, great care should be taken to select the pronoun in accordance with the meaning of that part of the sentence in which the pronoun stands; as, She was a conspicuous *flower, whom* he had sensibility to love, ambition to attempt, and skill to win." — *Wordsworth.* "Northumberland, thou *ladder,* by *which* my cousin Bolingbroke ascends my throne." — *Shakespeare.* "A dauntless *soul* erect, *who* smiled on death." — *Thomson.*

We shall arrange our remaining remarks under this head, according to the grammatical properties as given on page 2.

Gender. — To a class of persons, comprising both sexes, the masculine noun is applied, rather than the feminine. "The poets of America" may include the poetesses. When I say, "She is the best *poetess,*" I compare her with female poets only; but when I say, "She is the best *poet,*" I compare her with both male and female poets. It is proper to say, "An *authoress* sat next to me at the table"; because it may be a part of the speaker's wish to specify the sex, and there is no other word in the sentence to express it. But it would be hardly improper to say, "She is the *author* of the book"; because the sex is not important to the assertion, or it is sufficiently specified by the pronoun *she*. So, "She is my *accuser*," is a proper expression; for the word *accuseress* is uncommon, and is not needed to show the sex.

Our language is defective in not having, in the third person, a singular pronoun for the common gender. This often leads to an improper use of *they, their*, etc. In such cases the masculine pronoun is preferred when the antecedent is a noun of the common gender, and denotes a person; and both the masculine and the feminine pronoun are used when the antecedent comprises both a masculine and a feminine noun. To small children and to inferior animals the pronoun *it* is sometimes applied.

Person and Number. — In regard to number, writers occasionally allow themselves to be governed by the logical sense, or by euphony or attraction.

"In Hawick twinkled *many a light*,
Behind him soon *they* set in night." — *Scott.*

They, in this sentence, is allowable; because the clauses are not so closely connected that the pronoun *it* would preserve the full sense.

"Neither history nor tradition *furnish* such information." — *Robertson.*

"A silk dress or a flowered bonnet *were* then great *rarities*." — *Flint.*

"Where Leonidas, with his chosen band, *were cut* off." — *Kames.*

These plurals, though in accordance with the syntax of the Classic languages, are not allowable in modern English.

"A coach and six *is* in our time never seen except as a part of some pageant." — *Macaulay.* "Two thousand a year *was* a large revenue for a barrister." — *Id.*

"Early to bed, and early to rise,
Makes a man healthy, wealthy, and wise." — *Franklin.*

These singular verbs are probably allowable, because all that the subject denotes is taken as but one thing. — See p. 144.

Milton, in imitation of Greek and Latin syntax, frequently uses a singular verb after two nominatives joined by *and*, where, in modern English, a plural verb is required.

An abstract number may have a singular verb, where a concrete number would require a plural verb; as, "*Five* from *seven* | *leaves* two"; "*Five apples* [taken] from *seven apples* | *leave* two apples."

Most nominatives that consist of numbers may be classed with collective nouns; and they are about as indefinite in syntax. In *addition*, the verb must of course be *plural;* in *subtraction, division*, or *proportion*, it may be *singular* or *plural*, according as the number is abstract or concrete. In *fractions* and *compound numbers* that must be read *plurally*, the verb should, we think, be generally *plural;* though the principle that a plural term sometimes denotes a single object, or that two or more singular nominatives connected by *and* denote but one person or thing, may occasionally justify the use of the *singular* verb. In *multiplication*, the prevailing custom is, to make the verb plural when the word *times* is used. — See p. 224.

When a plural substantive precedes, some writers use *as follow;* but most writers prefer *as follows*, whether the preceding substantive is singular or plural.

"What *'s justice* to a man, or *laws*,
That never comes within *their* claws." — *Hudibras.*

Justice is nearer to *is*, and *laws* to *their* ; hence the difference, and both are proper by attraction. Such expressions as *one or more persons* are also now considered allowable on the same principle.

We say, "The Old and New *Testaments*," in stead of "The Old Testament and the New Testament"; and on the same principle, "Bancroft's and Palfrey's *Histories*" (Atlantic Monthly), "Glover's, Mason's, and Patterson's *regiments*" (Irving), seem to have been used. But English grammars teach that we should say, "Bancroft's and Palfrey's *History*."

Such expressions as "A ten-*foot* pole," "A twenty-*cent* piece," "A five-*dollar* note," etc., are proper; but a hyphen should always be used to connect the parts. The noun, in such expressions, being used as an adjective, loses the properties of a noun. If these singulars should be plural, then it would not seem unreasonable to require *he* to be *him* or *them* in the following example: "They brought *he*-goats."

Case. — In regard to the possessive case and kindred forms, there are some ambiguities, or shades of meaning, that are worthy of notice. The phrase "God's love," for instance, can be so used as to signify either his love toward us or our love to him; and "The doctor's treatment" is rather active, while "The treatment of the doctor" is rather passive.

It is remarkable that a possessive appositive noun does not always require the possessive form, while such a pronoun must always have it.

"Thy Maker's will has placed thee here,
A *Maker* wise and good." — *Brown's Grammar.*

The foregoing sentence is correct; but, misled by this grammar or principle, Mrs. Sigourney wrote improperly, —

"His curse be on him. *He*, who knoweth [, — *his*]
Where the lightnings hide." — *Mrs. Sigourney.*

By the figure enallage, the objective case is allowed in a few poetic or idiomatic expressions; as, —

"Fare *thee* well, thou first and fairest!
Fare *thee* well, thou best and dearest!" — *Burns.*

"Fare *thou* well" would be so grammatical as to spoil the poetry.

Voice. — The scarcity of verbal forms in our language has always caused some perplexity in regard to the mode of expressing verbs in the progressive passive sense. There was at one time a strong tendency to adopt the preposition *a* and the present participle; as, "Jack always liked to be present when money was *a paying* or *receiving*." — *Swift.* In the writings of Swift are many specimens of this construction; but the present and established practice seems to be what we have taught on pp. 141 and 307.

Mood. — Formerly, the subjunctive mood was extended over all the tenses of the indicative mood and the potential; or it was used when simply doubt was implied, as well as when both doubt and futurity affected the tense. The blundering and contradictory teachings of grammarians in regard to this mood have caused the public to discard it almost altogether. But there is for this mood a proper and well-established province, which we have endeavored to show on pp. 132, 133, 304; and if the mood should ever be expelled from this field of expression, our language will be the poorer for the change.

Tense. — See pp. from 136 to 160; also pp. 306 and 307.

We sometimes find an obsolescent subjunctive form in good modern writers; as, "If he *have given*," etc. — *Wayland*. Such forms are justifiable simply as being remnants or imitations of old style. We sometimes meet with a person who prefers some old-fashioned article of dress.

Comparison. — A word that is not a pure superlative, can sometimes be used in speaking of two objects only; as, "A trochee has the *first* syllable accented." And perhaps the superlative degree can be occasionally applied to one of two when we do not refer to inferior objects, but chiefly aim to impress the idea that the object is not exceeded. Since there are adjectives that have a fixed or absolute meaning, we are sometimes at a loss for words that express approximations to this fixed or high state of quality. In such cases it seems best to apply the words to the partial meaning, and then compare them. "Aristides was the *most just* of the Athenians," is better than "Aristides was the *least unjust* of the Athenians"; for the latter implies that the Athenians were all knaves, and he was simply not the worst one. Such expressions as "the *most nearly just*" have sometimes a stiff and pedantic air.

Position of Words.

A modifier naturally refers its meaning to the nearest word that is suitable to receive it; and since modifiers are numerous and various, and can refer to many different words, to give the best position to the words, phrases, and clauses, which are modifiers, becomes one of the chief concerns of every writer. Ambiguity, obscurity, and sometimes absurdity, harshness, or feebleness, are the chief faults of bad arrangement of words.

When a numeral and a cardinal adjective precede a noun, the numeral adjective is generally placed before the other; as, "The *first two* men," not "The *two first* men"; for there can not be two firsts. When adjectives or other modifiers precede their noun, the more accidental or comprehensive must generally be placed before those which are less so; as, "Mechanics' Bank," "National Mechanics' Bank," or "Mechanics' National Bank." The adjectives *all, such, many, what, both,* and adjectives preceded by *too, so, as,* or *how,* usually precede the article when used with it.

PART VI.

ORNAMENT AND FINISH.

FIGURES.

667. A **Figure** is a deviation from the ordinary form, construction, or application of words, for the sake of brevity, force, or beauty.*

668. Figures may be divided into three classes: —

1. **Figures of Orthography,** which are deviations from the ordinary spelling or pronunciation of words.

2. **Figures of Syntax,** which are deviations from the ordinary construction of words.

3. **Figures of Rhetoric,** which are deviations from the ordinary meaning or application of words.

FIGURES OF ORTHOGRAPHY.

669. The principal figures of orthography are, —

1. **Aphœr'esis**, the shortening of a word by taking a letter or syllable from the beginning; as, *'gainst* for *against.*

Ex. — There *'s* a bliss beyond all that the minstrel hath told.

A shortened word is thus sometimes made a part of an adjoining word.

2. **Syn'cope,** the shortening of a word by taking a

* The end to be reached is frequently gained indirectly rather than directly. Thus, in verse an inferior expression is sometimes allowed for the purpose of gaining the greater beauty of rhythm or rhyme.

letter or syllable from the middle; as, *red'ning* for *reddening*.

Ex. — *O'er* the land of the free and the home of the brave.

3. **Apoc'ope**, the shortening of a word by taking a letter or syllable from the end; as, *th'* for *the; Ben* for *Benjamin*.

Ex. — The *morn* is up again, the dewy *morn*.

4. **Pros'thesis**, the lengthening of a word by prefixing a syllable.

Ex. — Far *adown* the long aisle sacred music is streaming.

5. **Parago'ge**, the lengthening of a word by annexing a syllable; as, *Johnny* for *John*.

Ex. — Oft, in the *stilly* night, ere slumber's chain has bound me.

Elision is the omission of letters; **ellipsis**, the omission of words.

When a word is lengthened by pronouncing suppressed final *ed*, the figure may be called *Diær'esis;* and when a syllable is blended with another in pronunciation, the figure may be called *Synær'esis.*

6. **Tme'sis**, the inserting of a word between the parts of a compound; as, "on *which* side *soever*" for "on *whichsoever* side."

Ex. — The century-living crow that caws the *live* day *long*.

FIGURES OF SYNTAX.

670. The principal figures of syntax are, —

1. **Ellipsis**, the omission of words; usually, the omission of such words as must be supplied in parsing.

In analyzing and parsing, only such words should be supplied as are necessary to complete the construction. — See page 214.

Under the head of ellipsis can probably be included the following figures; though in parsing examples under them, it will generally be sufficient simply to mention the figure, without supplying words.

Aposiope'sis, the leaving of something unsaid.

Ex. — *Whom I* — but first 't is best the billows to restrain.

Say, in parsing, that *whom* is in the objective case; but, by the figure *aposiopesis*, it has no governing word expressed.

Zeug'ma; the referring of a word to two different ones, when in strict syntax it can agree with only one of them.

"In him who is, or him who finds, a *friend*." — *Pope*. Page 146, § 5.
"All of them knowing, and known by, our *coachman*." — *Dickens*.
"One or more scape-goats." — *Irving*. Supply *scape-goat* in parsing.

Say, in parsing, that *friend* is used, by the figure *zeugma*, as a predicate-nominative after *is*, and also as the object of *finds*. (It seems necessary to extend somewhat the ordinary meaning of *zeugma*, and we have done so accordingly.)

2. **Ple'onasm**, the use of more words than the sense or the syntax absolutely requires.

"One of the few, the *immortal* names, *that were not born to die*."

Either the same word is repeated, or an equivalent expression is used.

3. **Enal'lage**; the use of one part of speech, or of one form of a word, for another.

"*Thinks* I to myself, I 'll stop." — *J. Taylor*. So, "*Methinks*."
"The swallow sings *sweet* from her nest in the wall." — *Dimond*.
"And the idols are *broke* in the temple of Baal." — *Byron*.

Generally speaking, this figure should not be used when it can be avoided.

4. **Inversion**, or **Hyper'baton**; inverted syntax, or the transposition of words, as in verse.

---

671. An **Ar'chaism** is a word or expression imitative of ancient style or usage.

"On which *thilk wight* that has *y-gazing* been,
Kens the forthcoming rod — unpleasing sight, I *ween*." — *Shenstone*.

672. **Mimicry** is the imitation of another person's improper use of language.

Ex. — *Mrs. Gilpin*. So you must ride on horseback after *we*.

Say, in parsing, that the nominative *we* is used, by mimicry, for the objective *us*.

Justice Shallow. Let us *examination* these men.

To this figure should be referred all imitations of *brogues* and *dialects*.

The last two figures belong to both figures of orthography and figures of syntax.

FIGURES OF RHETORIC.

673. The following are the most important rhetorical figures: —

1. Sim'ile,
2. Met'aphor,
3. Al'legory,
4. Meton'ymy,
5. Synec'doche,
6. Personification,
7. Antith'esis,
8. I'rony,
9. Paralip'sis,
10. Hyper'bole,
11. Climax,
12. Allusion,
13. Eu'phemism,
14. Interrogation,
15. Exclamation,
16. Apos'trophe,
17. Vision,
18. Onomatopœ'ia.

674. A **Sim'ile** is an express comparison.

Ex. — "The music of Carryl was, *like the memory of joys that are past,* sweet and mournful to the soul." — *Ossian.*

A simile is a comparison usually expressed by means of *like* or *as.*

The teacher should read to the class, while he hears the lesson, what is said about each of these figures in Kerl's Comprehensive Grammar.

675. A **Metaphor** is an implied comparison.

Ex. — Life is an *isthmus* between two eternities.

A metaphor is a word suitable to one object, applied to another object, on account of some resemblance.

Sometimes a metaphor comprises two or more words; as, "Sin is a *bitter sweet,* and *the fine colors of the serpent by no means make amends for the poison of his sting.*" — South. But when the comparison extends beyond a sentence, the figure becomes an *allegory.*

676. An **Allegory** is a fictitious story about one thing, generally designed to teach some moral or practical wisdom about another. It is continued metaphor.

See Bunyan's Pilgrim's Progress.
The teacher should refer to an allegory in the reading-book.

To allegory belong *parables* and *fables.*

677. A **Metonymy** is the name of one object applied to a different one, from some other relation than resemblance.

Ex. — "They have *Moses* and the *prophets*"; *i. e.,* their *writings.*
"We drank but one *bottle*"; *i. e.,* the *contents* of but one bottle.

The most common instances of this figure are those in which the cause is put for the effect, the effect for the cause, the container for the thing contained, or the sign for the thing signified.

The transfer of an attribute to a related object may also be called *metonymy*; as, "my *adventurous* song;" "his *weary* way;" "*jovial* wine."

678. A **Synecdoche** is the name of a part applied to the whole, or that of the whole applied to a part.

As when we say *tea*, for supper; or *gold*, for money.

Synecdoche is simply the application of a word to more or less, of the same thing, than the word strictly denotes.

679. **Personification** represents as persons, or as rational or living beings, objects that are not such in reality.

Ex. — "There *Honor* comes a pilgrim gray." — *Collins.*

When the grammatical properties of a word are changed by personification or metonymy, the figure is sometimes called *Syllepsis*; as, "The *ship*, with *her* snowy sails." "Philip went down to the *city* of Samaria, and preached Christ unto *them*."

680. **Antithesis** is the contrasting of different objects, actions, qualities, or circumstances.

Ex. — Virtue ennobles, and vice debases.

"They heard the clarion's iron clang,
The breeze which through the roses sang." — *Croly.*

681. **Irony** is the sneering use of words with a contrary meaning.

To call a fool a Solomon, or to praise what we mean to disparage, is *irony*.

The expression becomes more sarcastic when the speaker seems to adopt the real thoughts or feelings of the person attacked.

682. **Paralipsis** is the pretended omission or concealment of what is thus really suggested and enforced.

Ex. — "I will not call him villain, for it would be unparliamentary." — *Grattan.* "Let me not think — Frailty thy name is woman." — *Shakespeare.*

683. **Hyperbole** is exaggeration. It usually represents things as greater or less, better or worse, than they really are.

Ex. — "Here Orpheus sings; trees, moving to the sound,
Start from their roots, and form a shade around." — *Pope.*

684. Climax means *ladder*. It is a gradual climbing, or rise of thought, from things inferior to greater or better. When reversed, it is called *anticlimax*.

Ex. — "A Scotch mist becomes a shower; and a shower, a flood; and a flood, a storm; and a storm, a tempest; and a tempest, thunder and lightning; and thunder and lightning, heaven-quake and earthquake." — *Wilson*.

Anticlimax: "Great men, — such as Washington, Adams, Jefferson, Aaron Burr, Stephen Arnold, and the worthy friend of my opponent."

685. Allusion is the use of an expression that recalls incidentally some interesting fact, custom, writing, or saying.

Ex. — "Hands that the rod of empire might have swayed,
Close at my elbow stir their lemonade." — *Holmes*.

Parody is a continued allusion or resemblance in style.

"'T is the last rose of summer left blooming alone;
All her lovely companions are faded and gone."

PARODY: "'T is the last golden dollar left shining alone;
All its brilliant companions are squandered and gone."

A Pun is a play on the sound or meanings of a word.

Ex — "The sutlers," says a newspaper, "are about to be organized into a military company. We rejoice to hear it; for we think if they were thoroughly organized in one body, no enemy could withstand their *charges!*"

686. Euphemism is a softened mode of speech for what would be disagreeable or offensive if told in the plainest language.

Cushi did not say to David, "Absalom is killed"; but, "*May all the enemies of the king be as that young man is.*"

687. Interrogation is a mode of strengthening a statement by an appeal in the form of question.

Ex. — Shall we gather strength by irresolution and inaction?

688. Exclamation is usually an abrupt or broken mode of speech, designed to express more strongly the emotions of the speaker.

Ex. — How glorious, how majestic, yonder setting sun!

689. Apostrophe is a sudden turning-away, in the fullness of emotion, to address some person or thing.

Ex. — "Death is swallowed up in victory. | *O Death!* where is thy sting? O Grave! where is thy victory?" — *Bible.*

690. Vision represents something that is past, future, absent, or simply imagined, as if it were really present.

Ex. — "Soldiers! from yonder pyramids, forty centuries look down upon you!" — *Bonaparte.*

691. Onomatopœia is such an imitation in the sound of the words as may correspond with the sense, or suggest it.

"The sound should seem an echo to the sense." — *Pope.*

Ex. — "Away they went, pell-mell, hurry-skurry, wild buffalo, wild horse, wild huntsman, with clang and clatter, and whoop and halloo, that made the forests ring." — *Irving.*

To this figure may also be referred such new-coined expressions as *bamboozle*, *skedaddle*, and *circumbendibus.*

Sometimes two or more figures are involved in the same expression; as,

"Here the *sword* and *sceptre rust;* —
Earth to earth, and dust to dust"; *metonymy* and *metaphor.*

In the use of rhetorical figures, there are four very common species of error that should be carefully avoided.

1. Figures should be well-founded or becoming, and more suitable than plain language. "The liberties of rising states were shackled by paper chains." — *Bancroft.*

The phrase *paper chains* suggests nothing formidable.

2. Figures should not be too numerous, nor carried too far.

3. Figures should not be improperly mixed, or incongruous figures should not be made parts of the same picture.

"I *bridle* in my struggling muse in vain,
That longs to *launch* into a bolder strain." — *Addison.*

That is, his muse is a monster, partly horse and partly ship.

4. Literal and figurative language should not be mixed.

"The colonies were not yet *ripe* | *to bid adieu* to British connection." — [*Jefferson.*

☞ Many of the meanings of words are but faded figures.

VERSIFICATION.

692. Versification is the art of making verse.

693. Verse is the musical arrangement of words, according to some regular accent.

Also pauses and rhymes are generally used as elements of verse.

Verse is to prose as dancing is to walking; and the accent in verse corresponds to the beat in music.

The word *verse* is sometimes applied to a single line of poetry, sometimes to a stanza, and sometimes to lines of poetry collectively considered.

The accent which runs through verse, affords pleasure to the mind by the regular pulsations; this pleasure is increased by final and cæsural pauses, which divide the verse into lines and shorter divisions by agreeable suspensions; these parts or lines are frequently made further agreeable by terminations similar in sound, which are called rhymes; and the pleasure of rhyming lines is enhanced by combining them into harmonious groups called stanzas. The language itself is colored, vivid, and striking, by being the language of passion or imagination as well as of good common sense. Such is, in a nutshell, the verse-making art.

To show the various elements of beauty to the best advantage, verse is usually arranged in lines, as in the following specimen: —

"Knów ye the lánd | where the cýpress and mýrtle |
Are émblems of déeds | that are dóne in their clíme; ||
Where the rage of the vulture, the love of the turtle,
Now melt into sorrow, now madden to crime?
Know ye the land of the cedar and vine,
Where the flowers ever blossom, the beams ever shine?"

694. Versification is comprised under the following heads: —

1. Poetic Accent and Feet.
2. Poetic Pauses and Lines.
3. Rhymes and Stanzas.
4. Poetic Licenses.

1. POETIC ACCENT AND FEET.

695. Poetic Accent is the accent which divides lines of poetry into small parts, called *poetic feet.*

Poetic accent passes through lines in four different ways, or rests on syllables as shown by the following numbers: —

Iambic.	2	4	6	8	10	12
Trochaic.	1	3	5	7	9	11
Anapestic.	3	6	9	12	15	18
Dactylic.	1	4	7	10	13	16

Iambic: "The cúrfew tólls the knéll of párting dáy."
Trochaic: "Roúnd us róars the témpest loúder."
Anapestic: "At the clóse of the dáy, when the hámlet is stíll."
Dactylic: "Báchelor's háll, — what a quéer-looking pláce it is!"

696. A **Poetic Foot** is a part of a line that consists generally of two or three syllables, one of which is accented.

697. There are four principal feet: —

1. The **Iambus**; a foot of two syllables, accented on the second; as, *enróll.*

2. The **Trochee**; a foot of two syllables, accented on the first; as, *gólden.*

3. The **Anapest**; a foot of three syllables, accented on the last; as, *entertáin.*

4. The **Dactyl**; a foot of three syllables, accented on the first; as, *dúrable.*

698. There are three secondary feet: —

1. The **Spondee**, a foot of two long or accented syllables.

2. The **Pyrrhic**, a foot of two short or unaccented syllables.

3. The **Cæsu'ra**, a long or accented syllable used as one foot.

Ex. — "Near the lake where drooped the willow
Lōng tīme ago." Spondee.

"*Of thĕ* | *lów sún*set clouds, *ánd thĕ* | *blūe skȳ.*" Pyrrhic and Spondee.

Sometimes the accent, in iambic verse, to avoid resting on a short syllable, passes to the first syllable (if long) of the next foot, making this foot a spondee, and the preceding one a pyrrhic. Spondees and pyrrhics are not always produced in this way; but they are generally best when made on this compensation principle.

"Thou wást that áll to mé, *lôve*, (Cæsura.)
For whích my sóul did píne." — *Poe.*

"*Gôld! góld! gôld! góld!* 4 feet }
Héavў tŏ gét ănd líght tŏ *hôld.*" — *Hood.* 4 feet } time equal.

699. The secondary feet are sometimes allowed to break the regular measure, in order to avoid a tedious sameness in the rhythm, or to secure onomatopœia.

700. The iambus and the anapest are kindred feet; and hence they are sometimes used promiscuously.

Ex. — "I cóme! I cóme! yĕ hăve cálled mĕ lóng;
I cóme ŏ'er thĕ moúntăins wĭth líght ănd sóng." — *Hemans.*

A pleasant rhythm is sometimes produced by throwing an anapest, or even two, into each iambic line.

701. The trochee and the dactyl are kindred feet, and hence they are sometimes used promiscuously.

Ex. — Boúndĭng ăwáy ŏvĕr híll ănd vállĕy.

702. Any word or syllable can be brought under the poetic accent, when there is no prevention from quantity or word-accent.

Quantity. — The quantity of a syllable is its relative quantity of sound, or it is the relative time occupied in uttering the syllable. In regard to quantity, some syllables are *long*, some are *short*, and some are *variable*. Ancient verse was made chiefly according to quantity; but modern verse is made chiefly according to *accent*.

703. It is sometimes inelegant or improper to make the poetic accent rest on a short syllable, especially when this syllable stands next to a long or accented one.

And it is also inelegant to make the poetic accent conflict with the emphasis of ordinary discourse.

We can not read, " As á friend thánk him, ánd with jóy see hím."
But we may read, " Seé him with jóy, and thánk him ás a friénd."

704. A word of two or more syllables can be admitted into the verse only when the poetic accent takes the place of the primary or secondary accent of the word.

2. POETIC LINES AND PAUSES.*

705. Feet are formed into lines of various length; and the lines are then called *iambic*, *trochaic*, *anapestic*, or *dactylic*, according to the kind of foot which prevails in them.

Lines are also named according to the number of feet composing them.

Monom'eter, a line of one foot.
Dim'eter, a line of two feet.
Trim'eter, a line of three feet.
Tetram'eter, a line of four feet.
Pentam'eter, a line of five feet.
Hexam'eter, a line of six feet.
Heptam'eter, a line of seven feet.
Octom'eter, a line of eight feet.

Iambic Lines.

I, iambus; *t*, trochee; *a*, anapest; *d*, dactyl; *c*, cæsura; +, syllable over.

1*i*. Refráin.
2*i*. The píbroch ráng.
3*i*. Beyónd the ócean blúe.
4*i*. The fréighted cloúds at ánchor líe.
5*i*. The cúrfew tólls the knéll of párting dáy.
6*i*. When thoú art nígh, it seéms a néw creátion roúnd.
7*i*. The mélanchóly dáys are cóme, the sáddest óf the yéar.

An iambic line of seven feet is sometimes broken, at the end of the fourth foot, into two lines.

706. Sometimes a line has a regular number of feet, and a part of another foot at the end. Such lines are called *hyper'meters*.

Iambic Hypermeters.

1*i*+. The lóss*es*.
2*i*+. To hálls of splénd*or*.
3*i*+. From Greénland's ícy moún*tains*.
4*i*+. Her heárt is líke a fáded flów*er*.
5*i*+. The deér, half-seén, are tó the cóvert wénd*ing*.
6*i*+. I thínk I wíll not gó with yoú to héar the tóasts and speéch*es*.

Trochaic Lines.

1*t*. Túrning.
2*t*. Dárkly wáving.
3*t*. Éarly bírds are sínging.
4*t*. Néver wédding, éver woóing.

* Strict adherence to truth probably requires that we should consider the poetic pauses — the final and the cæsural — as producing poetic lines and cæsural divisions; but to make the subject easier to the learner, we shall treat of lines first, and then regard them simply as having these pauses.

5*t*. Seé the dístant fórest dárk and wáving.
6*t*. Úp the déwy moúntain, Héalth is boúnding líghtly.
7*t*. Thén in theé let thóse rejoíce who seék theé sélf-denýing.
8*t*. Béams of noón, like búrning lánces, throúgh the treé-tops flásh and glísten.

Trochaic Hypermeters.

1*t*+. Ôver *wôôds.*
2*t*+. Dáys of sórrow *câme.*
3*t*+. Réstless mórtals tóil for *naûght.*
4*t*+. Thén, methóught, I héard a hóllow *soûnd.*
5*t*+. Faúns and drýads níghtly wátch the stárry *skŷ.*
6*t*+. Sóftly blów the évening breézes, softly fáll the déws of *nîght.*

The long or accented syllable which sometimes ends a trochaic or dactylic line, is so nearly equivalent to a foot, that it should rather be considered a cæsura than a mere hypermeter syllable.

Anapestic Lines.

1*a*. Far awáy.
2*a*. Far awáy in the Soúth.
3*a*. I am mónarch of áll I survéy.
4*a*. Far awáy in the Soúth is a beaútiful ísle.

Anapestic Hypermeters.

1*a*+. Strains entránc*ing.*
2*a*+. He is góne on the moún*tain.*
3*a*+. On the knólls the red clóver is grów*ing.*
4*a*+. Through the cóurts at deep mídnight the tórches are gléam*ing.*

Dactylic Lines.

2*d*. Lánd of the Pílgrim's pride.
2*dt*. Cóme to the moúntain of Zíon.
3*dc*. Shroúdless and tómbless they súnk to their rêst.
3*dt*. Paúse not to dréam of the fúture befóre us.
7*dc*. Nímrod the húnter was míghty in húnting, and fámed as the rúler of cíties of yôre.

Composite Verse. — Sometimes different kinds of feet, or different kinds of lines, are combined in the same poem. Such verse is called *composite;* and it is most frequently found in odes and songs.

See Kerl's Comprehensive Grammar, pp. 329, 330, 331.

POETIC PAUSES.

707. To improve the rhythm or verse, there are two pauses; the *final* and the *cæsu'ral.*

708. The **Final Pause** is a slight pause made at the end of each line, even when the grammatical sense does not require it.

Ex. — Ye who have anxiously and fondly *watched* |
Beside a fading friend, unconscious *that* | |
The cheek's bright crimson, lovely to the view,
Like nightshade, with unwholesome beauty bloomed.

709. The **Cæsural Pause** is a slight pause made within the line, most frequently about the middle of it; and it belongs chiefly to long lines.

Sometimes a line has two or more cæsural pauses, one of which is commonly greater than the rest. The secondary pause may be called a *demi-cæsural pause.*

Ex. — "Warms | in the sun, | | refreshes | in the breeze,
Glows | in the stars, | | and blossoms | in the trees." — *Pope.*

"No sooner had the Almighty ceased, | than all
The multitude of angels, | with a shout
Loud | as from numbers without number, | sweet
As from blest voices | uttering joy," etc. — *Milton.*

This versification is admirable. The cæsural pause after *loud*, and that before *sweet*, and the final pause after *sweet*, make us halt in reading, to enjoy the exquisite luxury of the sense. Long lines can sometimes be divided at the cæsural pause into two lines each.

3. RHYMES AND STANZAS.

710. **Rhyme** is a similarity of sound between the endings of poetic lines.

Also verse that consists of rhyming lines, is frequently called *rhyme.*

Sometimes the first half of a line rhymes to the second, and sometimes rhymes occur in immediate succession.

711. Rhymes must begin with different letters, and end with the same sound, or with nearly the same sound.

Rhymes that are not exact, yet authorized, are called *allowable rhymes.*

712. Rhymes may run back into lines one, two, or three syllables; and hence they are classified into *single* rhymes, *double* rhymes, and *triple* rhymes.

The rhyming part of each line must always be accented, or begin with an accented syllable.

713. **Blank Verse** is verse without rhyme.

Most of our blank verse consists of iambic pentameters.

714. **Heroic Verse** is verse that consists of iambic pentameters.

This verse is called so because it is chiefly used in epic poetry, or in poetry that relates the exploits of heroes. It allows greater license of versification than any other kind of verse, in the way of admitting other kinds of feet, as well as hypermeters. — See Milton and Shakespeare.

An iambic hexameter is usually called an *Alexandrine.*

715. A **Couplet** consists of two poetic lines that usually rhyme together. A *triplet*, of three.

716. A **Stanza** is a combination of three or more poetic lines that usually make a distinct chime of rhymes, and a regular division of the poem.

A stanza generally consists of four, six, eight, or nine lines.

The most common stanzas are the *common-metre*, the *long-metre*, the *short-metre*, the *elegiac*, and the *Spenserian.*

Common-Metre Stanza.

4*i.* When áll thy mércies, Ó my Gód,
3*i.* My rísing sóul survéys,
4*i.* Transpórted wíth the viéw, I 'm lóst
3*i.* In wónder, lóve, and práise.

Short-Metre Stanza.

3*i.* The dáy is pást and góne;
3*i.* The évening shádes appéar;
4*i.* O máy we áll remémber wéll
3*i.* The níght of déath draws néar.

Long-Metre Stanza.

4*i*. So blúe yon wínding ríver flóws,
4*i*. It seéms an oútlet fróm theský,
4*i*. Where, wáiting tíll the wést-wind blóws,
4*i*. The fréighted cloúds at ánchor líe.

Elegiac Stanza.

5*i*. Here résts his héad, upón the láp of Éarth,
5*i*. A yoúth to Fórtune ánd to Fáme unknówn;
5*i*. Fair Scíence frówned not ón his húmble bírth,
5*i*. And Mélanchóly márked him fór her ówn.

Scanning.

717. Scanning is the dividing of verse into its feet.

Each line is usually scanned by itself; but it seems best to scan continuously from one line into another when we can thus avoid irregularities.

Ex. — 'T is the lást rose of súmmer,
Left bloóming alóne; 4 feet.
All her lóvely compánions
Are fáded and góne. 4 feet.

Sometimes more than one mode of scanning can be applied to the same poem; but that mode should always be preferred which is most simple and musical.

For the various specimens of stanzas, and the modes of scanning them, see Kerl's Comprehensive Grammar.

POETIC LICENSES.

718. A **Poetic License** is an allowed deviation from the correctness of ordinary prose, or from the regular laws of versification, in order that the poet may be enabled to reach the requirements of verse.

Poetic licenses are allowed, —

1. In Spelling. Poets frequently shorten words by the elision of some letter or syllable. — See p. 318.

2. In Pronunciation. Poets sometimes change the accent of a word; and sometimes they adopt some old pronunciation, in order to make a rhyme. — See pp. 58, 59.

3. In the Choice of Words. Poets have gradually gathered and manufactured for themselves a little extra vocabulary of words. These consist of antiquated words, foreign words, and common words shortened or lengthened. The following are specimens : *Ken, wend, ween, trow, rife, yore, lone, guerdon, welkin, whilom, albeit, eyne, brand* (sword), *sylvan, steed, swain, morn, eve, fount, plaint, ope, meed, fane, yon, darksome, stilly, vasty, evanish, bedimmed, bewept.*

4. In the Meanings of Words. Poets sometimes vary the meanings of words, or employ a less appropriate word.

Ex. — " Chill Penury repressed their noble *rage.*" — Gray. (For *zeal.*)

A license in regard to the meaning or pronunciation of a word is always a blemish, rather than a beauty.

5. In Idioms. Poets sometimes use uncommon native idioms, and frequently borrow idioms from foreign languages.

Ex. — " Who would not sing for Lycidas? he *knew*
Himself *to sing*, and *build* the lofty rhyme." — See p. 223.

6. In Syntax. Violent inversion. Violent ellipsis. Violations of the minor rules or principles of grammar. In general, any inversion or ellipsis is allowable that will preserve the sense.

Omission of Article. " The why is plain as ^ way to ^ parish church."

Omission of Pronoun. " It was a tall young oysterman ^ lived by the river-side." — *Holmes.*

(Omission of *It.*) " Suffice ^ , to-night, these orders to obey."

Omission of Verb. " Sweet ^ the pleasure, rich ^ the treasure." (*is*)

Omission of Principal Verb. " Angels could ^ no more." (*do*)

Object before its Verb. " *Him* well I *knew.*"

Subject after the Verb. " *Echo* the *mountains* round."

Auxiliary after Principal Verb. " *Nestled* at its roots *is* beauty."

Adjective after its Noun. " *Violets blue* and *daisies white.*"

Predicate Adjective before its Verb. " *Purple grows* the primrose pale."

Pronoun before Antecedent. " Back to *its* mansion call the fleeting *breath.*"

Relative Clause severed from Antecedent. " From *things* too low *that lie.*" (Inelegant.)

Adverb between *to* and the rest of the Infinitive. " *To slowly trace* the forest's shady scenes."

Preposition after its Object. " Birds sang the leafy *dells within.*"

Adjuncts, participial phrases, infinitive phrases, and adjective phrases, are frequently transposed.

Self added to a Noun. " Bewept till Pity's *self* be dead."

Pleonastic Pronoun added to its Antecedent. " My banks *they* are furnished with bees."

Simple Pronoun for Compound. " I laid *me* [*myself*] down on a green bank."

Adjective used for Adverb. " So *sweet* she sung." (*sweetly*)

Adjective for Noun. " O'er the vast *abrupt.*"

Intransitive Verb made Transitive. " *To meditate* the blue *profound.*"

Past Tense for Perfect Participle. "The idols are *broke.*" — *Byron.*
First or Third Person Imperative in stead of *Let.* "*Turn we* to survey," etc.
Or — or, *nor — nor*, for *either — or*, *neither — nor.* "*Nor* in sheet *nor* in shroud we wound him."

7. In Figures. Poetic style abounds in figures, and is frequently set all aglow by the creative power of the imagination; as, "The native hue of resolution is sicklied o'er with the pale cast of thought." — *Shak.*

8. In Versification. Variations in the position of the poetic accent, or in the number of unaccented syllables, are allowable where the chief poetic pauses occur, — the final and the cæsural.

"Ye 've tráiled me throúgh the *fórest;* | ye 've tráiled me ó'er the stréam;
And strúggling throúgh the éverglåde | your brístling báyŏnĕts gléam."

Observe that *forest* makes here a syllable in excess; but the irregularity, occurring at the cæsural pause, is little noticed. It is just so in music: variations or extra flourishes can frequently be made where pauses occur. A distinguished poet, in speaking of licenses in versification, says, "To prevent metrical harmony from degenerating into monotony, occasional roughness must be interposed. *The rivulet is made musical by obstructions in its channel.*"

Iambic or anapestic lines sometimes end with one or two extra unaccented syllables. — See Rogers's Ginevra.

Iambic lines may occasionally begin with a trochee, a dactyl, or a spondee; or admit a trochee, a spondee, or an anapest within, especially where the cæsural pauses occur.

Ex. — "*Búrsts thĕ* | *wīld crȳ* | of térror ánd dismáy." — *Campbell.*
"*Lībĕrăl*, not lávish, ís kind Náture's hánd." — *Beattie.*
"*Wēēp*, *wēēp*, and rénd your háir for thóse who néver sháll retúrn."
"Of góod*līĕst treés* | *lóadĕn* with fáirest frúit." — *Milton.*
"And mánȳ *ă yoúth* and mánȳ *ă máid.*" — *Id.*
"With Héavĕn'*s ărtil* | *lĕrȳ fraúght*, come ráttling ón." — *Id.*

It is generally better to contract an excess of short syllables by synæresis, or by hasty pronunciation, than to reject any of them by elision.

Anapestic lines may occasionally begin with an iambus or a spondee; or admit a spondee or an iambus within, especially where the cæsural pause occurs.

Ex. — "*The póp*lars are felled, | *fārewēll* to the shade,
And the whíspering soúnds of the coól colonnáde." — *Cowper.*

UTTERANCE.

Utterance comprises, — 1. Articulation; 2. Degree of Loudness; 3. Degree of Rapidity; 4. Inflections; 5. Tones; 6. Emphasis; 7. Pauses.

1. Good *articulation* requires the words to be uttered with their proper sound, fully in all their syllables, and distinctly from one an-

other. It is opposed to mumbling, mouthing, mincing, muttering, slurring, drawling, clipping, lisping, hesitating, stammering, miscalling, and recalling.

"Words should drop from the lips as beautiful coins newly issued from the mint, — deeply and accurately impressed, perfectly finished, neatly struck by the proper organs, distinct, sharp, in due succession, and of due weight." — *Austin.*

2. and 3. The *degree* of *loudness* or *rapidity* must depend on the speaker, the hearer, the discourse, the place, or other circumstances. Scarcely any thing else is so disagreeable as utterance too rapid, low, and jumbled to be intelligible, and rather suggesting that the speaker is ashamed to let others know what he is saying.

4. *Inflections* refer to the passage of the voice from one key or pitch to another. There are three: the *rising* inflection, which implies elevation of the voice; the *falling* inflection, which implies a sinking of the voice; and the *circumflex*, which combines the other two. "Was it *yoú*, or *hè?*" "Madam, *yoŭ* have my father much offended."

5. *Tones* are voice as modulated by feeling. They should be adapted to the general discourse, and also to its distinct sentiments. Tones aim to awaken, by sympathy, the intended emotions in the hearer.

"In *exordiums*, the voice should be low, yet clear; in *narrations*, distinct; in *reasoning*, slow; in *persuasions*, strong: it should thunder in *anger*, soften in *sorrow*, tremble in *fear*, and melt in *love*." — *Hiley.*

6. *Emphasis* is an elevation of the voice on some words, word, or part of a word, by which the meaning is brought out more precisely or forcibly. Emphasis, properly used, adds greatly to the vigor of discourse.

Emphasis relates to words; and *accent*, to syllables.

7. *Pauses* are of three kinds: *sentential* or *grammatical* pauses, which show the grammatical sense; *rhetorical* pauses, which are used for emphasis, or for effect on the hearer; and *harmonic* or *metrical* pauses, which are used in poetry.

The pauses are relative rather than absolute. The semicolon requires a pause double that of the comma; the colon, double that of the semicolon; and the period, double that of the colon, and sometimes even longer. Most of the other points require pauses that depend chiefly on the sense. Grave or solemn discourse requires longer pauses than that which is lively and spirited.

PUNCTUATION.

719. Punctuation treats of the points or marks used in writing and printing.

Punctuation shows the joints or interruptions in the flow of sentences, and helps to bring out the meaning to better advantage. It is based almost wholly on grammatical sense, and is seldom influenced by delivery.

The principal marks of this kind are the following: —

. The **Period;** which denotes the longest pause or a full stop.

: The **Colon;** which denotes the next shorter pause.

; The **Semicolon;** which denotes the next shorter pause.

, The **Comma;** which denotes the shortest pause.

? The **Interrogation-Point;** which is placed after every direct question.

! The **Exclamation-Point;** which denotes great surprise, joy, or other emotion.

Hence it is generally placed after interjections or unusually earnest addresses.

— The **Dash;** which denotes emphasis or abruptness.

( ) The **Curves;** which enclose some explanation or remark that can be omitted.

[ ] The **Brackets;** which enclose some correction or explanation that is generally inserted by another person.

" " The **Quotation-Marks;** which enclose words taken from another person.

' ' "Single Quotation-Marks enclose 'a quotation within a quotation.'"

When a piece is quoted in paragraphs, quotation-marks are placed at the beginning of each paragraph, and only at the end of the last paragraph.

' The **Apostrophe;** which denotes possession, or the omission of some letter or letters. Page 52.

- The **Hyphen;** which joins the parts of most compound words, and is placed at the end of a line when a part of a word is carried to the next line.

´ The **Acute Accent;** which marks stress of voice.

` The **Grave Accent;** which shows a sinking of the voice, or brings out a syllable.

^ or ˇ The **Circumflex Accent;** which is a union of the other two accents. It sometimes denotes an unusual or long sound given to a vowel, as in *tête-à-tête*.

¯ The **Macron;** which marks a long sound, as in *līve*.

˘ The **Breve;** which marks a short sound, as in *lĭve*.

¨ The **Diær'esis;** which separates two vowels into two syllables, as in [*Menelaüs*.

ç The **Cedil'la;** which is a French mark joined to the lower part of *c*, to give this letter the sound of *s*, as in *façade*.

ñ The **Til'de**; which is a Spanish mark, placed over *ñ*, to annex to it the sound of *y*; as in *cañon*, a ravine.

^ The **Caret**; which is used in writing, to show where words or letters are to be inserted.

} The **Brace**; which serves to connect parts.

§ The **Section**; which is sometimes used to mark the small divisions of a book.

¶ The **Paragraph**; which shows where a new subject begins, or denotes a paragraph.

*, †, ‡ The **Star, Dagger,** and **Double Dagger**; which are used as marks of reference. Letters or figures are sometimes used for the same purpose.

***, ——, or ..... **Stars, Double Dash,** or **Periods**; which denote omission or suppression.

" or ,, The **Ditto**; a mark used in stead of repeating the word or expression above it.

☞ The **Hand**; which directs special attention to something.

⁂ The **Asterism,** or **Three Stars**; a mark sometimes placed before a note that has a general reference.

.... **Leaders**; which are periods that lead the eye from one part to another over a blank space, as in indexes.

________ The **Underscore**; which is a line drawn under words in writing, that are to be printed in Italics or capitals.

Also various marks are used to show the sounds of letters as in Webster's or Worcester's Dictionary.

PERIOD.

720. The **Period** is put at the end of every word, phrase, or sentence, complete by itself, and not interrogative or exclamatory; also after abbreviations.

Ex. — John W. Ringgold, Esq., addressed the assembly.

The abbreviating period supersedes no point except itself.

Exceptions. — Such abbreviations as *Tom*, *Ben*, and *per cent* do not take the abbreviating period, for they have themselves become words; and such expressions as *1st*, *2d*, *2dly*, *4th*, etc., do not take the abbreviating period, for they are not so much abbreviations as they are cardinal numerals made ordinal.

Other Uses. — To separate decimals from whole numbers; as, $ 5.055 +. After enumerating figures or letters; as, "I have two good reasons: 1. I can not give my attention to the business; 2. I have no money to invest in it."

COLON.

721. The **Colon** is used, —

1. As an intermediate point between the semicolon and the period.

Ex. — Powers depart,
Possessions vanish, and opinions change;
And passions hold a fluctuating seat:
But, by the storms of circumstance unshaken,
And subject neither to eclipse nor wane,
Duty exists.

2. After words that promise a series or statement, or something important.

That is, after a statement that ends with *as follows*, *the following*, *thus*, *these*, or other words suggestive of the same meaning; also generally after a formal address that begins a discourse or letter.

3. Before an important remark added to a sentence, especially when it sums up the sentence, or presents the meaning in another form.

Ex. — The boast of heraldry, the pomp of power,
And all that beauty, all that wealth, e'er gave,
Await alike the inevitable hour:
The paths of glory lead but to the grave.

The colon, in this sense, is frequently used in stead of a semicolon and conjunction.

SEMICOLON.

722. The **Semicolon** is used, —

1. To separate parts that have the comma, or parts that require a point greater than the comma and less than the colon.

Ex. — Though deep, yet clear; though gentle, yet not dull.

Obs. — Hence the semicolon is frequently placed before *and*, *but*, *for*, *though*, *yet*, *nor*, *nay*, *hence*, *therefore*, or a similar connective, when this unites two clauses that are rather long, and make but one sentence; and it is also frequently placed before an appositive phrase that is subdivided by the comma.

2. To separate the parts of a loose series.

Ex. — Every thing has its time to flourish; every thing grows old; every thing passes away.

Such a series may consist of clauses, subjects, predicates, or modifiers.

COMMA.

Serial Parts. **723.** The **Comma** is used, —

1. To separate the terms of a closely related series, or two such terms when the connective is omitted.

Ex. — Hedges, groves, orchards, and gardens, were in bloom.
It was a dark, desolate region.

Our captain then went to the camp, called upon the officer in command, and informed him who we were, whence we had come, and whither we intended to go.

2. To separate terms that are contrasted or otherwise distinguished, and terms of which a part in one might be referred improperly to the other.

Ex. — He is poor, but honest.
Now a peal of gunpowder was heard, and another, and another.
The troops landed, and killed a hundred Indians.

"The troops landed and killed a hundred Indians," has a different meaning.

Obs. — When a term relates to each of two or more separated terms, it must generally be set off to show its common dependence on them all; as, "The water was as bright and pure, and seemed as precious, *as liquid diamonds.*" "The classics have been the models, I might almost say the masters, *of composition and thought in all ages.*"

Parenthetic Parts. 3. To set off a word, phrase, or clause, that is parenthetic, or that comes between other parts and breaks their connection.

Ex. — You will then, *however*, be in no better condition.
Moral culture, *especially in youth*, is of the greatest importance.
They set out early, and, *before the dawn of day*, reached the place.
Columbus, *who was a Genoese*, discovered America.

Modifying Words, Phrases, and Clauses. 4. To set off a modifying word, phrase, or clause, that is not closely connected with what it modifies, or that is removed from it by inversion.

This is a very comprehensive rule, and partially includes the preceding rule.

Ex. — "In a central region, midway on the continent, though somewhat nearer the Pacific than the Atlantic ocean, at an elevation of nearly seven thousand five hundred feet, lies the remarkable valley of Mexico, encircled by a colossal rampart of the hardest rocks, and forming a circumference of about sixty-seven leagues, with a sky of the deepest blue, a serene atmosphere, and a magnificent landscape." — *Prescott.* (Lies where? What kind of valley ?)

Obs. — Hence, also, an appositive word or phrase that is parenthetic rather than restrictive, or that produces a separate impression on the mind, is generally set off by the comma; as, "The greatest Roman orator, *Cicero*, was distinguished for his patriotism." "Such was Tecumseh, *the celebrated Indian warrior*."

Independent Parts. 5. To set off words or phrases used independently or absolutely.

Ex. — This book, *Mary*, is yours. *O*, *yes*, *sir*, I do know.
Shame being lost, all virtue is lost. — See Note V.

Subject and Predicate. 6. To separate the predicate from its subject, when the subject is very long, has a clause, or consists of punctuated parts.

Ex. — That one bad example spoils many good precepts, is true.
He who falls in love with himself, will have few rivals.
Neither time nor distance, neither weal nor woe, can separate us.

Obs. 1. — A predicate consisting of two parts that are rather long, or equivalent to two clauses, generally needs a comma between them; as, "The prairies of Iowa are covered with a rich coat of grass, and not unfrequently spotted with hazel thickets."

Obs. 2. — A clause or long infinitive phrase, that is used in the sense of a predicate-nominative, is generally set off by the comma; as, "The unanimous decision of this little party now was, that a desperate effort should be made to reach the ship again before the approach of night."

Clauses. 7. To separate clauses that are neither very closely nor very loosely connected.

Ex. — There mountains rise, and circling oceans flow.
If Homer was the greater genius, Virgil was the better artist.
We next went to London, which is the largest city in the world.

No Point. 8. Short simple sentences or clauses seldom require a point within them; and phrases or clauses that stand in close connection with that on which they depend, seldom require a point before them.

Ex. — " And the deep-pealing organ rolled
Contrition from its lips of gold." — *Funeral of Lincoln.*

" Tell me when it was that you saw him after he returned."

Other Uses. — The comma is generally placed between a word and its repetition; as, " Sweet, sweet home!" It is placed after a surname when this is put before the given name; as, "Tyler, George W. It is used to separate numbers into periods; as, " Population of the United States," 31,443,790. And it is sometimes used to supply the place of an omitted verb or conjunction; as, " Indolence produces poverty; and poverty, misery."

INTERROGATION-POINT.

724. The **Interrogation-Point** is placed after every complete direct question, whether it forms a complete sentence or only a part of a sentence.

Ex. — Shall we never have any rest?
What have you to say, Charles? for I am waiting.
" Will you go?" said he, " or will you stay?"
Is my name Talbot? and am I your son? and shall I fly?
Which are the interjections of joy? — of grief? — of wonder?

When a sentence consists of interrogative parts, it is sometimes very difficult to decide whether only the comma or semicolon should be used within the sentence, and the interrogation-point at the end, or whether the interrogation-point should be used after each interrogative part. The following direction may afford some assistance in doubtful cases.

Obs. 1. — When each of the interrogative parts requires a distinct answer, or when the interrogative nature of the parts is not sufficiently obvious without the point, the interrogation-point is placed after each of the parts. (See above.) But when only one answer is needed, or when the question is not complete before the end is reached, the comma or semicolon is used within the sentence, and the interrogation-point at the end; as, " Will you go, or stay?" " Which is more, — six inches square or six square inches?"

Obs. 2. — A question that is merely mentioned, and not asked, is called indirect, and does not admit the interrogation-point after it; as, " He asked me, '*Why do you weep?*'" Direct. " He asked me *why I wept.*" Indirect.

Hence the following sentence from Dr. Johnson is punctuated incorrectly: " When Diog'enes was asked what wine he liked best? he answered, That which is drunk at the expense of others." CORRECTED: " When Diogenes was asked what wine he liked best, he answered," etc.

EXCLAMATION-POINT.

725. The **Exclamation-Point** is placed after a word, phrase, clause, or sentence, that indicates great surprise, grief, joy, or other emotion in the speaker.

Ex. — O home! magical, all-powerful home! how strong must have been thy influence, when thy faintest memory could make these bronzed heroes of a thousand battles weep like children!

Obs. 1. — The exclamation-point is frequently placed after interjections; as, "Fie! such a man!"

Obs. 2. — The exclamation-point is placed after unusually emotional or earnest addresses; as, "O Absalom, Absalom! my son, my son!"

Obs. 3. — The exclamation-point is sometimes repeated, for greater effect; as, "Selling off below cost!! great sacrifices!!!"

Obs. 4. — The interrogation or exclamation-point is sometimes used sneeringly to express the disbelief of the speaker; as, "The measures which he introduced to Congress, and which ought to have been carried by overwhelming majorities (?), proved him to have been in every sense a great statesman (!)."

A sentence that is interrogative in form but exclamatory in sense, is followed by the exclamation-point; as, "What business could the honest man have in my room!" — *Shak.*

DASH.

726. The **Dash** is used, —

1. To show omission caused by interruption.

Ex. — "HERE LIES THE GREAT —" False marble! where?

2. To show emphasis or suppressed feeling, or to show an unexpected turn in thought or style.

Ex. — The pulse fluttered — stopped — went on — throbbed — stopped again — moved — stopped.

This world, 't is true, was made for Cæsar — but for Titus too.

3. To set off a parenthesis, especially when emphatic, or when there are other points within it.

Ex. — He was dressed — and, indeed, so were they nearly all — in coarse homespun.

If the separated parts require a point between them, this point is usually placed before each dash.

4. Before echoes, or where *that is* or *namely* is understood.

Ex. — They were governed by the worst passions, — malice and revenge.

Other Uses. — The dash is generally used after side-heads, and also before authorities when in the same line with the end of the paragraph. It is sometimes added to the common points to lengthen the pause or supply the want of an intermediate point, to show emphasis, or to mark transition. In dialogue that is not paragraphed, it is now commonly used when the speakers' names are omitted. It is generally used in composite headings, as in newspapers. It is often used where a line is broken off, and the subject is resumed in the next line. It is sometimes used to show omission of letters or figures And it is often used at the left of newspaper extracts, to show that they are such, or as a more modest request to notice than the ☞. (The teacher should explain what is meant. — See Kerl's Comprehensive Grammar.)

CURVES.

727. The **Curves** are used to enclose some incidental remark or explanation that breaks the regular construction of the sentence, and can be omitted without injuring the grammatical sense. What is enclosed, is properly called a parenthesis.

Ex. — "*Orthoepy*, a word derived from the Greek *orthos* (correct) and *epo* (I speak), signifies the right utterance of words." — *Sargent.*

"Know then this truth (enough for man to know):
Virtue alone is happiness below." — *Pope.*

Obs. — If the parts separated by the parenthesis require a point between them, this point is frequently placed before each curve; sometimes it is placed only after the latter curve, especially when the parenthesis is more closely related to the first part than to the second; and it is placed only before the first curve when the parenthesis requires a different point at its end, which point is then placed before the latter curve. The parenthesis, within, is punctuated as if it stood alone.

Ex. — "I gave (and who would not have given?) my last dollar."

"The Frenchman, first in literary fame,
(Mention him, if you please. Voltaire? — The same.)
With spirit, genius, eloquence, supplied,
Lived long, wrote much, laughed heartily, and died." — *Cowper.*

"At the opening of a new year it is pleasant — (*tling-a-ling-a-ling*, rings the front-door bell; and Bridget breaks upon our privacy with, 'Plase, Sir, it 's the butcher's boy with the bill.') — it is pleasant — (*tling-a ling*: 'Plase, Sir, it 's the baker's bill.') — it is pleasant, we say, to dwell upon the delightful memories of the past, — (*tling-a-ling-a-ling-a-ling*: 'Plase, Sir, it 's the milliner's girl left mistress's bill! ') — and — and — What?" *Harper's Weekly.*

BRACKETS.

728. The **Brackets** are properly used to enclose what one person puts into the writings of another.

Explanation: "Yours [the British] is a nation of great resources," etc.
Correction: "Do you know if [whether] he is at home?"
Omission: "Abbotsford, May 12th, [1820]."

729. The writer himself may sometimes use the brackets to enclose a detached explanation or remark, or some digression or apparent interpolation.

Ex. — "DISMISSION (-mish′-un), n. [Lat. *dismissio.*]" — *N. Webster*

"I never liked him, never, in my days!"
["O, yes! you did," said Ellen with a sob.]
"There always was a something in his ways" —
["So sweet — so kind," said Ellen with a throb.] — *Hood.*

HYPHEN.

730. The **Hyphen** is used, —

1. At the close of a syllable that ends a line, when the remaining syllable or syllables of the word must be carried to the next line.

2. To join the parts of most compound words.

Ex. — "There is pretty, *ten-year-old*, *rosy-cheeked*, *golden-haired* Mary." — *Wilson.*

Compound Words.

731. A phrase is generally made a compound word when it expresses a complex idea rather than two or more distinct ideas, when it is used as one adjective, when it has become the common name of an object, or when it differs in meaning from that of the separated words.

Ex. — The *tree-and-cloud-shadowed* river; a *ten-dollar* note; *humming-bird*, *honeysuckle*, *apple-orchard;* the *live-oaks* of Texas.

"*Time-tutored age* and *love-exalted* youth" is very different from "*Time tutored age*, and *love exalted youth.*" *To-night* has not the meaning of *to* and *night.* A *paper-mill* is not made of paper, nor *is* a *tin-peddler* made of tin. *Boston-Neck Meat-Market* is a more definite expression than "Boston Neck Meat Market." — See p. 56.

Obs. 1. — Phrases in which the words are separately significant, are usually not compounded; as, "*brick wall*," "*gold cup.*" Phrases made proper names, when sufficiently distinguished by having each principal word commenced with a capital letter, are usually not compounded; as, "*Union Square*," "*Baffin's Bay.*" Idiomatic phrases are usually not compounded; as, *to and fro*, *by and by.* Cardinal numerals are compounded from twenty to hundred, as *twenty-one;* but not above, as "*five hundred and twenty* dollars."

Can not and *in stead of* have as good right to separation as *may not* and *in lieu of.*

Obs. 2. — A part common to two or more consecutive compounds, should either be left separate, or be made a part of each.

Ex. — "Riding and dancing schools;" or, "Riding-schools and dancing-schools;" not, "Riding and dancing-schools," nor, "Riding- and dancing-schools." "Six and seventeen" = 23; "sixteen and seventeen" = 33.

Hyphened.

732. A compound word is generally hyphened when it is first formed, when it has been but little used, when its parts are rather long, when each part retains its own accent, when some letter of one part might be improperly referred to the other part, or when the parts do not coalesce as smoothly as syllables of one word.

Ex. — Zephyr-haunted, festal-sounding, knitting-needle, ant-hill, red-hot.

Unhyphened.

733. A compound word is generally not hyphened when it has been long or much used, and when its parts are short or coalesce as smoothly as syllables of one word under one chief accent.

See § 156. Most compound words that are used as adverbs, prepositions, or conjunctions, are not hyphened; and prefixes are very seldom set off from the remainder of the word by a hyphen. A hyphen should be placed after a prefix, when two vowels come together that might be mistaken for a diphthong; as, *re-elect.*

UNDERSCORE.

734. The **Underscore** is a line drawn under words in writing, that are to be printed in Italics or capitals.

One line is drawn under a written word, to denote *slanting* or *Italic letters;* two lines are drawn under, to denote SMALL CAPITALS; and three lines, to denote CAPITALS.

735. Italic letters, and sometimes small capitals, are used for emphasis or distinction.

Ex. — "Here *I* reign king, and, to enrage thee more, *thy* king and lord." — *Milton.*

1. Italics are generally used to distinguish foreign words, and also common words when we speak of them merely as being words.

Ex. — "He was secretary *pro tempore.*"
"*Secretary* is a common noun."

2. Italics are frequently used to distinguish the names of boats, ships, newspapers, and magazines.

Ex. — "The *Neptune* sailed yesterday."

"This article appeared in the *Atlantic Monthly*."

In the common version of the Bible, Italics show what words were supplied by the translators.

☞ For exercises in punctuation, let the reading-books be used. The pupil may give rules for the points which he finds; and he may also be required to capitalize and punctuate paragraphs transcribed without capitals or points.

OBSERVATIONS.

Poetry. — Poetry, in its highest perfection, is thought, feeling, imagery, and music, expressed in language. It should possess the accuracy, the solid sense, and the other good qualities of good prose; and all deviations should be such as tend to make it poetry, or to elevate it above prose. Care should always be taken to select that mode of versification which accords best with the spirit of the intended poem; and when a certain stanza, or a certain mode of versification, has been adopted, there can seldom be allowed, throughout the same poem, any departure from it. Regularity in versification is one of the chief beauties of poetry; and deviations are allowable only when they would not be noticed, or when they serve to produce a better harmony than unvaried regularity could afford.

Punctuation. — The punctuation of standard English literature, as well as of our newspapers and other journals, is one of the most chaotic subjects that ever perplexed investigation. As an art, punctuation is one of the nicest; and long experience is needed to secure a reliable amount of skill. That most people know so little of this art, is because they are too ignorant of grammar, of the construction of sentences, and of the niceties of syntax and thought; for without a thorough knowledge of these things, rules of grammar are unavailable, or can not strike root in the mind. So far as there can be a difference of opinion in regard to the meaning of what is written, there will always be room for diversity of punctuation; but punctuation, as a science, can never rest on any firm basis except the principles of grammatical "Analysis."

There are two modes of punctuating, called *close punctuation* and *free punctuation*. The former is the older system, and it consists in the use of many points; the latter is the later system, and it consists in the use of but few points. CLOSE PUNCTUATION: "To carve for others, is, to starve yourself." — *G. Brown.* "So that the term, *language*, now signifies, any series," etc. — *Id.* In free punctuation, the foregoing commas would be omitted; as, "To carve for others is to starve yourself." "So that the term *language* now signifies any series," etc. The two modes of punctuation differ chiefly in regard to the comma. Free punctuation is preferred by the best printers; and it has become so far established that much of the punctuation now taught in most of the school grammars is rather obsolete.

In punctuation, the elements of sentences are clauses, phrases, and words; and the kinds of sense which must be regarded, are serial sense, modified sense, and broken sense. The points mostly used are the comma and the semicolon.

Simple Sentences. — Most printers now hold the opinion that no comma should be inserted between the subject and the predicate, and that Mr. Murray took the wrong end of the principle for his rule. A comma may be inserted between a series of nominatives and their predicate, to show the common dependence of the predicate on all the nominatives; though many printers omit the comma when a conjunction stands before the last nominative. To show whether a dubious word or phrase belongs to the subject or the predicate, a comma must be inserted; and sometimes a comma is admissible after a long subject. When the subject or the predicate consists of two parts that suggest the idea of two clauses, the parts are separated; as, "He, *as well as I*, was deceived." "Overhead the branches arch, *and make a pleasant bower*." An object or a predicate-nominative, closely depending on its verb, is not set off. Any phrase that makes a separate impression on the mind, rather than combines with some other part to make a whole with it, must be set off by the comma; as, "And then the flowers, so modest, so lovely, of such exquisite hue, enameled in the grass, sparkling amidst it, 'a starry multitude,' underneath such awful mountains and icy precipices — how beautiful!" Any phrase that is equivalent to a clause which would require a point, is set off as if it were the clause. When an infinitive phrase, a participial phrase, or an adjective phrase, that makes a part of the predicate, stands before the subject, it is set off by the comma; as, "*To be rightly estimated*, he must be judged by the times in which he lived." When such a phrase is placed between the nominative and the verb, and is parenthetic rather than restrictive, it is also set off. When it holds its proper syntactical position, it is not set off by the comma if it stands in close connection with the word on which it depends. But if somewhat removed from it, it is set off. An emphatic adjunct, at the beginning of a sentence, is set off by the comma. A forcibly parenthetic adjunct must also be set off. An adjunct that follows another, but depends on a preceding word, must generally be set off by the comma. An adjunct that is very long, or that has the force of a clause, must generally be set off by the comma. Two words in close apposition, especially when they consist of a pronoun and a noun, are not separated by the comma. When *or* annexes an appositive or explanatory noun, a comma is inserted; as, "The skull, *or cranium*." But when *or* joins equivalent adjectives or adverbs, they are not separated; as, "In a *careless or indifferent* manner." A point is seldom used between the word *price* and the number; though the strict sense requires the comma. A term immediately preceded by two or more others that govern or qualify it, is generally not set off by the comma; as, "Lend, lend *your wings*." "It was a bright, lovely *day*." But in other cases, and when there is something of suspense or contrast, the part is set off; as, "The liberties, the rights, *of our citizens*." "The former are called voluntary, and the latter involuntary, *muscles*." Parts that are compared or slightly contrasted, and depend closely on something after them, are seldom separated; as, "It is a *small but thrifty* tree." But an intermediate phrase that begins with *if not*, is always set off. When two or more adjoining modifiers are parenthetic, the less coalescent one is set off; as, "And her eyes, *on all my motions*, with a mute observance hung." A word is frequently set off by the comma, or not set off, according as it has the sense of a conjunction or that of an adverb. "You did not see him, *then?*" "You did not see him *then?*" "*However*, I will not shrink, *however* great the responsibility may be." The pointing sometimes depends on how smoothly the words of the sentence flow together; as, "*Perhaps* we shall never see him again." "We shall *perhaps* never see him again." "We shall never, *perhaps*, see him again." When two phrases of moderate length are united by *both — and*, *either — or*, or *neither — nor*, they seldom need the comma between them. A comma should be inserted before *and*, *or*, or *nor*, that is used only before the last term of a series; as, "A, B, and Co." "John, James and William are studying," implies that I am telling John what the other two boys are doing. Insert a comma before *and* and the sense is clear. When a conjunction is repeated throughout a series of terms, it is generally better to insert the comma; as, "The health, and strength, and freshness, and sweet sleep of infancy, are yours." — *R. G. Parker*. But when no greater point than the comma can be used at the end of the series, the comma within may be omitted; as, "Dividing and gliding and sliding, and falling and brawling and sprawling," etc. — *Southey*. Indeed, the comma is sometimes excluded within, because no greater point can be admitted at the end. But sometimes the comma must be used within a part that is itself set off only by the comma; as, "And therefore will I take the Nevil's part, and, when I spy advantage, claim the crown." — *Shakespeare*. But when the nominative is repeated, the semicolon should be used. Between the number and the name of a street, the comma is generally needed; as, "No. 75, Spruce Street." The comma is, however, frequently omitted. (See Kerl's Comprehensive Grammar, p 371.) Any element of a simple sentence can sometimes run into so long and loose a series of particulars that the semicolon is allowable between them.

Complex Sentences. — When the dependent clause of a complex sentence is used as a subject-nominative or a predicate-nominative, it is set off by the comma. When it is used as a noun in any other relation, a comma is seldom needed. (See pp. 246, 247.) When *that* begins a clause which depends closely on *it*, preceding it, or on a governing or controlling verb, or on *so* or *such*, the clause does not require the comma; as, "It is reported *that he is coming*." "I know *that he is honest*." "It was so heavy *that I could not carry it*." When *such* or *so* begins the previous clause, a comma must be inserted between the clauses. When an objective clause is a quotation, it must generally be set off by a comma; as, "Seneca says, 'Life is a voyage.'" When a relative clause is restrictive, it is not set off by the comma; but when it is simply explanatory, it is set off. "The great principles of government *which are easily understood*, are known everywhere," implies that only some of the great principles of government are easily understood. "The great principles of government, *which are easily understood*, are known everywhere," implies that all great principles of government are easily understood. A clause that begins with *as, because, how, if, than, that, when, where, whether, while, why*, or a similar word, and depends closely on a preceding clause, seldom needs a point before it. But when such a clause stands *before the principal clause*, it must be set off by the comma; as, "I will go when he comes"; "*When he comes*, I will go." Sometimes even a semicolon or a colon can be used between the principal and the subordinate element of a complex sentence. When the dependent element of a complex sentence is extended into a series, sometimes the comma is used, and sometimes the semicolon. The latter point implies greater deliberation.

Compound Sentences. — The clauses or members of compound sentences are sometimes separated by the comma, and sometimes by the semicolon. (See pp. 338, 340.) In stead of the semicolon, the period can also be used, when there is a design to give still greater importance to the particulars. When the verb of one of the clauses is omitted, a comma must generally be put in its place; as, "Industry produces wealth; and wealth, corruption."

When the name of a person, and a complimentary address, are both used at the beginning of a letter, a period is placed after the name, and a comma or a colon after the address; the comma in the familiar style, and the colon in the solemn or formal style. When the letter begins in the line below, a dash may be added to the point above.

QUESTIONS FOR REVIEW.

1. Into what four great classes can all the errors in the use of language be divided?
2. What is the first General Rule
3. What is said, in the special rules, about superfluous pronouns? — two negatives? — double comparison? — too many articles? superfluous prepositions? — poverty of language?
4. What is the second General Rule?
5. What is said, in the special rules, about the insertion of articles? — improper comparison? — parts emphatically distinguished? — serial parts? — nominatives improperly omitted? — participial nouns?
6. What is the third General Rule?
7. Repeat the Rules of Syntax; — the Notes.
8. What is said, in the special rules, of *them* used for *those?* — of adverbs and adjectives? — of two objects compared? — of the leading term, in comparison? — of compared adjectives and plural nouns, improperly expressed? — of words that should not be compared, or made plural? — of *a* and *an?* — of *a* or *an* and *the?* — of the subject of passive verbs? — of the possessive apostrophe? — of a compound word or a complex term expressed in the possessive case? — of a pair or series of nouns expressed in the possessive case? — of harsh or inelegant possessives? — of ambiguous pronouns? — of relative pronouns? — of mixing different pronouns, or different forms of the verb? — of *shall* and *will?* — of past tense and perfect participle? — of improper passive forms? — of the indicative and the subjunctive mood? — of the tenses? — of the infinitives? — of clumsy participial forms?
9. What is the fourth General Rule?
10. What is said, in the special rules, of the position of nouns and pronouns? — of the position of adjectives, adverbs, and adjuncts? — of adverbs that modify infinitives? — of a part of a sentence that relates to each of two or more other parts?
11. What is a Figure? 667
12. Into what classes are figures divided? 668
13. Mention the figures of orthography. 669
14. What is aphæresis? — syncope? — apocope? — prosthesis? — paragoge? — tmesis?
15. Mention the figures of syntax. . 670
16. What is ellipsis? — aposiopesis? — zeugma — pleonasm? — enallage? — inversion, or hyperbaton?
17. What is an archaism? . . . 671
18. What is mimicry? 672
19. Mention the figures of rhetoric. 673
20. What is a simile? — a metaphor? — an allegory? — a metonymy? — a synecdoche? — personification? — antithesis? — irony? — paralipsis? — hyperbole? — climax? — allusion? — euphemism? interrogation? — exclamation? — apostrophe? — vision? — onomatopœia?
21. What is parody? What is a pun?
22. What is Versification? . . . 692
23. What is verse? 693
24. To what four heads is versification reduced? 694
25. What is poetic accent? . . 695
26. What is a poetic foot? . . . 696
27. Mention and define the principal feet. 697
28. Mention and define the secondary feet. 698
29. What is said of poetic lines? . 705
30. What is an hypermeter? . . 706
31. What pauses are peculiar to verse? 707
32. Define them. 708, 709
33. What is rhyme? 710
34. Describe rhymes. . . 711, 712
35. What is blank verse? — heroic verse? — a couplet? — a stanza? — scanning?
36. What is a poetic license? . . 718
37. Mention the eight principal kinds.
38. What does utterance comprise?
39. What is said of articulation? — the degree of loudness or rapidity? — inflections? — tones? — emphasis? — pauses?
40. What is Punctuation? . . . 719
41. How many of the points and marks can you mention?
42. What is said of the period? — the colon? — the semicolon? — the interrogation-point? — the exclamation-point? — the dash? — the curves? — the brackets? — the hyphen? — the underscore? — Italics?
43. What is said of the comma in regard to series of terms? — parenthetic terms? — loose modifiers? — independent words? — subject and predicate? — clauses? — simple sentences?

www.ingramcontent.com/pod-product-compliance
Lightning Source LLC
LaVergne TN
LVHW010145110826
845151LV00002B/425

* 9 7 8 1 4 2 5 5 3 8 2 6 2 *